VIRTUAL REALITY SYSTEMS

VIRTUAL REALITY SYSTEMS

Edited by:

Zoran Gacovski

ARCLER PRESS

www.arclerpress.com

Virtual Reality Systems

Zoran Gacovski

Arcler Press
2010 Winston Park Drive,
2nd Floor
Oakville, ON L6H 5R7
Canada
www.arclerpress.com
Tel: 001-289-291-7705
001-905-616-2116
Fax: 001-289-291-7601
Email: orders@arclereducation.com

ISBN: 978-1-77407-350-6 (Hardcover)

DECLARATION

Some content or chapters in this book are open access copyright free published research work, which is published under Creative Commons License and are indicated with the citation. We are thankful to the publishers and authors of the content and chapters as without them this book wouldn't have been possible.

ABOUT THE EDITOR

Dr. Zoran Gacovski has earned his PhD degree at Faculty of Electrical engineering, Skopje. His research interests include Intelligent systems and Software engineering, fuzzy systems, graphical models (Petri, Neural and Bayesian networks), and IT security. He has published over 50 journal and conference papers, and he has been reviewer of renowned Journals. Currently, he is a professor in Computer Engineering at European University, Skopje, Macedonia.

TABLE OF CONTENTS

SECTION IV- BRAIN AND NEURAL APPLICATIONS OF THE VR

LIST OF CONTRIBUTORS

Woong Choi
Advanced Production Systems Engineering Course, National Institute of Technology, Gunma College, Maebashi, Japan

Liang Li
College of Information Science and Engineering, Ritsumeikan University, Kusatsu, Japan

Satoru Satoh
Gungin System Service Co., Ltd., Maebashi, Japan

Kozaburo Hachimura
College of Information Science and Engineering, Ritsumeikan University, Kusatsu, Japan

Gert Pfurtscheller
Laboratory of Brain-Computer Interfaces (BCI-Lab), Institute for Knowledge Discovery, Graz University of Technology, Austria

Robert Leeb
Chair on Non-Invasive Brain-Machine Interface, School of Engineering, Ecole Polytechnique Fédérale de Lausanne, Switzerland

Josef Faller
Laboratory of Brain-Computer Interfaces (BCI-Lab), Institute for Knowledge Discovery, Graz University of Technology, Austria

Christa Neuper
Laboratory of Brain-Computer Interfaces (BCI-Lab), Institute for Knowledge Discovery, Graz University of Technology, Austria

Bernhard E. Riecke
Simon Fraser University Canada

Siti Soleha Muhammad Nizam
Mixed Reality and Pervasive Computing Lab, Centre of Artificial Intelligence Technology, Faculty of Information Science and Technology, Universiti Kebangsaan Malaysia, 43600 Bangi, Selangor, Malaysia

Meng Chun Lam
Mixed Reality and Pervasive Computing Lab, Centre of Artificial Intelligence Technology, Faculty of Information Science and Technology, Universiti Kebangsaan Malaysia, 43600 Bangi, Selangor, Malaysia

Haslina Arshad
Mixed Reality and Pervasive Computing Lab, Centre of Artificial Intelligence Technology, Faculty of Information Science and Technology, Universiti Kebangsaan Malaysia, 43600 Bangi, Selangor, Malaysia

Nur Asylah Suwadi
Mixed Reality and Pervasive Computing Lab, Centre of Artificial Intelligence Technology, Faculty of Information Science and Technology, Universiti Kebangsaan Malaysia, 43600 Bangi, Selangor, Malaysia

Alexander Paz
University of Nevada, Las Vegas, Civil and Environmental Engineering and Construction, Las Vegas, NV 89154, USA

Naveen Veeramisti
University of Nevada, Las Vegas, Civil and Environmental Engineering and Construction, Las Vegas, NV 89154, USA

Romesh Khaddar
University of Nevada, Las Vegas, Electrical and Computer Engineering, Las Vegas, NV 89154, USA

Hanns de la Fuente-Mella
Pontificia Universidad Católica de Valparaíso, Facultad de Ciencias Económicas y Administrativas, Escuela de Comercio, Avenida Brasil 2830, 2340031 Valparaíso, Chile

Luiza Modorcea
Faculty of Law, Transilvania University of Brasov, 500036 Brasov, Romania

Katy Tcha-Tokey
Arts et Métiers ParisTech, LAMPA EA 1427, 2 bd du Ronceray, 49000 Angers, France

Olivier Christmann
Arts et Métiers ParisTech, LAMPA EA 1427, 2 bd du Ronceray, 49000 Angers, France

Emilie Loup-Escande
Université de Picardie Jules Verne, CRP-CPO EA 7273, chemin du Thil, 80025 Amiens, France

GuillaumeLoup
Université Bretagne Loire, LIUM EA 4023, avenue Olivier Messiaen, 72085 Le Mans, France

Simon Richir
Arts et Métiers ParisTech, LAMPA EA 1427, 2 bd du Ronceray, 49000 Angers, France

Haipeng Mi
Interaction Technology Laboratory, Department of Electrical Engineering and Information Systems, University of Tokyo, 7-3-1 Hongo, Bunkyo-ku, 113-8656 Tokyo, Japan

Aleksander Krzywinski
The Interaction Research Group, Department of Information Science and Media Studies, University of Bergen, Fosswinckelsgate 6, 5020 Bergen, Norway

Tomoki Fujita
Interaction Technology Laboratory, Department of Electrical Engineering and Information Systems, University of Tokyo, 7-3-1 Hongo, Bunkyo-ku, 113-8656 Tokyo, Japan

Masanori Sugimoto
Interaction Technology Laboratory, Department of Electrical Engineering and Information Systems, University of Tokyo, 7-3-1 Hongo, Bunkyo-ku, 113-8656 Tokyo, Japan

Hui-Chin Chang
Department of Mechanical Engineering, De Lin Institute of Technology, Taipei, Taiwan, China

Patorn Piromchai
Department of Otolaryngology, Royal Victorian Eye and Ear Hospital, University of Melbourne, East Melbourne, Australia
Department of Otorhinolaryngology, Faculty of Medicine, Khon Kaen University, Khon Kaen, Thailand

Ronei M. Moraes
Federal University of Paraíba Brazil

Liliane S. Machado
Federal University of Paraíba Brazil

Eder H. Govea-Valladares
Facultad de Ingeniería, Universidad Autónoma de San Luis Potosí, 78290, San Luis Potosí, Mexico

Hugo I. Medellin-Castillo
Facultad de Ingeniería, Universidad Autónoma de San Luis Potosí, 78290, San Luis Potosí, Mexico

Jorge Ballesteros
Instituto Tecnológico de Canarias, Playa Pozo Izquierdo s/n, 35119, Las Palmas, Islas Canarias, Spain

Miguel A. Rodriguez-Florido
Instituto Tecnológico de Canarias, Playa Pozo Izquierdo s/n, 35119, Las Palmas, Islas Canarias, Spain

Irene Alice Chicchi Giglioli
Applied Technology for Neuro-Psychology Lab, IRCCS Istituto Auxologico Italiano, 20145 Milan, Italy

Federica Pallavicini
Applied Technology for Neuro-Psychology Lab, IRCCS Istituto Auxologico Italiano, 20145 Milan, Italy

Elisa Pedroli
Applied Technology for Neuro-Psychology Lab, IRCCS Istituto Auxologico Italiano, 20145 Milan, Italy

Silvia Serino
Applied Technology for Neuro-Psychology Lab, IRCCS Istituto Auxologico Italiano, 20145 Milan, Italy

Giuseppe Riva
Applied Technology for Neuro-Psychology Lab, IRCCS Istituto Auxologico Italiano, 20145 Milan, Italy
Department of Psychology, Catholic University of Milan, 20123 Milan, Italy

Rafael D. de C. Silva
Programa de Pós-Graduação em Informática Aplicada, Laboratório de Bioinformática, Universidade de Fortaleza, Fortaleza, CE, Brazil

Saulo G. C. Albuquerque
Hospital de Saúde Mental de Messejana, Fortaleza, CE, Brazil
Internato em Saúde Coletiva e Mental, Universidade de Fortaleza, Fortaleza, CE, Brazil

Artur de V. Muniz
Hospital de Saúde Mental de Messejana, Fortaleza, CE, Brazil

Pedro P. Rebouças Filho
Laboratório de Processamento de Imagens e Simulação Computacional, Instituto Federal de Educação, Ciência e Tecnologia do Ceará, Maracanaú, CE, Brazil

Sidarta Ribeiro
Instituto do Cérebro, Universidade Federal do Rio Grande do Norte, Natal, RN, Brazil

Plácido Rogerio Pinheiro
Programa de Pós-Graduação em Informática Aplicada, Laboratório de Bioinformática, Universidade de Fortaleza, Fortaleza, CE, Brazil

Victor Hugo C. Albuquerque
Programa de Pós-Graduação em Informática Aplicada, Laboratório de Bioinformática, Universidade de Fortaleza, Fortaleza, CE, Brazil

Dr. Christiane Eichenberg
University of Cologne (Institute of Clinical Psychology and Psychological Diagnosis) Germany

Beatriz Rey
Instituto Interuniversitario de Investigación en Bioingeniería y Tecnología Orientada al Ser Humano, Universidad Politécnica de Valencia Spain

Mariano Alcañiz
Instituto Interuniversitario de Investigación en Bioingeniería y Tecnología Orientada al Ser Humano, Universidad Politécnica de Valencia Spain

LIST OF ABBREVIATIONS

APIs	Application Programming Interface
APIs	Application-programmer interfaces
ABL	Auditory Biophysics Laboratory
AR	Augmented Reality
AV	Augmented virtuality
BP	Band power
BAT	Behaviour avoidance test
BPPV	Benign paroxysmal positional vertigo
BOLD	Blood Oxygen Level Dependent method
BT	Bluetooth
BMH	Bone marrow harvest
B-Rep	Boundary Representation
BCI	Brain-Computer Interface
CORBA	Common Object Request Broker Architecture
CFI	Comparative Fit Index
CSG	Constructive solid geometry
DI	Diffused illumination
DLPFC	Dorso lateral prefrontal cortex
DES	Driving Environment Simulator
ED	Eating disorders
EEG	Electroencephalogram
ES3	Endoscopic sinus surgical simulator
ERPs	Event-related potentials
ERP	Evoked Response Potential
FSQ	Fear of Spiders Questionnaire
FTIR	Frustrated total internal reflection
FESS	Functional endoscopic sinus surgery

fMRI	Functional magnetic resonance imaging
GBNs	General Bayesian Networks
GPS	Global Positioning System
GUI	Graphic user interface
HMDs	Head-mounted displays
HR	Heart rate
HRI	Human-robot interaction
IVE	swImmersive virtual environments
IPL	Inferior parietal cortex
IR	Infrared
IC	Intended control
INC	Intended non-control
MEG	Magnetoencephalography
MFC	Microsoft Foundation Classes
MIST	Minimally invasive system
MR	Mixed reality
MT4J	MultiTouch for Java
NADS	National Advanced Driving Simulator
NHTSA	National Highway Traffic Safety Administration
NFI	Normed Fit Index
OSATS	Objective Structured Assessment of Technical Skills
OSM	Open Street Maps
OST	Optical see-through
PAMELA	Pedestrian Accessibility and Movement Environment Laboratory
PTSD	Posttraumatic stress disorder
PWM	Power width modulation
PRISMA	Preferred Reporting Items for Systematic Reviews and Meta-Analysis
PRJQ	Presence and Reality Judgment Questionnaire
RMSEA	Root Mean Square Error of Approximation
RHI	Rubber Hand Illusion

SEP	Secretariat of Public Education
SSM	Social spatial mashup
SDK	Software Development Kit
SAR	Spatial augmented reality
SPBQ	Spider Phobia Beliefs Questionnaire
SSEPs	Steady-state evoked potentials
SSVEP	Steady-state visual evoked potential
SEM	Structural Equation Modelling
SUDS	Subjective Units of Discomfort Scale
SPL	Superior parietal cortex
TUIs	Tangible user interfaces
TL	Therapeutic lamp
3D)	Three-dimensional (
TCD	Transcranial Doppler
UMTRI	University of Michigan Transportation Research Institute
UWO	University of Western Ontario
UXIVE Model	User eXperience in Immersive Virtual Environment Model
UX	User eXperience
VST	Video see-through
VE	Virtual environment
VHI	Virtual Hand Illusion
VOSS	Virtual Osteotomy Simulator System
VR	Virtual reality
VADE	Visual assembly design environment
VTK	Visualization Toolkit libraries
WHO	World Health Organization

PREFACE

The world is recognized through our senses and the perception system. At school we all learned that there are 5 basic senses: taste, touch, smell, vision and hearing. It is true that people have a lot more senses than these, such as e.g. sense of balance. All the senses that exist - in fact provide us with a rich flow of information from our surroundings to the brain.

All we know about reality is because of our senses. In other words, the whole experience of reality is simply a combination of all these senses and information that our brain reasons in a certain way. Therefore, if we succeed in any way to add additional information that our senses are collecting, we could change the perception of them in our brain. It would be like second version of reality that does not actually exist, but from our perspective - it seems to be real. Something we can call - virtual reality.

So in essence, virtual reality presents us with a modified reality with the help of a computer - with which we can interact and explore it in some way.

Responding to the question 'What is a Virtual Reality' in the technical sense is very simple. Virtual reality is a term used to describe a three-dimensional, computer-generated environment with which the user can interact. The user becomes part of a virtual world in which he is able to manipulate various objects and perform possible actions.

This may seem like a lot of effort, as it is. The reason for this is that VR is in constant development. The huge potential of the entertainment applications is a clear evidence for VR usage. Movies and games are also a great example. In an industry that entertains people in various ways, companies invest billions of dollars and users are always in favor of novelties.

The VR is already used in various industries such as: Architecture, Sport, Medicine, Art, Entertainment etc. It can lead to new exciting discoveries that will affect our everyday life.

Whether it's something dangerous, costly or impractical to do in reality, virtual reality is the answer to that. From pilots training to medical applications for training of surgeons, virtual reality allows us to take risks - in order to gain a real experience. As the price of real environments rises - VR becomes more and more used, so we can expect more serious benefits in education, medicine, various researches, and the like.

Section 1 focuses on Motion control and movements in VR, describing multisensory integration in the virtual hand illusion with active movement, brain-computer interface systems used for virtual reality control, self-motion through virtual environments without actual self-motion, review on tangible and spatial awareness interaction technique, and a traffic and driving simulator based on architecture of interactive motion.

Section 2 focuses on Robotics and Virtual Environments, describing model of user experience in immersive virtual environments, an infrastructure for intuitive interaction with mobile robots in a mixed-reality environment, an augmented reality game as a new business model to present artworks, and a novel training system of lathe works on virtual operating platform.

Section 3 focuses on Medical applications of VR, describing virtual reality surgical training in ear, nose and throat surgery medical training system with integration of users' assessment, potential of virtual reality for the elderly and people with disabilities, development of virtual reality scenarios for computer-assisted biomedical applications, design and validation of an augmented reality system for laparoscopic surgery in a real environment.

Section 4 focuses on Brain and Neural Applications of the VR, describing augmented reality: a brand new challenge for the assessment and treatment of psychological disorders, a new cognitive approach based on augmented reality, application of 'virtual realities' in psychotherapy, virtual reality-based assessment of social skills, and research in neuroscience and virtual reality.

SECTION I - MOTION CONTROL AND MOVEMENTS IN VR

Chapter 1

Multisensory Integration in the Virtual Hand Illusion with Active Movement

Woong Choi[1], Liang Li[2] , Satoru Satoh[3] , and Kozaburo Hachimura[2]

[1]Advanced Production Systems Engineering Course, National Institute of Technology, Gunma College, Maebashi, Japan

[2]College of Information Science and Engineering, Ritsumeikan University, Kusatsu, Japan

[3]Gungin System Service Co., Ltd., Maebashi, Japan

ABSTRACT

Improving the sense of immersion is one of the core issues in virtual reality. Perceptual illusions of ownership can be perceived over a virtual body in a multisensory virtual reality environment. Rubber Hand and Virtual Hand Illusions showed that body ownership can be manipulated by applying suitable visual and tactile stimulation. In this study, we investigate the

Citation: Woong Choi, Liang Li, Satoru Satoh, and Kozaburo Hachimura, "Multisensory Integration in the Virtual Hand Illusion with Active Movement," BioMed Research International, vol. 2016, Article ID 8163098.

effects of multisensory integration in the Virtual Hand Illusion with active movement. A virtual xylophone playing system which can interactively provide synchronous visual, tactile, and auditory stimulation was constructed. We conducted two experiments regarding different movement conditions and different sensory stimulations. Our results demonstrate that multisensory integration with free active movement can improve the sense of immersion in virtual reality.

INTRODUCTION

The mutual interaction of the sensory signals is a critical aspect in human perception and cognition. Recently, with the development of virtual reality (VR) technology, increasing researches were carried out on projecting multisensory information to virtual representations of the actual body. Ideally, the virtual representations in VR space should be identical to the actual body. However, in practice, physical differences arise due to the spatial limitation when constructing the VR space. The real-time representation of multisensory information plays a pivotal role in an immersive VR environment.

The shifts between physical stimuli and human perceptions are known as illusions. Using these sensory distortions, more realistic perceptions can be represented despite the physical limitations of sensory display interfaces.

Body ownership illusion, which is typically induced by VR, has been widely studied in the past few decades. Self-recognition is necessary for human cognition adapting to changes in the environment [1]. Mental representation of one's own body, which is called body image, is not limited to the sense of body ownership but also comprises the multisensory perceptions such as visual and tactile information [2]. In addition, body image can be extended to an object or an artificial limb attached to the human body. Therefore, body image can be intentionally manipulated by displaying coherent multisensory information.

A famous illusion of body ownership is the Rubber Hand Illusion (RHI) [3–7]. In the RHI, the subjects viewing stimulation of a rubber hand being stroked synchronously with their own unseen hand feel that the rubber hand is part of their own body [8].

The displacement of body ownership has also been observed in VR environment, in which a virtual hand was displayed as the visual stimulation [9, 10]. This illusion is called the Virtual Hand Illusion (VHI). As reported by IJsselsteijn et al., the VR environment produced a weaker illusion than the RHI but a more convincing subjective illusion than the mixed reality environment [11]. Furthermore, connectivity of the virtual hand with the rest of the virtual body has a significant effect on the subjective illusion of ownership [12].

It is relatively easy to evoke the illusory ownership by displaying synchronous visual and tactile stimulation with multisensory display interface. Therefore, with a proper integration and display of multisensory stimulation, a more realistic experience can be elicited in an immersive virtual reality environment.

Many researchers investigated the effect of synchrony for visual, tactile, and auditory stimulation. The results showed that the synchronous conditions led to stronger illusions of body ownership than the asynchronous conditions [4, 12–14]. In other words, synchronous stimulation is critical for inducing the VHI. Most studies on synchrony of multisensory stimulation are focused on examining the minimum conditions necessary to induce the illusion of body ownership. However, considering that the synchronous stimulation is the basis of multisensory integration, we aimed to investigate the most effective combination for inducing the illusion of ownership over the virtual hand in a 3D virtual reality environment.

In practice, a human being moves his/her body parts initiatively and receives subsequent multisensory feedback. Therefore, investigation of active movement in the VHI is necessary for answering the question of how to properly extend body image in VR space. Recent research showed that the change of body image is affected not only by passive sensory stimulation but also by the feedback from active movement. When visual and felt movements were synchronized, active movement arises stronger illusion than passive movement [15]. It has confirmed that illusory body ownership existed during active virtual games in an immersive VR space [16]. There is also evidence that the VHI can be induced by only synchronous visual and motor stimulation, in the absence of tactile stimulation [14].

In VR environment, active movement and multisensory feedback produce the sense of ownership and the sense of agency [17]. Most researches on the VHI in active movement using VR representation were focused on the visual and tactile stimulation. It was reported that the inclusion of a sound cue heightened the effects of the illusion and caused participants to more readily accept the rubber hand into the body schema [18]. Under the invisible hand illusion, the influence of visual-tactile integration on proprioceptive updating is modifiable by irrelevant auditory cues merely through the temporal correspondence between the visual-tactile and auditory events [19]. However, the effects of visual, tactile, and auditory integration in the VHI have not been studied yet.

The purpose of our study was to investigate the effects of multisensory integration in the VHI with active movement. In this paper, we constructed a VR system that interactively generates synchronous visual, tactile, and auditory stimulation. Our system enables participants to perform active movement in a VR environment. We conducted two experiments: (1) the VHI in different active movement conditions and (2) multisensory integration in the VHI. The effect of the visual presentation of the virtual hand was also evaluated.

MATERIALS AND METHODS

Participants

Twenty participants (19 males) with mean age 19.0 ± 1.83 (SD) were recruited for the experiments. All participants had normal or corrected-to-normal vision and were right-handed. None had previously participated in similar studies.

All of the participants gave written informed consents prior to their participation. The protocol was approved by the ethics committees of Gunma National College of Technology.

Experimental Setup

The virtual reality setup consisted of a stereoscopic three-dimensional (3D) display (LG FLATRON W2363D), a six degree-of-freedom haptic device (SensAble Technologies Phantom Omni), and a pair of stereo speakers (Figure 1). The display had a resolution of 1,920 × 1,080 and synchronized with active shutter 3D glasses (NVIDIA 3D Vision) at 120 Hz. The haptic device provided force feedback and positional sensing in a 160*W* × 120*H* × 70D mm workspace with a 0.88 N continuous exertable force and a 3.3 N maximum exertable force at nominal position. A purpose-built frame with the display mounted on its top was constructed. The haptic device and the speakers were hidden inside the frame with a curtain during the experiments.

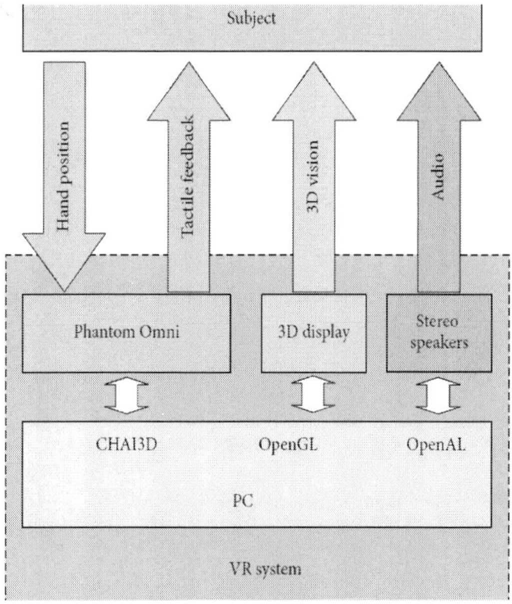

Figure 1: Configuration of the virtual reality system.

A virtual xylophone system was designed for this study. The system allowed active movement and interactively provided synchronous visual, tactile, and auditory stimulation in real time. In a xylophone playing task, participants saw a horizontally placed 3D virtual xylophone with a mallet (Figure 2). A 3D virtual right hand matched to their own hand sizes was also displayed in certain experimental conditions. Participants could operate the virtual hand and play the xylophone with their own unseen hand by holding and moving a pen-shaped tool of the haptic device. A tactile feedback with the resilience of a rubber-headed mallet was received when participants virtually struck the xylophone. A synchronous sound was played by the stereo speakers. The pitch and the volume of the sound were determined according to the struck bar and the striking speed. Libraries of CHAI3D, OpenGL, and OpenAL were used to build the system.

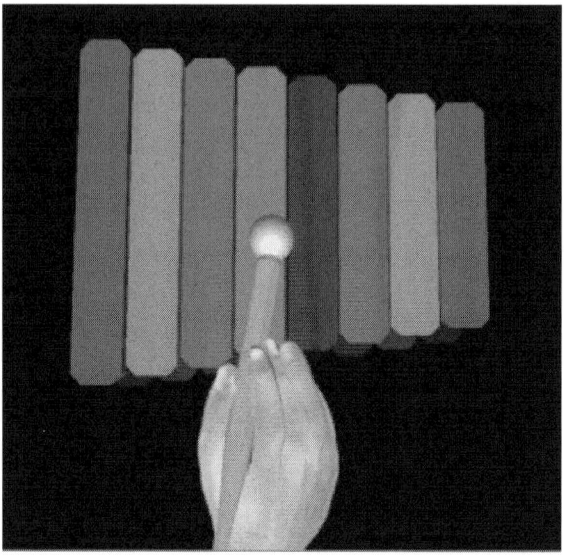

Figure 2: Virtual xylophone, mallet, and the virtual hand rendered and displayed in the experiments.

Procedure

Two experiments were performed in a quiet and dimly lit laboratory room.

Experiment 1: The VHI in Different Active Movement Conditions

This experiment was aimed to investigate the VHI in different active movement conditions. Participants were seated in front of the system with their right sleeve rolled up. They were directed to correctly hold the pen-shaped tool of the haptic device with their right hand while the device remained unseen. They were then asked to look at the display through 3D glasses. The virtual hand (without the xylophone and the mallet) was displayed as the visual stimulation (Figure 3). Participants were asked to perform left/right, forward/backward, up/down, rotatory, and free movements. The duration for each condition was 30 seconds. The order of the five conditions was counter-balanced across participants.

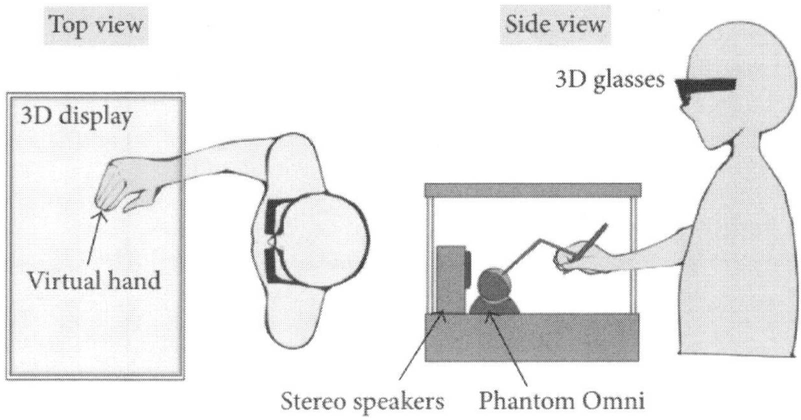

Figure 3: Experimental setup in experiment 1.

After the experiment, participants filled in a 11-item questionnaire in Japanese as shown below.

Questionnaire for Experiment 1

(Q-a1)Sometimes it seemed as if my hand were located where I saw the virtual hand.

(Q-a2)Sometimes I felt as if the virtual hand were my hand.

(Q-a3)Sometimes I felt as if my hand were made by computer graphics.

(Q-a4)At some moments, it seemed as if the virtual hand began to resemble my own hand.

(Q-a5)Sometimes it seemed as if I might have more than one right hand.

(Q-a6)Sometimes I felt as if my hand were existed in the virtual environment.

(Q-a7)I had the sensation in questions (Q-a1) to (Q-a6) during left/right movements.

(Q-a8)I had the sensation in questions (Q-a1) to (Q-a6) during forward/ backward movements.

(Q-a9)I had the sensation in questions (Q-a1) to (Q-a6) during up/down movements.

(Q-a10)I had the sensation in questions (Q-a1) to (Q-a6) during rotatory movements.

(Q-a11)I had the sensation in questions (Q-a1) to (Q-a6) during free movements.

Each question was scored on a 7-point Likert scale, with 1 indicating strongly disagree and 7 strongly agree. Questions (Q-a1) to (Q-a6) were partially adapted and modified from [3]. Questions (Q-a7) to (Q-a11) were introduced to apply to different conditions. For questions (Q-a7) to (Q-a11), reasons for their choice were asked.

Measurement of the displacement of the perceived hand position (proprioceptive drift) is a major way to evaluate the strength of the feeling of ownership in the RHI [20, 21]. However, most of these studies were carried out in passive movement conditions, in which the participant was asked to rest his/her hand on a table. The perceived hand positions were recorded before and after the participant's hand was tapped or stroked passively by the experimenter.

The task in our study was an active movement one, which was designed to resemble a typical dynamic operation in VR environment. Measurement of the proprioceptive drift in the traditional RHI studies is difficult for us because the active hand is constantly moving. Therefore, we used the questionnaire to evaluate the strength of the illusory ownership.

Experiment 2: Multisensory Integration in the VHI

This experiment was aimed at investigating the effect of multisensory integration in the VHI with active movement. The experimental setup was similar to that in experiment 1. In this experiment, eight different experimental conditions with different combinations of visual, tactile, and auditory stimulation were designed (Table 1). It should be noted that, for visual stimulation, the xylophone and the mallet were displayed in all conditions, whereas the virtual hand was only displayed in conditions C1, C3, C5, and C7. Visual, tactile, and auditory stimulation were synchronized in all conditions. The order of the eight conditions was counter-balanced across participants. Figure 4 illustrated the experimental setup of conditions C1, C3, C5, and C7 as an example.

Table 1: The eight experimental conditions

Conditions	Visual stimulation: the xylophone and the mallet	Visual stimulation: the virtual hand	Auditory stimulation	Tactile stimulation
C1	Yes	Yes	No	No
C2	Yes	No	No	No

C3	Yes	Yes	Yes	No
C4	Yes	No	Yes	No
C5	Yes	Yes	No	Yes
C6	Yes	No	No	Yes
C7	Yes	Yes	Yes	Yes
C8	Yes	No	Yes	Yes

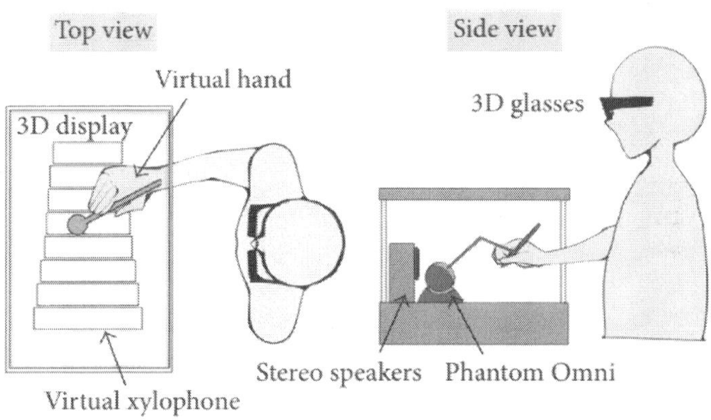

Figure 4: Experimental setup in experiment 2 (conditions C1, C3, C5, and C7).

Participants were directed to move their hand to the reference point to begin the experiment of each condition. They were asked to strike each bar of the virtual xylophone once in an ascending scale. They were then asked to play the xylophone freely for 15 seconds. After the experiment of each condition, participants filled in a 5-item, 7-point Likert scaled questionnaire in Japanese as shown below.

Questionnaire for Experiments 2: Common Questions

(Q-b1)It seemed as if I were playing the xylophone with the mallet.

(Q-b2)It seemed as if I were holding the mallet.

(Q-b3)I could move the mallet to any position at my will.

(Q-b4)I felt as if I were striking an object in the virtual environment.

(Q-b5)I felt an increasing virtual reality experience during the experiment.

For conditions C1, C3, C5, and C7, five more questions that referred to the virtual hand were included as shown below.

Questionnaire for Experiments 2: Questions for Conditions C1, C3, C5, and C7

(Q-c1)Sometimes I felt as if the virtual hand were my hand.

(Q-c2)I felt as if my real hand were located at the virtual hand.

(Q-c3)Sometimes I felt as if my hand were made by computer graphics.

(Q-c4)At some moments, it seemed as if the virtual hand began to resemble my own hand.

(Q-c5)Sometimes it seemed as if I might have more than one right hand.

For conditions C3, C4, C7, and C8, one more question that referred to auditory stimulation was included. For conditions C5–C8, one more question that referred to tactile stimulation was included as shown below.

Questionnaire for Experiments 2: Questions for Conditions C3–C8

(Q-d1)It seemed as if the sound were coming from the xylophone bars where I struck.

(Q-d2)It seemed as if the force were coming from the xylophone bars where I struck.

RESULTS

Figure 5 shows the mean scores and standard deviations regarding questions (Q-a1) to (Q-a6) in experiment 1. Figure 6, regarding questions (Q-a7) to (Q-a11), shows that free movement condition (Q-a11) has a significantly higher mean score than other conditions (paired t-test, (19) = 3.57, (19) = 3.44, $t(19) = 3.21$, $t(19) = 2.94$, and $p < 0.01$).

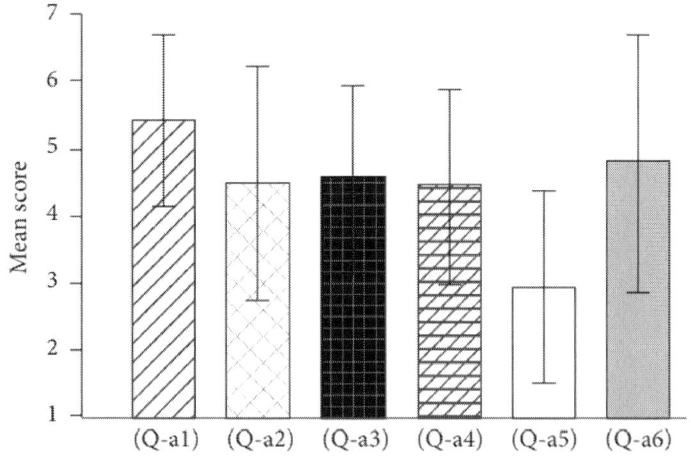

Figure 5: Questionnaire results for (Q-a1) to (Q-a6) in experiment 1.

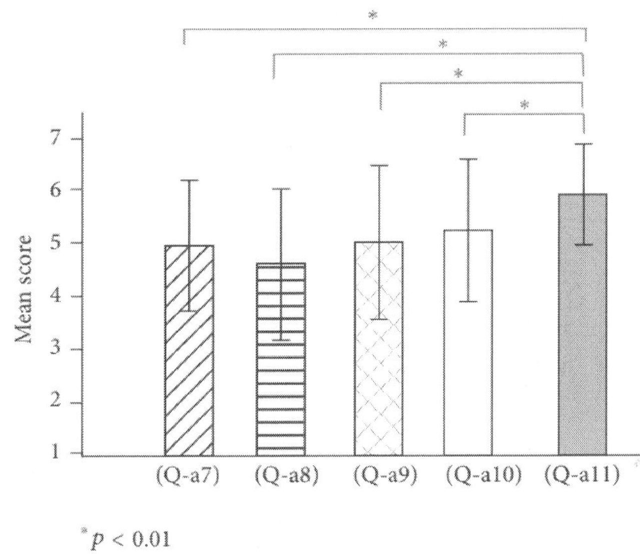

Figure 6: Questionnaire results for (Q-a7) to (Q-a11) in experiment 1.

Figure 7 shows the results of questions (Q-b1) to (Qb5) for conditions C1 and C2 (visual stimulation only) in experiment 2. For conditions C1 and C2, the existence of the virtual hand showed a significant effect in (Q-b2), (Q-b5) ((19) = 4.29, (19) = 3.57, and $p < 0.01$), and (Q-b4) ($t(19) = 2.10$, and $p < 0.05$).

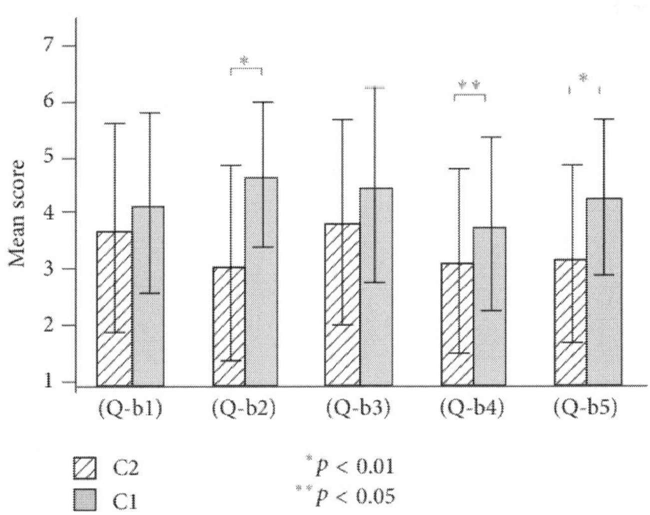

Figure 7: Questionnaire results of (Q-b1) to (Q-b5) for conditions C1 and C2 in experiment 2.

Figure 8 shows the results of questions (Q-b1) to (Q-b5) for conditions C3 and C4 (visual and auditory stimulation) in experiment 2. For conditions C3 and C4, the existence of the virtual hand showed a significant effect in (Q-b1), (Q-b2), and (Q-b3) ((19) = 5.08, (19) = 3.34, $t(19) = 3.12$, and $p < 0.01$) and (Q-b4) and (Q-b5) ($t(19) = 2.34$, $t(19) = 2.24$, and $p < 0.05$).

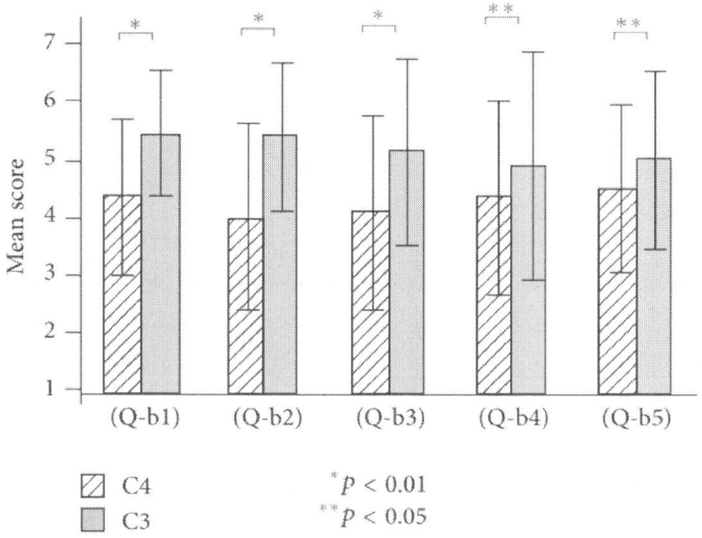

Figure 8: Questionnaire results of (Q-b1) to (Q-b5) for conditions C3 and C4 in experiment 2.

Figure 9 shows the results of questions (Q-b1) to (Q-b5) for conditions C5 and C6 (visual and tactile stimulation) in experiment 2. For conditions C5 and C6, the existence of the virtual hand showed a significant effect in (Q-b1), (Q-b2), and (Q-b3) ((19) = 2.93, (19) = 4.08, $t(19) = 3.29$, and $p < 0.01$) and (Q-b4) and (Q-b5) ($t(19) = 2.18$, $t(19) = 2.65$, and $p < 0.05$).

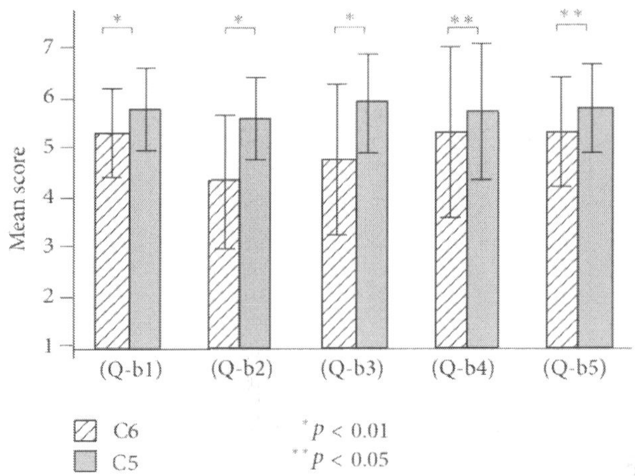

Figure 9: Questionnaire results of (Q-b1) to (Q-b5) for conditions C5 and C6 in experiment 2.

Figure 10 shows the results of questions (Q-b1) to (Qb5) for conditions C7 and C8 (visual, auditory, and tactile stimulation) in experiment 2. For conditions C7 and C8, the existence of the virtual hand showed a significant effect in (Qb1), (Q-b2), (Q-b3), and (Q-b4) ((19) = 5.10, (19) = 3.65, $t(19) = 3.47$, $t(19) = 3.39$, and $p < 0.01$).

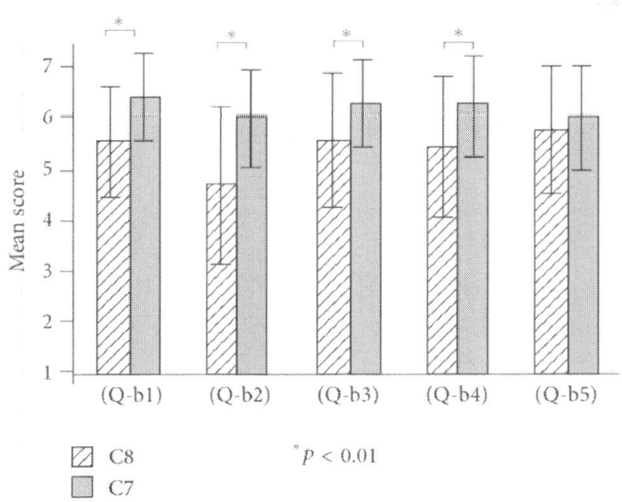

Figure 10: Questionnaire results of (Q-b1) to (Q-b5) for conditions C7 and C8 in experiment 2.

Figure 11 shows the results of questions (Q-c1) to (Q-c5) for conditions C1, C3, C5, and C7 (with the virtual hand) in experiment 2.

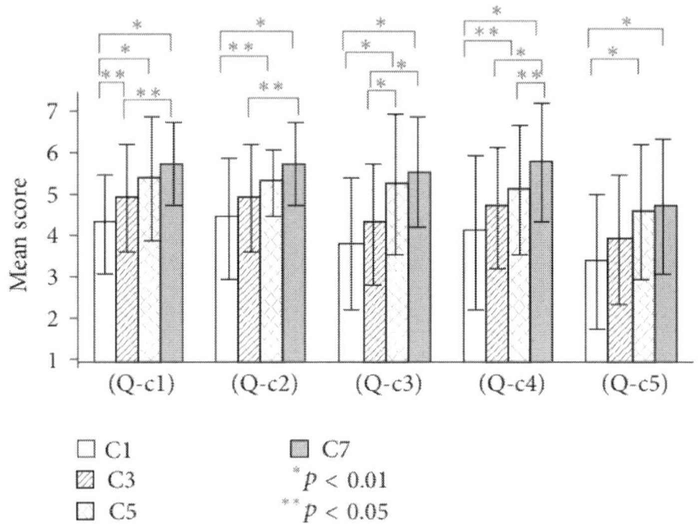

Figure 11: Questionnaire results of questions (Q-c1) to (Q-c5) for conditions C1, C3, C5, and C7 in experiment 2.

For question (Q-c1), there were significant differences between conditions C1 and C5 ((19) = 3.17, $p < 0.01$), conditions C1 and C7 ((19) = 5.25, $p < 0.01$), conditions C1 and C3 ($t(19) = 2.56$, $p < 0.05$), and conditions C3 and C7 ($t(19) = 2.63$, $p < 0.05$).

For question (Q-c2), there were significant differences between conditions C1 and C7 ((19) = 3.27, $p < 0.01$), conditions C1 and C5 ((19) = 2.67, $p < 0.05$), and conditions C3 and C7 ($t(19) = 2.38$, $p < 0.05$).

For question (Q-c3), there were significant differences between conditions C1 and C5 ((19) = 4.92, $p < 0.01$), conditions C1 and C7 ((19) = 6.05, $p < 0.01$), conditions C3 and C5 ($t(19) = 2.97$, $p < 0.01$), and conditions C3 and C7 ($t(19) = 4.08$, $p < 0.01$).

For question (Q-c4), there were significant differences between conditions C1 and C7 ((19) = 3.61, $p < 0.01$), conditions C3 and C7 ((19) = 3.17, $p < 0.01$), conditions C1 and C5 ($t(19) = 2.50$, $p < 0.05$), and conditions C5 and C7 ($t(19) = 2.67$, $p < 0.05$).

For question (Q-c5), there were significant differences between conditions C1 and C5 ((19) = 3.74, $p < 0.01$) and conditions C1 and C7 ((19) = 4.35, $p < 0.01$).

Figures 12 and 13 show the result of questions (Q-d1) and (Q-d2). For (Q-d1), the conditions with the virtual hand (conditions C3 and C4) had significantly higher mean scores than those without the virtual hand (conditions C7 and C8) ((19) = 2.83, (19) = 2.13, and $p < 0.05$). For conditions C7 and C8, the existence of the virtual hand also showed a significant effect in (Q-d2) ((19) = 3.05, $p < 0.01$). No significant difference was observed between conditions C5 and C6 in (Q-d2).

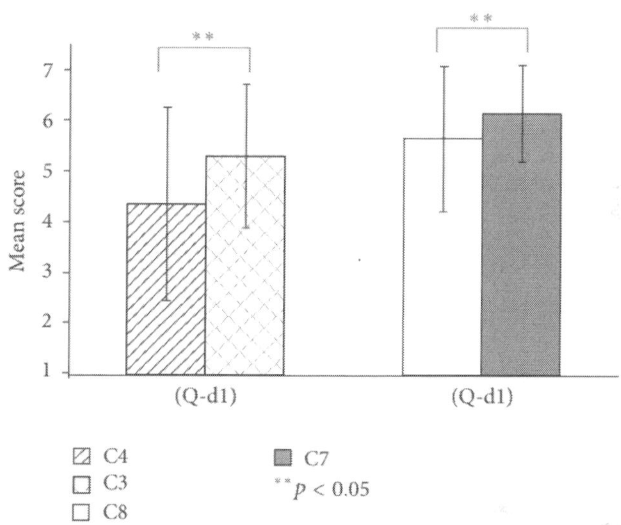

Figure 12: Questionnaire results of (Q-d1) in experiment 2.

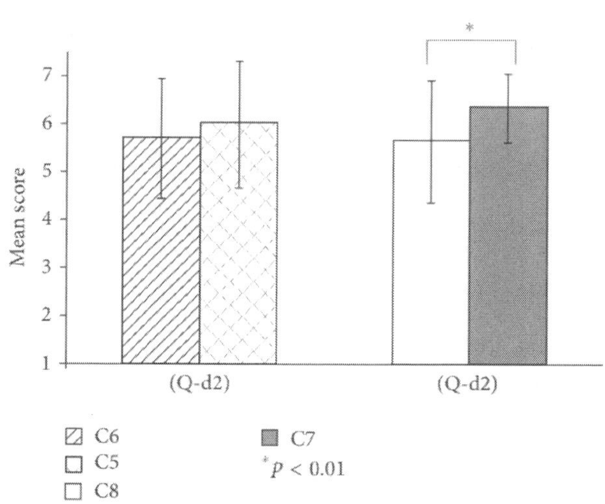

Figure 13: Questionnaire results of (Q-d2) in experiment 2.

DISCUSSIONS

We investigate the effects of multisensory integration in the VHI with active movement.

Experiment 1 examined the VHI in different active movement conditions.

The experimental results showed that, in translation (the movements without rotation), left/right and forward/backward movements yielded less illusion than up/down movements. Because it is relatively difficult to perceive the depth for human, the perception gap between the virtual space and the real space in vertical movements (up/down) was smaller than that in horizontal movements (left/right and forward/backward) [22, 23].

Participants reported that they had a strong illusion at the near side and felt sense of incongruity during forward/backward movements. This result that might have been caused by the difference between camera view in the virtual space and participant's view in the real space has been increased in forward/backward movements. As shown in Figure 6, questionnaire results were in agreement with that the forward/backward movement yielded least illusion.

Rotatory movements had a higher mean score than translation movements. Participants experienced stronger illusion because they felt less incongruity of spatial coordinates between virtual and real spaces especially during rotatory movements performed at the near side. Not only objective spatial parameters but also subjective impressions informed by previous experiences have an effect on the VHI [24]. Rotatory hand movements, which were less experienced than translation hand movements for participants, evoked greater illusion in our experiment.

Participants felt significantly stronger illusion in the condition of free movement. This result indicates that free-willed active movement can enhance the illusion of body ownership.

Previous studies suggested that the strongest illusion was reported when the rubber hand and the real hand were in the closest positions [25]. Furthermore, efference copy and the sensory feedback should be coincided in time for having the sense of agency [26]. Neurons in the parietal lobe related to the sense of agency function as mirror neuron [27]. It fires when an action is performed or the same action is performed by another. In the parietal lobe, the visual feedback and the predicted sensory feedback which is generated by the efference copy are compared [28]. During the free movements performed in our experiments, when the two feedbacks matched, the participants felt as if their real hand was moving in the virtual space and experienced a stronger illusion.

Experiment 2 examined the effects of multisensory integration in VHI with active movement.

We assumed that the VHI in VR space can be enhanced by applying multisensory integration to the virtual hand.

In experiment 2, conditions C1 and C2 (visual stimulation only conditions) had lower mean scores compared to the other six conditions. In addition, only three out of five items showed a significant effect of the existence of the virtual hand (Figure 7). In contrast, the existence of the virtual hand showed a significant effect in all items of the visual-auditory (Figure 8) and visual-tactile (Figure 9) conditions. It indicates that, with only the visual stimulation, it is relatively difficult to induce the illusion of body ownership despite the existence of the virtual hand. Note that, although conditions C7 and C8 (visual, tactile, and auditory conditions) had highest mean scores, the virtual hand showed less importance in one item (Figure 10). We consider that strong illusion was induced by multisensory integration even without visual existence of the virtual hand. Figure 11 showed that multisensory integration enhanced the strength of the illusory ownership. Furthermore, except for question (Q-c1), visual-auditory stimulation did not show significant advantage over visual only stimulation. However, visual-tactile stimulation showed a significantly greater effect on the illusion than visual only stimulation. This result shows that tactile signal is more critical than auditory signal in inducing the illusion of body ownership.

Figure 12 showed a significant effect of the existence of the virtual hand. It indicates that the auditory stimulation has been enhanced by the visually displayed virtual hand. The integration of visual and action auditory signals is one of the most important cues for human's spatial position perception [29].

In contrast, no significant effect of the virtual hand was observed in visual-tactile conditions (Figure 13, C5 and C6). Iriki et al. studied behavioral effects of tool-use in humans and monkeys [30, 31]. The results indicated that body representation in the brain could be changed following tool-use. Body image has been extended to the tool. Studies in VHI also reported that the illusion of body ownership can be extended to noncorporeal objects by synchronous movements [32]. Note that wooden stick shaped object without movement was reported to be not capable of inducing the illusion [21]. In our experiments, participants extended their body image to the virtual mallet instead of the virtual hand by performing active movements with synchronous visual-tactile stimulation. The strength of the illusory ownership has not reduced because the effect of the virtual hand has been substituted by the virtual mallet.

We conclude that not only visual stimulation but also multisensory integration with active movement is important to induce a strong illusion of body ownership in VR space. Furthermore, a stronger sense of immersion can be expected by performing a free movement task before the operation in VR space.

CONCLUSION

In this study, we constructed a VR system that provided interactive feedback of visual, tactile, and auditory stimulation. We investigated the effects of different hand moving conditions and multisensory integration in the illusion of body ownership with active movement. We designed a virtual xylophone playing task for the VHI experiments. The VR system provided synchronous visual, tactile, and auditory stimulation when the participants played the xylophone in VR environment. Furthermore, we evaluated the effect of the visual existence of the virtual hand under different sensory stimulation conditions.

The experiments showed that (1) free movement yielded strongest illusion in different active movement conditions, (2) tactile stimulation had more significant influences than auditory stimulation on the VHI, and (3) multisensory integration of visual, tactile, and auditory signals induced strongest illusion. We conclude that free active movement with multisensory feedback is the most effective way to induce the illusory ownership in VR space. This study suggested a possibility to improve the sense of immersion in VR space, provide multisensory feedback, and perform a set of free active movements before the formal operation.

We also expect that our study can improve the sense of immersion in VR based clinical applications, such as treatment for phantom limb pain [33] and pain relief during acupuncture [34]. A network of multisensory and homeostatic brain areas was reported to be responsible for maintaining a "body-matrix" [35]. We consider that, by using multisensory integration in VR space, training with virtual limb can be an effective therapeutic method for phantom limb pain experienced by amputees. The VR system used in this study can be extended to virtual rehabilitation training for patients' recovery after stroke. For further study, experiments for investigating the effectiveness of different multisensory synchrony conditions will be carried out. The changes of electromyography (EMG) [36] and position of the arm/hand [37] will be measured and analyzed quantitatively. The spatial information of the arm/hand during active movement can be obtained by using a motion capture system, which we used to develop a gesture based VR system [38].

AUTHORS' CONTRIBUTIONS

Woong Choi, Liang Li, Satoru Satoh, and Kozaburo Hachimura conceived and designed the experiments. Woong Choi and Satoru Satoh performed the experiments. Woong Choi, Liang Li, and Satoru Satoh analyzed the data. Woong Choi, Liang Li, and Satoru Satoh wrote the paper.

REFERENCES

1. M. Jeannerod, "The mechanism of self-recognition in humans," Behavioural Brain Research, vol. 142, no. 1-2, pp. 1–15, 2003.
2. S. Gallagher, "Philosophical conceptions of the self: implications for cognitive science," Trends in Cognitive Sciences, vol. 4, no. 1, pp. 14–21, 2000.
3. M. Botvinick and J. Cohen, "Rubber hands 'feel' touch that eyes see," Nature, vol. 391, no. 6669, p. 756, 1998.
4. H. H. Ehrsson, N. P. Holmes, and R. E. Passingham, "Touching a rubber hand: feeling of body ownership is associated with activity in multisensory brain areas," The Journal of Neuroscience, vol. 25, no. 45, pp. 10564–10573, 2005.
5. M. Samad, A. J. Chung, and L. Shams, "Perception of body ownership is driven by Bayesian sensory inference," PLoS ONE, vol. 10, no. 2, Article ID e0117178, 2015.
6. X. Fuchs, M. Riemer, M. Diers, H. Flor, and J. Trojan, "Perceptual drifts of real and artificial limbs in the rubber hand illusion," Scientific Reports, vol. 6, article 24362, 2016.
7. F. Pavani, C. Spence, and J. Driver, "Visual capture of touch: out-of-the-body experiences with rubber gloves," Psychological Science, vol. 11, no. 5, pp. 353–359, 2000.
8. M. Costantini and P. Haggard, "The rubber hand illusion: sensitivity and reference frame for body ownership," Consciousness and Cognition, vol. 16, no. 2, pp. 229–240, 2007.
9. M. Slater, D. Perez-Marcos, H. H. Ehrsson, and M. V. Sanchez-Vives, "Towards a digital body: the virtual arm illusion," Frontiers in Human Neuroscience, vol. 2, article 6, 2008.
10. F. Short and R. Ward, "Virtual limbs and body space: critical features for the distinction between body space and near-body space," Journal of Experimental Psychology: Human Perception and Performance, vol. 35, no. 4, pp. 1092–1103, 2009.
11. W. A. IJsselsteijn, Y. A. W. De Kort, and A. Haans, "Is this my hand I see before me? The rubber hand illusion in reality, virtual reality, and mixed reality," Presence: Teleoperators and Virtual Environments, vol. 15, no. 4, pp. 455–464, 2006.
12. D. Perez-Marcos, M. V. Sanchez-Vives, and M. Slater, "Is my hand

connected to my body? The impact of body continuity and arm alignment on the virtual hand illusion," Cognitive Neurodynamics, vol. 6, no. 4, pp. 295–305, 2012.

13. H. H. Ehrsson, C. Spence, and R. E. Passingham, "That's my hand! Activity in premotor cortex reflects feeling of ownership of a limb," Science, vol. 305, no. 5685, pp. 875–877, 2004.
14. M. V. Sanchez-Vives, B. Spanlang, A. Frisoli, M. Bergamasco, and M. Slater, "Virtual hand illusion induced by visuomotor correlations," PLoS ONE, vol. 5, no. 4, article e10381, 2010.
15. T. Dummer, A. Picot-Annand, T. Neal, and C. Moore, "Movement and the rubber hand illusion," Perception, vol. 38, no. 2, pp. 271–280, 2009.
16. Y. Yuan and A. Steed, "Is the rubber hand illusion induced by immersive virtual reality?" in Proceedings of the IEEE Virtual Reality Conference (VR '10), pp. 95–102, Boston, Mass, USA, March 2010.
17. N. David, A. Newen, and K. Vogeley, "The 'sense of agency' and its underlying cognitive and neural mechanisms," Consciousness and Cognition, vol. 17, no. 2, pp. 523–534, 2008.
18. B. O'Mera, Auditory information in the form of a scratching sound enhances the effects of the rubber hand illusion [Honors thesis], University of Dayton, Dayton, Ohio, USA, 2014.
19. G. Darnai, T. Szolcsányi, G. Hegedüs et al., "Hearing visuo-tactile synchrony—sound-induced proprioceptive drift in the invisible hand illusion," British Journal of Psychology, 2016.
20. M. Rohde, M. Luca, and M. O. Ernst, "The rubber hand illusion: feeling of ownership and proprioceptive drift do not go hand in hand," PLoS ONE, vol. 6, no. 6, Article ID e21659, 2011.
21. M. Tsakiris and P. Haggard, "The rubber hand illusion revisited: visuotactile integration and self-attribution," Journal of Experimental Psychology: Human Perception and Performance, vol. 31, no. 1, pp. 80–91, 2005.
22. V. Interrante, B. Ries, and L. Anderson, "Distance perception in immersive virtual environments, revisited," in Proceedings of the IEEE Virtual Reality Conference, pp. 3–10, IEEE, Albuquerque, NM, USA, March 2006.
23. L. Kaufman and J. H. Kaufman, "Explaining the moon illusion," Proceedings of the National Academy of Sciences of the United States of America, vol. 97, no. 1, pp. 500–505, 2000.

24. J. Zhang, K. Ma, and B. Hommel, "The virtual hand illusion is moderated by context-induced spatial reference frames," Frontiers in Psychology, vol. 6, article 1659, 2015.
25. D. M. Lloyd, "Spatial limits on referred touch to an alien limb may reflect boundaries of visuo-tactile peripersonal space surrounding the hand," Brain and Cognition, vol. 64, no. 1, pp. 104–109, 2007.
26. E. von Holst and H. Mittelstaedt, "Das Reafferenzprinzip—wechselwirkungen zwischen zentralnervensystem und peripherie," Die Naturwissenschaften, vol. 37, no. 20, pp. 464–476, 1950.
27. G. Rizzolatti and L. Craighero, "The mirror-neuron system," Annual Review of Neuroscience, vol. 27, no. 1, pp. 169–192, 2004.
28. A. Murata and H. Ishida, "Representation of bodily self in the multimodal parieto-premotor network," in Representation and Brain, S. Funahashi, Ed., pp. 151–176, Springer, Berlin, Germany, 2007.
29. A. Tajadura-Jiménez, A. Väljamäe, I. Toshima, T. Kimura, M. Tsakiris, and N. Kitagawa, "Action sounds recalibrate perceived tactile distance," Current Biology, vol. 22, no. 13, pp. R516–R517, 2012.
30. A. Maravita and A. Iriki, "Tools for the body (schema)," Trends in Cognitive Sciences, vol. 8, no. 2, pp. 79–86, 2004.
31. A. Iriki and M. Taoka, "Triadic (ecological, neural, cognitive) niche construction: a scenario of human brain evolution extrapolating tool use and language from the control of reaching actions," Philosophical Transactions of the Royal Society B: Biological Sciences, vol. 367, no. 1585, pp. 10–23, 2012.
32. K. Ma and B. Hommel, "Body-ownership for actively operated non-corporeal objects," Consciousness and Cognition, vol. 36, pp. 75–86, 2015.
33. C. D. Murray, E. Patchick, S. Pettifer, F. Caillette, and T. Howard, "Immersive virtual reality as a rehabilitative technology for phantom limb experience: a protocol," CyberPsychology & Behavior, vol. 9, no. 2, pp. 167–170, 2006.
34. D.-S. Chang, Y.-J. Kim, S.-H. Lee et al., "Modifying bodily self-awareness during acupuncture needle stimulation using the rubber hand illusion," Evidence-based Complementary and Alternative Medicine, vol. 2013, Article ID 849602, 7 pages, 2013.
35. G. L. Moseley, A. Gallace, and C. Spence, "Bodily illusions in health and disease: physiological and clinical perspectives and the concept of

a cortical 'body matrix'," Neuroscience and Biobehavioral Reviews, vol. 36, no. 1, pp. 34–46, 2012.

36. T. Tsuji, H. Yamakawa, A. Yamashita et al., "Analysis of electromyography and skin conductance response during rubber hand illusion," in Proceedings of the IEEE Workshop on Advanced Robotics and Its Social Impacts (ARSO '13), pp. 88–93, Tokyo, Japan, November 2013.
37. I. Olivé and A. Berthoz, "Combined induction of rubber-hand illusion and out-of-body experiences," Frontiers in Psychology, vol. 3, article 128, 2012.
38. J. Minagawa, W. Choi, S. Tsurumi et al., "Supporting system with hand gesture for location-based augmented reality," in Proceedings of the IEEE 4th Global Conference on Consumer Electronics (GCCE '15), pp. 479–480, Osaka, Japan, October 2015.

Chapter 2

Brain-Computer Interface Systems used for Virtual Reality Control

Gert Pfurtscheller[1], Robert Leeb[2], Josef Faller[1] and Christa Neuper[1]

[1]Laboratory of Brain-Computer Interfaces (BCI-Lab), Institute for Knowledge Discovery, Graz University of Technology, Austria

[2]Chair on Non-Invasive Brain-Machine Interface, School of Engineering, Ecole Polytechnique Fédérale de Lausanne, Switzerland

INTRODUCTION

A Brain-Computer Interface (BCI) is a non-muscular communication channel for connecting the brain to a computer or another device. Currently, non-invasive BCIs transform thoughtrelated changes in the electroencephalogram (EEG) online and in real time into control signals. In such an EEG-based BCI, specific features are extracted from brain-signals, transformed

Citation: Gert Pfurtscheller, Robert Leeb, Josef Faller and Christa Neuper (January 8th 2011). Brain-Computer Interface Systems Used for Virtual Reality Control, Virtual Reality, Jae-Jin Kim, IntechOpen, DOI: 10.5772/13467.

into a control signal, and used to restore communication to patients with locked-in-syndrome or to control neuroprosthesis in patients with spinal cord injuries (Birbaumer et al., 1999; Pfurtscheller et al., 2008b; Wolpaw et al., 2002). In addition to these applications, which focus on communication and control, the related field of neurofeedback supports feedback training in people suffering from epilepsy, autism, stroke, and emotional or attentional disorders (Birbaumer & Cohen, 2007).

Today the world of BCI applications is expanding and new fields are opening. One new direction involves BCIs to control virtual reality (VR), including BCIs for games, or using VR as a powerful feedback medium to reduce the need for BCI training (Leeb et al., 2007b; Scherer et al., 2008). Virtual environments (VE) can provide an excellent testing ground for procedures that could be adapted to real world scenarios, especially for patients with disabilities. If people can learn to control their movements or perform specific tasks in a VE, this could justify the much greater expense of building physical devices such as a wheelchair or robot arm that is controlled by a BCI. BCIs are more and more moving out of the laboratory and becoming also useful for healthy users in certain situations (Nijholt et al., 2008).

One of the first efforts to combine VR and BCI technologies was Bayliss and Ballard (2000) and Bayliss (2003). They introduced a VR smart home in which users could control different appliances using a P300-based BCI. Pineda et al. (2003) showed that immersive feedback based on a computer game can help people learn to control a BCI based on imagined movement more quickly than mundane feedback, a finding we later validated with other immersive feedback (Leeb et al., 2006; 2007b). Lalor et al. (2005) used a steady-state visual evoked potential (SSVEP)-based BCI to control a character in an immersive 3-D gaming environment. Recently, Leeb et al. (2007b) have reported on exploring a smart virtual apartment using a motor imagery-based BCI, and Holzner et al. (2009) in an experiment for P300-based BCI for smart home control.

This short overview about BCI applications in VR shows that there are many different types of BCIs. The next section provides a short introduction to BCIs.

DEFINITION AND BASIC PRINCIPLES OF A BCI

Wolpaw et al. (2002) defined a BCI as a "...new non-muscular channel for sending messages and commands to the external world". Here, we clarify this definition to emphasize that any BCI must have the 4 following components (Pfurtscheller et al., 2010a):

- Direct recording: The BCI must rely at least partly on direct measures of brain activity, such as through electrical potentials, magnetic fields, or hemodynamic changes.
- Real time processing: The signal processing must occur online and yield a communication or control signal.
- Feedback: Goal-directed feedback, about the success or failure of the control, must be provided to the user.
- Intentional control: The user must perform an intentional, goal-directed mental action to control, such as imagining movement or focusing on a stimulus.

These definitions implicate that each BCI is a closed-loop system with two adaptive controllers: the user's brain, which produces the signals and provides the input to the BCI; and the BCI itself, which analyses the brain signals and transforms them to a control signal as the BCI output (Figure 1).

The EEG is the most widely used brain signal in BCIs (Mason et al., 2007), and is also the most common signal when using a BCI system for VR control. Two types of changes can be extracted from the ongoing EEG signals: one change is time and phase-locked (evoked) to an externally or internally-paced event, the other is non-phase-locked (induced). Evoked signals include event-related potentials (ERPs), including the P300 and SSVEPs (Allison et al., 2008). Induced signals include the dynamic amplitude changes of oscillations in different frequency bands (Pfurtscheller & Lopes da Silva, 1999; Pfurtscheller & Neuper, 2010). Thus, we can differentiate between 2 types of BCI systems. One is based on predefined mental tasks and classifying induced brain activities (Figure 1a), while the other is based on sensory stimulation (e.g. visual) and classifying evoked potential changes (Figure 1b).

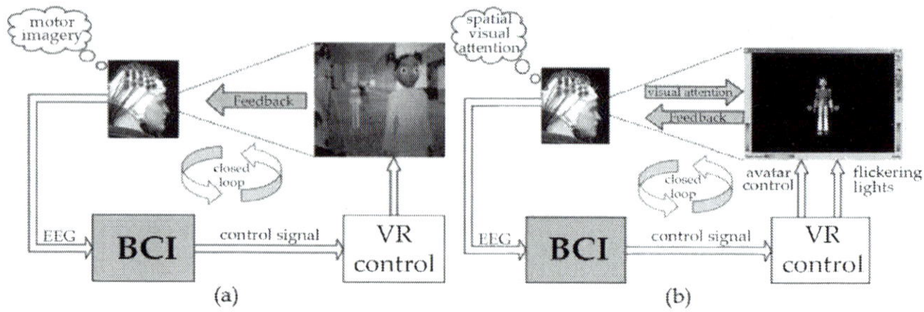

Figure 1: Principles of BCI systems without (a) and with external stimulation (b). Motor imagery is the most common mental strategy in BCIs which do not rely on external stimulation to generate the necessary brain activity. BCIs that do rely on external stimulation to elicit brain activity typically involve spatial visual attention.

Three different BCI approaches have received the most attention in recent years:

- ***P300-based BCI (P300 BCI):*** The P300 is the positive component of the evoked potential that may develop about 300 ms after an item is flashed. The user focuses on one flashing item while ignoring other stimuli. Whenever the target stimulus flashes, it yields a larger P300 than the other possible choices. P300 BCIs are typically used to spell (Allison & Pineda, 2006; Donchin et al., 2000; Farwell & Donchin, 1988), but have been validated with other tasks such as control of a mobile robot (Bell et al., 2008) or a smart home control (Holzner et al., 2009).
- ***SSVEP-based BCI (SSVEP BCI):*** Steady-state evoked potentials (SSEPs) occur when sensory stimuli are repetitively delivered rapidly enough that the relevant neuronal structures do not return to their resting states. In a BCI application, the user focuses on one of several stimuli, each of which flicker at a different rate and/or phase. Flickering light sources are typically used to trigger steady-state visual evoked potentials. Gao et al. (2003) described a BCI with 48 flickering lights and a high information transfer rate of 68 bits/min. This was the fastest BCI reported in the published literature until recently, when the same group described some improved approaches (Bin et al., 2009). Like P300 BCIs, SSVEP BCIs require no training and can facilitate rapid communication

(Allison et al., 2008; Krusienski et al., 2006). SSVEP BCIs have also recently expanded to tasks beyond spelling, such as controlling a virtual character (avatar) in a computer game (Faller et al., 2010; Lalor et al., 2005; Martinez et al., 2007) or controlling an orthosis (Pfurtscheller et al., 2010b).

- ***ERD-based BCI (ERD BCI, SMR BCI):*** Brain rhythms can either display an event-related amplitude decrease or desynchronization (ERD) or an event-related amplitude increase or synchronization (ERS) (Pfurtscheller & Lopes da Silva, 1999). The term ERD BCI describes any BCI system that relies on the detection of amplitude changes in sensorimotor rhythms (mu and central beta rhythms) and/or other brain oscillations, also including short-lasting postimagery beta bursts (beta ERS, beta rebound) (Blankertz et al., 2007; Pfurtscheller et al., 2006a; 2008b; Pfurtscheller & Solis- Escalante, 2009). The term SMR BCI is frequently used when only sensorimotor rhythms are classified (Birbaumer & Cohen, 2007). In the standard protocol, the user performs a motor imagery task to consciously modify brain rhythms. Motor imagery results in a somatotopically organised activation pattern, similar to that observed when the same movement is really executed (Lotze et al., 1999; Pfurtscheller & Neuper, 2010). In particular, hand and feet motor imagery affect sensorimotor EEG rhythms in ways that allow a BCI to detect such changes online and generate a reliable control signal.

The ERD BCI can operate in two different modes: the input data are either processed in a predefined time windows of a few seconds each following cue stimuli (synchronous or cuebased BCI), or continuously sample-by-sample (asynchronous or self-paced BCI). In a synchronous protocol, the user performs a mental task after each cue; the EEG processing is time-locked to externally-paced cues that are repeated in intervals of several seconds because the onset of motor imagery is precisely known. No cue is presented in the asynchronous mode. Hence, the system is continuously available for control, allowing users to freely decide when they wish to generate a control signal. The output (control) signal of a BCI can be either the result of the user's intended control (IC) or intended non-control (INC). In the latter case, during the resting state, undefined mental tasks (thoughts) or artifacts may be erroneously classified as control signals. Such an asynchronous BCI is more complex and demanding for developers, even though it may be easier for the user. However, asynchronous BCIs have been validated even in advanced situations, such as navigating in a virtual environment (Leeb et al., 2007a; 2007d; Scherer et al., 2008).

VIRTUAL REALITY SYSTEM

In order to carry out the VE experiments, two different and complex systems had to be integrated: the BCI and the VR system. Figure 2 shows that both systems run on two different machines (hardware) and different platforms (software). The interaction between them is realized via a network connection (usually TCP/IP).

The participant is placed in the middle of a multi-projection based stereo and head-tracked VR system commonly known as a "CAVE" (Cruz-Neira et al., 1993). The surround projection system consists of three rear-projected active stereo screens (left, right and front wall on which the images are projected from outside) and a front-projected screen on the floor (image for the floor is projected from above), as shown in the right part of Figure 2. It generates three-dimensional stereoscopic representations of computer animated worlds, depending on the current viewing position and direction of the visitor.

The projections on the screens are continuously adapted to the movements of the visitor by re-computing the projected images for the respective current viewing position and direction (update rate of 30 – 50 times per second). The position of the subject is determined using four infrared cameras that keep track of a number of highly retro-reflective balls that are attached to the shutter glasses. This makes it possible to compute images for every screen that accurately fit the visitor's view on the simulated scene.

A special feature of any multi-wall VR system is that the images on the adjacent walls are seamlessly joined together, so that participants do not see the physical corners but the continuous virtual world that is projected with active stereo (Slater et al., 2002). The basic idea is to let a user become immersed in a 3-D scene (Slater & Usoh, 1993). Therefore, the subject has to wear shutter glasses (CrystalEyes, StereoGraphics Corporation, San Rafael, USA) to see the two separate stereoscopic images generated for each eye of the observer. The creation of the 3-D virtual environment entails two consecutive steps: first, the creation of a 3-D model of the scene; and second, the generation of a VR-application that controls and animates the modeled scene.

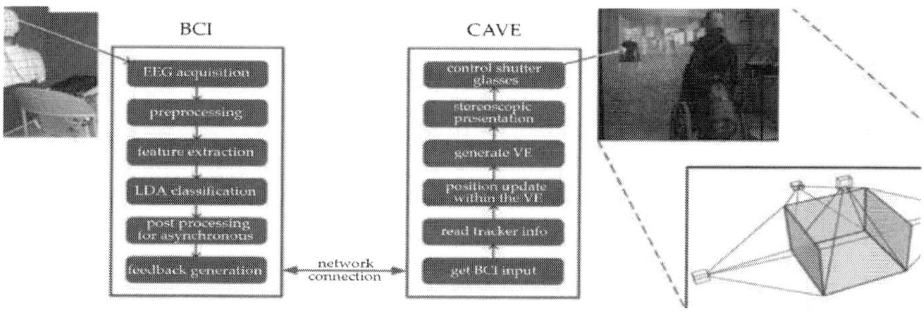

Figure 2: System diagram of the hardware setup. The BCI system on the left analyses the EEG signals, and the extracted control commands are transferred into movements with the VE projected in the CAVE system. On the right bottom side is the physical CAVE installation with indicated projection screens. Modified from Leeb (2008).

SETUP OF AN EEG-BASED BCI

The first step is always the same. The computer (classifier) has to learn how subject-specific EEG data (trials) look during execution of a predefined mental task. In general, each trial starts with a warning stimulus followed by a cue stimulus, indicating the type of mental task. The task depends on whether the BCI requires external stimulation to generate the necessary brain signals. P300 BCI and SSVEP BCIs do require such stimuli, while ERD BCIs do not. In the former BCI approaches, the user typically must pay attention to one out of 2 or more flickering lights or to flashing letters, numbers, and/or other symbols or commands. In the latter case the user has to perform a motor imagery task (e.g. hand or foot movement imagery) as indicated by the cue stimulus. During this training, about 80 trials of EEG data (each lasting several seconds) are recorded without any feedback to the user and used to set up the classifier. In a second step, the user has to perform the cue-paced mental task, and real-time feedback informs the user about success or failure of the online classification. P300- based and SSVEP-based BCIs have an apparent advantage in that both require no or only minimal user training. In contrast, ERD-based BCIs often need extensive user training, sometimes lasting many weeks (for details see Pfurtscheller et al., 2000; 2006a).

The experimental procedure commonly used with ERD-based BCI research can be divided into the following steps:

- The (new, naive) subject must be instructed on what exactly is going to be done. It is crucial that the subject performs kinesthetic motor imagery (Neuper et al., 2005).
- Training without feedback is done to acquire subject specific data for the imagery task used.
- The most discriminative features (e. g., frequency bands) are extracted from this data.
- The classifier is set up based on the features from step 3. If the classification accuracy is above 70 %, move on the next step, otherwise continue with step 2. This involves the selection of the best mental strategy, the localization of the best electrode recording sites and the optimal frequency bands.
- Training with feedback; that is, online processing of EEG signals.
- Classifier update, if the frequency bands have been modified or the EEG patterns have been changed.
- Online applications like virtual environments can be controlled.

In general, multi-EEG channel recordings using various mental strategies can be performed at the beginning of step 2. Furthermore, offline optimization can be applied to determine the best mental strategies, electrode positions and frequency bands.

A BCI-system is, in general, composed of the following components: Signal acquisition, signal processing (which includes preprocessing, feature extraction, classification / detection, and post processing), application interface and an output device or application (left part of Figure 2; see also Wolpaw et al., 2002). For the experiments reported here, the Graz-BCI system was used (for details see Pfurtscheller et al., 2006c). It consisted of a biosignal amplifier (gBSamp, g.tec medical engineering, Graz, Austria), one data acquisition card (E-Series, National Instruments Corporation, Austin, USA), and a standard personal computer running Windows XP operating system (Microsoft Corporation, Redmond, USA) The recording was handled by rtsBCI (Scherer, 2004), based on MATLAB 7.0.4 (MathWorks, Inc., Natick, USA) in combination with Simulink 6.2, Real-Time Workshop 6.2 and the open source package BIOSIG (BioSig, 2010). In the case of an ERD BCI band power (BP) features were estimated from the ongoing EEG by digitally band-pass filtering the EEG recordings (Butterworth IIR filter of order 5) and squaring and averaging the samples over the past second. Finally, the logarithm was computed from this time series. To distinguish between the two motor imagery tasks, Fisher's linear discriminant analysis

(LDA, Bishop, 1995) was applied to the BP estimates (sample-by-sample).

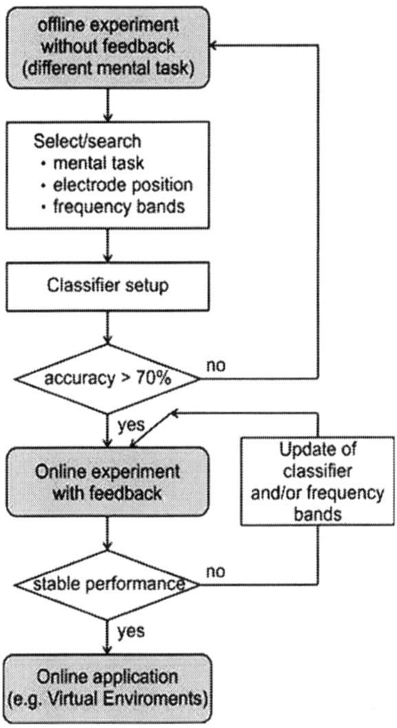

Figure 3: General workflow of an experiment with a motor imagery-based BCI.

In the case of a SSVEP BCI, after calculation of the power spectrum, the first, second and third harmonic components are individually defined for each target frequency. For selecting one class, the sum of all its harmonic frequency components need to be larger than that of the other classes (for details see Müller-Putz et al., 2005).

The philosophy of the Graz-BCI is to use as few electrodes as possible for online experiments, which makes the BCI both, more comfortable and easier to apply, especially for subjects out of laboratory (e.g. at home or in working space). In all of the 4 experiments reported, EEG was recorded with an electrode cap (Easycap, Germany) fitted to the subject's head. EEG electrodes were mounted bipolarly over the sensorimotor cortex (ERD BCI) or over the occipital cortex (SSVEP BCI). The EEG was amplified (power-line notch filter was activated), band pass filtered between 0.5 and 100 Hz (EEG acquisition and preprocessing block, see Figure 2, left part) and recorded with a sampling frequency of 250 Hz.

WALKING FROM THOUGHT - IMPACT OF IMMERSIVE ENVIRONMENTS

The goals of the first study were: (i) to demonstrate that it is possible to move forward – "to walk" – within a VE (e.g. a virtual street) without any muscular activity, using only the imagination of movements recorded with a BCI and (ii) to compare the influences of different feedback types (common BCI feedback versus VE feedback (HMD and CAVE)) on the BCI performance. Therefore, the results from three different feedback (FB) conditions were compared: First, the results of the standard BCI with a simple bar graph; second, using a head-mounted display (HMD) as a FB device; and finally, using a highly immersive "CAVE" projection environment (see Figure 4a). In case of the HMD and CAVE conditions, the idea was to use the imagination of foot movement to walk through the VE, based on a synchronous BCI paradigm. The subject was instructed by a cue to imagine a right hand movement (single beep) or a foot movement (double beep). Three healthy volunteers participated several times over 5 months in this study. The task given to each participant was to walk to the end of a virtual street (see Figure 4a), and only in the case of successful foot motor imagery would a motion occur (for further details see Leeb et al., 2006; Pfurtscheller et al., 2006a). Correct classification of foot motor imagery was accompanied by forward movement at a constant speed in the virtual street, whereas a correct classification of hand motor imagery stopped the motion. Incorrect classification of foot motor imagery resulted in halting, and incorrect classification of hand motor imagery in backward motion (same speed). The walking distance was scored as "cumulative achieved mileage" (CAM, Leeb & Pfurtscheller, 2004; Leeb et al., 2006), which was the integrated forward/backward distance covered during foot movement imagination and was used as the performance measurement. So the BCI output of the online classification was either used to control the length and orientation of the bar graph feedback (control condition) or to move through a virtual street (HMD or CAVE condition). The CAM performances of the bar graph feedback experiments were simulated offline to enable comparison.

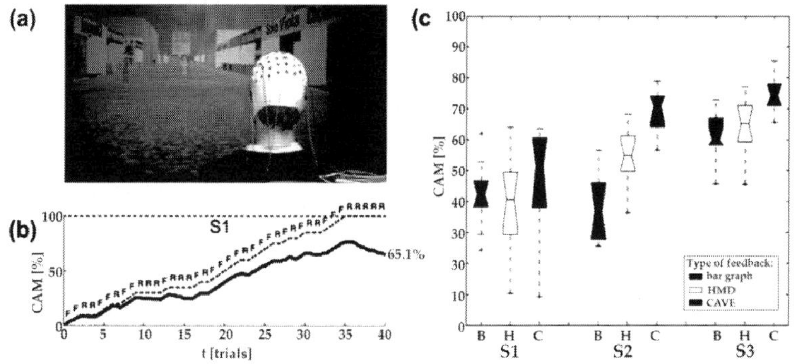

Figure 4: (a) Participant in the virtual main street with shops and animated avatars. The subject wears an electrode cap and shutter glasses. (b) Examples of task performances displayed in the theoretical possible CAM (dashed line) and the real CAM (full line) of one run of one subject. The cue class indicated is written above the line. Due to the random cue sequence, each participant had a different theoretical pathway (dashed line). (c) Boxplot of all achieved CAMs of all subjects and feedback types. The diagram consists of 3 groups, each corresponding to a subject. Within these groups the left plots corresponds to standard bargraph feedback (B), the middle to HMD feedback (H) and the right one to CAVE feedback (C). Modified from Leeb et al. (2007c).

The CAM of an example result of subject S1 (session 2, run 4) is plotted in Figure 4b. Both the theoretically possible CAM (dashed line) and the real achieved CAM (full line) are plotted. A CAM of 100 % corresponds to a correct classification of all 40 imagery tasks over the entire feedback time. A random classification would result in an expected CAM of 0 %. It is almost impossible to achieve the maximum attainable CAM of 100 %, because even a small procrastination or hesitation reduces mileage.

All the subjects were able to walk through the virtual street, and the resulting BCI performance in the VR tasks was comparable to standard BCI recordings. The use of VR as feedback stimulated the participant's performances and provided motivation. All the subjects achieved their best results within the CAVE and the worst in the standard BCI conditions. The mean achieved CAM of all participants and condition is plotted in Figure 4c. Two participants showed an increase over the condition, but participant S1 achieved worse results with the HMD (for further details see Leeb et al., 2006). These data indicate that foot motor imagery is a suitable mental strategy to control events within the VEs. Imagination of feet movement is a mental task which comes very close to that of natural walking. In the CAVE condition (highest immersion) the performance of two participants was especially outstanding (up to 100 % BCI classification accuracy of single trials), although we observed a variability in the classification results between individual runs.

EXPLORING A VIRTUAL APARTMENT USING AN ERD-BASED BCI

The second study shows that ten naive subjects can be trained in a synchronous paradigm within 3 sessions to navigate freely through a virtual apartment (see Figure 5a), whereby, at every junction, the subjects could decide on their own how they wanted to explore the VE. The very important and crucial step away from a synchronized or cue-based BCI and from laboratory conditions towards real world applications is performed in this experiment. The virtual apartment was similarly designed to a real world application, with a goal-oriented task, a high mental workload and a variable decision period for the subject. All the subjects were able to perform long and stable motor imagery over a minimum time of two seconds (for further details see Leeb et al., 2007b).

In this paradigm, only the start of the decision period was indicated with a "neutral" cue consisting of two arrows (see Figure 5b). The subject could decide for him/herself which motor imagery he/she wanted to perform and therefore which direction he/she wanted to select, but walking was only possible along predefined pathways through the corridors or rooms. The subject received feedback by viewing the size of the arrows, which were modulated depending on the BCI classification output. In this case, the corresponding arrow was huge and the subject was turned to the right/left/straight. Afterwards, the system automatically guided the subject to the next junction. As stated above, a "neutral cue" was used to indicate the starting point of the decision period (similar to the cue-based BCI), but the neutral cues were completely embedded in the given task and the duration of the decision periods (similar to trials) was variable, depending only on the performance of the subject. The subjects were instructed to go to a predefined target room. A small flag pole on the map indicated the destination which should be reached by using the shortest route through the maze-like apartment (see Figure 5a). The performance error was calculated by dividing the number of wrong decisions by the total number of junctions.

Each of the ten participating subjects performed 12 runs of variable duration in the virtual apartment. All the runs started at the same point (entrance door). During the first run, no instructions were given to the subjects, so they could walk freely through the apartment for 5 minutes to become familiar with the VE. In all the other runs, the subjects were instructed to go to a predefined target room. A small flag pole on the map indicated the destination which should be reached by using the shortest route through the maze-like apartment (see Figure 5a). Only one target was given in the first two runs, but in further runs, the number of targets was increased and only one target was visible each time. If this target was reached, either the follow-up target was inserted or the run was finished. Each run was limited to 5 minutes in total.

For comparison, synchronous BCI sessions with a standard bar-graph feedback were performed before and after the sessions with the virtual apartment, whereby the experiments with the virtual apartment were performed in front of a normal TFT monitor (TFT) and within an immersive virtual environment (iVE). In Figure 5c, the mean and standard error over all subjects is given and the statistical differences between the sessions are marked. All the subjects were able to deal with the variable trial length (the duration of the trial depended on how fast or slow the subject could perform a decision) and the variable inter-trial interval. The subjects noted that the task in the virtual apartment was much harder compared to the prior feedback training, because it was not only necessary to perform the "correct" imagination, but also the shortest way through the apartment had to be found. Therefore, the cognitive load was much higher compared to the standard BCI paradigm (for further details see Leeb et al., 2007b). According to our hypothesis, we found that the performance improves (that is, reduced error) over the sessions, and the lowest error was found during the sessions with virtual feedback. The slight but stable performance improvement of all subjects is very well known as the training effect (Pfurtscheller & Neuper, 2001; Wolpaw et al., 2002).

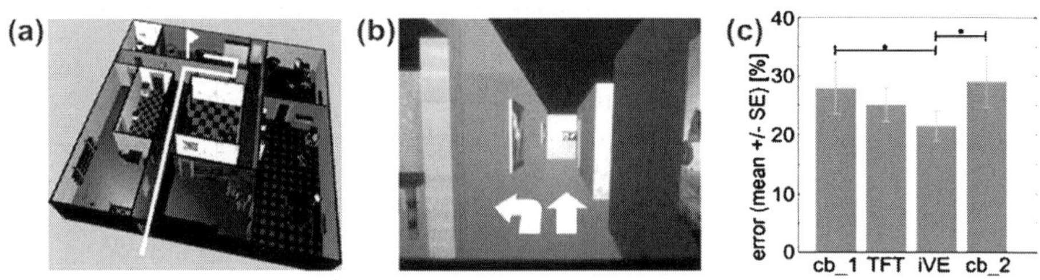

Figure 5: (a) View into the virtual apartment, with one possible pathway plotted in white. The target room is marked with a small flag pole (in this example, the room at the upper end of the apartment). (b) First-person view of the virtual apartment with two arrows indicating the possible directions to go ("neutral cue"). (c) Mean ± standard error (SE) over all subjects of the integrated classification error and performance error. The asterisk (* $p< 0.05$) shows statistically significant post-hoc differences. Cb_1 and cb_2 are the two sessions with standard BCI feedback before and after the VR sessions. TFT is the session with VR feedback presented on a normal TFT monitor and iVE in an immersive environment. Modified from Leeb (2008).

EXPLORING A VIRTUAL APARTMENT USING AN SSVEP-BASED BCI

Another study involving seven healthy participants (see Faller et al., 2010) presented an even more flexible, asynchronous navigation paradigm within the same apartment scenario as in Leeb et al. (2007b) using an SSVEP-based BCI. The participants were instructed to navigate an avatar to two waypoints (see Figure 6a) along a given path in two runs, by alternately focusing attention on one of three visual stimuli that were flickering at the different frequencies 12, 15 and 20 Hz. Successful classifications of the according classes triggered the associated commands (i) turn 45° left (ii) turn 45° right and (iii) walk one step ahead.

In contrast to the work presented in Chapter 6, this system requires minimal setup and training time and offers faster, more accurate control, with the trade-off that it requires the user to visually fixate certain stimuli in order to communicate a control signal. The stimuli were presented directly within the 3D environment (see Figure 6b). Compared to systems that rely on external stimuli (e.g. LEDs), this approach is more dynamic and allows the user to better focus on goal-directed interactions and deal with a higher mental workload in the task.

Six out of seven subjects were able to navigate to the first waypoint in the first run halfway through the apartment. Five participants successfully reached the second waypoint in the second run. The average positive predictive value (precision, PPV = TP/(TP+FP), whereby TP stands for true positive and FP for false positive detections) over all participants was 91.7 ± 9.9 %, which resulted in an average of 6.5 ± 2.3 TP and 0.4 ± 0.4 FP activations per minute given a dwell-time of 1.5 s and a refractory period of 4s. These fixed temporal restrictions do of course limit the number of possible control commands per minute. However, some factors other than speed may be more important for the user. For instance, choosing a higher refractory period (Townsend et al., 2004) makes the SSVEP BCI easier to use, more likely to provide effective communication for a broader population of users, more reliable, and less fatiguing. This system demonstrates a virtual feedback environment that allows both disabled and healthy users to seamlessly communicate and interact through an intuitive, natural and friendly interface.

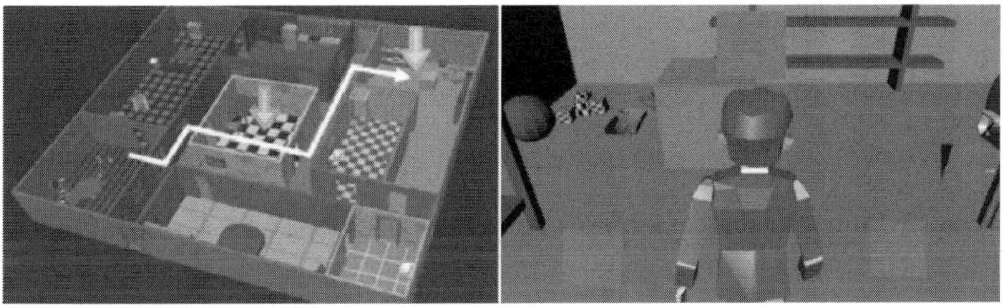

(a) (b)

Figure 6: (a) Overview of the apartment showing the path along the two way-points (marked by the arrows) that the participants are supposed to reach in the runs 1 and 2 respectively. (b) Screenshot of an in-game scene, showing the avatar in third person perspective along with the three navigation stimuli on the left, the right and over the avatar's head.

MOVING A WHEELCHAIR IN VR

Finally, we report on a 35 year old male tetraplegic subject. After a traumatic injury of the spinal cord in 1998, he has a complete motor and sensory lesion below C5 and an incomplete lesion below C4. During an intensive training period of approximately 4 months, he learned to control the cue-based Graz-BCI (details about this training are reported elsewhere (Pfurtscheller et al.,

2000). Specifically, the midcentral focused beta oscillations with a dominant frequency of approximately 17 Hz allowed a brain-switch like application and control of a VE (recorded close to Cz, foot representation area). Only one single EEG channel was recorded bipolarly at Cz (foot representation area). One single logarithmic band power feature was estimated from the ongoing EEG (see Figure 7b-c). A simple threshold (TH) was used to distinguish between foot movement imagination (IC) and rest (INC). For further details see Leeb et al. (2007a).

The tetraplegic participant was placed with his wheelchair in the middle of a multiprojection based stereo VR system ("CAVE"). The VE used was a virtual street with shops on both sides (Leeb et al., 2006) and populated with 15 avatars, who were lined up along the street (see Figure 7a). The participant was instructed to "move" from avatar to avatar towards the end of the virtual street (65 length units) by movement imagination of his paralyzed feet. Only when foot MI was detected (IC) did the subject move forward (see Figure 7d, walking speed 1.25 units/second). Every time he was about to pass an avatar, he had to stop very close to it. The avatar started talking to the subject if he was standing close and still to it for one second. Each avatar was surrounded by an invisible communication sphere (0.5 – 2.5 units) and the subject had to stop within this sphere.

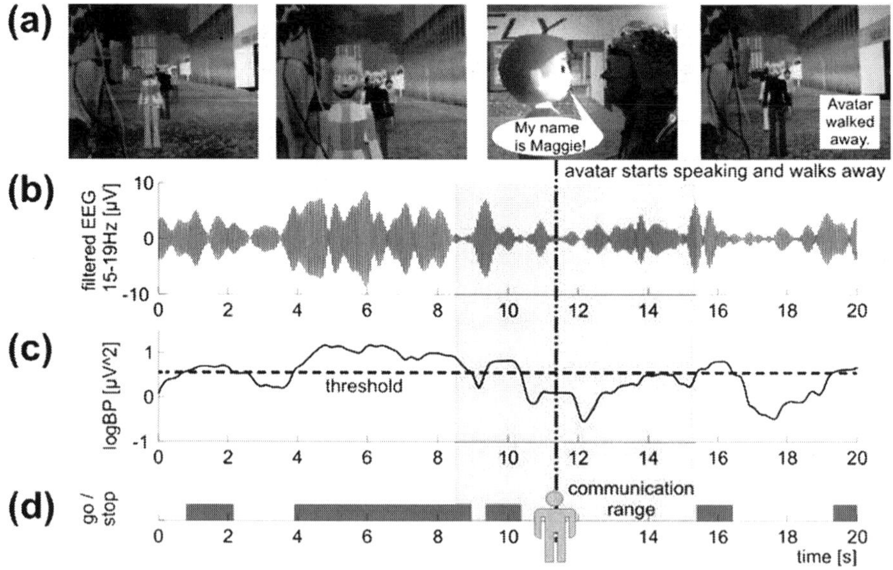

Figure 7: (a) Picture sequence before, during and after the contact with an avatar. (b) Band-pass filtered (15–19 Hz) EEG and (c) logarithmic band power

time course with threshold. (d) Indicated periods of moving and stopping. The contact with the avatar occurred at second 11.4. Modified from Leeb (2008).

The size of the sphere approximated the distance for a conversation in the real world. The avatar started talking to the subject if he was standing still for one second within this sphere. After finishing a randomly chosen short statement (like: "Hi", "My name is Maggie", "It was good to meet you"…), the avatar walked away. Communication was only possible within the sphere; if the subject stopped too early or stopped too close to the avatar, nothing happened. After a while, and with his own free will, the subject could imagine another foot movement and started moving again towards the next avatar, until the end of the street was reached.

The tetraplegic subject performed ten runs on two days, and he was able to stop at 90 % of the 150 avatars and talk to them. In four runs, he achieved a performance of 100 %. In 11 of the 15 missed avatars (of all runs), the subject stopped within the communication range, but the stopping time was too short (between 0.08 to 0.88 s mean ± SD = 0.47 s ± 0.27 s).

In an interview after the experiment, the patient confirmed that "moving" occurred only during periods of foot motor imagery, but he reported that it was hard to stop precisely. When the avatars were placed very laterally, it was especially hard to find the correct distance to the avatar. Concerning the experience with the interaction, he mentioned that "It has never happened before, in the sense of success and interaction. I thought that I was on the street and I had the chance to walk up to the people. I just imagined the movement and walked up to them. However, I had the sensation that they were just speaking but not talking to me..." He said that he had the feeling of being in that street and forgot that he was in the lab and people were around him. "Of course the image on the CAVE wall didn't look like you or me, but it still felt as if I was moving in a real street, not realistic, but real. I checked the people (avatars). We had 14 ladies and 1 man." The subject stated that he felt surprised as one avatar walked through him; he wanted to get out of the way, to go backwards. This suggests that the subject felt very absorbed in the virtual reality environment.

This work demonstrated for the first time that a tetraplegic subject, sitting in a wheel chair, could control his movements in a VE by the usage of a self-paced (asynchronous) BCI based on one single EEG recording (for further details see Leeb et al., 2007a). The mentally induced beta oscillation in our patient is a unique phenomenon and probably the result of the intensive and long-lasting BCI feedback training with the goal of achieving control over brain waves. The use of visually rich and stimulating VE, involving avatars that were interacting with the subject, accounted for a diverse and challenging experimental paradigm. The simulation power of the VE ensured that he had the sense of being in the street and going to the people; therefore the experiment was similar to a task in a real street. VEs are especially attractive for a person who is wheelchair-bound. First, simply using a VE can give such persons access to experiences that may be long forgotten (or which they have never had). The fact that the subject could still perform feet motor imagery, years after an injury that rendered him unable to use his feet, is a testament to the plasticity of the human brain (see also Kübler et al., 2005). Another advantage here is that VEs can be used to create virtual prototypes of new navigation or control methods, and give potential users experience of them in a safe environment before they are ever physically built.

IMPORTANCE OF VR FEEDBACK IN BCI RESEARCH

The increasing availability of VR technology has generated a high interest in studying BCI interaction with VEs.

Compared to traditional, abstract interfaces like mouse or keypad, BCI systems could potentially promise a more direct and intuitive way of interacting and thereby overcome some limitations of navigating within VEs (Usoh & Slater, 1995). This is especially obvious for stimulus-dependent BCI-VR systems (Figure 1b), where users can control appliances in the VE by simply directing their eye gaze and/or focus of attention towards the desired element (e.g., looking at the TV to switch it on, looking at the door to open it; Allison et al., 2008). In a typical independent BCI paradigm (Figure 1a) as described above, users learn to direct, e.g., a computer cursor towards a highlighted target via certain changes of specific EEG features. To accomplish this task, each participant develops a specific mental strategy to modify the relevant brain signals and use a BCI effectively. As ERD BCIs mostly rely on motor imagery, the mental process of imagining different types of movements offers an intuitive way of VE control like, for example, imagining foot movements for moving forward in a VE (Leeb et al., 2007a; Pfurtscheller et al., 2006a). A further advantage of using sensorimotor rhythms in BCI-based VE control is that they are typically modulated by motor activity (including both actual and imagined movements), but unaffected by changes in visual stimulation. Therefore people can use an ERD BCI while performing other visual tasks. Indeed, we have successfully shown that people can use an ERD BCI (based on motor imagery) at the same time as an SSVEP BCI (based on visual attention) (Allison et al., 2010; Brunner et al., 2010; Pfurtscheller et al., 2010a; 2010b).

Furthermore, research that explores BCI training in VEs is important for many reasons. VEs can help focus the training on the specific target application. For example, different training settings and paradigms may be more or less efficient, depending on whether the user's task is to select certain characters or icons for communication, control a neuroprosthesis to restore grasping, or navigate a wheelchair in a realistic environment. Moreover, it is a matter of ongoing research whether BCI training in stimulus-rich virtual environments is more effective than the standard training procedure using simple, more or less abstract, visual cues and feedback stimuli. The literature suggests that a realistic VE enhances the feeling of presence, task performance and also cortical activation (Jäncke et al., 2009; Lee and Kim, 2008; Slater et al., 2002). Combining BCI and VR technologies can lead to highly realistic and immersive BCI feedback scenarios that make participants more engaged and motivated. Thus, it is not unexpected that a rich visual representation of the feedback signal, such as a 3-dimensional video game or VE, may facilitate learning to use a BCI (Leeb, 2008; Pineda et al., 2003; Ron-Angevin et al., 2005).

The feedback is a very important component of the BCI as it provides the user with information about the efficiency of his/her strategy and enables learning. The studies mentioned above support realistic and engaging feedback scenarios which are closely related to the specific target application. However, the processing of such a realistic feedback stimulus may also interfere with the mental motor imagery task, and thus might impair the development of BCI control (Neuper et al., 2009). This could be the case when the realistic feedback presentation showing (for instance) a moving visual scene is not compatible with the specific mental action the user creates to induce the relevant brain signals. Therefore, the mutual interaction between a mentally simulated movement (for BCI control) and simultaneous watching of a moving scene should be further investigated in future studies.

Another interesting aspect is that mental simulation of movement (motor imagery) results in cardiovascular changes explained by two factors, i.e. function of anticipation of movement and central preparation of movement (Damen & Brunia, 1987; Oishi et al., 2000). The heart rate (HR) generally decreases during motor imagery in laboratory conditions without VR feedback (Leeb, 2008; Pfurtscheller et al., 2006b), but can be increased during effortful imagery and/or enhanced mental effort (Decety et al., 1991), such as during VR feedback in BCI experiments (Pfurtscheller et al., 2006b; 2008a). This underlines the importance of VR feedback in modifying emotional experiences and enhances autonomic and visceral responses. The HR changes can be in the order of several beats per minute and therewith used to increase the classification accuracy of an ERD-based BCI when both the EEG and the HR are analyzed simultaneously.

CONCLUDING REMARKS

One important component of a BCI system is feedback. VR offers a powerful possibility not only to rehearse scenarios that are otherwise too dangerous or expensive to set up, such as simulation of wheel chair movement, but also to modify emotional experiences and enhance therewith autonomic responses as e.g. heart rate changes. This opens a new way to improve the performance of a BCI by simultaneously analyzing and classifying brain and heart rate changes and to realize a "hybrid BCI" (Pfurtscheller et al., 2010a). Furthermore, VR environments may offer numerous other benefits, such as reduced training time, improved classification accuracy, increased sense of immersion/presence in an artificial setting, and reduced boredom or fatigue.

ACKNOWLEDGMENT

This work was carried out as part of the "PresenCCia" project, an EU funded Integrated Project under the IST program (project no. 27731) and the EU funded project "BrainAble" (project no. ICT-2010-247447). The authors are grateful to Brendan Allison for proofreading the manuscript.

REFERENCES

1. Allison, B. Z.; Brunner, C.; Kaiser, V.; Müller-Putz, G. R.; Neuper, C. & Pfurtscheller, G. (2010). Toward a Hybrid Brain-Computer Interface Based on Imagined Movement and Visual Attention, J Neural Eng, Vol. 7, No. 2, 26007
2. Allison, B. Z.; McFarland, D. J.; Schalk, G.; Zheng, S. D.; Jackson, M. M. & Wolpaw, J. R. (2008). Towards an Independent Brain-Computer Interface Using Steady State Visual Evoked Potentials, Clin Neurophysiol, Vol. 119, No. 2, 399-408
3. Allison, B. Z. & Pineda, J. A. (2006). Effects of SOA and Flash Pattern Manipulations on ERPs, Performance, and Preference: Implications for a BCI System, Int J Psychophysiol, Vol. 59, No. 2, 127-40
4. Bayliss, J. D. (2003). Use of the Evoked Potential P3 Component for Control in a Virtual Apartment, IEEE Trans Neural Syst Rehabil Eng, Vol. 11, No. 2, 113-6
5. Bayliss, J. D. & Ballard, D. H. (2000). A Virtual Reality Testbed for Brain-Computer Interface Research, IEEE Trans Rehabil Eng, Vol. 8, No. 2, 188-90
6. Bell, C. J.; Shenoy, P.; Chalodhorn, R. & Rao, R. P. (2008). Control of a Humanoid Robot by a Noninvasive Brain-Computer Interface in Humans, J Neural Eng, Vol. 5, No. 2, 214- 20
7. Bin, G.; Gao, X.; Yan, Z.; Hong, B. & Gao, S. (2009). An Online Multi-Channel SSVEP-Based Brain-Computer Interface Using a Canonical Correlation Analysis Method, J Neural Eng, Vol. 6, No. 4, 046002
8. BioSig (2003-2010). An Open Source Software Package for Biomedical Signal Processing under Matlab, Available online at http://biosig.sf.net/
9. Birbaumer, N. & Cohen, L. G. (2007). Brain-Computer Interfaces: Communication and Restoration of Movement in Paralysis, J Physiol, Vol. 579, No. Pt 3, 621-36
10. Birbaumer, N.; Ghanayim, N.; Hinterberger, T.; Iversen, I.; Kotchoubey, B.; Kübler, A.; Perelmouter, J.; Taub, E. & Flor, H. (1999). A Spelling Device for the Paralysed, Nature, Vol. 398, No. 6725, 297-8
11. Bishop, C. M. (1995). Neural Networks for Pattern Recognition. Clarendon Press, Oxford, UK
12. Brunner, C.; Allison, B. Z.; Krusienski, D. J.; Kaiser, V.; Müller-Putz, G. R.; Pfurtscheller, G. & Neuper, C. (2010). Improved Signal Processing Approaches in an Offline Simulation of a Hybrid Brain-

Computer Interface, J Neurosci Methods, Vol. 188, No. 1, 165-73

13. Cruz-Neira, C.; Sandin, D. J. & DeFanti, T. A. (1993). Surround-Screen Projection-Based Virtual Reality: The Design and Implementation of the Cave, Proceedings of the 20th annual conference on Computer graphics and interactive techniques, 135-42
14. Damen, E. J. & Brunia, C. H. (1987). Changes in Heart Rate and Slow Brain Potentials Related to Motor Preparation and Stimulus Anticipation in a Time Estimation Task, Psychophysiology, Vol. 24, No. 6, 700-13
15. Decety, J.; Jeannerod, M.; Germain, M. & Pastene, J. (1991). Vegetative Response During Imagined Movement Is Proportional to Mental Effort, Behav Brain Res, Vol. 42, No. 1, 1-5
16. Donchin, E.; Spencer, K. M. & Wijesinghe, R. (2000). The Mental Prosthesis: Assessing the Speed of a P300-Based Brain-Computer Interface, IEEE Trans Rehabil Eng, Vol. 8, No. 2, 174-9
17. Faller, J.; Müller-Putz, G. R.; Schmalstieg, D. & Pfurtscheller, G. (2010). An Application Framework for Controlling an Avatar in a Desktop Based Virtual Environment via a Software SSVEP Brain-Computer Interface, PRESENCE Special Issue, "BrainComputer Interface (BCI) Systems in Virtual Reality Environments." Vol. 19, No. 1, 25- 34
18. Farwell, L. A. & Donchin, E. (1988). Talking Off the Top of Your Head: Toward a Mental Prosthesis Utilizing Event-Related Brain Potentials, Electroencephalogr Clin Neurophysiol, Vol. 70, No. 6, 510-23
19. Gao, X.; Xu, D.; Cheng, M. & Gao, S. (2003). A BCI -Based Environmental Controller for the Motion-Disabled, IEEE Trans Neural Syst Rehabil Eng, Vol. 11, No. 2, 137-40
20. Holzner, C.; Guger, C.; Edlinger, G.; Gronegress, C. & Slater, M. (2009). Virtual Smart Home Controlled by Thoughts, Proc. of the 2009 18th IEEE International Workshops on Enabling Technologies: Infrastructures for Collaborative Enterprises - Volume 00, 236-39
21. Jäncke, L.; Cheetham, M. & Baumgartner, T. (2009). Virtual Reality and the Role of the Prefrontal Cortex in Adults and Children., Front Neurosci., Vol. 3, No. 1, 52-59
22. Krusienski, D. J.; Sellers, E. W.; Cabestaing, F.; Bayoudh, S.; McFarland, D. J.; Vaughan, T. M. & Wolpaw, J. R. (2006). A Comparison of Classification Techniques for the P300 Speller, J Neural Eng, Vol. 3,

No. 4, 299-305

23. Kübler, A.; Nijboer, F.; Mellinger, J.; Vaughan, T. M.; Pawelzik, H.; Schalk, G.; McFarland, D. J.; Birbaumer, N. & Wolpaw, J. R. (2005). Patients with Als Can Use Sensorimotor Rhythms to Operate a Brain-Computer Interface, Neurology, Vol. 64, No. 10, 1775-7
24. Lalor, E.; Kelly, S.; Finucane, C.; Burke, R.; Smith, R.; Reilly, R. B. & McDarby, G. (2005). Steady-State Vep-Based Brain-Computer Interface Control in an Immersive 3-D Gaming Environment, EURASIP J on Appl Sig Proc, Vol. 19, 3156-64
25. Lee, S. & Kim, G. J. (2008). Effects of Visual Cues and Sustained Attention on Spatial Presence in Virtual Environments Based on Spatial and Object Distinction, Interact. Comput., Vol. 20, No. 4-5, 491-502
26. Leeb, R. (2008). Brain-Computer Communication: The Motivation, Aim, and Impact of Virtual Feedback. Graz University of Technology, PhD thesis
27. Leeb, R.; Friedman, D.; Müller-Putz, G. R.; Scherer, R.; Slater, M. & Pfurtscheller, G. (2007a). Self-Paced (Asynchronous) BCI Control of a Wheelchair in Virtual Environments: A Case Study with a Tetraplegic, Computational Intelligence and Neuroscience, special issue: "Brain-Computer Interfaces: Towards Practical Implementations and Potential Applications", Vol. 2007, No. Article ID 79642, 1-8
28. Leeb, R.; Keinrath, C.; Friedman, D.; Guger, C.; Scherer, R.; Neuper, C.; Garau, M.; Antley, A.; Steed, A.; Slater, M. & Pfurtscheller, G. (2006). Walking by Thinking: The Brainwaves Are Crucial, Not the Muscles! Presence Teleoper Virtual Environ., Vol. 15, No. 5, 500-14
29. Leeb, R.; Lee, F.; Keinrath, C.; Scherer, R.; Bischof, H. & Pfurtscheller, G. (2007b). BrainComputer Communication: Motivation, Aim and Impact of Exploring a Virtual Apartment, IEEE Trans Neural Syst Rehabil Eng, Vol. 15, No. 4, 473-82
30. Leeb, R. & Pfurtscheller, G. (2004). Walking through a Virtual City by Thought, Proc. of the 26th A Int Conf IEEE EMBS - EMBC 2004, San Francisco, USA, 4503-6
31. Leeb, R.; Scherer, R.; Friedman, D.; Lee, F.; Keinrath, C.; Bischof, H.; Slater, M. & Pfurtscheller, G. (2007c). Combining BCI and Virtual Reality: Scouting Virtual Worlds, In: Toward Brain-Computer Interfacing, edited by G. Dornhege, J. del R. Millan, T. Hinterberger, D. J. McFarland & K.-R. Müller, 393-408. MIT Press, Cambridge,

MA, USA

32. Leeb, R.; Settgast, V.; Fellner, D. W. & Pfurtscheller, G. (2007d). Self-Paced Exploring of the Austrian National Library through Thought, Int J Bioelectromagnetism, Vol. 9, No. 4, 237-44
33. Lotze, M.; Montoya, P.; Erb, M.; Hulsmann, E.; Flor, H.; Klose, U.; Birbaumer, N. & Grodd, W. (1999). Activation of Cortical and Cerebellar Motor Areas During Executed and Imagined Hand Movements: An Fmri Study, J Cogn Neurosci, Vol. 11, No. 5, 491-501
34. Martinez, P.; Bakardjian, H. & Cichocki, A. (2007). Fully Online Multicommand BrainComputer Interface with Visual Neurofeedback Using SSVEP Paradigm, Comput Intell Neurosci, 94561
35. Mason, S. G.; Bashashati, A.; Fatourechi, M.; Navarro, K. F. & Birch, G. E. (2007). A Comprehensive Survey of Brain Interface Technology Designs, Ann Biomed Eng, Vol. 35, No. 2, 137-69
36. Müller-Putz, G. R.; Scherer, R.; Brauneis, C. & Pfurtscheller, G. (2005). Steady-State Visual Evoked Potential (SSVEP)-Based Communication: Impact of Harmonic Frequency Components, J Neural Eng, Vol. 2, No. 4, 123-30
37. Neuper, C.; Scherer, R.; Reiner, M. & Pfurtscheller, G. (2005). Imagery of Motor Actions: Differential Effects of Kinesthetic and Visual-Motor Mode of Imagery in SingleTrial EEG, Cogn Brain Res, Vol. 25, No. 3, 668-77
38. Neuper, C.; Scherer, R.; Wriessnegger, S. & Pfurtscheller, G. (2009). Motor Imagery and Action Observation: Modulation of Sensorimotor Brain Rhythms During Mental Control of a Brain-Computer Interface, Clin Neurophysiol, Vol. 120, No. 2, 239-47
39. Nijholt, A.; Tan, D.; Pfurtscheller, G.; Brunner, C.; Millan Jdel, R.; Allison, B. Z.; Graimann, B.; Popescu, F.; Blankertz, B. & Müller, K. R. (2008). Brain-Computer Interfacing for Intelligent Systems, IEEE Intelligent Systems, Vol. 23, No. 3, 72-79
40. Oishi, K.; Kasai, T. & Maeshima, T. (2000). Autonomic Response Specificity During Motor Imagery, J Physiol Anthropol Appl Human Sci, Vol. 19, No. 6, 255-61
41. Pfurtscheller, G.; Allison, B. Z.; Brunner, C.; Bauernfeind, G.; Solis-Escalante, T.; Scherer, R.; Zander, T. O.; Müller-Putz, G.; Neuper, C. & Birbaumer, N. (2010a). The Hybrid BCI, Front Neurosci, Vol. 4, 42
42. Pfurtscheller, G.; Guger, C.; Müller, G.; Krausz, G. & Neuper, C.

(2000). Brain Oscillations Control Hand Orthosis in a Tetraplegic, Neurosci Lett, Vol. 292, No. 3, 211-4

43. Pfurtscheller, G.; Leeb, R.; Friedman, D. & Slater, M. (2008a). Centrally Controlled Heart Rate Changes During Mental Practice in Immersive Virtual Environment: A Case Study with a Tetraplegic, Int J Psychophysiol, Vol. 68, No. 1, 1-5
44. Pfurtscheller, G.; Leeb, R.; Keinrath, C.; Friedman, D.; Neuper, C.; Guger, C. & Slater, M. (2006a). Walking from Thought, Brain Res, Vol. 1071, No. 1, 145-52
45. Pfurtscheller, G.; Leeb, R. & Slater, M. (2006b). Cardiac Responses Induced During ThoughtBased Control of Virtual Environments, Int J Psychophysiol, Vol. 62, No. 1, 134-40
46. Pfurtscheller, G. & Lopes da Silva, F. H. (1999). Event-Related EEG / MEG Synchronization and Desynchronization: Basic Principles, Clin Neurophysiol, Vol. 110, No. 11, 1842-57
47. Pfurtscheller, G.; Müller-Putz, G. R.; Scherer, R. & Neuper, C. (2008b). Rehabilitation with Brain-Computer Interface Systems, Computer, Vol. 41, No. 10, 58
48. Pfurtscheller, G.; Müller-Putz, G. R.; Schlögl, A.; Graimann, B.; Scherer, R.; Leeb, R.; Brunner, C.; Keinrath, C.; Lee, F.; Townsend, G.; Vidaurre, C. & Neuper, C. (2006c). 15 Years of BCI Research at Graz University of Technology: Current Projects, IEEE Trans Neural Syst Rehabil Eng, Vol. 14, No. 2, 205-10
49. Pfurtscheller, G. & Neuper, C. (2010). Dynamics of Sensorimotor Oscillations in a Motor Task, In: Brain Computer Interfaces: Revolutionizing Human-Computer Interaction, edited by B. Graimann, B. Z. Allison & G. Pfurtscheller. Springer
50. Pfurtscheller, G. & Neuper, C. (2001). Motor Imagery and Direct Brain-Computer Communication, Proceedings of the IEEE, Vol. 89, No. 7, 1123-34
51. Pfurtscheller, G. & Solis-Escalante, T. (2009). Could the Beta Rebound in the EEG Be Suitable to Realize a "Brain Switch"? Clin Neurophysiol, Vol. 120, No. 1, 24-9
52. Pfurtscheller, G.; Solis-Escalante, T.; Ortner, R.; Linortner, P. & Müller-Putz, G. R. (2010b). Self-Paced Operation of an SSVEP -Based Orthosis with and without an ImageryBased "Brain Switch": A Feasibility Study Towards a Hybrid BCI., IEEE Trans Neural Syst

Rehabil Eng

53. Pineda, J. A.; Silverman, D. S.; Vankov, A. & Hestenes, J. (2003). Learning to Control Brain Rhythms: Making a Brain-Computer Interface Possible, IEEE Trans Neural Syst Rehabil Eng, Vol. 11, No. 2, 181-4
54. Ron Angevin, R.; Diaz-Estrella, A. & Reyes-Lecuona, A. (2005). Development of a Braincomputer Interface Based on Virtual Reality to Improve Training Techniques, Cyberpsychol Behav, Vol. 8, No. 4, 353-54
55. Scherer, R. (2004-2006). RtsBCI: Graz brain-computer interface real-time open source package. Available at http://sourceforge.net/projects/biosig
56. Scherer, R.; Lee, F.; Schlögl, A.; Leeb, R.; Bischof, H. & Pfurtscheller, G. (2008). Toward SelfPaced Brain–Computer Communication: Navigation through Virtual Worlds, IEEE Trans Biomed Eng, Vol. 55, No. 2, 675-82
57. Slater, M.; Steed, A. & Chrysanthou, Y. (2002). Computer Graphics and Virtual Environments: From Realism to Real-Time. Addison-Wesley, Harlow, UK
58. Slater, M. & Usoh, M. (1993). Presence in Immersive Virtual Environments, Proc. IEEE Virtual Reality Annual International Symposium, Seattle, WA, 90-96
59. Townsend, G.; Graimann, B. & Pfurtscheller, G. (2004). Continuous EEG Classification During Motor Imagery-Simulation of an Asynchronous BCI, IEEE Trans Neural Syst Rehabil Eng, Vol. 12, No. 2, 258-65
60. Usoh, M. & Slater, M. (1995). An Exploration of Immersive Virtual Environments, Endeavour, Vol. 19, No. 1, 34-38
61. Wolpaw, J. R.; Birbaumer, N.; McFarland, D. J.; Pfurtscheller, G. & Vaughan, T. M. (2002). Brain-Computer Interfaces for Communication and Control, Clin Neurophysiol, Vol. 113, No. 6, 767-91

Chapter 3

Compelling Self-Motion Through Virtual Environments without Actual Self-Motion – Using Self-Motion Illusions ("Vection") to Improve User Experience in VR

Bernhard E. Riecke

Simon Fraser University Canada

INTRODUCTION

While modern computer graphics and virtual reality (VR) simulations can have stunning photorealism, they are often unable to provide a life-like and compelling sensation of moving through the simulated world. This is in stark contrast to our real-world experience, where locomotion through the environment is naturally accompanied by the embodied sensation of self-motion, even when we are not actively walking but using other transportation

Citation: Bernhard E. Riecke (January 8th 2011). Compelling Self-Motion Through Virtual Environments Without Actual Self-Motion – Using Self-Motion Illusions ('Vection') to Improve VR User Experience, Virtual Reality, Jae-Jin Kim, IntechOpen, DOI: 10.5772/13150.

devices like bicycles, cars, or buses. This fundamental difference in which we perceive simulated versus actual motions might negatively impact the perceived realism, behavioural effectiveness, user acceptance, and commercial success of virtual reality technology and applications. In this chapter, I propose and discuss how investigating, utilizing, and optimizing self-motion illusions ("vection") might be a lean and elegant way to overcome such shortcomings and provide a truly "moving experience" in computermediated environments without the need to physically move, thus reducing overall cost and effort.

The aim of this chapter is to provide an overview of the state of the art in research on visually-induced self-motion illusions in real and virtual environments. Specific focus will be on a topic that is of particular interest in the context of VR but has not been thoroughly reviewed before: Namely how self-motion illusions are not only affected by physical stimulus parameters themselves via bottom-up perceptual processes (as discussed in section 3), but also by the way we look at, perceive, and interpret the stimulus, how it is integrated into the overall display setup, and whether or not actual motion might be possible (see section 4). Knowledge of these factors can not only deepen our understanding of the complex processes underlying self-motion perception, but might also be of particular interest for VR simulations and other immersive/multi-media applications like gaming or movies, as these factors can often be manipulated with relatively little effort. Section 5 will provide a brief overview on recent studies on multi-modal contributions and interactions for vection. These indicate significant cross-modal benefits, which could, together with the results presented in earlier sections, be employed to design more effective-yet-affordable VR interfaces, as will be discussed in the final section and throughout this chapter. Possible side-effects of vection in VR are discussed in section 6.

SELF-MOTION ILLUSIONS ("VECTION")

Self-motion illusions induced by moving visual stimuli that cover a large part of the visual field have been first described more than a century ago (Mach, 1875; Wood, 1895), and were termed circular and linear vection for rotational and translational self-motion illusions, respectively (Fischer & Kornmüller, 1930; Tschermak, 1931). Many readers might have experienced the compellingness of visually-induced self-motion illusions themselves, as they can easily occur under natural conditions – for example, when sitting in a train waiting to depart from the station and looking out of the window where a train on the adjacent track starts moving, many people experience a rather convincing illusion that there own train started moving ("train illusion"). Similarly, when waiting in a car in front of a red light and a large truck slowly pulls up on the side, many of us instinctively hit the break as for a moment we believed that our own car was moving. One of the earliest occurrences of vection might have been when our ancestors were gazing at fast-moving clouds or looking down on a river and fixating onto a stationary object (like a rock) in the river and experienced a tilting sensation in the direction opposite of the visual (river) motion. More recently, large-screen theme park rides and cinemax or I-Max theatres utilize self-motion illusions to provide more compelling experiences to their audience, as was already done more than a century ago with the "haunted swing" illusion described by Wood (1895).

Why might we want to care about self-motion illusions in the context of VR and other immersive media? As mentioned above, most VR and immersive media setups and applications do not provide a compelling and believable sensation of moving through the simulated environments; despite often impressive visual realism, perceptual and behavioural realism is often lacking. That is, seeing a simulated self-motion does not necessarily imply experiencing and believing it, thus reducing overall believability and simulation quality. So what conditions are conducive to experiencing believable self-motion illusions?

There is more than a century of vection research investigating under what precise conditions moving visual and non-visual stimuli can induce embodied sensations of self-motion. I propose that revisiting, utilizing, and extending this body of knowledge can provide both inspiration and guidance for improving VR and other immersive media from the human/ user perspective. In a nutshell, if we could provide users with a compelling illusion of moving through simulated worlds, we would not have to go through the effort of allowing for large-scale physical locomotion or could at least relax the requirement of those. One of the biggest challenges in self-motion simulation is that some modalities simply cannot (yet) be simulated easily or switched off noninvasively: In particular, vestibular and most somatosensory cues cannot be simply "turned off" like visual cues (closing ones' eyes) or auditory cues (wearing earplugs and/or listening to masking noise). Hence, whenever self-motions are only simulated and not physically performed, there is a conflict between those cues suggesting self-motion (e.g., the visual simulation) and other cues indicating stationarity (e.g., vestibular cues indicating that there was no acceleration and we should thus still be stationary, or somatosensory cues from our feet touching solid ground). So how is this conflict and ambiguity resolved by the human system to form a coherent percept of one's current state of motion?

Indeed, self-motion perception is a complex phenomenon that includes multiple sensory and motor systems as well as both bottom-up processes and higher-level, cognitive influences, as will be discussed in the subsequent sections. There are several mathematical frameworks modelling how the different sensory and motor inputs might be integrated to form a coherent percept of self-motion despite conflicting or ambiguous information (e.g., Mergner & Becker, 1990; Mergner et al., 2000; Wertheim, 1994; Zacharias & Young, 1981). While vestibular motion cues immediately yield a sensation of self-motion, large-field visual motion can be interpreted as either object motion (where the observer is stationary) or selfmotion (where the visual stimulus is stationary) or a combination thereof. When presented with coherent large-field visual motion, the observer typically perceives object motion during the first few seconds after motion onset (1-30s, depending on various stimulus parameters), followed by a sometimes very brief period of mixed object and self-motion, and finally exclusive self-motion and saturated vection (Dichgans & Brandt, 1978). During saturated vection, the moving stimulus is typically (but not always) perceived as earthstationary, and vection occurs in the direction opposite of the visual motion (just as if we would be physically moving).

There is a long history of investigating how different stimulus parameters affect the onset, strength, and velocity of vection. General reviews on self-motion illusions can be found in (Andersen, 1986; Dichgans & Brandt, 1978; Howard, 1982, 1986; Mergner & Becker, 1990; Warren & Wertheim, 1990). Auditory vection has recently been reviewed by (Riecke et al., 2009; Väljamäe, 2009). Neurophysiological correlates of vection have been described in, e.g., (Hettinger, 2002; Kovacs et al., 2008) and references therein. Vection with a specific focus on motion simulation, virtual environments, and undesirable side-effects has been reviewed in (Hettinger, 2002).

The goal of the following section is to provide a current review on different stimulus parameters affecting visually-induced vection, and how these factors might be utilized in the design of VR and other immersive applications. Section 4 will focus on recent findings indicating that vection is not only affected by physical stimulus parameters themselves, but also by how we look at, perceive, and interpret the stimulus, by what is beyond the display itself, and by our sensation/knowledge whether actual motion might or might not be possible. The presented research findings lead to a number of possible applications and implications for VR and other immersive applications. Instead of summarizing them in a separate section, I decided to integrate them with the respective research findings to provide a stronger link and an improved understanding of their origin and underlying processes.

STIMULUS PARAMETERS AFFECTING VISUALLY-INDUCED VECTION

Vection induced by moving visual stimuli has clearly received the most research attention so far and will thus be discussed in more detail below. Self-motion illusions can, however, also be induced by other modalities including auditory (see reviews by Riecke et al., 2009; Väljamäe, 2009), tactile (Dichgans & Brandt, 1978), or biomechanical cues (Bles, 1981; Brandt et al., 1977) or from direct galvanic stimulation of the vestibular system (Cress et al., 1997; Lepecq et al., 2006). In the following, I will review different factors that have been shown to facilitate vection, and how they might be utilized in VR and other immersive situations. Note that this information can, of course, equally be used to inhibit self-motion illusions were desired to avoid possible undesired side-effects, as discussed in section 6.

Up to an Optimal Velocity, Higher Stimulus Velocities Yield Stronger Vection

Higher stimulus velocities in general enhance vection, indicated by earlier vection onset, higher perceived self-motion velocity, and increased intensity and convincingness of the self-motion illusion (Allison et al., 1999; Brandt et al., 1973; Dichgans & Brandt, 1978; Schulte-Pelkum et al., 2003; Howard, 1986). For example, Brandt et al. (1973) showed that circular vection velocity increased linearly with increasing stimulus movement up to 120!/s and roughly matched the stimulus velocity. Further increasing stimulus velocity did not increase perceived self-rotation velocity further, such that the moving stimulus was no longer perceived to be earth-stationary. In terms of VR applications, this suggests that there might be maximum movement and/or optic flow velocities beyond which simulation effectiveness could deteriorate and the simulated world might no longer be perceived as stable.

Larger Stimulus Sizes Increase Vection

One major factor determining the onset and strength of vection is the solid angle (field of view, FOV) subtended by the moving visual stimulus. Although stimulus sizes as small as 7.5° have been shown to induce linear vection under carefully designed lab conditions (Andersen & Braunstein, 1985), larger stimulus sizes generally enhance vection in all measures, and full-field stimulation results in the strongest vection to a point where it cannot be suppressed any more and can be indistinguishable from actual self-motion (Berthoz et al., 1975; Brandt et al., 1973; Dichgans & Brandt, 1978; Held et al., 1975).

Central and Peripheral Vision is Equally Effective in Inducing Vection

While earlier studies reported that peripheral visual motion is more effective in inducing vection than central motion (Brandt et al., 1973; Dichgans & Brandt, 1978; Johansson, 1977), later studies demonstrated that peripheral and central motion have similar influences on vection when their display areas are equated (Andersen & Braunstein, 1985; Howard & Heckmann, 1989; Nakamura, 2008; Post, 1988; Wolpert, 1990). In fact, the peripheral dominance effect observed earlier was likely caused by peripheral stimuli being perceived as farther away than central stimuli. When perceived depth is held constant, vection strength linearly increases with increasing stimulus size, independent of stimulus eccentricity (Nakamura, 2008).

Optimal Spatial Frequency for Vection Depends on Stimulus Eccentricity

There is, however, an interaction between optimal frequency for central versus peripheral stimulation: Palmisano & Gillam (1998) showed that the most compelling circular vection is achieved when lower spatial frequency patterns are presented peripherally (where the eye's spatial resolution is also lower) and higher-spatial frequency stimuli are presented to central vision (where acuity is higher). From an applied perspective of improving self-motion simulations, the decreased peripheral sensitivity to high-frequency stimuli relaxes the need for high-resolution displays or imagery in the periphery unless the user needs to focus there (see also discussion in Wolpert, 1990). Even without a central display, vection can be reliably induced by peripheral stimulation: Brandt el al. (1973) demonstrated that circular vection was hardly reduced when the central 120° of the human visual field was blocked and participants saw motion only in the far periphery. Similar amounts of vection were achieved when visual motion was restricted to a horizontal streak of 60° height and full-field width. These results suggest that adding affordable low-resolution displays in the periphery of VR or other immersive setups might have surprisingly strong effects on perceived self-motion (and likely also presence and immersion).

Density of Moving Contrasts Enhances Vection

While single moving dots or objects can hardly induce vection, increasing their number and density can eventually induce vection, and vection strength seems to generally increase with the density of moving contrasts (Brandt et al., 1975; Dichgans & Brandt, 1978). Thus, care needs to be taken for simulations where there are only few objects (e.g., for flight, space, or diving simulations), especially if they are also far away (and thus have low image velocity for translations). If compelling vection is desired, it might thus be necessary to carefully add nearby objects to increase overall optic flow and relative motion with respect to stationary foreground objects. Ideally, this should be done in the context of the simulation scenario to ensure ecological validity. For flight simulations, this could, e.g., be achieved by adding clouds or haze.

Linear vs. Circular vs. Curvilinear Vection

Trutoiu et al. (2009) demonstrated that linear vection in a panoramic projection setup was less convincing than circular vection, whereas curvilinear vection was perceived to be as convincing as circular vection. This has interesting implications for motion simulations, suggesting that even slight curvatures in the path might be able to increase the convincingness of the motion percept. Linear vection could be enhanced by adding a floor projection, though, possibly due to the special role that a perceivable moving ground plane seems to play in vection (Sato et al., 2007).

Overall, however, up-down (aka "elevator") vection tends to be more compelling and occur earlier than left-right or forward-backward vection, likely because up-down movements do not change the direction of the gravito-inertial vector, such that accelerational and gravitational forces are parallel (Giannopulu & Lepecq, 1998; Trutoiu et al., 2009). Similarly, continuous circular vection around the earth-vertical axis can be induced more easily than vection around earth-horizontal axes (roll or pitch). The latter can lead to paradoxical sensations of limited body tilt despite continuous sensations of tilting (Allison et al., 1999; Held et al., 1975; Young et al., 1975). This has been attributed to the conflict between the visually-suggested tilt in the gravitoinertial vector and the actual gravitoinertial vector (sensed by the otoliths in the vestibular system and the somatosensory system) which does not tilt. Without full-field stimulation and a naturalistic visual stimulus, it seems difficult to obtain pitch or roll vection that includes head-over-heels orientations. As most real-world situations do not include those extreme orientations, this might not be a major limitation for most VR and immersive media applications, though.

Simulated Viewpoint Jitter Facilitates Vection Despite Visuo-vestibular Conflict

Traditionally, it was often believed that vection should be facilitated if the sensory conflict between visual cues (simulating motion) and vestibular cues (indicating stationarity) was reduced. This view is supported by findings that bilaterally labyrinthine defective participants perceive visual vection much earlier and more intense (Johnson et al., 1999), and can perceive unambiguous roll or pitch vection through head-over-heels orientations (Cheung et al., 1989). In a series of studies, Palmisano and colleagues challenged this notions by showing that forward linear vection occurred earlier, lasted longer, and was more compelling when coherent viewpoint jitter was added to the expanding optic flow display (Palmisano et al., 2000), whereas incoherent jitter impaired vection (Palmisano et al., 2003). Moreover, viewpoint jitter alone induced weak vection sensations, without any overall radial or lamellar optic flow (Palmisano et al., 2003).

Perceived Rigidity of Optic Flow Field Enhances Vection

Nakamura (2010) extended these findings in showing that coherent visual jitter can facilitate linear vection even when the stimulus does not contain any depth cues and appears flat, whereas incoherent jitter impaired vection. Nakamura proposed that coherent jitter increasing the perceived rigidity of the random dot display, which in turn facilitated vection. Increasing the perceived rigidity of a vection-inducing stimulus seems, however, not to be the only mechanism underlying the vection-facilitating effect of stimulus jitter, as the effect can also be observed for naturalistic stimuli, which are arguably readily perceived as inherently rigid: Using videos of translations along a hallway, Bubka & Bonato (2010) showed that adding image oscillations induced by walking motions considerably enhanced linear forward vection strength while reducing vection onset latencies. Similar facilitation of forward linear vection when including slow viewpoint oscillations has been reported for more abstract optic flow displays (Palmisano et al., 2007). Surprisingly, it did not matter whether the viewpoint oscillations were caused by active head oscillations or just passively viewed without any head motions (Kim & Palmisano, 2008).

While it is tempting to suggest to add coherent image jitter or oscillations to VR simulations in order to enhance self-motion perception and perceptual realism, this should be carefully evaluated on a case-by-case basis, as adding image jitter/oscillations has also been shown to increases motion sickness (Palmisano et al., 2007), likely due to the increased sensory conflict between visual and non-visual cues.

BEYOND PHYSICAL STIMULUS PARAMETERS: HOW WE LOOK AT, PERCEIVE, AND INTERPRET THE STIMULUS CAN ALSO AFFECT VECTION

As described above, previous vection research mostly focussed on how various physical parameters of the moving stimulus like the stimulus contrast or field of view affect vection via lower-level, bottom-up perceptual processes. As I will argue in this section, there is, however, increasing evidence that vection can also be affected by what is outside of the moving stimulus itself, by the way we move and look at a moving stimulus, our preconceptions, intentions, and how we perceive and interpret the stimuli. Vection might even be directly or indirectly affected by higher-level and cognitive/top-down processes (Andersen & Braunstein, 1985; Lepecq et al., 1995; Mergner & Becker, 1990; Riecke et al., 2005). While many of these findings are exploratory in nature and await further careful experimentation, they provide a fascinating glimpse into the complex processes and interactions underlying the phenomenon of perceived self-motion without actual selfmotion. Apart from its theoretical relevance, potential higher-level/cognitive/intentional contributions to vection might be of considerable interest for many applications, as these factors can often be manipulated with relatively small effort and cost.

Eye Movements and Relative Motion Perception

Intent and Eye Movements: Fixation and Staring Facilitate Vection, as Compared to Smooth Pursuit

In the following, I will review research demonstrating that vection is not only determined by the physical parameters of the moving stimulus (i.e., strictly bottom-up perceptual processes), but also strongly influenced by our intent and specifically the way we look at a moving stimulus. When viewing a moving visual stimulus without explicit viewing instruction, our eyes smoothly follow the stimulus (optokinetic nystagmus). Likely one of the first observations on vection-facilitating factors was that fixating on a stationary foreground object (like our outstretched hand) facilitated vection (Fischer & Kornmüller, 1930; Mach, 1875; Wallach, 1940; Warren, 1895). However, fixation is not necessarily required, and inattentively staring at a moving pattern can also facilitate vection (Fischer & Kornmüller, 1930). Careful experimentation by Becker et al. (2002) showed that suppressing the optokinetic reflex by fixating a stationary fixation point yields higher perceived vection velocities and lower vection onset latencies, as compared to trying to suppress the optokinetic reflex without a fixation point or merely staring at the stimulus. Attentively following the moving pattern yielded the lowest vection velocity and highest onset latencies, although eye movements were similar to the staring condition. This suggests that not only retinal slip and the pattern of eye movements, but also one's intent (e.g., to follow vs. stare) can affect self-motion illusions, as has been shown and mathematically modeled in a series of studies (Becker et al., 2002; Mergner et al., & Becker, 2000; Mergner et al., 2000).

In terms of applications like motion simulations, differences in the user task, instructions, and intentions could thus have a considerable effect on the perceived self-motion and consequently on the overall believability and effectiveness of a simulation. For instance, instructions that require users to fixate on foreground objects moving with the observer instead of the simulated outside scene (e.g., checking the speedometer or operating the radio in a car or aircraft cockpit instead of looking at the surrounding outside environment) might somewhat surprisingly enhance self-motion perception and thus potentially overall simulation realism and effectiveness.

Note, however, that the combination of fast-moving stimuli and a limited update rate (typically 60Hz) of VR displays can induce undesirable perceptual artifacts like flicker and ghost images, especially when observers fixate or stare at the display and thus do not follow the visual motion with their eyes. Moreover, color-sequential displays like 1-chip dlp projectors or the commonly-used LCoS head-mounted displays (HMDs) can induce color separation for fast-moving sharp contrast edges, even without fixation or staring. Thus, applications where fast object or observer motion is required should be carefully tested and tuned to limit display artifacts.

Increasing retinal slip, local image velocities, and relative motion between moving stimulus and observer-fixed reference frame facilitates vection

Apart from fixation and staring, peripheral looking and gaze shifts between central and peripheral regions can also improve forward linear vection (Palmisano & Kim, 2009). Potential factors underlying this effect include faster local image velocities and increased retinal slip (local image velocity is higher in the periphery for radially expanding flow fields) as well as screen boundary effects as described in the following. Several studies demonstrated that vection depends not only on characteristics of the moving visual stimulus itself, but also on the relative motion between the moving visual stimulus and stationary reference objects. For example, circular vection was facilitated when the moving visual stimulus was surrounded by a stationary rectangular foreground viewing window (Howard & Heckmann, 1989). Merely adding two vertical thin bars as stationary foreground objects also enhanced vection, in particular for slowly (5°/s) moving stimuli where vection is otherwise hard to achieve (Howard & Howard, 1994). Howard and colleagues argued that the effect originated from the relative motion signal between the stationary foreground objects and the moving stimulus, although it seems that perceived object-background separation might also have contributed (Seno et al., 2009, see also subsection below). Even without physical depth separation, stationary objects can facilitate vection, as was shown by Lowther & Ware (1996) when adding a rectangular 5”5 grid to a projection screen displaying the moving stimulus or by Riecke et al. (2005, exp. 2) when adding hardly noticeable marks (scratches) to the projection screen.

This opens up interesting avenues and future research areas for facilitating vection in nonobtrusive ways, without the need for fixation or other restrictions of eye movements. Especially for slow image motions, adding a stationary (foreground) reference frame can provide relative motion cues that facilitate motion detection and vection. This can be achieved, e.g., though the frames of multi-monitor setups, through real or simulated window frames (like the windscreen pillar in driving or flight simulators), or through other means that should ideally be inspired by and match the motion metaphor and application scenario. Ironically, although large-FOV spherical or cylindrical projection setups have many advantages, they typically provide only limited relative motion cues due to the lack of visible screen boundaries or other foreground objects, which can reduce their vection-inducing potential.

Perceived Background Motion, Not Just Physical Depth Determine Vection

Already in 1975, Wist et al. (1975) demonstrated that the perceived self-rotation velocity (which is often used as a measure of the strength of circular vection) increases not only with the angular velocity of the visual stimulus as one might expect, but also linearly increases with the perceived distance of the moving stimulus. However, later research demonstrated that not only the absolute perceived distance, but in particular the relative depth structure and figure-ground (or object-background) separation seems critical, in that the stimulus that is perceived to be further away typically determines the occurrence, direction, and strength of vection (Brandt et al., 1975; Howard & Heckmann, 1989; Ito & Shibata, 2005; Nakamura, 2008; Nakamura & Shimojo, 1999; Ohmi & Howard, 1988; Ohmi et al., 1987). Several of these studies used perceptually bistable displays and demonstrated that not only physical stimulus parameters themselves, but in particular how the stimulus is perceived and interpreted at any moment in time can modulate or even determine self-motion perception. For example, monocular viewing of two optic flow displays in Ohmi et al. (1987) caused spontaneous reversals in their perceived depth order, without any physical stimulus changes. Results showed that the display that was currently perceived to be the further away dominated the self-motion percept, irrespective of the physical depth order and irrespective of which of the two displays was fixated or pursued.

Importance of perceived object-background relation for vection

As our visual system readily organizes visual stimuli into figure versus ground (i.e., perceptual objects versus background), the findings by Ohmi et al. (1987) could be interpreted as the perceived background dominating vection, whereas "figures" (e.g., objects in the foreground) having less, if any, effect on vection (Kitazaki & Sato, 2003; Ohmi et al., 1987). This hypothesis was confirmed and extended in a clever series of experiments by Seno et al. (2009), who used two independently moving luminance-defined gratings organized to form perceptually bistable displays like a Rubin's vase that show spontaneous reversals of the figure-ground (i.e., the object-background) relationship. When a moving stimulus was currently perceived as an "object", it's vection-inducing potential decreased to a point where it could no longer induce vection. Conversely, the part of the stimulus that was currently perceived as the "ground" or background determined vection responses, even if it was stereoscopically defined to be closer than the "object". Moreover, Experiment 5 of Seno et al. (2009) showed that upright shapes (face, apple, or human figure) produced stronger vection than inverted (upside-down) shapes, arguable because the inverted shapes were less likely to be perceived as an object.

Object-background and rest frame hypothesis provide a unifying framework

Seno et al. (2009) proposed that the object versus background hypothesis could provide a unifying framework for investigating and better understanding vection and vection-inducing stimuli. In particular, many factors that have been shown to facilitate vection are also typical properties of the perceived background, like occupying a large field of view, peripheral stimulation, lower spatial frequencies, rigidity and coherent visual motion, being a ground plane, being unattended, or being further away than other parts of the display. For example, paying particular attention to one of the two motion components in Kitazaki & Sato (2003) might have emphasized it's "object" or "foreground" status, such that other aspects of the stimulus were more likely to be perceived as a background and thus dominated vection. Similarly, fixating a stationary part of the display might have perceptually enhanced its objectlikelihood, such that the other (now "background") stimulus dominated vection.

Note that the object-background hypothesis bears similarity with the rest frame hypothesis proposed earlier by Prothero (1998) and Prothero & Parker (2003). This hypothesis states that "a particular reference frame, the 'rest frame,' is selected as the comparator for spatial judgments" (Prothero & Parker, 2003, p. 47). In this sense, spatial presence as well as vection are proposed to be (in part) determined by the extent to which a presented stimulus is accepted and selected as a primary reference or rest frame, which in turn is related to the likelihood of it being perceived a as background (see also theoretical framework by von der Heyde & Riecke, 2002; Riecke, 2003, chap. IV).

The findings by Riecke et al. (2006) could also be interpreted in the context of the objectbackground hypothesis and rest frame hypothesis: They observed that vection was reduced when the naturalism of the visual stimulus was decreased by inverting the presented scene or making it globally inconsistent via scene scrambling (see section 4.6 for details). Both stimulus inversion and scrambling decreased spatial presence and arguably might also have reduced the likelihood that the moving stimulus was perceived as a background and accepted as a stable reference frame with respect to which visual motion is more likely to be interpreted as self-motion rather than object-motion. In particular, I propose that spatial presence and immersion in a real or simulated environment are tightly linked to the likelihood of the stimulus being perceived and accepted as a "background" or scene. That is, in order for strong spatial presence and immersion to emerge, the visual stimulus should not be perceived as an object, but instead as a scene or background that can act as a stable reference or rest frame (von der Heyde & Riecke, 2002; Prothero, 1998; Prothero & Parker, 2003; Riecke, 2003, chap. IV). Although further research is needed to explore the concept of perceptual object-background separation and rest/reference frames for vection, the simplicity and unifying nature of these concepts if promising and might ultimately enable a deeper understanding of the underlying processes and allow us to better predict how vection and other phenomena like spatial presence depend on various stimulus parameters.

Stationary Foreground vs. Background

In agreement with the object-background hypothesis and the rest frame hypothesis, adding stationary background stimuli has been found to reduce or even inhibit circular vection, especially when presented peripherally, whereas stationary foreground stimuli can facilitate circular vection, especially if centrally presented (Brandt et al., 1975; Howard & Howard, 1994; Nakamura, 2006). Moreover, stationary foreground stimuli in front of a moving background are typically perceived to be moving with the observer, suggesting they are localized in body coordinates (Brandt et al., 1975; Fischer & Kornmüller, 1930), whereas during saturated vection the moving background stimulus is perceived as stationary in external coordinates and thus might act like an allocentric reference frame or rest frame. This situation is similar to riding a vehicle, where close-by objects (being part of the vehicle) move with the observer and are thus likely represented in an egocentric (body-centered) reference frame, whereas the more distant (outside) stimuli are likely to be part of the stationary environment. This can easily be utilized in motion simulator design and other applications (Nakamura, 2006). If the goal is to enhance perceived self-motion and overall realism, providing centrally located physical foreground objects like a cockpit, instruments, or other objects that match the overall simulation/ application metaphor would be instrumental. This way, the simulated scene (outside of the cockpit) will be more easily perceived as the background, thus facilitating vection and enhancing overall simulation effectiveness. Conversely, if desired, vection (and potentially also motion sickness) can be reduced or even suppressed by providing peripheral static backgrounds (Prothero & Parker, 2003). Incidentally, this mimics typical desktop VR/ gaming situations, where the static visible background of the room typically suppresses self-motions that might otherwise occur from the visual motions presented on the centrally located monitor in the foreground.

Consistent Stereoscopic Depth Cues Facilitate Vection

Displaying the vection-inducing stimulus stereoscopically has been shown to facilitate both circular and linear vection (Lowther & Ware, 1996; Palmisano, 1996). Furthermore, consistent stereoscopic cues can increase the speed and travelled distance for optic flow-induced linear forward vection, which might have mediated the vection-enhancing effect of stereoscopic cues (Palmisano, 2002). Palmisano argued that the vection-enhancing effect of stereoscopic presentation goes beyond merely increasing the perceived distance of the visual stimulus. With stereoscopic presentation becoming increasingly available and affordable, this opens up new opportunities for increasing vection and the overall simulation experience by not only providing stereoscopic information of the simulated scene, but also purposefully enhancing object-background separation, providing unobtrusive stationary foreground object that increase the relative perceived motion between the stationary (observer-fixed) foreground and background movement through the simulated scene, or by providing a more realistic and believable scene that can more easily be accepted as a primary reference or rest frame.

Head-tracking can Facilitate Vection for Moving Observers

Lowther & Ware (1996) demonstrated that vection occurs later when observers moved in front of the stationary display used to present the vection-inducing motion, possibly because of the increased cue conflict between visual and vestibular/somatosensory cues. Using head tracking to couple the simulated perspective to the observers' motion mitigated most of the motion-induced vection deterioration.

This highlights the importance of including head tracking whenever observer head position is not fixed, such as to provide a simulated scene that "behaves" like the real world and can be perceived as stable in 3D space despite head movements. Head tracking might have facilitated vection by stabilizing the simulated scene, thus making it more believable and increasing the likelihood that it is selected and accepted as a primary reference frame or rest frame with respect to which scene relative motions are more easily perceived as self-motion instead of object-motions (von der Heyde & Riecke, 2002; Prothero & Parker, 2003; Riecke, 2003, chap. IV).

Attention and Cognitive Demand can Modulate Vection

To investigate potential attentional biases in visual vection, Kitazaki & Sato (2003) presented participants with vertically moving patterns of red and green dots moving in opposite (up vs. down) direction, and asked participants to attend to either the red or the green dots. The perceived direction of vection was largely determined by the non-attended stimulus, both when the red and green dots were spatially separated (exp. 1) or superimposed (exp. 2). When the upward and downward moving patterns were presented in different depth planes, however, the far stimulus dominated the attentional modulation, although there was still some attentional contribution. Apart from a direct effect of attention on vection, it is also conceivable that the attended stimulus was perceived to be closer, such that perceived depth ordering and not attention per se determined vection (see discussion in Seno et al. 2009). Furthermore, the attended stimulus might have become the perceptual "object" or "figure", such that attention might have modulated the perceptual object-background relationship, which in turn might have determined vection. Recently, Trutoiu et al. (2008) showed that forward linear visual vection occurs earlier if participants were performing an attentiondemanding working-memory task (counting specific targets moving by in the visual stimulus). This suggests that vection can be enhanced if one does not pay particular attention to the vection-inducing stimulus.

In summary, although it seems likely that attention can modulate vection, it remains to be determined if attention can directly affect vection or whether the effect is mediated by other factors like eye movement patterns or changes in the perceived depth structure or objectbackground relationships.

No matter what the underlying processes, it is clear that we can modify the vection experience intentionally to some degree, which is relevant for both fundamental research, where task instructions should be carefully phrased, and for applications, where task requirements and expectations can likely affect the effectiveness of a motion simulation and the overall user experience.

Reference Frames, Naturalism, and Ecological Validity of Vection-inducing Stimuli

Already in 1954, Gibson put forth that "Perceived motion occurs in a perceptually stable space or environment. Another way of saying this is to assert that the perception of stability is part and parcel of the perception of motion; you cannot have the latter without the former" (Gibson, 1954, p. 310). Thus, when we see environmental motion, (illusory) selfmotion might be inferred due to our conscious or unconscious assumption of a stable environment (Dichgans & Brandt, 1978; Prothero & Parker, 2003). If this were the case, one might posit that moving visual or auditory stimuli that depict objects that normally do not move (e.g., houses or the sound of church bells) should enhance vection, compared to moving objects where our experience does not suggest stationarity (e.g., the sight or sound of a moving car). In the following, I will review studies that explicitly tested this hypothesis for visual vection. Note that auditory vection can also be facilitated when the moving sound sources represent objects that normally do not move (so-called "acoustic landmarks" like church bells) as compared to objects that move (e.g., the sound of a driving car) or are ambiguous (e.g., pink noise) (Larssonet al., 2004; Riecke et al., 2005; Väljamäe et al., 2009).

While most of the classic visual vection studies used abstract stimuli like polka-dotted or striped patterns, several researchers stressed that complex, naturalistic, and ecologically relevant stimuli should instead be used for studying self-motion perception (Gibson, 1954; Wann & Rushton, 1994). Indeed, when using naturalistic stimuli projected on a wide (142° " 110°) FOV dome projection of a flight simulator, van der Steen & Brockhoff (2000) observed surprisingly rapid vection buildup with saturated linear (forward) and circular (yaw) vection after only 2.7s and 3s, respectively. This is considerably faster than for abstract, nonnaturalistic stimuli, where vection takes between 10s (Brandt et al., 1973) to 20-30s (Howard & Howard, 1994) until reaching saturation. This led van der Steen & Brockhoff (2000) to propose that the natural scene might have contributed to the unusually fast vection buildup. Unfortunately, this hypothesis was not directly tested, and a multitude of differences in the experimental setup, procedure, and response measures compared to classic vection studies makes direct comparisons problematic.

Naturalistic, Globally Consistent Stimuli Facilitate Vection

To provide a more conclusive answer and assess if naturalistic stimuli do indeed enhance vection, we performed a series of experiments that directly manipulated the degree of naturalism and global scene consistency (i.e., higher-level factors) within one experimental paradigm (Schulte-Pelkum et al., 2003; Riecke et al., 2006). In a first study, circular yaw vection was induced by seating participants behind a curved projection screen (84°"63° FOV) displaying a rotating virtual environment created from either a naturalistic roundshot photograph (see Figure 1b) or a mosaic-like scrambled version of the same photograph (see Figure 1c)(Schulte-Pelkum et al. 2003, see also Schulte-Pelkum 2007, exp. 1). While the globally consistent scene was rendered perspectively correct and contained ample pictorial depth cues and might thus facilitate vection by providing a reference frame of a naturalistic environment on could feel spatially present in, the scrambled stimulus contained the same local image information and statistics, but could not be interpreted as a naturalistic scene one could feel present in. In addition, the scene scrambling procedure introduced additional high-contrast edges, which are known to increase perceived motion and facilitate vection (Dichgans & Brandt, 1978; Diener et al., 1976; Palmisano & Gillam, 1998). These lower-level factors thus worked against our higher-level hypothesis that naturalistic stimuli might enhance vection. Nevertheless, the naturalistic stimulus resulted in earlier vection onset and higher perceived vection intensity and convincingness than the scrambled stimulus.

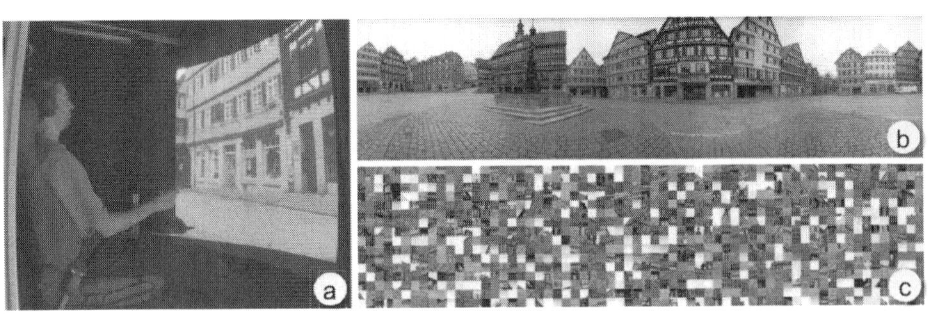

Figure 1: (a): Participant seated behind curved projection screen showing the

naturalistic circular vection stimulus based on a panoramic image (b). A globally inconsistent scene was created by mosaic-like scrabbling of the panoramic image (c).

Riecke et al. (2006) replicated and extended these results by systematically varying the degree of stimulus degradation and global inconsistency (see Figure 2, a-f). Results showed enhanced vection and presence for the naturalistic stimulus as compared to any of the sliced or scrambled stimuli, and hardly any influence of the type or degree of stimulus degradation. Figure 2, g-i contrasts the vection measures for the intact versus the least degraded stimulus. Together, these results suggest that higher-level factors related to scene consistency dominated over lower-level factors (more high-contrast edges for the scrambled stimulus) that would have predicted the opposite result.

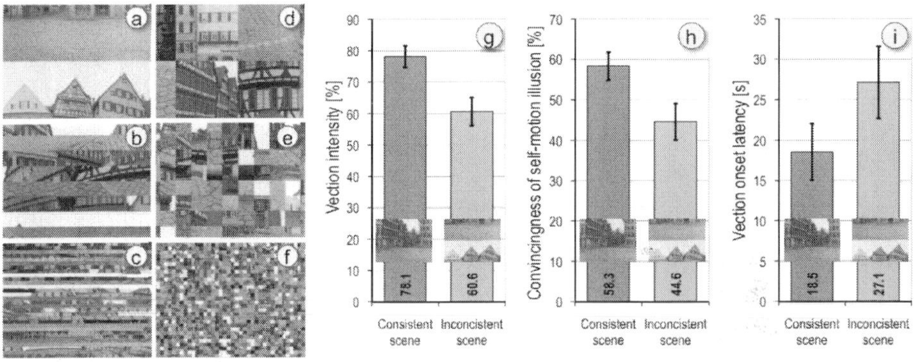

Figure 2: 54°»45° view of the different horizontally sliced (a-c) and mosaic-like scrambled (d-f) vection-inducing stimuli as seen by participants in (Riecke et al., 2006) in addition to the globally consistent stimulus (cf. Figure 1, a & b). (g) – (i): Circular vection measures for the comparison of the globally consistent stimulus (left bar) and one of the globally inconsistent stimuli (the sliced version depicted in (a)). Note the vection impairment for the globally inconsistent (less naturalistic) stimulus, suggesting higher-level/cognitive influences. Depicted are mean # one standard error of the mean, re-plotted from a subset of the original data of Riecke et al. (2006) for 40°/s stimulus velocity without data normalization.

There are at least three underlying mechanism that might explain the observed vectionfacilitating effect of globally consistent, naturalistic stimuli:

- The globally consistent stimulus contained ample pictorial depth cues arranged in a consistent, naturalistic environment. This might have increased the perceived distance of the stimulus, which is known to increase perceived vection velocity (Wist et al., 1975), which in turn is associated with enhanced vection. In fact, increasing stimulus velocities in (Schulte-Pelkum et al., 2003) from 20°/s to 40°/s to 60/s reduced vection onset latencies and increased vection intensity and convincingness.

- Previous studies showed that perceived foreground-background separation can affect vection: When vection-inducing stimuli are comprised of multiple parts (e.g., superimposed or spatially separated), vection is dominated by the motion of the perceived background (Howard & Heckmann, 1989; Nakamura & Shimojo, 1999; Ohmi et al., 1987; Seno et al., 2009). In our study, the naturalistic scene stimulus and pictorial depth contained therein might have resulted in a perceived foreground-background separation between the physical screen and setup acting as the foreground and the projected scene being perceived as further away and thus acting as a moving background, thus indirectly facilitating vection.
- Presence ratings were significantly higher for the naturalistic stimulus than any of the sliced or scrambled stimuli, and were consistently correlated with vection measures. Thus, the naturalistic scene might have provided a more believable and convincing, stable reference frame and primary rest frame than the globally inconsistent stimuli, such that stimulus motion might be more easily perceived or interpreted as self-motion than image or object motion (Dichgans & Brandt, 1978; Gibson, 1954; Prothero, 1998).

In sum, the data suggest that not only lower-level factors, but also higher-level factors like the interpretation of the stimulus as a believable and ecologically valid scene can affect selfmotion perception.

Natural stimulus orientation enhances vection and presence

In a second experiment, Riecke et al. (2006) showed that inverting the naturalistic scene such that it appears upside-down reduced both the convincingness of vection and rated presence in the scene. Note that lower-level factors (e.g., image statistics) and scene consistency were identical between the upright and upside-down stimulus. This corroborates the relevance of higher-level/cognitive factors like the ecological validity and naturalism of the stimulus and the existence of optic flow from a believable ground surface, which has been shown to facilitate vection (Sato et al., 2007).

Naturalistic stimuli induce stronger vection than abstract geometric patterns

Further indication of potential higher-level influences stem from Richards et al. (2004), who investigated how postural stability during linear treadmill walking is affected by different moving visual stimuli presented on a projection screen (FOV: 65°"48°). Body sway in roll and pitch direction was more pronounced for a simple textured room display that contained intrinsic upright orientation cues (i.e., visual polarity defined by room geometry and clearly distinguishable ceiling, walls, and floor) as compared to a black and white polka-dotted cylindrical room that had no intrinsic upright cues. Furthermore, the room environment were rated as perceptually more compelling and resulted anecdotally in more frequent and intense vection experiences and reduced vection drop-outs. This supports findings by Riecke et al. (2006) and Schulte-Pelkum et al. (2003) that consistent, naturalistic visual cues enhance vection. Similarly, Wann & Rushton (1994) observed stronger circular vection for a naturalistic 3D environment presented via HMD as compared to the 2D texture stripes of a simulated optokinetic drum. Note, however, that the room versus polka-dotted stimuli in Richards et al. (2004) and the 3D environment versus texture stripes in Wann & Rushton (1994) differed not only in terms of naturalism and inherent upright-direction, but also with regards to other factors that are known to affect vection and could thus have contributed to the observed effects, including their spatial frequency content and the number of moving contrasts (Diener et al., 1976; Palmisano & Gillam, 1998; Hu et al., 1997) or perceived depth and foreground-background separation (Howard & Heckmann, 1989; Seno et al., 2009).

Tumbling sensation (roll vection) is facilitated by cue-rich, naturalistic environment

Additional support for the importance of naturalistic 3D environments comes from tumbling room studies, where stationary observers are surrounded by an (empty or fully furnished) room that can be rotated around the observers' roll axis. The perception of body tilt and roll vection was facilitated by a number of factors including the availability of a visual frame of reference, objects with clear visual polarity (i.e., intrinsic "up" direction), rotation velocity of the tumbling room, and field of view (Allison et al., 1999; Howard & Childerson, 1994). With 30°/s rotation of a fully furnished room with ample visual polarity cues and unrestricted FOV, up to 80% of observers experienced strong tumbling sensations including head-over-heels (cartwheel) roll vection. Tumbling (roll vection) occurred less frequently for smaller rotational velocities (15°/s instead of 30/s) and reduced field of views. These results highlight the vection-inducing power of naturalistic full-field visual motion. Further, carefully conducted research is, however, needed to more deeply understand what parameters of the visual stimulus make it more effective, and to disambiguate lower-level, bottom-up factors (like number of moving contrasts and edges) from higher-level perceptual and cognitive factors (like the "known" visual polarity of objects or the familiarity of "rooms"). Using wide-FOV VR simulators would give us the flexibility to more easily investigate these issues without the need to equip physical tumbling rooms with different objects and having to secure them for roll rotations.

Does the possibility of actual motion affect the illusion of self-motion?

Whenever self-motions are only simulated (e.g., through visual cues or a motion platform) and not actually performed, there is a conflict between some cues suggesting self-motion and others indicating stationarity. Apart from sensory cues directly indicating motion or nomotion, there are typically also other factors that might affect perceived self-motion. In particular, we are typically aware whether actual motion is, in fact, possible (e.g., when sitting on a moveable platform or vehicle) or not (e.g., when we stand/sit on solid ground). Thus, in order to provide compelling sensations of (illusory) self-motion, we might not only need to overcome the sensory conflict between sensory information suggesting self-motion versus stationarity, but potentially also "convince" us that actual motion is indeed possible. Theme parks have long recognized the importance of providing a cognitive-perceptual framework of movability, e.g., by guiding users of a star wars fun ride (at Disney's Hollywood Studio theme park) through a (fake) space-craft airport before entering the "space-craft", which is a motion platform carefully disguised as a space ship such that users are unaware of the actual motion limitations of the system. Apart from being entertaining and avoiding that visitors get bored while waiting for the next ride, providing such a scenario and suggesting movability of the space craft might help to prime visitors to expect actual motion and more easily accept and believe the motion simulation. Although such suspension of disbelief is frequently used in consumer-market applications like theme parks and video arcades, there is surprisingly little published research investigating whether providing a cognitive-perceptual framework of movability can not only increase user enjoyment and fun but also enhance the effectiveness and believability of self-motion simulations.

As providing a cognitive-perceptual framework of movability can often be created at much lower cost and effort than increasing the actual motion range of VR simulations, pursuing this question could be of considerable interest for many applications. In addition, it can extend our understanding of higher-level influences on vection, and in particular on the integration of multi-modal sensory cues with higher-level cognitive/perceptual information. In the following, I will review and discuss research that explicitly investigated whether the perceived possibility of actual self-motion can enhance vection, for example by designing for situational awareness of movability by providing a cognitive-perceptual framework suggesting the possibility of actual self-motion.

Participants are often seated on movable devices to facilitate vection

In order to suggest movability and facilitate vection, a number of vection researchers have seated participants on rotating chairs when investigating circular vection (Lackner, 1977; Väljamäe, 2009) or on moveable carts when studying linear vection (Berthoz et al., 1975; Lackner, 1977; Pavard & Berthoz, 1977; Andersen & Braunstein, 1985) and demonstrated the possibility of motion prior to the actual vection experiments. Andersen & Braunstein (1985, p. 124) stated, for example, that "several subjects in pilot studies and other observers had previously reported that the experience of self-motion was inhibited by the observation that they were in an environment in which they could not be physically moved". Surprisingly, however, none of the above-mentioned studies provided actual data that vection was indeed facilitated when participants were seated on a moveable chair or cart.

Children experience vection earlier when sitting on moveable platform

To the best of our knowledge, the first study that explicitly addressed this issue was conducted by Lepecq et al. (1995) with children of seven and eleven years. Half of the participants were seated on a chair with rollers ("movement possible" condition) and were demonstrated prior to the actual experiment how the chair could move. The other half of the participants were seated on a stationary chair ("movement impossible" condition) and shown that the chair could not be moved. Although participants were always stationary during the subsequent backward linear visual vection experiment, knowledge about the possibility of motion reduced vection onset latencies. The frequency of vection occurrences remained unaffected by this cognitive manipulation, though. Nevertheless, Lepecq et al. (1995) provided first evidence that the knowledge and prior experience that actual motion is possible could facilitate vection, suggesting higher-level, cognitive contributions. Is there a similar effect of perceived movability on vection in adults, or are they less easily "fooled to believe"? There are only a few studies that investigated this issue in adults, and the results provide somewhat mixed evidence.

Self-motion-bias versus object-motion-bias instructions affect vection reporting

Palmisano & Chan (2004) used adult participants and a similar overall procedure as Lepecq et al. (1995) to investigate if linear forward linear vection induced by an optic flow display is modulated by creating situations were physical movements are possible vs. impossible. While the "movement possible" (or self-motion-bias) group was instructed to report the onset and offset of self-motion as in Lepecq et al. (1995), the "movement impossible" (or object-motion-bias) group in Palmisano & Chan (2004) was instructed to report the onset and offset of object motion, and vection was inferred when no object motion was reported. This object-motion-bias reduced the occurrence of vection reports as compared to the selfmotion-bias, although vection onset latencies were unaffected by the cognitive manipulation. Note that these results differ from Lepecq et al.'s findings, where the cognitive manipulation affected the onset latency, but not the occurrence of vection. It is conceivable that the object-motion-bias introduced a criterion shift and response bias in favor of reporting object-motion. Moreover, trials with only partial vection, where objectand self-motion co-exist, would have been identified as vection trials for the self-motion-bias group but as no-vection trials for the object-motion-bias group. Hence, it remains unclear whether the cognitive manipulation in Palmisano & Chan (2004) did indeed affect perceived self-motion.

Elevator vection occurs earlier if actual motion is possible

In a vertical oscillatory ("elevator") vection study with adults, Wright et al. (2006) showed that participants who were seated in a vertical oscillator and shown prior to the actual experiment how they could be moved reported more compelling vection than participants who saw the same vection stimulus, but were sitting on a stationary chair in a different room. Vection amplitudes and onset latencies remained unaffected by the cognitive manipulation, though. To explain their data, Wright et al. (2006) proposed two dissociable factors underlying vection: One process determining the compellingness of vection that is susceptible to cognitive manipulations, and a second process primarily driven by visual (bottom-up) cues that mainly affects vection onset latencies and the extend of the selfmotion illusion. Note that this distinction does not fit the data by Lepecq et al. (1995), where the cognitive manipulation affected the onset latency, but not the occurrence of vection.

Visual circular vection not facilitated if actual motion is possible

While by Lepecq et al. (1995) and Wright et al. (2006) found a significant facilitation of linear visual vection when participants were previously demonstrated that actual motion is possible, circular visual vection might be less affected by such cognitive manipulations (Schulte-Pelkum, 2007; Schulte-Pelkum et al., 2004): When participants were seated on a 6 degree of freedom Stewart motion platform and previously shown how the platform can move, 2/3 of them did indeed believe that they were physically moving in at least some of the trials where the platform was switched on (see Figure 3, middle), and many of them were fairly certain that actual motion occurred (see Figure 3, right). Nevertheless, vection reports were unaffected by this cognitive manipulation, and vection onset times, intensity, and convincingness were identical between movement-possible and movement-impossible trials. As discussed in detail in Riecke (2009) and Schulte-Pelkum (2007), the lack of a clear vection-facilitating effect of the cognitive manipulation might be due to a number of differences in experimental procedures, as compared to Lepecq et al. (1995) and Wright et al. (2006), and we are currently planning experiments to assess if visual circular vection can indeed be affected by providing a cognitive-perceptual framework of movability.

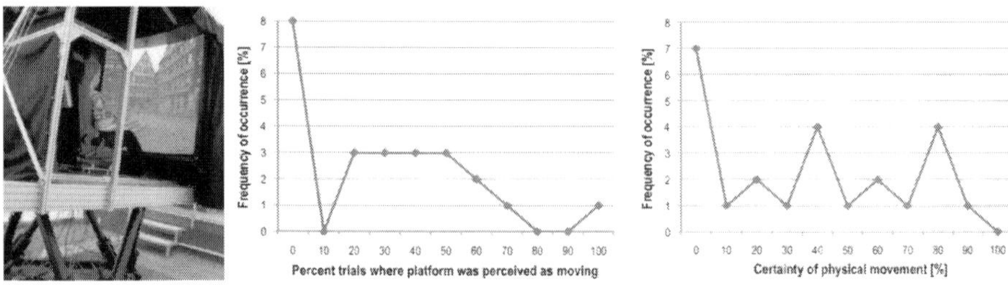

Figure 3: Left: Participant seated on a motion platform that was either switched on ("motion possible" condition) or not ("motion impossible"). Middle: Histogram of participants' responses. Participants were asked to rate in what percentage of trials they perceived the platform to be physically moving. 8/24 participants (33.3%) stated that it never moved, whereas the remaining 66.7% stated that the platform moved in at least 10% of the trials. One participant stated that it always moved. Right: Participants were asked to rate how certain they were (on a 0-100% scale) that the platform did move in at least some trials. Only seven participants were certain that it never moved, and five participants were at least 80% certain that it moved. Data re-plotted from (Schulte-Pelkum et al., 2004; Schulte-Pelkum, 2007).

Auditory vection can be facilitated by cognitive-perceptual framework of movability

While it remains to be demonstrated if a cognitive-perceptual framework of movability can affect visually-induced circular vection, there is recent evidence that it can affect auditorilyinduced circular vection (Riecke, Feuereissen, & Rieser, 2009). In order to provide highquality recordings of rotating sound fields for the auditory vection experiments, the lab was equipped with two easily distinguishable and localizable sound sources positioned 90! apart, and participants were seated on a hammock chair mounted above a circular treadmill (see Figure 4a) and passively rotated. Small in-ear microphones were used to generate individualized binaural recordings of what participants hear when actually rotating in the lab. During the subsequent vection experiment, participants sat on the hammock chair with the circular treadmill switched off while wearing blindfolds and noise-cancelling headphones displaying the previously recorded rotating sound fields. Participants' feet were either suspended by a chair-attached footrest (see Figure 4b, "movement possible" condition) or positioned on solid ground ("movement impossible" condition). Providing a cognitive-perceptual framework of movability in the "motion possible" condition yielded higher vection intensity ratings (see Figure 4d), and there was a marginally significant trend ($p<.1$) towards more frequent occurrence of vection (84% vs. 68%, see Figure 4c), reduced vection onset latencies (41s vs. 31s, see Figure 4e), and higher perceived realism of actually rotating in the lab. Hence, the common practice of seating participants on moveable chairs or platforms (Lackner, 1977; Väljamäe, 2007, 2009) does indeed seem to benefit auditory vection.

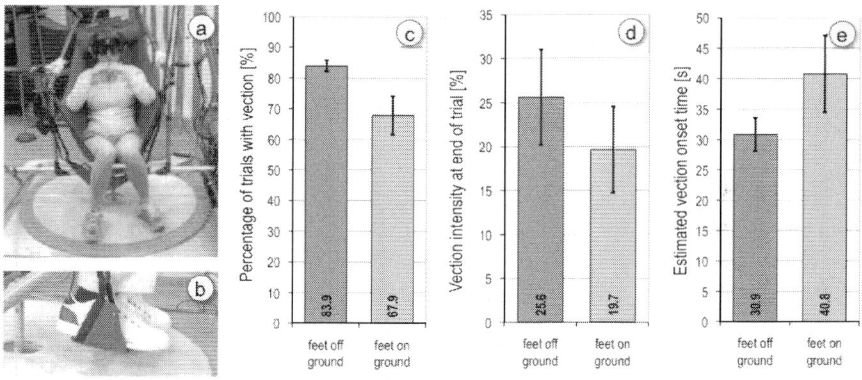

Figure 4: (a): Participant wearing blindfold and noise-cancelling headphone, seated on a hammock chair mounted stationary above a circular treadmill. (b) In a "feet off ground" condition, participants' feet were suspended by a footrest, whereas in a "feet on ground" condition (a) participants' feet were on solid ground, thus acting as a "motion impossible" condition. (c) – (e): Auditory circular vection measures show slightly enhanced vection when participants' feet did not touch solid ground. Depicted are mean # 1SEM, re-plotted from a subset of the original data of (Riecke et al., 2009) with no jitter.

The exact mechanisms underlying this effect await further experimentation, though: In the current experiment, both cognitive and perceptual factors might have contributed. On the one hand, resting one's feet on solid ground provides somatosensory and thus lower-level, perceptual cues indicating stationarity. On the other hand, it provides higher-level, cognitive "knowledge" that could have primed participants to believe that physical motion was impossible. From the current data, it is not possible to disambiguate between cognitive and perceptual factors, and they likely contributed both and might even support or depend on each other.

Touching the floor attenuates visual roll vection in weightlessness

The influence of touching the stationary floor on vection was also investigated by Young et al. (1983) and Young & Shelhamer (1990): While in weightlessness, visually induced roll vection was compared between a "free floating" condition, where only a bite bar fixated participants' orientation and position in space, and a "tactile" condition, where an additional shoulder harness pressed participants to the floor using elastic bands. Thus touching the floor resulted in more vection drop-outs and reduced the strength of roll vection. Some participants also reported prolonged vection onset latencies. Similar to the auditory vection study discussed above (Riecke et al., 2009) touching and being restrained to the floor in Young et al. (1983) and Young & Shelhamer (1990) might have attenuated visual roll vection via both lower-level perceptual processes, namely somatosensory cues indicating being tied to a stationary floor, and higher-level, cognitive factors like the knowledge that actual motion was impossible due to the restraints.

Conclusions

In summary, although it is often difficult to disentangle the possible influence of cognitive versus perceptual processes, there is converging evidence that providing a cognitiveperceptual framework of movability can under certain conditions facilitate self-motion perception. This is consistent with informal reports and common practice of seating participants on moveable platforms in situations where vection is difficult to achieve, as is the case for auditory vection (e.g., Lackner 1977; Väljamäe 2007) or visual vection with small field of views (Andersen & Braunstein, 1985). Although the above-mentioned results are promising, further research is necessary to enable us to more deeply understand why, how, and under which conditions perceptual and/or cognitive information suggesting movability versus stationarity can affect self-motion perception. While of clear theoretical interest, there is also a clear applied benefit, as cognitive-perceptual frameworks of movability can often be implement with relatively little effort, especially compared to the costs involved in allowing for large-scale physical locomotion or full-fledged motion simulators.

CROSS-MODAL FACILITATION OF VECTION

While an in-depth review of multi-modal aspect of vection would go beyond the scope of this chapter, it is important to realize that there are a number of cross-modal effects and facilitations of vection that could help to optimize VR simulations and other immersive applications. For example, galvanic vestibular stimulation can both directly induce self-tilt and affect visually simulated self-motions (Cress et al., 1997; Lepecq et al., 2006). Adding subtle vibrations to the observers' seat and footrest has been shown to enhance visual vection (Riecke et al., 2005; Schulte-Pelkum, 2007). Similarly, vibrations can enhance auditory vection (Riecke et al., 2009), especially if accompanied by a matching simulated engine sound (Väljamäe et al., 2006; Väljamäe et al., 2009). Although moving sound fields by themselves can only induce vection in about 20-75% of blindfolded listeners, they have been shown to enhance vection induced by other modalities, including visual circular vection (Riecke et al., 2009) and biomechanical circular vection induced by stepping along a circular treadmill (Riecke et al., 2010). Adding small physical motions (simple jerks) to the onset of visually simulated self-motion has been shown to significant enhance visually induced vection, both for passive movement (Berger et al., 2010; Riecke et al., 2006; Schulte-Pelkum, 2007; Wong & Frost, 1981) and for simple self-initiated motion cueing (Riecke, 2006). Note that these jerks facilitated vection despite being only qualitatively correct (i.e., they matched the direction and precise temporal onset of the visual motion, but not the extent or acceleration). This suggests that there might be a surprisingly large coherence zone within which visuo-vestibular conflicts go unnoticed or at least have little detrimental effect (Steen, 1998). Finally, applying vibrations and small physical movements (jerks) together enhanced visual vection more then either of them alone (Schulte-Pelkum, 2007, exp. 6). Together, these results suggest considerable cross-modal benefits for self-motion perception, even when cross-modal stimuli are only qualitatively matched. While proper motion cueing using 6DOF motion platforms is clearly desirable in many applications including flight or driving simulations, budgets and space are often limited. In such situations, vibrations and spatialized auditory cues can often be included at moderate cost and effort. Even simple commercially available motion seats or gaming seats might provide considerable benefits to self-motion perception and overall simulation effectiveness.

POTENTIAL UNDESIRABLE SIDE-EFFECTS OF VECTION IN VR

For all applications, the potential benefits of providing compelling self-motion illusions need to be carefully evaluated against potential undesirable side-effects (for a detailed discussion, see Hettinger 2002; Kennedy et al. 2003 and references therein). The occurrence of vection can, for example, correlate with undesirable side-effects like motion sickness or motion after-effects. It is, however, still unclear whether or how vection might be causally related to motion sickness, as vection generally seems to occur when visuo-vestibular cue conflicts are small, whereas motion sickness tends to occur for larger cue conflicts (Kennedy et al., 2003; Palmisano et al., 2007). Moreover, visually-induced motion sickness can occur without either vection or optokinetic nystagmus (Ji, So, & Cheung, 2009). Vection is also known to co-occur with body sway in standing observers (Howard, 1982). While small infants can indeed tip over due to large-field visual stimulation (Lee & Aronson, 1974), children older than five years and adults seem less affected and sway less. While vection and visually induced body sway likely share similar pathways and vection strength can be indicative of body sway, body sway occurs well before the onset of vection and does not necessarily match the direction of perceived self-motion, again questioning a direct causal relation between vection and body sway (Guerraz & Bronstein, 2008; Wang et al., 2010). In sum, further research is needed to carefully assess factors promoting undesirable sideeffects like motion/simulator sickness, postural responses, after-effects, and (re)adaptation effects, and to what degree there might or might not be any causal relationships to vection.

CONCLUSIONS AND OUTLOOK

Self-motion illusions are embodied illusions that can be quite compelling and thus critically affect the overall experience and effectiveness of VR and other immersive media. Hence, it is important to better understand the nature of the phenomenon of vection and the different contributing factors and their interactions, such that the illusion can be purposefully elicited or suppressed, depending on the specific goals and requirements of a given application. While this chapter provides a review on different factors that can enhance vection, this information can, of course, also be used to purposefully inhibit the illusion where desired. Depending on the goals and user task of an application, different degrees of vection and overall presence/immersion might be desirable, and it should be carefully evaluated on a case-by-case basis to what degree vection can or cannot contribute to the overall goal.

Given the increased availability and affordability of large, multi-screen displays setups, care should be taken that self-motion is only perceived where intended. For example, when manipulating 3D objects or CAD models on a screen, this should be perceived as object motion and not self-motion. Especially when users have to quickly switch between different tasks, screens, or simulated environments, vection as well as spatial presence and immersion should be avoided. Conversely, for architecture walkthroughs, vehicle simulation, telepresence, and other applications where perceptual/ behavioral realism is of the essence, simulated observer motions should be perceived as self-motion and not object motion; else, the 3D model might be perceived as a small toy mockup instead of a full-sized, naturalistic environment. For disambiguating between perceived object versus self motion, manipulating the perceived object-background separation might be the most effective means, as discussed above.

Interestingly, many sought-after attributes in the design of VR systems and other immersive media seem to also be factors that are known to enhance vection, such as large FOVs, naturalistic and ecologically valid stimuli, stereoscopic presentation, perceived background motion, or multi-modal stimulation and consistency. In particular, presence in the simulated environment frequently correlates with vection, seems to benefit from similar factors as vection, and might even be mediated by vection (Riecke et al., 2006; Väljamäe, 2009), as predicted by the rest frame hypothesis (Prothero & Parker, 2003). I propose that utilizing and further developing promising comprehensive frameworks like the rest frame hypothesis (Prothero, 1998; Prothero & Parker, 2003), the object-background hypothesis (Seno et al., 2009), or the reference frame model (von der Heyde & Riecke, 2002; Riecke, 2003, chap. 4) can foster a deeper understanding of the mechanisms underlying phenomena like vection, presence, or spatial orientation and enable us to devise operation definitions and novel measurement methods (Prothero & Parker, 2003; Riecke, 2003, chapter IV). Ultimately, being able to integrate seemingly disparate findings into a conceptual framework will allow us to derive testable hypothesis and predictions that can guide future research and applications.

In conclusion, a growing body of evidence suggests that vection and overall simulation effectiveness is not only determined by physical stimulus parameters themselves, but also by other factors including how we look at, perceive, and interpret the stimulus, the perceived foreground-background separation, and a variety of higher-level phenomena like cognitive-perceptual frameworks of movability, naturalism and ecological validity, spatial presence, and reference/rest frames. Clearly, these factors deserve more attention both in basic research and applications. These factors might also turn out to be crucial especially in the context of VR applications and self-motion simulations, as they have the potential of offering an elegant and affordable way to optimize simulations in terms of perceptual and behavioral effectiveness. Compared to other means of increasing the convincingness and effectiveness of self-motion simulations like increasing the visual field of view or using a motion platform, higher-level factors can often be manipulated rather easily and without much cost, such that they might be an important step towards a lean and elegant approach to effective self-motion simulation. This is nicely demonstrated by many theme park rides, where setting up the proper cognitive framework and expectation (both highly cognitive factors) helps to draw users more easily and effectively into the simulation and into "believing". Thus, I posit that an approach that is centered around the perceptual and behavioral effectiveness and not only the physical stimulus realism is important both for gaining a deeper understanding in basic research and offering a lean and elegant way to improve a number of applications, especially in the advancing field of virtual reality simulations. This might ultimately allow us to come closer to fulfilling the promise of VR as a believable "window onto the simulated world", such that the virtual reality can be perceived and accepted as an alternate reality that enables natural and unencumbered human behavior.

REFERENCES

1. Allison, R. S., Howard, I. P., & Zacher, J. E. (1999). Effect of field size, head motion, and rotational velocity on roll vection and illusory self-tilt in a tumbling room. Perception, 28(3), 299-306.
2. Andersen, G. J. (1986). Perception of Self-Motion - Psychophysical and Computational Approaches. Psychological Bulletin, 99(1), 52-65.
3. Andersen, G. J., & Braunstein, M. L. (1985). Induced Self-Motion in Central Vision. Journal of Experimental Psychology – Human Perception and Performance, 11(2), 122-132.
4. Becker, W., Raab, S., & Jürgens, R. (2002). Circular vection during voluntary suppression of optokinetic reflex. Experimental Brain Research, 144(4), 554-557.
5. Berger, D. R., Schulte-Pelkum, J., & Bülthoff, H. H. (2010). Simulating believable forward accelerations on a stewart motion platform. ACM Trans. Appl. Percept., 7(1), 1-27. doi:10.1145/1658349.1658354
6. Berthoz, A., Pavard, B., & Young, L. R. (1975). Perception of linear horizontal self-motion induced by peripheral vision (linearvection) - basic characteristics and visualvestibular interactions. Experimental Brain Research, 23(5), 471-489.
7. Bles, W. (1981). Stepping around: circular vection and Coriolis effects. In J. Long & A. Baddeley (Eds.), Attention and performance IX (pp. 47–61). Erlbaum, Hillsdale, NJ.
8. Brandt, T., Büchele, W., & Arnold, F. (1977). Arthrokinetic nystagmus and ego-motion sensation. Experimental Brain Research, 30(2), 331-338. doi:10.1007/BF00237260
9. Brandt, T., Dichgans, J., & Koenig, E. (1973). Differential effects of central versus peripheral vision on egocentric and exocentric motion perception. Experimental Brain Research, 16, 476-491.
10. Brandt, T., Wist, E. R., & Dichgans, J. (1975). Foreground and Background in Dynamic Spatial Orientation. Perception & Psychophysics, 17(5), 497-503.
11. Bubka, A., & Bonato, F. (2010). Natural visual-field features enhance vection. Perception, 39(5), 627 – 635. doi:10.1068/p6315
12. Cheung, B. S. K., Howard, I. P., Nedzelski, J. M., & Landolt, J. P. (1989). Circularvection About Earth-horizontal Axes in Bilateral Labyrinthine-defective Subjects. Acta OtoLaryngologica, 108(5), 336. doi:10.3109/00016488909125537

Resources for Ecological Psychology. Erlbaum, Hillsdale, NJ.

105. Zacharias, G. L., & Young, L. R. (1981). Influence of combined Visual and Vestibular Cues on Human Perception and Control of Horizontal Rotation. Experimental Brain Research, 41, 159-171.

Chapter 4

A Scoping Review on Tangible and Spatial Awareness Interaction Technique in Mobile Augmented Reality-Authoring Tool in Kitchen

Siti Soleha Muhammad Nizam, Meng Chun Lam, Haslina Arshad, and Nur Asylah Suwadi

Mixed Reality and Pervasive Computing Lab, Centre of Artificial Intelligence Technology, Faculty of Information Science and Technology, Universiti Kebangsaan Malaysia, 43600 Bangi, Selangor, Malaysia

ABSTRACT

The interaction paradigm has changed with the emerging technology, mobile augmented reality, and spatial awareness mobile device. The traditional way for designing a kitchen can cause mistake in measurement and user's

---

Citation: Siti Soleha Muhammad Nizam, Meng Chun Lam, Haslina Arshad, and Nur Asylah Suwadi, "A Scoping Review on Tangible and Spatial Awareness Interaction Technique in Mobile Augmented Reality-Authoring Tool in Kitchen," Advances in Multimedia, vol. 2018, Article ID 5320984.

imagination is different from kitchen advisor's sketch design due to limitation of human imagination. Using mobile augmented reality technology, the user can overlay the virtual kitchen outcome that could fit with the actual kitchen environment. Interaction technique is required in order to allow the user to change the characteristic of the virtual kitchen to suite their need. Thus, this paper is intended to propose the tangible and spatial awareness interaction techniques in the kitchen design authoring tool. A scoping review related to the previous research on tangible and spatial awareness interaction is presented in this paper. The proposed techniques were based on the review on the existing interaction technique and the interview section with the Malaysian kitchen designer by understanding the kitchen design elements and flow. The proposed techniques will be further improved by going through the heuristic evaluation with the augmented reality expert.

INTRODUCTION

Augmented Reality (AR) receives a lot of attention globally. There are a lot of efforts in research and ongoing development in this area as it is the newest technology. Augmented Reality can provide attractive and interactive experience in kitchen design. Interior design has gained tons of attention among the users in order to make a convenient and comfortable kitchen environment. Based on the previous finding, AR offers many advantages in digital architectural design and construction fields [1]. It is a new design approach for interior design, where AR environment is able to display virtual furniture and it can be modified in real-time where the user can directly see the virtual outcome of the design.

Some of the kitchen design companies are using physical board to show rough design by arranging the physical blocks into the empty kitchen layout as shown in Figure 1. However, with the limitation of human imagination, it is challenging to visualize how the cabinet will look like or align in the real kitchen space [2]. Mobile Augmented Reality (MAR) application allows the virtual furniture to overlay into real scene. Thus, the user can see the outcome of the kitchen design whether the design outcome could fit with the actual kitchen environment. The interaction with the augmented reality environment plays an important role in this authoring type application. It could affect the performance and user preference such as to discourage the user if the interaction is too complicated. Thus, this paper is focusing on the interaction technique design in kitchen design. There are two types of potential interaction techniques, which are suitable for the kitchen design:

tangible and spatial awareness interaction technique. This work reviews the existing studies on the tangible and spatial awareness technique in order to identify and design a new interaction technique for the kitchen design in MAR environment.

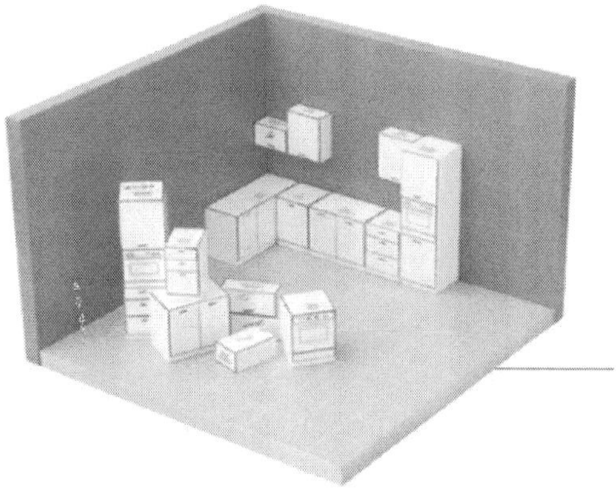

Figure 1: Physical kitchen miniature modelling kit [3].

This paper consists of six parts: the first part is the introduction of the study. The second part discusses the documents selection process. The third part is the reviews of the studies related to tangible and spatial awareness interaction technique to explore their possibilities in kitchen design MAR authoring tool. Next, the kitchen design process is defined based on the interview section with the Malaysian kitchen design company. The fifth part of the paper discusses the proposed tangible and spatial awareness interaction techniques in mobile augmented reality setting. The conclusion and the future works are in the final part of the paper.

DOCUMENTS SELECTION

This study focused on two types of interaction techniques, which are tangible interaction technique and spatial awareness interaction technique. Tangible interaction technique is an approach of designing the AR interfaces that focus on interactions using related physical object to interact with the virtual object [4, 5]. Tangible interaction technique registers the virtual object to a physical object, and a user interacts with the virtual objects by manipulating the corresponding physical objects [1]. In the designing session, it allows the user to interact with the virtual furniture in order to move, rotate, and copy them as in the real environment using physical object. With the latest development, RGB and depth camera embedded in the smart phone have enabled the spatial awareness interaction technique in a mobile setting [6]. It allows the user to measure the depth of the object by using depth sensor. Spatial awareness interaction technique involves motion tracking, depth sensing, and area learning where the environment properties could be recognized by the AR system. Both types of interaction techniques require further exploration on their effectiveness in helping design process between the kitchen designer and customer.

Documents (Tangible Interaction Technique)

Based on Figure 2, the initial result of query search is 1768 from SCOPUS database. Then, the result was filtered by the document type, field, language, and year. The filtration ended up with 1528 documents. After title and abstract filtering, 1528 documents have been reduced to 145. Then, full text reading process excluded 133 documents, resulting in 12 documents as the final document to be analysed.

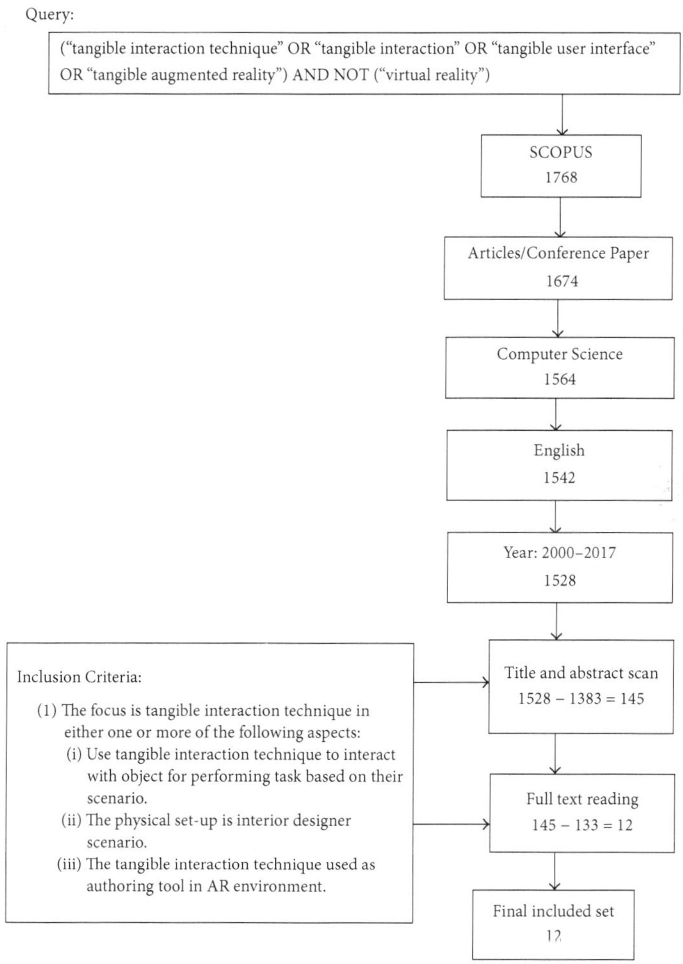

Figure 2: Document selection for tangible interaction technique.

Documents (Spatial Interaction Technique)

Based on Figure 3, the initial query shows 3565 raw results in SCOPUS. The field was then specified to computer science leaving 771 results. 717 articles and conference papers were then chosen to be included in this filtering. The documents from year 2000 until 2017 were chosen, reducing the documents into 650 documents. After scanning the title and abstract, only 116 documents were applicable. At the end, 8 documents were chosen after finishing the full text reading.

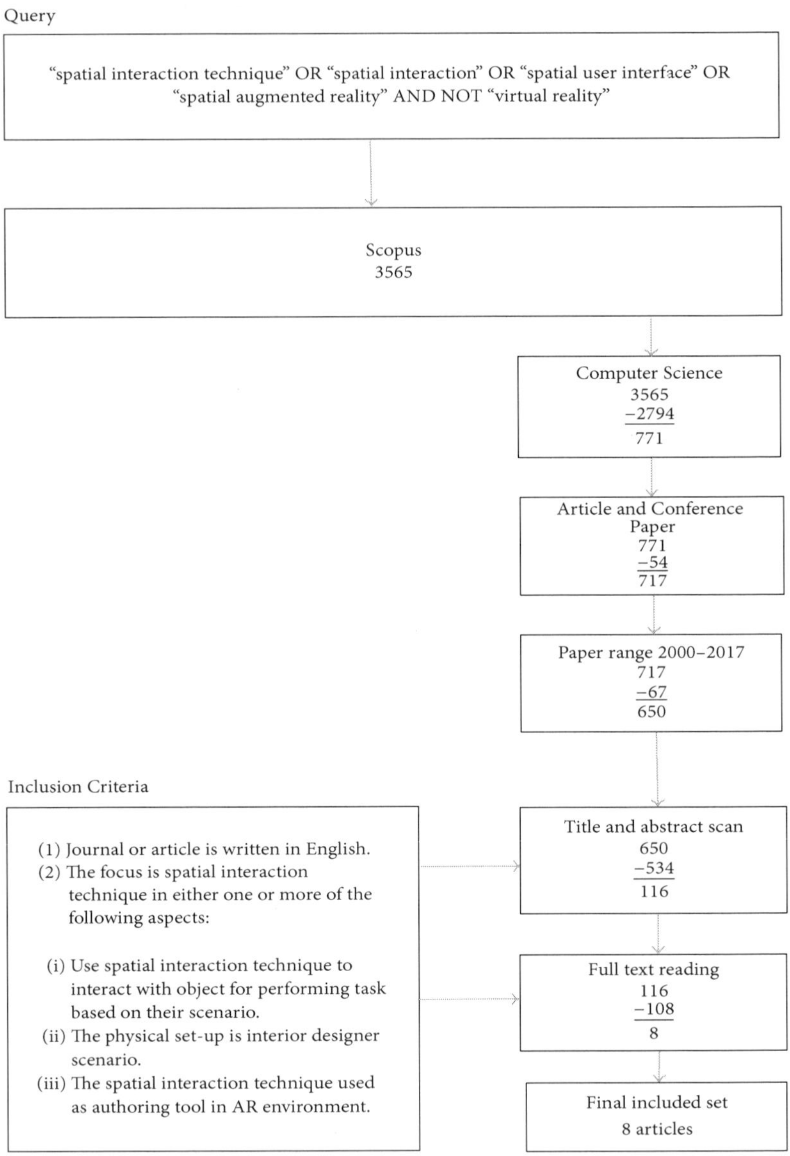

Figure 3: Document selection for spatial interaction technique.

RESULT AND STATISTICAL INFORMATION OF DOCUMENTS

In summary, 20 articles have been selected from the SCOPUS database and reviewed in which 60% are in tangible interaction technique and 40%

are related to spatial awareness interaction technique. All the papers were published in proceedings and journals from 2002 until 2017. Study on spatial awareness interaction technique is a new topic and the reviewed papers are from 2013 to 2017. 50% of the reviewed papers for tangible interaction technique are proceeding papers and another 50% are from journal articles. Meanwhile, all the reviewed papers for spatial awareness interaction technique are proceeding papers. The selection process will be discussed in Section 2. There are 6 scenarios that used tangible interaction technique in their study as shown in Table 1.

Table 1: Scenarios

Interaction	Scenario	Percentage
Tangible	Product design	8%
	Rapid Prototype	8%
	Game	18%
	Music	8%
	Interior design	25%
	Education	33%
Spatial awareness	Architecture	37%
	Information Sharing	37%
	Game	13%
	Medical	13%

Based on the review there are four types of AR, which are projection based, see-through based, PC based, and mobile based which used tangible and spatial awareness interaction techniques. The statistics of the types of AR used in the reviewed papers are shown in Table 2.

Table 2: Type of AR

Type of AR	Type of interaction	
	Tangible	Spatial awareness
Projection	17%	50%
See-through	58%	12.5%
PC	17%	12.5%
Mobile	8%	25%

22. M. R. Marner and B. H. Thomas, "Poster: Spatial Augmented Reality user interface techniques for room size modeling tasks," in Proceedings of the 8th IEEE International Symposium on 3D User Interfaces, 3DUI 2013, pp. 155-156, usa, March 2013.
23. J. Lee, "4-1:," SID Symposium Digest of Technical Papers, vol. 48, no. 1, pp. 17-18, 2017.

Chapter

5 Traffic and Driving Simulator Based on Architecture of Interactive Motion

Alexander Paz[1] , Naveen Veeramisti[1] , Romesh Khaddar[2] , Hanns de la Fuente-Mella[3] , and Luiza Modorcea[4]

[1]University of Nevada, Las Vegas, Civil and Environmental Engineering and Construction, Las Vegas, NV 89154, USA

[2]University of Nevada, Las Vegas, Electrical and Computer Engineering, Las Vegas, NV 89154, USA

[3]Pontificia Universidad Católica de Valparaíso, Facultad de Ciencias Económicas y Administrativas, Escuela de Comercio, Avenida Brasil 2830, 2340031 Valparaíso, Chile

[4]Faculty of Law, Transilvania University of Brasov, 500036 Brasov, Romania

Citation: Alexander Paz, Naveen Veeramisti, Romesh Khaddar, Hanns de la Fuente-Mella, and Luiza Modorcea, "Traffic and Driving Simulator Based on Architecture of Interactive Motion," The Scientific World Journal, vol. 2015, Article ID 340576.

in the driving simulator experiences a realistic journey and reveals a behavior that is not artificially affected by unrealistic modeling. This driver is termed in this study the virtual driver. In the experimental framework, a SimCraft motion-based driving simulator with 3 Degrees of Freedom (3DoFs) is used.

- A Pedestrian Simulator. This simulator comprises Microsoft Kinect to capture and display the movements of walking human.
- A Bicycle and Motorcycle Simulator. This is a motion-based simulator with capabilities to simulate a self-powered or fuel-powered bike. It consists of a computer CPU with a graphics card, a Head-Up-Display setup or LCD screen, a motion base, and a joystick.
- A Central Simulation Server. This server runs simultaneously on parallel CPUs the mesoscopic and microscopic simulations and provides the background traffic to the driving, pedestrian, and bike simulators. It also takes care of the communication and data transfer between the different simulators. The implementation involves a high end supercomputer running Microsoft Windows 7 64-bit edition and networking hardware including a 1000BaseT Gigabit Ethernet as well as the necessary routers and switches to complete the network.

The data flow diagram illustrated in Figure 2 includes a server module and client modules. There are various types of clients to represent different traffic entities such as cars, bikes, or pedestrians. Each client module in turn includes the following modules:

- Hybrid Simulation Module. This hybrid simulation module is required to provide realistic and consistent traffic around the vicinity of the virtual driver and to capture the consequences of the driver actions on the entire system. It combines a microscopic and a mesoscopic traffic flow simulators. In this module, the actions and location of the virtual driver are directly and continuously incorporated into the microscopic model. The microscopic simulator continuously receives traffic from and sends traffic to the mesoscopic simulator considering the boundary established by the location of the virtual driver.
- Virtual Reality (VR) Module. This module creates a simulated world around the vicinity of the virtual driver and provides the associated audio and 3D graphics. It receives information from

Chapter

5

Traffic and Driving Simulator Based on Architecture of Interactive Motion

Alexander Paz[1], Naveen Veeramisti[1], Romesh Khaddar[2], Hanns de la Fuente-Mella[3], and Luiza Modorcea[4]

[1]University of Nevada, Las Vegas, Civil and Environmental Engineering and Construction, Las Vegas, NV 89154, USA

[2]University of Nevada, Las Vegas, Electrical and Computer Engineering, Las Vegas, NV 89154, USA

[3]Pontificia Universidad Católica de Valparaíso, Facultad de Ciencias Económicas y Administrativas, Escuela de Comercio, Avenida Brasil 2830, 2340031 Valparaíso, Chile

[4]Faculty of Law, Transilvania University of Brasov, 500036 Brasov, Romania

Citation: Alexander Paz, Naveen Veeramisti, Romesh Khaddar, Hanns de la Fuente-Mella, and Luiza Modorcea, "Traffic and Driving Simulator Based on Architecture of Interactive Motion," The Scientific World Journal, vol. 2015, Article ID 340576.

ABSTRACT

This study proposes an architecture for an interactive motion-based traffic simulation environment. In order to enhance modeling realism involving actual human beings, the proposed architecture integrates multiple types of simulation, including: (i) motion-based driving simulation, (ii) pedestrian simulation, (iii) motorcycling and bicycling simulation, and (iv) traffic flow simulation. The architecture has been designed to enable the simulation of the entire network; as a result, the actual driver, pedestrian, and bike rider can navigate anywhere in the system. In addition, the background traffic interacts with the actual human beings. This is accomplished by using a hybrid mesomicroscopic traffic flow simulation modeling approach. The mesoscopic traffic flow simulation model loads the results of a user equilibrium traffic assignment solution and propagates the corresponding traffic through the entire system. The microscopic traffic flow simulation model provides background traffic around the vicinities where actual human beings are navigating the system. The two traffic flow simulation models interact continuously to update system conditions based on the interactions between actual humans and the fully simulated entities. Implementation efforts are currently in progress and some preliminary tests of individual components have been conducted. The implementation of the proposed architecture faces significant challenges ranging from multiplatform and multilanguage integration to multievent communication and coordination.

INTRODUCTION

A vast number of studies have illustrated the potential of driving simulators to analyze actual driver behavior for multiple purposes, such as traffic safety and information provision [1–5]. The history of driving simulators can be traced back to the 1920s, with research for various purposes [6]. In the 1980s, Daimler-Benz [7] developed a high-fidelity driving simulator, encouraging others to develop even better simulators. Several researchers and commercial companies have developed driving simulators ranging from fixed-based simulators to the most advanced motion-based simulators known today. Some of the newest driving simulators include the National Advanced Driving Simulator (NADS), funded by NHTSA and maintained by the University of Iowa [8]; the Driving Environment Simulator (DES), developed by the University of Minnesota [9] in collaboration with AutoSim and Realtime Technologies; the VTI Simulator IV by the Swedish National Road and Transport Research Institute [10]; the University of Leeds driving simulator [11]; DriveSafety driving simulator by the University of Michigan Transportation Research Institute (UMTRI) [12]; the STISIM Drive driving simulator by System Technology Inc.; [13] and the UC-win/Road driving simulator by FORUM8 [14].

The National Advanced Driving Simulator (NADS) Laboratory [8] at the University of Iowa has very advanced driving simulators including NADS-1, NADS-2, and the MiniSim simulator. NADS-1 is an advanced motion-based ground vehicle simulator. NADS-2 is similar to NADS-1 but fixed-based. The MiniSim is a PC-based, high-performance driving simulator that uses the same technology as NADS-1. However, MiniSim can be used at a lower cost than NADS-1 and NADS-2 because it is portable and easy to set up and operate.

The Human Factors Interdisciplinary Research in Simulation and Transportation Program (HumanFIRST) at the University of Minnesota has the Driving Environment Simulator (DES) [9]. DES is an immersive driving simulator that provides high fidelity simulation to generate a realistic presence within the simulated environment. DES measures psychophysiological responses, including brain activity—for example, Evoked Response Potential (ERP). DES also includes highly accurate eye-tracker software. HumanFIRST has a portable, low-cost driving simulator that uses the same technology as DES.

UC-win/Road [14] is a Virtual Reality (VR) environment where the driver can navigate in a three-dimensional (3D) space. The environment, including a traffic simulation and visualization tool, uses ground texture maps and can include 3D building images. The environment also includes traffic generation models to generate traffic on various lanes and roads.

This study proposes an architecture for an interactive motion-based traffic simulation environment. Although the existing driving simulation models provide tremendous capabilities to study driving behavior in a safe and controlled environment, there are multiple aspects of the real-world that can be addressed to significantly enhance modeling realism. The proposed architecture integrates multiple types of simulation, including (i) a motion-based driving simulation; (ii) a pedestrian simulation; (iii) a motorcycling and bicycling simulation; and (iv) a traffic flow simulation. This integration enables the simultaneous and interactive interaction between actual and simulated drivers, pedestrians, and bike riders. In addition, the architecture provides capabilities to simulate the entire network at a reasonable price; in this way, the drivers, pedestrians, and bike riders can navigate anywhere in the system. To increase modeling realism, the proposed architecture enables actual humans to experience background traffic and the background traffic to be affected by the decisions and behavior of the actual humans navigating the system. To achieve this interaction, the background traffic is modeled using a hybrid mesomicroscopic modeling approach for traffic flow simulation. The mesoscopic traffic flow simulation module of the hybrid model loads the results of a user equilibrium traffic assignment solution and propagates the corresponding traffic throughout the entire system. The microscopic traffic flow simulation model provides background traffic around the vicinities where actual human beings are navigating the system. The two traffic flow simulation models interact continuously to update system conditions, based on the interactions between actual humans and the fully simulated entities. The interaction between actual and background traffic has tremendous implications. For example, in the real-world, an accident, as consequence of a human error, can affect a large portion of the traffic system. These types of scenarios of significant interest for a number of applications cannot be modeled realistically without using the proposed architecture that integrates the driving simulator and the microscopic traffic flow simulator. Such scenario requires capabilities to propagate traffic and represent congestion related phenomena including queue formation and dissipation as well as spillback and spillover. Existing driving simulation models do not provide such capabilities because they do not model background traffic using realistic traffic flow models.

Depending upon the nature of the experiment, a scenario can be designed using a single simulator or any instances of simulators. Some examples for which the proposed system can be used include the following:

- The evaluation of driver and pedestrian behavior for traffic safety projects including distracted driving and/or walking and driving and/or walking under the influence of alcohol or drugs [1–5].
- The evaluation of multiple mechanisms or technologies designed to assist the driving task and to improve traffic safety. Some of these mechanisms and technologies include crosswalks, flashing lights, infrared sensors to detect pedestrians, distance warning systems, dynamic cruise control, automatic braking systems, and dynamic navigation.
- The simultaneous study of the interactions among drivers, pedestrians, and bikers as well as the interactions of them with the infrastructure and the control and information mechanisms

and the different technologies used influencing behavior and/ or assisting the navigation tasks. The existing literature [15–17] relies on models that do not use actual humans during the experimental part of the analysis.

- The training of first responders and emergency personnel. Multiple potential emergency scenarios can be designed and used to provide adequate training in safe and controlled environment. Burke et al. [18] documents the importance of training such personnel. Accidents involving emergency vehicles were analyzed using several sources of information including video data as well as interviews. The results highlighted that drivers' errors were responsible for most of the accidents.

In this study, implementation efforts are currently in progress, and some preliminary tests of individual components have been conducted. The implementation of the proposed architecture faces significant challenges, ranging from multiplatform and multilanguage integration to multievent communication and coordination. To address some of those challenges and achieve the greatest benefits at the lowest cost, state-of-the-art technologies currently are being used to implement the proposed architecture. Some of these technologies include (i) Open Street Maps (OSM) [19]; (ii) Blender [20]; (iii) DynusT© [21]; CORBA; and free SDKs, such as MS Kinect [22] and Ardunio [23]. The proposed architecture is called Networked Motion-Based Interactive PEdestrian and Driving Simulator (n-MIPEDS). Although particular suggestions to implement the proposed architecture are provided in this paper, the conceptual architecture is general and can be implemented using multiple technologies. Appropriate modules can be developed depending on available hardware. In particular, this study uses a SimCraft three-axis motion-based driving simulator.

MATERIALS AND METHODS

The proposed architecture uses a multiplayer framework where each player is connected to the traffic system through a communication network (LAN or internet). The corresponding system architecture diagram and data flow diagram are shown in Figures 1 and 2, respectively. Figure 1 illustrates the following:

- A Car Simulator. This simulator generates motion and the corresponding forces based on the roadway conditions and the driver's behavior and actions. Hence, the human being driving in the driving simulator experiences a realistic journey and reveals a behavior that is not artificially affected by unrealistic modeling. This driver is termed in this study the virtual driver. In the experimental framework, a SimCraft motion-based driving simulator with 3 Degrees of Freedom (3DoFs) is used.

- A Pedestrian Simulator. This simulator comprises Microsoft Kinect to capture and display the movements of walking human.
- A Bicycle and Motorcycle Simulator. This is a motion-based simulator with capabilities to simulate a self-powered or fuel-powered bike. It consists of a computer CPU with a graphics card, a Head-Up-Display setup or LCD screen, a motion base, and a joystick.
- A Central Simulation Server. This server runs simultaneously on parallel CPUs the mesoscopic and microscopic simulations and provides the background traffic to the driving, pedestrian, and bike simulators. It also takes care of the communication and data transfer between the different simulators. The implementation involves a high end supercomputer running Microsoft Windows 7 64-bit edition and networking hardware including a 1000BaseT Gigabit Ethernet as well as the necessary routers and switches to complete the network.

The data flow diagram illustrated in Figure 2 includes a server module and client modules. There are various types of clients to represent different traffic entities such as cars, bikes, or pedestrians. Each client module in turn includes the following modules:

- Hybrid Simulation Module. This hybrid simulation module is required to provide realistic and consistent traffic around the vicinity of the virtual driver and to capture the consequences of the driver actions on the entire system. It combines a microscopic and a mesoscopic traffic flow simulators. In this module, the actions and location of the virtual driver are directly and continuously incorporated into the microscopic model. The microscopic simulator continuously receives traffic from and sends traffic to the mesoscopic simulator considering the boundary established by the location of the virtual driver.
- Virtual Reality (VR) Module. This module creates a simulated world around the vicinity of the virtual driver and provides the associated audio and 3D graphics. It receives information from

the hybrid simulation module and provides information to the virtual driver.

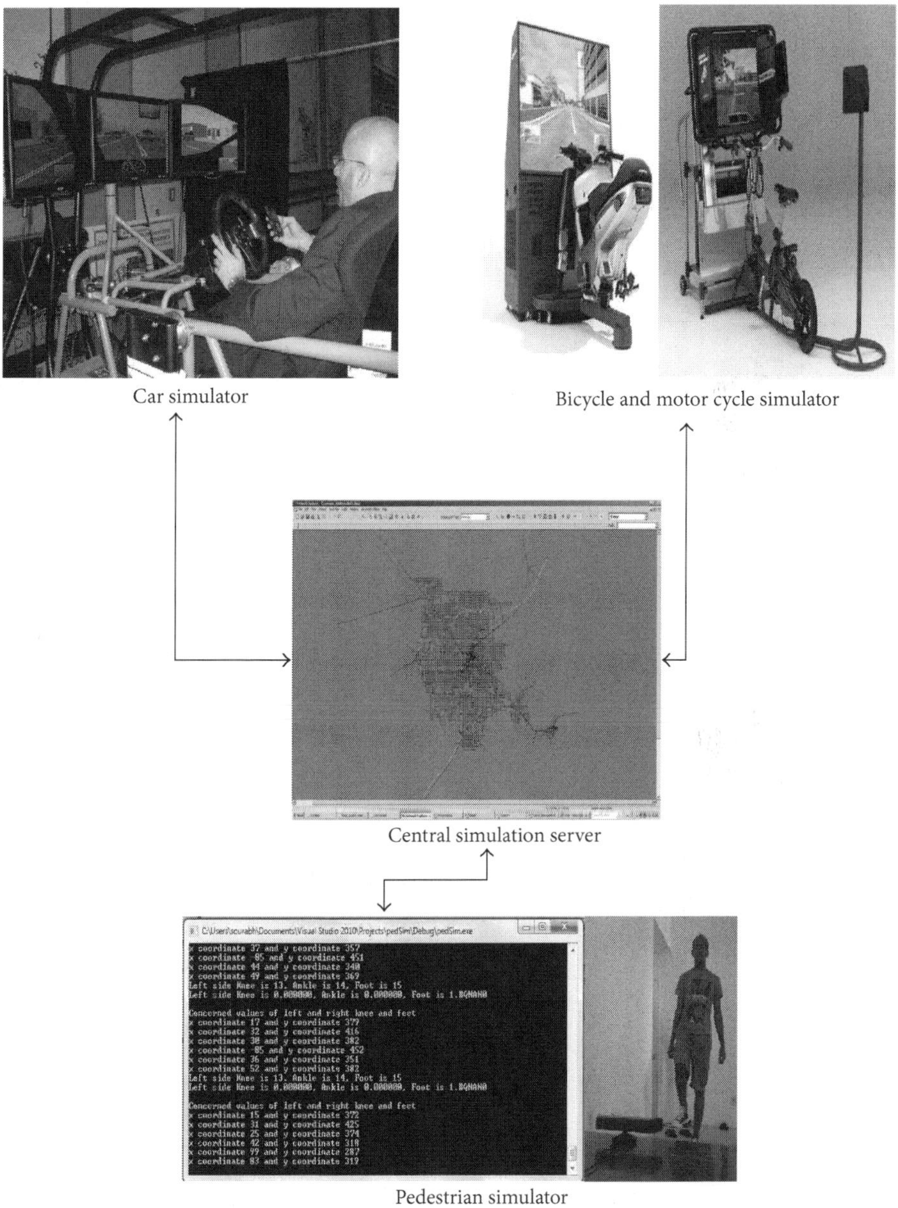

Figure 1: System architecture of n-MIPEDS. (The images for the bicycle and motorcycle simulators are used here for illustrative purposes only. Copyright: Honda.).

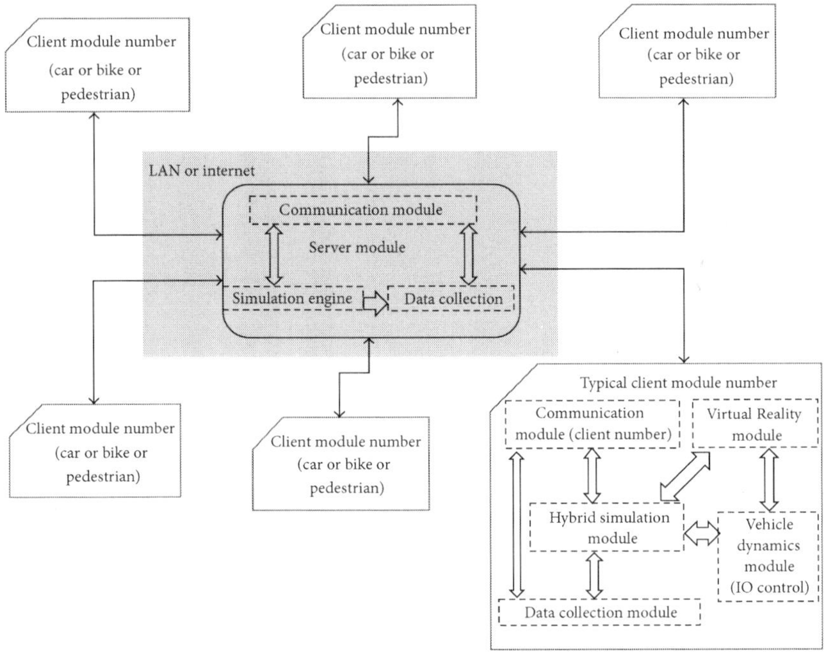

Figure 2: Data flow diagram.

- Vehicle Dynamics Module. This module generates the motion related information for each of the simulators based on the traffic conditions and the users' actions.
- Communication Module. This module enables communication between the server and the client module. It is responsible for synchronizing the transfer of information between the client and the server. For various reasons, the modules proposed in this architecture are being developed using different environments. Hence, the Common Object Request Broker Architecture (CORBA) is to enable interoperability across different language and platforms [24].
- Data Collection Module. This module collects a vast array of data including drivers' and pedestrians' behavior as well as the associated traffic characteristics.

The server module integrates all the information and it is responsible for tracking the entire system performance using a communication and data collection module and a simulation engine. The simulation engine receives information from all the clients via the communication. That information is stored via the data collection module. Information about system states is also sent to each of the clients using the communication module.

Roadway Network Geometry

Some simulators such as STISIM Drive [13] only support modeling of corridors without enabling network-level representation. The proposed architecture enables the modeling of generalized networks. Geometric and control characteristics are particularly important for microscopic traffic flow simulation. Data about actual road network geometry for a given city can be obtained from Open Street Maps (OSM) [19] in .xml format. This type of data includes latitude, longitude, street names, intersection details, and horizontal curve information. The OSM data is an open source of world maps maintained by users across the globe. It includes all the freeways, major roads, and many minor streets of every major city. The OSM data can be used to generate the network of roads for the Virtual Reality module in Figure 2. Missing data, such as lane information, traffic control, and signal timings, needs to be obtained from local or state agencies or any existing model.

The proposed architecture can be used for any network with the required information. In this study and for demonstration purposes, the Las Vegas road network was created using OSM data. Lane data, traffic control, and signal settings were obtained from an existing traffic simulation model. To obtain the correct mapping, the coordinates from OSM were matched with those in the existing model. A portion of the roadway network created using this approach is shown in Figure 3. This approach reduces the time required to generate a roadway network for the proposed architecture. Details about this approach are discussed below in Section 2.2.

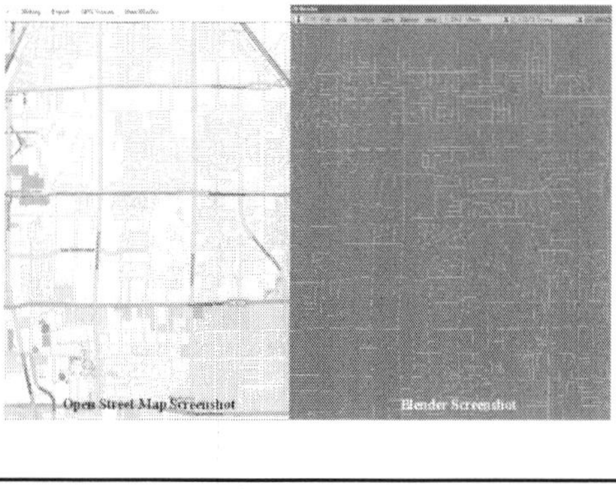

Figure 3: Generated network on Blender using Open Street Map.

Hybrid Simulation Model

Most driving simulators provide background traffic around the virtual driver using survey data and hourly volumes/distributions [13] or the desired traffic density [25, 26]. This approach has limitations to capture congestion related phenomena such as spillback and spillover. Microscopic simulation can be used to capture congestion related phenomena. However, the computational burden and the simulation time can increase significantly with network size. In addition, data needs and modeling time are prohibitively expensive for large-scale micro simulation models.

In order to adequately represent both the microlevel vehicle dynamics around the virtual driver and the traffic dynamics in the rest of the network, a hybrid simulation model that integrates a microscopic and a mesoscopic traffic flow simulation model is proposed. Félez et al. [27] have envisaged the required environment by integrating a driving simulation engine, SCANeR II, and a microscopic traffic-flow simulation model, AIMSUN. The authors have discussed and proposed solutions for various integration issues such as the matching of roadway geometry, computing speed for data exchange, simulation step size, and autonomous vehicle visualization. The paper also discusses some limitations of the integration including issues with control of the autonomous vehicles, vehicle kinematics in curve sections, and lane changing behavior. The proposed architecture in this study envisions higher consistency at a lower computation cost by integrating various simulators as interdependent components in a single framework. To the best of our knowledge, only Olstam et al. [28] have used a hybrid simulation model to provide background traffic to a driving simulator. The area surrounding the virtual driver was divided into one inner region and two outer regions. Vehicles in the inner region were simulated according to a microscopic model, while vehicles in the outer regions were updated according to a mesoscopic model. The authors mentioned that further research is required to address the following issues: (i) arterials and freeways with three or more lanes; (ii) ramps on freeways and intersections on rural roads; (iii) simulation of urban traffic conditions; and (iv) simulation on roadway networks.

Critical aspects in the development of hybrid simulation models are the compatibility of two different traffic flow streams and the propagation of traffic conditions at the interfaces [29]. Traffic propagation at interfaces should be analyzed both at free-flow conditions and at congested conditions. In mesoscopic models, vehicles move in an aggregate fashion while, in microscopic models, vehicles move according to individual vehicle dynamics. Hence, at the interfaces of meso to micro and micro to meso, traffic propagation both upstream and downstream has to be considered. It is necessary to define the time when both the models will transfer data based on the updating time intervals for the two models [30].

The proposed hybrid simulation model integrates the DynusT© [21], a mesoscopic simulation-based dynamic traffic assignment model, with a microscopic simulation model. The microscopic model includes a car-following model, a lane changing model, and a gap-acceptance model. Background traffic around the virtual driver is provided by the micro simulation model. Hence, the region covered by the micro simulation, called the μSim zone, is defined by the position of the virtual driver. The following methods can be used to define this region:

- Method 1 (Moving μSimlink). Use the microscopic simulation model only on the roadway link where the virtual driver is present. Show the Virtual Reality Environment to the extent of the driver's visibility limit. Use mesoscopic simulation on all the other links. Thus, the μSim zone is the link where the virtual driver is located and it changes according to the position of the virtual driver.
- Method 2 (Moving μSimzone). Use the microscopic simulation model in a zone around the position of the virtual driver. Show the Virtual Reality Environment to the extent of the driver's visibility limit. Use mesoscopic simulation on links other than those modeled using micro simulation. Thus, the μSim zone is the fixed zone with respect to position of the virtual driver.

In both methods, the problem of conserving vehicles should be solved at the boundary of mesoscopic and microscopic integration. In each simulation interval of the mesoscopic model, the entire network is updated based on the mesoscopic logic and the states at the boundary between the meso and micro models. However, the network states covered by the micro simulation model govern that zone.

User-Driven Vehicle Dynamics Model

The objective here is to generate actual vehicle motion dynamics so as to enhance modeling realism. This motion produces physiological and psychological reactions similar to those present in a real-world driving experience. Motion-axis simulators can be used to generate vehicular motion dynamics using DOFs ranging from two to fourteen [8–14, 25]. Implementation should be based on the required aspects for the particular problem context in order to avoid unnecessary computations. Vehicle motion dynamics are generated using SimCraft 3DOFs motion-based simulator. Although 6DOFs are desired to reproduce most vehicle dynamics, the 3DOFs can realistically reproduce the most important motions such as the effects of acceleration/deceleration as well as changes on roadway geometry. The motion dynamics are generated based on the actions of the virtual driver, the geometric characteristics of the roadway, and the interactions with other vehicles. Hence, motion dynamics must be seamlessly synchronized with the Virtual Reality module.

Pedestrian, Bicycle, and Motorcycle Simulator

Existing pedestrian models [31, 32] require detailed data to capture the interactions between pedestrians and vehicles. Some studies [33] have focused on the study of pedestrian and driver behavior at crosswalk locations, where pedestrians and vehicles often interact. Numerous data has been collected about both pedestrians and drivers. However, the data collection process can be expensive and limited by the physical and operational characteristics of the location where the data is being collected. Hence, it is difficult to analyze multiple alternatives and the effects of critical factors. Pedestrian simulators enable circumventing some of these issues. The University College London has a Pedestrian Accessibility and Movement Environment Laboratory (PAMELA) [34] to study pedestrian movements under various environmental conditions. PAMELA has been used to better understand roadway aspects that affect pedestrian's ability to navigate the traffic system. The proposed pedestrian, bicycle, and motorcycle simulators have the unique capability of interacting together with a car or driving simulator. This capability enables studying a broad range of transportation phenomena using actual human beings in a safe and controlled environment.

Sensors can be used to capture the movements of various entities as well as human behavior including, for example, a pedestrian observing traffic while crossing a street and the walking speed relative to the traffic conditions. Traffic safety is highly influenced by users' behavior and their interactions. According to a report by the National Highway Traffic Safety Administration (NHTSA) [35], every year at least 50% of the motorcycle fatal crashes involve multiple vehicles; of that percentage, 41% had a blood alcohol concentration of 0.08 g/dL or higher. Safety is a primary concern not only for cars, but also for motorcycles and pedestrians. The proposed simulation framework enables the study of traffic safety for all these users.

The pedestrian simulator consists of a state-of-the-art Natural Interaction Sensor (Microsoft Kinect) and a head-mounted display. The movements of human walking are captured using the Microsoft Kinect. The Kinect consists of sensors that identify joints, body structure, facial features, and voice. The head-mounted display is to project the traffic conditions for the pedestrian. These traffic conditions are obtained using the communication module in the pedestrian simulation client.

Virtual Reality Environment

The Virtual Reality Environment is used to provide all the background as well as the traffic conditions representing the real-world to the various human beings navigating the system using the proposed simulators. The Virtual Reality Environment includes seven different components: simulation, interaction, artificiality, immersion, telepresence, full-body immersion, and network communication [36]. These components are used to provide an immersive traffic experience subject to hardware and software limitations.

In this study, the Virtual Reality Environment is created using 3D models [14]. To accelerate the modeling process and to achieve cost-effective development, an automated modeling process is required. A challenging problem for automation is creating and deploying 3D models at the required exact locations without deforming their sizes and shapes. Here, a hierarchical multilayer and data-driven approach is proposed. Each layer includes different types of objects which are recreated using data obtained from various sources.

Figure 4 illustrates the proposed multilayer approach for the generation of the Virtual Reality Environment. A list of landmarks is created and imported from Google Earth. Similarly, 3D images for the imported list are obtained from Google SketchUp [37] or created in Blender [20]. Landmarks are used to provide a perception of familiarity in the Virtual Reality Environment. The location of these models is automated using their latitudes and longitudes. The locations of other objects including trees and buildings and such roadside components as mailboxes, water pumps, fire hydrants, bus stop shelters, and street lights are defined as realistic as possible.

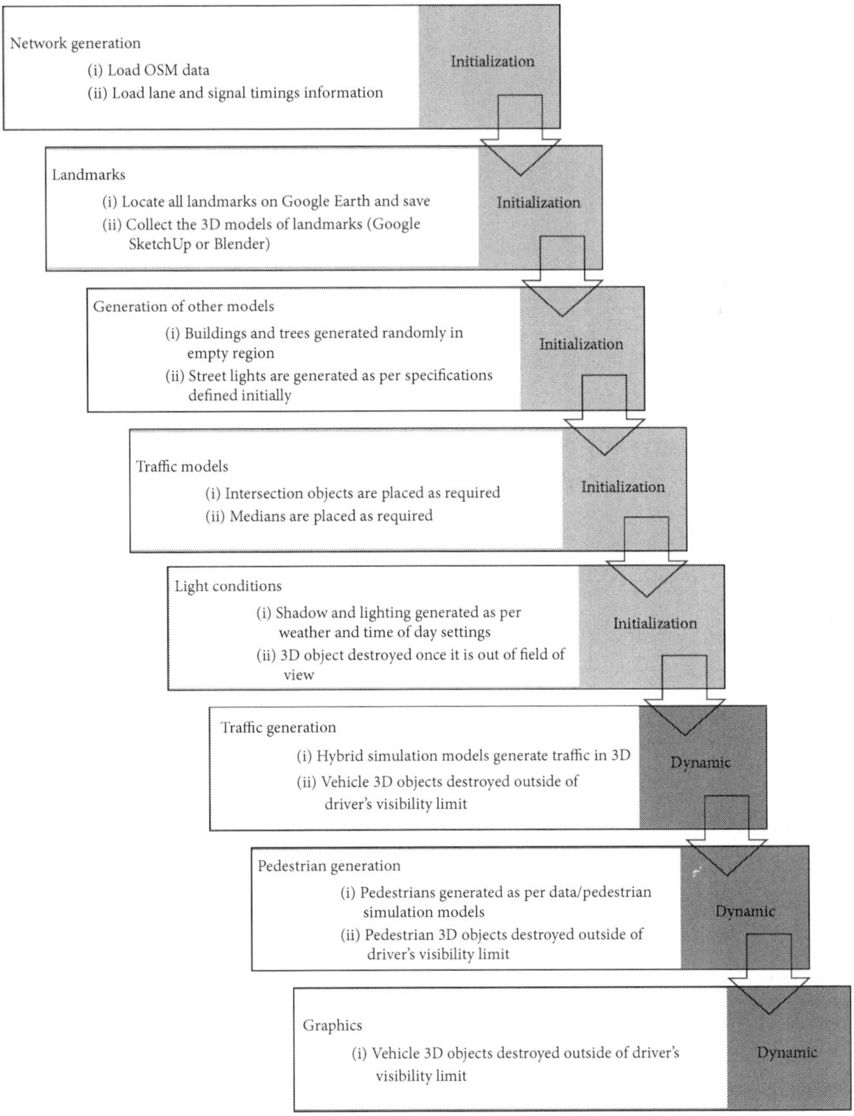

Figure 4: Layer-architecture for Virtual Reality generation.

The Virtual Reality Environment is generated only to include the visibility limits for the virtual driver(s) and virtual pedestrian(s). The generated Virtual Reality Environment includes pedestrians as well as different classes of vehicles, such as cars and trucks. Different levels of visibility are available according to weather and time of day conditions. These conditions are recreated using various rendering techniques such as shading and reflecting.

RESULTS AND DISCUSSION

One of the primary objectives of the proposed architecture is the collection of data about the vehicles, the users, and the system performance. Vehicle data includes variables such as lateral position, vehicle trajectories, vehicle heading angle, acceleration/deceleration, and braking times. Users' data includes variables such as perception-reaction times, physiological data obtained from electrocardiograms, galvanic skin response, and body temperature. The hybrid simulation model will collect system performance data. The data collection module is included in every single client so as to collect the corresponding information.

The initial implementation of the proposed architecture began with control of the driving simulator using the Software Development Kit (SDK) provided by the manufacturer, SimCraft. A control module was created using a Dynamic Link Library (.dll) file provided in SDK. Blender [20] was chosen for the development of graphics because it provides the required minimum capabilities. Blender is open source and has a big user base and a support community. In addition, Blender [20] is supported in both Linux and Windows. Once the graphics of roadway network were developed, a vehicle model was created to drive in the network. The scripts developed in this study can be used to generate models of the transportation network of any city. This requires using Open Street Maps.

Microsoft Kinect is currently being used for the development of the pedestrian simulator. A walk identification module has been created with a text output. This will later be developed and integrated into the pedestrian simulator. Blender [20] is used for creating 3D models for various transportation components, such as different roadways, traffic signal displays, buildings, and trees. The proposed architecture requires views inside the Virtual Reality Environment for cars, motorcycles, bicycles, and pedestrians. Multiple CPUs are used to generate these views. A networking module was developed to enable data transfer across the multiple CPUs. CORBA is used for this purpose along with omniORB C++ and Python.

Future work includes (i) the implementation of hybrid simulation model for the driving and pedestrian simulators; (ii) the graphics module for Virtual Reality Environment; (iii) the development of hardware for bicycle and motorcycle simulator; and (iv) the integration, coordination, and synchronization of all the components of the proposed architecture.

CONCLUSIONS

This study has proposed an architecture for an interactive and motion-based simulation of a vehicular and pedestrian traffic system. The proposed architecture increases the realism of existing alternative modeling approaches by explicitly and simultaneously including actual drivers, pedestrians, and bikers. In addition, the architecture enables the modeling of the entire network with reasonable investment of resources. To the best of our knowledge, there is no alternative architecture that simultaneously considers all the elements of reality considered here. Existing modeling frameworks focus on a particular component of the real-world system; the reaming components are ignored or modeled using artificial entities. State-of-the-art modeling and analysis tools such as simulation-based Dynamic Traffic Assignment, CORBA, and Open Street Maps enable the implementation of the proposed architecture. Implementation of the architecture will provide the unique capability to study countless traffic problems using actual human beings.

ACKNOWLEDGMENTS

The authors would like to thank the Nevada Department of Transportation, the Research and Innovative Technology Administration of the US Department of Transportation, University Transportation Center, UNLV, and the Transportation Research Center at UNLV for their support.

REFERENCES

1. F. Yang, K. Zhang, and X. Sun, "Behavior analysis of traffic accidents with high fidelity driving simulator," in Proceedings of the 2nd International Conference on Transportation Engineering, vol. 345, pp. 3231–3235, Chengdu, China, July 2009.
2. F. Bella and G. D'Agostini, "Combined effect of traffic and geometrics on rear-end collision risk: driving simulator study," Transportation Research Record, vol. 2165, pp. 96–103, 2010.
3. E. Blana, "Driving simulators as research and training tools for improving road safety," in Progress in System and Robot Analysis and Control Design, vol. 243 of Lecture Notes in Control and Information Sciences, pp. 289–300, Springer, 1999.
4. D. Liao, "A high-fidelity immersive cluster-based driving simulator for transportation safety research," in Proceedings of the ACM International Conference on Virtual Reality Continuum and Its Applications (VRCIA '06), pp. 361–364, ACM, Hong Kong, 2006.
5. S. Daniels, J. Vanrie, A. Dreesen, and T. Brijs, "Additional road markings as an indication of speed limits: results of a field experiment and a driving simulator study," Accident Analysis and Prevention, vol. 42, no. 3, pp. 953–960, 2010.
6. J. Watchel, "Brief history of driving simulators," TR News, no. 179, pp. 26–45, 1995.
7. J. Drosdol and F. Panik, "The daimler-benz driving simulator," SAE Papcr 85-0334, SAE International, 1985.
8. The National Advanced Driving Simulator, University of Iowa, Iowa City, Iowa, USA, 2010, http://www.nads-sc.uiowa.edu.
9. Human Factors Interdisciplinary Research in Simulation and Transportation, University of Minnesota, Minneapolis, Minn, USA, 2010, http://www.humanfirst.umn.edu/capabilities/simulation/.
10. VTI, Swedish National Road and Transport Research Institute, Linköping, Sweden, 2010, http://www.vti.se/templates/Page____11862.aspx.
11. University of Leeds Driving Simulator (UoLDS), October 2011, http://www.its.leeds.ac.uk/itsresearch/facilities/uolds/.
12. University of Michigan Transportation Research Institute, University of Michigan, Ann Arbor, Mich, USA, 2006, http://umich.edu/~driving/.

13. T. J. Rosenthal, STISIM Drive User's Manual, Systems Technology Inc, Hawthorne, Calif, USA, 2011.
14. FORUM8, UC-Win/Road Ver.4 Operation Guidance Manual, FORUM8, 2010.
15. W. W. Hunter, J. C. Stutts, W. E. Pein, and C. L. Cox, "Pedestrian and bicycle crash types of the early 1990's," Publication No FHWA-RD-95-163, Federal Highway Administration, McLean, Va, USA, 1996.
16. W. W. Hunter, An Evaluation of Red Shoulders as a Bicycle and Pedestrian Facility, Florida Department of Transportation, Bicycle/Pedestrian Safety, Tallahassee, Fla, USA, 1999.
17. A. Flannery, L. L. Ledbetter, L. Arnold, and M. Jones, "Analysis of bicycle, pedestrian, and auto interaction at multilane roundabouts in the US," in Proceedings of the 4th International Symposium on Highway Geometric Design, Valencia, Spain, June 2010.
18. C. S. Burke, E. Salas, and J. P. Kincaid, "Emergency vehicles that become accident statistics: understanding and limiting accidents involving emergency vehicles," in Proceedings of the Human Factors and Erogonomics Society 45th Annual Meeting, pp. 508–512, Minneapolis, Minn, USA, October 2001.
19. OpenStreetMap: The Free Wiki World Map, 2011, http://www.openstreetmap.org/.
20. Blender v2.49a, 2011, http://www.blender.org/.
21. Y.-C. Chiu and T. Dynus, "Simulation-based Dynamic Traffic Assignment Mesoscopic Model Software," 2011, http://dynust.net/.
22. Microsoft Kinect, 2011, http://www.xbox.com/en-US/xbox-one/consoles/xbox-one-plus-kinect.
23. Arduino, April 2011, http://www.arduino.cc/.
24. Common Object Request Broker Architecture, 2011, http://en.wikipedia.org/wiki/Common_Object_Request_Broker_Architecture.
25. V. Punzo and B. Ciuffo, "Integration of driving and traffic simulation: issues and first solutions," Journal of IEEE Transactions on Intelligent Transportation Systems, vol. 12, no. 2, pp. 354–363, 2011.
26. Q. Yang and H. N. Koutsopoulos, "A microscopic traffic simulator for evaluation of dynamic traffic management systems," Transportation Research Part C: Emerging Technologies, vol. 4, no. 3, pp. 113–129, 1996.

27. J. Félez, J. Maroto, G. Romero, and M. J. Cabanellas, "A full driving simulator of urban traffic including traffic accidents," Simulation, vol. 83, no. 5, pp. 415–431, 2007.
28. J. Olstam, J. Lundgren, M. Adlers, and P. Matstoms, "A framework for simulation of surrounding vehicles in driving simulators," ACM Transactions on Modeling and Computer Simulation, vol. 18, no. 3, article 9, 2008.
29. H. Shi, A. K. Ziliaskopoulos, and J. Zhang, "A hybrid mesoscopic-microscopic traffic simulation model: design, implementation and computational analysis," in Proceedings of the 85th Annual Meeting Transportation Research Board, CD-ROM Transportation Research Board of the National Academies, Washington, DC, USA, January 2006.
30. S. Espie, D. Gattuso, and F. Galante, "A hybrid traffic model coupling macro and behavioural micro simulation," in Proceedings of the 85th Annual Meeting Transportation Research Board, CD-ROM Transportation Research Board of the National Academies, Washington, DC, USA, January 2006.
31. E. Papadimitriou, G. Yannis, and J. Golias, "A critical assessment of pedestrian behaviour models," Transportation Research Part F: Traffic Psychology and Behaviour, vol. 12, no. 3, pp. 242–255, 2009.
32. W. Daamen and S. P. Hoogendoorn, "Experimental research of pedestrian walking behavior," Transportation Research Record, vol. 1828, pp. 20–30, 2003.
33. R. L. Knoblauch, B. H. Tustin, S. A. Smith, and M. T. Pietrucha, "Investigation of exposure based pedestrian accident areas: crosswalks, sidewalks, local streets and major arterials," Tech. Rep. FHWA/RD-88/038, Federal Highway Administration, Washington, DC, USA, 1988.
34. Pedestrian Accessibility and Movement Environment Laboratory (PAMELA), University College London, October 2011, http://www.cege.ucl.ac.uk/arg/pamela/Pages/PAMELA-home.aspx.
35. National Highway Traffic Safety Administration, "Fatally injured motorcycle operators by license status," NHTSA Report, National Highway Traffic Safety Administration, Washington, DC, USA, 2008, http://www-nrd.nhtsa.dot.gov/Pubs/810892.PDF.

36. M. R. Heim, The Metaphysics of Virtual Reality, Oxford University Press, Oxford, UK, 1993.
37. Google SketchUp, 2010, http://sketchup.google.com.

SECTION II - ROBOTICS AND VIRTUAL ENVIRONMENTS

Chapter 6 Towards a Model of User Experience in Immersive Virtual Environments

Katy Tcha-Tokey[1], Olivier Christmann[1], Emilie Loup-Escande[2], GuillaumeLoup[3], and Simon Richir[1]

[1]Arts et Métiers ParisTech, LAMPA EA 1427, 2 bd du Ronceray, 49000 Angers, France

[2]Université de Picardie Jules Verne, CRP-CPO EA 7273, chemin du Thil, 80025 Amiens, France

[3]Université Bretagne Loire, LIUM EA 4023, avenue Olivier Messiaen, 72085 Le Mans, France

Citation: Katy Tcha-Tokey, Olivier Christmann, Emilie Loup-Escande, Guillaume Loup, and Simon Richir, "Towards a Model of User Experience in Immersive Virtual Environments," Advances in Human-Computer Interaction, vol. 2018, Article ID 7827286.

ABSTRACT

There are increasing new advances in virtual reality technologies as well as a rise in learning virtual environments for which several studies highlighted the pedagogical value, knowledge transfer, and learners' engaged-behaviors. Moreover, the notion of user experience is now abundant in the scientific literature without the fact that there are specific models for immersive environments. This paper aims at proposing and validating a model of User eXperience in Immersive Virtual Environment, including virtual learning environments. The model is composed of 10 components extracted from existing models (i.e., presence, engagement, immersion, flow, usability, skill, emotion, experience consequence, judgement, and technology adoption). It was validated in a user study involving 152 participants who were asked to use the edutainment application Think and Shootand to complete an immersive virtual environment questionnaire. The findings lead us to a modified user experience model questioning new paths between user experience components (e.g., the influence of experience consequence on flow).

INTRODUCTION

The digital age has led to the emergence of digital games for learning [1]. These games are now too limited to conventional techniques such as Web, e-mail, or video conferencing [2]. So, new types of games known as "virtual learning environments" have succeeded in fully exploiting advanced technologies such as virtual reality. These virtual environments have opened up new perspectives in the field of education, increasing the number of stimuli by an immersive experience and then improving motivation [3].

Immersion should increase the motivation of users, and immersive virtual environments should provide a good User eXperience (UX) [4]. UX has been defined as "the user's perceptions and responses resulting from the use of a system or a service [...]" by the ISO 9241-210 (2009) norm. However, only few UX models are identified for immersive virtual environments (IVE) in the scientific literature. The UX approaches for virtual environments discussed in literature focus on a single or a couple of components, particularly presence and immersion (i.e., [5–8]). Indeed, all of the UX components in IVE are not dealt with in the literature. The IVE should be useful, usable, and acceptable, provide a high level of presence, immersion, and flow, and cause little cybersickness. This led us to propose holistic model of the UX in IVE that considers the multiple components of the UX. The aim of the present study is to propose and validate a conceptual model of the UX in IVE named User eXperience in Immersive Virtual Environment Model (UXIVE Model) in the field of edutainment. In Section 2, the UXIVE conceptual model is described in relation to UX models referenced in literature. An empirical study aiming at validating the UXIVE Model is detailed in Section 3. In Section 4, the validity of our model and component relationships with regard to the literature are discussed. In conclusion, suggestions on how to use our model to improve the UX in IVE, particularly in the field of edutainment, are evoked.

PROPOSITION OF A MODEL MEASURING THE UX IN IVE

The UXIVE Model is based on four UX models [9–12]. These models are reviewed in Section 2.1. The hypothesized model was designed based on these four models and presented in Section 2.2. We chose these four precursor models for two reasons: they are—to our knowledge—the only ones to precisely identify and describe the relationships between components of the UX; they are suitable or adaptable immersive virtual environments in the field of edutainment. These models are complementary to more recent works but not specific to virtual environments as, for example, [13, 14].

User Experience Models Review

User Experience Based on Flow

The flow is defined as "holistic sensation that people feel when they act with total involvement" ([15], p. 36) as "an enjoyable experience in which a participant feels an important level of behavioral control, happiness and enjoyment" ([9], p. 174) when interacting within the virtual environment. These authors propose a model designed in a context of a virtual entertainment environment and its components are structured around the concept of flow in a virtual environment. Their model comprises 10 components identified as interactivity, involvement, vividness, skill, challenge, focused attention, flow, telepresence, positive effect, and loyalty. They consider that the user enters in a flow state when he interacts and perceives that the whole virtual environment is in his grip, when there is a balance between his skills and the challenge given, when he focuses on the current activity, and when he feels "telepresent". Moreover, this model suggests that vividness stimulates the sensory perceptions of the user improving his interactivity and enhancing the sense of telepresence. The model also reveals that higher level of involvement (expert/novice distinction, importance) increases the likelihood of forming positive telepresence, creates greater user challenge, and yields the user to develop stronger skills. The authors also found that mediated environment with higher interaction increases user attention (i.e., concentration) on the current activity, increases the perceived challenge for even the most experienced, and improves user perceptions of control skills. They observed that the user who focuses on stimuli in the virtual environment perceives a higher level of telepresence and that strong flow creates an emotional state in users and positively affects users' attitude and future usage desirability, thus, loyalty.

User Experience Based on Acceptance and Continuance

The technology acceptance is defined as the actions and decisions taken by the user for a future use of the virtual environment. The continuance intention is the intention of the user to continue using such system. A second model created in the virtual learning environment context is built on acceptance and continuance theories [10]. This model includes 9 components known as immersion, presence, flow, confirmation, satisfaction, perceived usefulness, perceived ease of use, previous experience, and intention. The authors stated that the three constructs of flow, presence, and immersion coinfluence each other. They also revealed that users perceived immersion, flow, and presence as having impact on confirmation of what they expected regarding the technology. They observed that satisfaction, perceived usefulness, and perceived ease of use are influenced by the users' confirmation of the level of technology services and that user satisfaction is impacted by perceived usefulness, perceived ease of use, and confirmation. The author found that users' continuance intention is primarily determined by their satisfaction with prior technology use and that previous learning experience with technologies is a factor influencing intention directly.

User Experience Influenced by Virtual Environment Features

Lin and Parker [12] proposed a model designed in a context of virtual environment for entertainment which aims at identifying the virtual environment features (i.e., field-of-view, stereopsis, visual motion frequency, level of interactivity, and visual interventions predictability to visual motion) leading to an optimal UX. The authors define the UX through three components: presence, enjoyment, and simulator sickness. According to their model, there is a positive correlation between presence and enjoyment, a negative correlation between enjoyment and simulator sickness, no specific correlation between presence and simulator sickness, and a decline in presence or a growth in simulator sickness results from a decrease in enjoyment.

User Experience and Interaction

Mahlke [11] proposed a model which introduces the UX resulting from the interaction with a technical system. This model comprises 8 components defined as system properties, user characteristics, context parameters, human-technology interaction, perceptions of instrumental qualities, perception of noninstrumental qualities, emotional user reaction, and consequences of the UX. System properties, user characteristics, and context parameters are defined as categories of factors that determine the UX. The author observed that system properties lead to differences in objective measures of the interaction (e.g., number of accomplished tasks and time on task) as well as differences in UX (i.e., instrumental and noninstrumental quality perceptions as well as emotional user reactions) and in consequences of the experience (i.e., overall judgements and alternative choices). Their model suggests that user characteristics influence subjective feelings and context parameters influence overall judgement. The model also shows that emotional user reactions are assumed to be influenced by instrumental and noninstrumental quality perceptions. This suggests that consequences of UX are based on instrumental and noninstrumental quality perceptions as well as emotional user reactions.

Towards the UXIVE Model

Presence, Flow, and Experience Consequence

Presence is a component defined as the user's "sense of being there" in the virtual environment. Presence is achieved as soon as another reality is evoked, e.g., reading a book, watching TV, and experiencing virtual reality [16]. The concept of presence can be divided into three categories: presence or telepresence, copresence, and social presence in a collective or collaborative virtual environment [9, 17, 18]. Experience consequence is a component we defined as the symptoms (e.g., the "simulator sickness", stress, dizziness, and headache) the user can experience in the virtual environment. As we saw previously in the user experience models review, for [9], the user enters in a flow state when he feels "telepresent". Shin, Biocca, and Choo [10] have investigated the role of flow and presence and found that all two coinfluence each other; it can be said that they play enhancing roles for each other. As for [12], they investigated the degree of presence, enjoyment, and simulator sickness users experience in a virtual environment; they found that there is a positive correlation between presence and enjoyment, a negative correlation between enjoyment, and simulator sickness. Zhou and Lu [19] noted that flow experience includes perceived enjoyment and attention focus. Consequently, we may hypothesize that a low experience consequence and a high sense of presence greatly enhance the state of flow which influences back the two components (Hypothesis 1).

Presence, Immersion, and Engagement

Immersion is a component defined as the "objective level of sensory fidelity a virtual reality system provides"([20], p. 38). The immersive dimension in a virtual environment is created by "complex technologies that replace real-world sensory information with synthetic stimuli" ([20], p. 36). Engagement is a component defined as "a psychological state experienced because of focusing one's energy and attention on a coherent set of stimuli or meaningfully related activities and events" ([21], p. 227). Following the Witmer and Singer's approach, immersion and engagement are two elements that contribute to the idea of presence [21]. Shin et al. [10] consider immersion as clearly related to the widely research concept of presence. Hence, we may hypothesize that the sense of presence enhances the degree of engagement and the feeling of immersion; the same way the two components enhance presence (Hypothesis 2).

Flow, Usability, Skill, and Emotion

Usability is a component defined as the ease of using (i.e., efficiency, effectiveness, and satisfaction) the virtual environment. Skill is a component defined as the knowledge the user gain in mastering his activity in the virtual environment. Emotion is a component defined as the subjective feelings (i.e., joy, pleasure, satisfaction, frustration, disappointment, and anxiety) of the user in the virtual environment that varies with his prior experience with virtual reality [22]. According to Shin et al. [10] users feeling present and in a state of flow may want to perceive what is useful and easy to use and thus feel satisfied. Given the widely accepted factors, perceived usefulness, perceived ease of use, and satisfaction can be indicators of perceived usability [10]. Cheng et al. [9] asserted that the user can derive emotions from the human-machine interaction experience and that strong flow creates this emotional state. They also suggest that skill affects flow. In fact, the state of flow results from an equilibrium between the user's perceived skill and the challenge given. Thus, we may hypothesize that the perceived skills influence the state of flow which in turn influences the perceived usability and the emotion (Hypothesis 3).

Experience Consequence, Judgement, and Technology Adoption

Judgement is a component defined as the overall judgement (i.e., positive, indifferent or negative) of the virtual environment. Technology adoption is a component defined as the actions and decisions taken by the user for a future use or intention to use of the virtual environment. According to Shin et al. [10], experience consequence can alter the user's prior use and thus the intention to use the virtual environment. Indeed, as revealed by Lin and Parker [10], simulator sickness (i.e., a UX after effect) severity could make the users feel uncomfortable and even withdraw from a virtual environment exposure. Thus, simulator sickness could contribute negatively to UX. According to Mahlke [11] the consequence of the experience incorporates the acceptance of the system (overall judgement of the system), intention to use the system, and usage behavior. Consequently, we may hypothesize that the experience consequence influences the overall virtual environment judgement and the propensity of adopting the technology (Hypothesis 4).

These four hypotheses, justified by the literature, lead to a hypothesized model named User eXperience in Immersive Virtual Environment Model or UXIVE Model (Figure 1). This model has been validated through an empirical study.

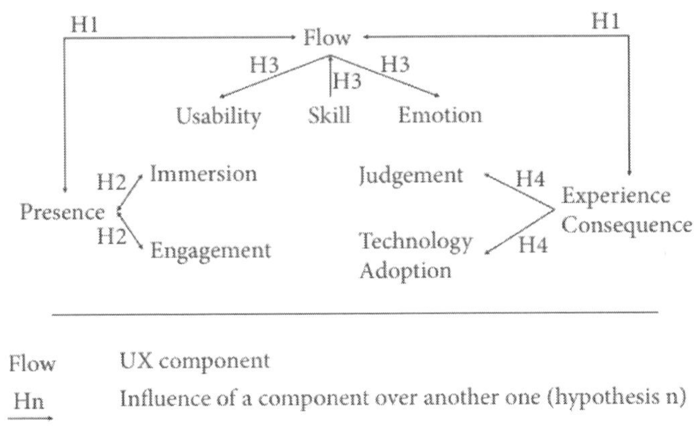

Figure 1: The hypothesized UXIVE Model.

VALIDATION OF THE USER EXPERIENCE IN IMMERSIVE VIRTUAL ENVIRONMENT MODEL

After explaining the purpose of the study, methodology detailing participants, material, measures and the procedure, and results of the structural equation modelling analysis of the UXIVE Model are exposed.

Aim of the Study

This study aims at validating the theoretical UXIVE Model defining relationships between ten UX components specific to IVE: presence, immersion, engagement, skill, emotion, flow, usability, technology adoption, judgement, and experience consequence (Figure 1). In other words, this aim was to validate the following four hypotheses:(i)Hypothesis 1: a low experience consequence and a high sense of presence greatly enhance the state of flow which influences back the two components.(ii)Hypothesis 2: the sense of presence enhances the degree of engagement and the feeling of immersion; the same way the two components enhance presence.(iii) Hypothesis 3: the perceived skills influence the state of flow which in turn influences the perceived usability and the emotion.(iv)Hypothesis 4: the experience consequence influences the overall virtual environment judgement and the propensity of adopting the virtual environment technology.

Method

Participants

One hundred fifty-two participants (28 women and 124 men; 37 inexperienced and 115 experienced in virtual reality; students or professionals) had volunteered to take part in this study. The sample mean age was 23.96 years and the standard deviation was 6.93 (ranging from 18 to 63).

Material and Measures

Think and Shoot on Oculus DK2. Think and Shoot is an edutainment virtual environment aiming at familiarizing the participants with the notions of function and parameters. It consists of two main actions which are collecting balls and shoot on evil creatures. The participants are given instructions in a pseudo programming language where the action of shooting is represented by a function and the three parameters of the function are represented by the type of evil creature to shoot on (i.e., two different types of creatures), the type of ball to shoot (i.e., three different types of balls), and the remaining balls that can be used. An example of instruction could be "Shoot (fire creature, ice ball, 0)" (Figure 2), the participant should understand that there is no ice ball left to shoot on the fire creature, and he must collect more.

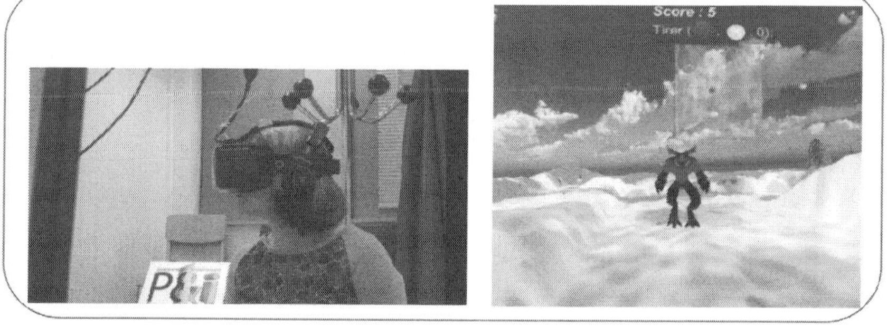

Figure 2: A participant (left) playing the "Think and Shoot" virtual environment (right).

This edutainment virtual environment was designed with the development tool UNITY © and ran on a Dell 64bits with 4 GB of RAM computer, an Intel® Xeon® processor, CPU E5-16030 2.80 GHz. A Logitech wireless gamepad and an Oculus development kit 2 (DK2) allowed the participant to collect balls and to shoot on three different sphere targets in the training session and on two different evil creatures in the regular session according the instructions given on a panel in the application. 3D spatialized sound was rendered in a Tritton AX 180 audio headset.

Questionnaires. Participants had to answer two questionnaires before and after the task.

The questionnaire filled in before the task contained 11 questions: four demographic items (age, gender, marital status, and occupation) and seven items on prior knowledge about programming and familiarity with virtual reality (e.g., "Among the following devices (such as virtual reality headsets, data glove...), which ones have you used and how often (never, little, sometimes, often, very often)?").

The subjective questionnaire completed after the task was a UX questionnaire consisting of 84 items rated on 10-point Likert scales. It contained 12 items to measure presence taken from [21] (Cronbach's $\alpha = 0.76$; e.g.,"The virtual environment was responsive to actions that I initiated"), 3 items to measure engagement translated from [21] (Cronbach's α = 0.74; e.g., "The sense of moving around inside the virtual environment was compelling"), 7 items to measure immersion inspired by [21] (Cronbach's $\alpha = 0.74$; e.g., "I felt stimulated by the virtual environment"), 11 items to measure flow taken from [23] (Cronbach's $\alpha = 0.82$; e.g., "I felt I could perfectly control my actions"), 6 items to measure skill translated from [24] (Cronbach's $\alpha = 0.80$; e.g., "I felt confident selecting objects in the virtual environment"), 15 items to measure emotion taken from [25] (Cronbach's $\alpha = 0.72$; e.g., "I enjoyed being in this virtual environment"), 9 items to measure experience consequence inspired by [26] (Cronbach's α = 0.91; e.g., "I suffered from fatigue during my interaction with the virtual environment"), 12 items (grouped in 4) to measure judgement taken from [27] (Cronbach's $\alpha = 0.82$; e.g.,"Personally, I would say the virtual environment is impractical/practical"), and 9 items to measure technology adoption inspired by [28] (Cronbach's $\alpha = 0.75$; e.g., "If I use again the same virtual environment, my interaction with the environment would be clear and understandable for me").

Usability Measures. Usability was measured through level completion time, number of errors, total levels score, and level reached. Participants evolved from one level to the next after having eliminated all the creatures in the level. Level completion time is the time the users took to complete the level n°2 (i.e., level reached by all participants). The number of errors are the points the user had lost when he collided with a creature (i.e., one point was lost for every collision with a creature) during the whole session. The total levels score is the total score gained in all levels, and the level reached is the level the users reached at the end of the session.

Procedure

The experiment took place in a research laboratory in computer sciences. Once participant had filled in the pretask questionnaire (personal details), the experimenter introduced and gave the participant instructions about the experiment. The first one was an orally guided training session of about 5 minutes (the participants could ask for more or less training time if they felt more or less comfortable in the IVE). The second session was a regular session of 5 minutes. For each session, participants followed the instructions in a pseudo programming language written on a panel in the application. A questionnaire on UX completed the session. Each participant spent between 30 to 45 minutes in the experiment room.

Statistical Analyses

A Structural Equation Modelling (SEM) analysis was used to validate the hypothesized UXIVE Model. This statistical method has long been associated with the idea that a high sample size was necessary [29], recent studies show that the association between sample size and result is much more complex. For example, Wolf, Harrington, Clark, and Miller (2013) indicate that the recommended minimum sample size may decrease if the number of components to be measured and the number of items per component is high (e.g., 8 items per component) [30]. Moreover, the reality on the field demonstrates the difficulty in obtaining the recommended minimum sample size. This gives rise to SEM studies with small samples [31]. According to these authors, our sample size (i.e., N = 152) and the complexity of the UXIVE Model (i.e., 10 components) are suitable for SEM analysis. Scale scores of the UX questionnaire and usability measures (i.e., level completion time, the number of errors, the levels score, and the level reached) for all participants were both taken into account in the structural model designed on the IBM® SPSS® AMOS 24 software. To assess how well the model represented the data, four goodness-of-fit recommended indices were evaluated in a structural model: Comparative Fit Index (CFI), Normed Fit Index (NFI), Root Mean Square Error of Approximation (RMSEA), and the ratio Chi-square and the degree of freedom. The recommended fit indices of these analyses are presented in Table 1.

Table 1: The recommended value of fit indices for SEM analysis

Fit index	Recommended value	Reference
CFI	> 0.9	Bagozzi and Yi (1988)
NFI	> 0.9	Bentler (1990)
RMSEA	< 0.08	Kline (2005)
$\chi 2$/df	< 5	Bagozzi and Yi (1988)

Note. CFI: Comparative Fit Index; NFI: Normed Fit Index; RMSEA: Root Mean Square Error of Approximation; $\chi 2$/df: the ratio between Chi square and degrees of freedom.

Results: From a Hypothesized UXIVE Model to a Modified UXIVE Model

Structural Model of the Hypothesized UXIVE Model. The structural model analysis—based on a SEM analysis—should reveal significance and fit of the components relations with the data collected. The test from the structural model (Figure 3) revealed three statistically significant relations and nine nonsignificant relations. We rejected these nine relations (Table 2).

Table 2: Evaluation of the structural model with supported and rejected paths estimations.

Hypothesis	From	To	Path estimation	Test Result
1	Presence	Flow	0.641	Reject
1	Flow	Presence	0.651	Reject
1	Flow	Experience consequence	-0.215	Reject
1	Experience consequence	Flow	-0.193	Reject
2	Presence	Engagement	0.860	Reject
2	Engagement	Presence	1.627**	Support
2	Presence	Immersion	9.368	Reject
2	Immersion	Presence	-1.279	Reject
3	Flow	Usability	0.067	Reject
3	Flow	Emotion	0.962***	Support

3	Skill	Flow	0.078	Reject
4	Experience consequence	Judgement	-0.236*	Support
4	Experience consequence	Technology adoption	-0.381***	Support

* p<0.05** p<0.01***p<0.001.

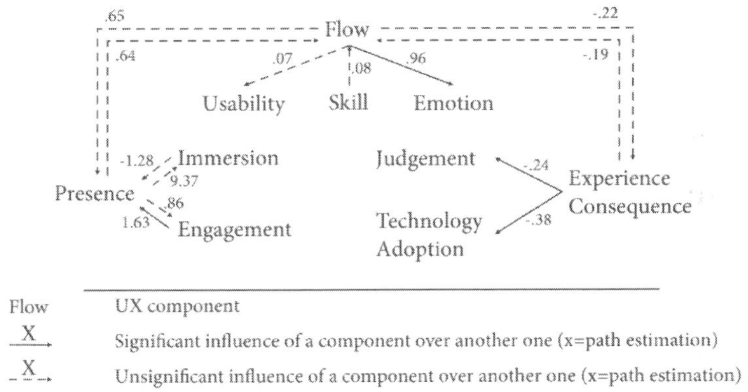

Figure 3: Standardized path estimation coefficient of the structural model of the hypothesized UXIVE Model.

Furthermore, the model fit according to the SEM fit indices indicated that CFI is 0.539, NFI is 0.390, and RMSEA is 0.086 which also indicate poor fit of our hypothesized UXIVE Model. However, χ^2/df falls into the acceptable range (i.e., 2.098). Indeed, Kline (1998) suggested that there should be a minimum of four indices that are acceptable and compatible with the model fit, we only have one acceptable index fit for this tested structural model [32]. The hypothesized UXIVE Model is then poorly acceptable.

Modified UXIVE Model. To improve the structural model of the hypothesized UXIVE Model, a covariance analysis was conducted. The analysis revealed 32 hypothesized covariances within which 15 statistically significant covariances matched with the tested structural model (i.e., the statistically significant relations from the tested structural model were preserved). According to the covariance analysis, nine hypothesized new relations were added to the conceptual model and six relations were dropped. All the 15 relations of the modified UXIVE Model were statistically significant (Table 3).

Table 3: Evaluation of the modified UXIVE Model

H	From	To	Estimate	S.E.
Previous relations				
1	Flow	Presence	.168*	.066
1	Experience consequence	Flow	-.098*	.046
2	Engagement	Presence	.365***	.082
3	Skill	Flow	.190*	.093
3	Flow	Emotion	1.427***	.298
4	Experience consequence	Technology adoption	-.158**	.054
4	Experience consequence	Judgement	-.092*	.044
Added relations				
	Skill	Experience consequence	-.694***	.208
	Skill	Usability	.328***	.078
	Experience consequence	Emotion	-.283***	.061
	Engagement	Immersion	.924***	.154
	Engagement	Technology adoption	.147*	.074
	Flow	Technology adoption	.288*	.128
	Presence	Emotion	.791***	.237
	Presence	Judgement	1.128***	.293
	Usability	Technology adoption	.430***	.130

H: hypothesis; S.E.: Standard Error; $*p < 0.05$; $**p < 0.01$; $***p < 0.001$.

So, in the modified UXIVE Model (Figure 4), the hypothesis 4 is fully validated, and the hypotheses 1, 2, and 3 are partially validated.

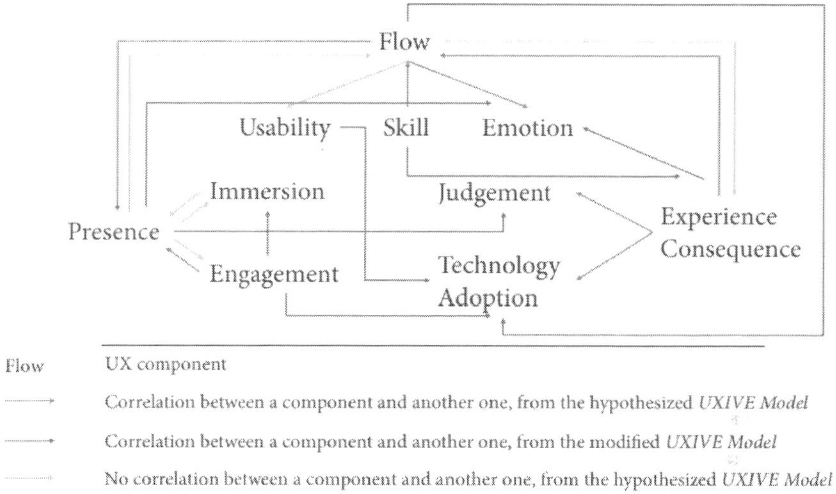

Figure 4: The modified UXIVE Model.

DISCUSSION

This present research set out to integrate the fragmented theories and research on UX into a unified UX in IVE model named UXIVE Model. We analyzed our UXIVE Model and questioned the relationships between UX components.

Our first hypothesis stating that a low experience consequence and a high sense of presence greatly enhance the state of flow which influences back the two components is partially validated in the modified model. The results rather show influence of experience consequence on flow and influence of the latter on presence. According to several studies there is indeed a correlation between presence and flow and this relationship is of great interest for game fields (e.g., [9, 10, 33]) due to the immersive experience provided by the two components. However, no known studies focused on the relationship between experience consequence and flow.

Furthermore, the modified model revealed a significant path estimation from flow to technology adoption and from experience consequence to emotion. Studies show interest in the relationship between flow and technology adoption (e.g., [34, 35]) in online games or e-learning fields; studies in this area wish to predict user technology acceptance by measuring the flow. Experience consequences such as motion sickness are known to be affected by emotional factors such as fear, anxiety, and nervousness [36].

Our second hypothesis stating that the sense of presence enhances the degree of engagement and the feeling of immersion, and the same way the two components enhance presence, is partially validated in our modified model. The results rather show influence of engagement on both presence and immersion and no correlation between presence and immersion contrary to other studies (e.g., [5, 10, 37]). In addition, the modified model shows correlation between engagement and technology adoption, presence and emotion, and presence and judgement. The relationship between presence and engagement is indeed well known and studied in several works (i.e., [12, 37–39]), other studies in the game field investigated engagement as being the first state of immersion (i.e., [40, 41]), and more studies in the education field and technology adoption issues investigated engagement through technology adoption (i.e., [42, 43]). Emotional reactions and presence are related according to studies in virtual environment and game fields (i.e., [44, 45]).

Our third hypothesis stating that the perceived skills influence the state of flow which in turn influences the perceived usability and the emotion is again partially validated in our modified model. The results rather show skill influence on flow which in turn influences emotion. As shown by [46], flow is highly correlated with the user's emotions and just as [47]; he relates flow and skill in their studies.

The modified model revealed a significant correlation between usability and technology adoption, skill and experience consequence, and skill and usability. Perceived usability as enhancing technology adoption is indeed confirmed by other studies (i.e., [10, 48]). Several other studies confirmed that usability perception depends on user skill (i.e., [5, 49]), whereas no studies are known that report on the effects of perceived skill on experience consequence.

Our fourth hypothesis stating that the experience consequence influences the overall judgement and the propensity of adopting the VE technology is validated in the modified model. These findings are in line with Mahlke's model [11] and specify that the judgement is a moderator between the experience consequence and the technology adoption.

Finally, this study revealed new UX components relationships to investigate. Indeed, the modified model states that flow and engagement are the two components influencing presence. Experience consequence and skill are the two components influencing flow. Presence, flow, and experience consequence are the three components influencing emotion. Engagement is the unique component influencing immersion. Skill is the unique component influencing experience consequence and usability. Presence and experience consequence are the two components influencing judgement. Flow, experience consequence, engagement, and usability are the four components influencing technology adoption.

CONCLUSION

This paper examines new relationships among UX components in an IVE framework and confirms others through two steps. First, a review of UX models led us to propose the hypothesized UXIVE Model. Second, we assessed the whole theoretical structure with analyses based on SEM and correlations. Results do not allow us to validate hypothesized UXIVE Model but allowed us to propose a modified UXIVE Model validated in the field of edutainment.

The most significant limitation of this study is the sample size, even if this sample is sufficient according to [30, 31]. To resolve this limitation, the experimental protocol could be pursued in the same conditions to gather a larger participation rate. Another solution to gather a larger participation rate would be to conduct an online experimental protocol. Tools such as "webvr" websites (see, for example, webvr.info) allow the user to experience virtual reality in his browser with any type of virtual reality device. Online experiments usually gather many users (e.g., 1000). Indeed, the SEM analysis recommend that the more variables are included in an SEM analysis; the more participants are needed to guarantee the stability of the results. In addition, more experiments are needed to corroborate the findings in this study as some relationships revealed by the study are relatively new and have not been investigated in previous studies.

The second limitation of this study is the sample profile. 48% of the participants share the same characteristics (e.g., age, sex, studies or work area, and experience with 3D technologies). Although, the target population of virtual edutainment environment is young, it could be interesting to apply these findings to other population because virtual reality devices are more and more reaching every type of profile. This limitation is directly linked to the third limitation which involves the device and content types.

The third limitation of this study is that other types of immersive virtual devices and other types of content are excluded. Indeed, the experiment is conducted with a Head Mounted Display (HMD) with an edutainment application. So, our modified UXIVE Model is only valid for Think and Shoot on HMD. First, this model should be validated for other immersive edutainment applications such as REARTH [50]). Second, this framework could be extended to different fields such as therapeutic, industrial, or collaborative applications. Third, the UXIVE Model can be experienced through different types of devices such as 6 axes virtual simulators, 6 walls CAVEs, and Z-spaces. Indeed, using our model in other studies from several fields and with different immersive virtual technologies may contribute to generalize our modified UXIVE Model.

ACKNOWLEDGMENTS

The authors acknowledge Laval Agglomération and the Mayenne Department for their financial support and the participants who took time to engage and provide feedback on this project.

REFERENCES

1. D. Hatfield and D. W. Shaffer, "Press play: designing an epistemic game engine for journalism," in Proceedings of the 7th International Conference of the Learning Sciences (ICLS '06), pp. 236–242, July 2006.
2. N. K. Boots and J. Strobel, "Equipping the designers of the future: Best practices of epistemic video game design," Games and Culture, vol. 9, no. 3, pp. 167–181, 2004.
3. G. Loup, A. Serna, S. Iksal, and S. George, "Immersion and persistence: improving learners engagement in authentic learning situations," in Adaptive and Adaptable Learning, EC-TEL 2016, K. Verbert, M. Sharples, and M. Klobučar, Eds., vol. 9891 of Lecture Notes in Computer Science, p. 9891, Springer, Cham, 2016.
4. K. Tcha-Tokey, E. Loup-Escande, O. Christmann, and S. Richir, "Effects on user experience in an edutainment virtual environment: comparison between CAVE and HMD," in Proceedings of the 35th Annual Conference of the European Association of Cognitive Ergonomics (ECCE '17), pp. 1–8, September 2017.
5. A. E. Blandford, R. Butterworth, and P. Curzon, "PUMA Footprints: linking theory and craft skill in usability evaluation," in Proceedings of the Human-Computer Interaction (INTERACT '01), M. Hirose, Ed., pp. 577–584, 2001.
6. S. Nichols, C. Haldane, and J. R. Wilson, "Measurement of presence and its consequences in virtual environments," International Journal of Human-Computer Studies, vol. 52, no. 3, pp. 471–491, 2000.
7. T. Schubert, F. Friedmann, and H. Regenbrecht, "The experience of presence: factor analytic insights," Presence: Teleoperators and Virtual Environments, vol. 10, no. 3, pp. 266–281, 2001.
8. C. Dede, "Immersive interfaces for engagement and learning," Science, vol. 323, no. 5910, pp. 66–69, 2009.
9. L.-K. Cheng, M.-H. Chieng, and W.-H. Chieng, "Measuring virtual experience in a three-dimensional virtual reality interactive simulator environment: A structural equation modeling approach," Virtual Reality, vol. 18, no. 3, pp. 173–188, 2014.
10. D.-H. Shin, F. Biocca, and H. Choo, "Exploring the user experience of three-dimensional virtual learning environments," Behaviour & Information Technology, vol. 32, no. 2, pp. 203–214, 2013.

11. S. Mahlke, "User Experience of Interaction with Technical Systems. Theories, Methods, Empirical Results, and Their Application to the Design of Interactive Systems," Tech. Rep., VDM Verlag, Saarbrücken, Germany, 2008.
12. J. J. W. Lin and D. E. Parker, "User experience modeling and enhancement for virtual environments that employ wide-field displays," in Digital Human Modeling, ICDHM 2007, V. G. Duffy, Ed., vol. 4561 of Lecture Notes in Computer Science, Springer, Berlin, Heidelberg, 2007.
13. M. Pereira de Aguiar, B. Winn, M. Cezarotto, A. L. Battaiola, and P. Varella Gomes, "Educational digital games: a theoretical framework about design models, learning theories and user experience," in Design, User Experience, and Usability: Theory and Practice. DUXU 2018, A. Marcus and W. Wang, Eds., vol. 10918 of Lecture Notes in Computer Science, Springer, 2018.
14. C. Rico-Olarte, D. M. López, and S. Kepplinger, "Towards a conceptual framework for the objective evaluation of user experience," in Design, User Experience, and Usability: Theory and Practice. DUXU 2018, A. Marcus and W. Wang, Eds., vol. 10918 of Lecture Notes in Computer Science, Springer, 2018.
15. M. Csikszentmihalyi, "Beyond boredom and anxiety," Jossey-Bass, 1975.
16. J. S. Pillai, C. Schmidt, and S. Richir, "Achieving presence through evoked reality, 'Consciousness Research'," Frontiers in Psychology, vol. 4, no. 86, 2013.
17. M. Pallot, R. Eynard, B. Poussard, O. Christmann, and S. Richir, "Augmented sport: exploring collective user experience," in The ACM Proceedings of Virtual Reality International Conference, 2013.
18. R. Eynard, M. Pallot, O. Christmann, and S. Richir, "Impact of Verbal Communication on User Experience in 3D Immersive Virtual Environments," in Proceedings of the 21st ICE/IEEE International Technology Management Conference, Belfast, Ireland, 2015.
19. T. Zhou and Y. Lu, "Examining mobile instant messaging user loyalty from the perspectives of network externalities and flow experience," Computers in Human Behavior, vol. 27, no. 2, pp. 883–889, 2011.
20. D. A. Bowman and R. P. McMahan, "Virtual reality: how much

immersion is enough?" The Computer Journal, vol. 40, no. 7, pp. 36–43, 2007.

21. B. G. Witmer and M. J. Singer, "Measuring presence in virtual environments: a presence questionnaire," Presence: Teleoperators and Virtual Environments, vol. 7, no. 3, pp. 225–240, 1998.
22. E. Geslin, S. Bouchard, and S. Richir, "Gamers' versus non-gamers' emotional response in virtual reality," Journal of CyberTherapy and Rehabilitation, vol. 4, no. 4, 2011.
23. J. Heutte, F. Fenouillet, C. Martin-Krumm, I. Boniwell, and M. Csikszentmihalyi, "Proposal for a conceptual evolution of the flow in education (EduFlow) model," in Proceedings of the 8th European Conference on Positive Psychology (ECPP '16), Angers, France, 2016.
24. C. A. Murphy, D. Coover, and S. V. Owen, "Development and validation of the computer self-efficacy scale," Educational and Psychological Measurement, vol. 49, no. 4, pp. 893–899, 1989.
25. R. Pekrun, T. Goetz, A. C. Frenzel, P. Barchfeld, and R. P. Perry, "Measuring emotions in students' learning and performance: the achievement emotions questionnaire (AEQ)," Contemporary Educational Psychology, vol. 36, no. 1, pp. 36–48, 2011.
26. R. S. Kennedy, N. E. Lane, K. S. Berbaum, and M. G. Lilienthal, "Simulator sickness questionnaire: an enhanced method for quantifying simulator sickness," The International Journal of Aviation Psychology, vol. 3, no. 3, pp. 203–220, 1993.
27. M. Hassenzahl, M. Burmester, and F. Koller, "AttrakDiff: Ein Fragebogen zur Messung wahrgenommener hedonischer und pragmatischer Qualität," in Mensch & Computer, G. Szwillus and J. Ziegler, Eds., vol. 57 of Berichte des German Chapter of the ACM, 2003.
28. V. Venkatesh, M. G. Morris, G. B. Davis, and F. D. Davis, "User acceptance of information technology: toward a unified view," MIS Quarterly: Management Information Systems, vol. 27, no. 3, pp. 425–478, 2003.
29. J. C. Nunnally, Psychometric theory, McGraw-Hill, New York, NY, USA, 1967.
30. E. J. Wolf, K. M. Harrington, S. L. Clark, and M. W. Miller, "Sample size requirements for structural equation models: an evaluation of power, bias, and solution propriety," Educational and Psychological

Measurement, vol. 73, no. 6, pp. 913–934, 2013.

31. P. M. Bentler and K.-H. Yuan, "Structural equation modeling with small samples: Test statistics," Multivariate Behavioral Research, vol. 34, no. 2, pp. 181–197, 1999.
32. R. B. Kline, Principles and Practice of Structural Equation Modeling, Guilford, New York, NY, USA, 1998.
33. D. Weibel and B. Wissmath, "Immersion in computer games: the role of spatial presence and flow," International Journal of Computer Games Technology, vol. 2011, Article ID 282345, 14 pages, 2011.
34. S.-H. Liu, H.-L. Liao, and J. A. Pratt, "Impact of media richness and flow on e-learning technology acceptance," Computers & Education, vol. 52, no. 3, pp. 599–607, 2009.
35. C.-L. Hsu and H.-P. Lu, "Why do people play on-line games? An extended TAM with social influences and flow experience," Information and Management, vol. 41, no. 7, pp. 853–868, 2004.
36. A. Uno, N. Takeda, A. Horii, Y. Sakata, A. Yamatodani, and T. Kubo, "Effects of amygdala or hippocampus lesion on hypergravity-induced motion sickness in rats," Acta Oto-Laryngologica, vol. 120, no. 7, pp. 860–865, 2000.
37. A. McMahan, "Immersion, engagement and presence," in The Video Game Theory Reader, D. M. J. Wolf and B. Perron, Eds., pp. 67–86, 2003.
38. S. Dow, M. Mehta, E. Harmon, B. MacIntyre, and M. Mateas, "Presence and engagement in an interactive drama," in Proceedings of the 25th SIGCHI Conference on Human Factors in Computing Systems (CHI '07), pp. 1475–1484, May 2007.
39. L. Jarmon, "Learning in virtual world environments: Social-presence, engagement, and pedagogy," Encyclopedia of Distance and Online Learning, pp. 1610–1619, 2009.
40. E. Brown and P. Cairns, "A grounded investigation of game immersion," in Proceedings of the ACM CHI'04 Extended Abstracts on Human Factors in Computing Systems, pp. 1297–1300, 2004.
41. J. H. Brockmyer, C. M. Fox, K. A. Curtiss, E. McBroom, K. M. Burkhart, and J. N. Pidruzny, "The development of the Game Engagement Questionnaire: a measure of engagement in video game-playing," Journal of Experimental Social Psychology, vol. 45, no. 4, pp. 624–634, 2009.

42. A. Kai-ming and P. Enderwick, "A cognitive model on attitude towards technology adoption," Journal of Managerial Psychology, vol. 15, no. 4, pp. 266–282, 2000.
43. M. Manuguerra and P. Petocz, "Promoting student engagement by integrating new technology into tertiary education: The role of the iPad," Asian Social Science, vol. 7, no. 11, pp. 61–65, 2011.
44. D. Västfjäll, "The subjective sense of presence, emotion recognition, and experienced emotions in auditory virtual environments," Cyberpsychology, Behavior, and Social Networking, vol. 6, no. 2, pp. 181–188, 2003.
45. N. Ravaja, T. Saari, M. Turpeinen, J. Laarni, M. Salminen, and M. Kivikangas, "Spatial presence and emotions during video game playing: does it matter with whom you play?" Presence: Teleoperators and Virtual Environments, vol. 15, no. 4, pp. 381–392, 2006.
46. M. Csikszentmihalyi, The Psychology of Optimal Experience, Harper and Row, New York, NY, USA, 1990.
47. D. L. Hoffman and T. P. Novak, "Flow online: lessons learned and future prospects," Journal of Interactive Marketing, vol. 23, no. 1, pp. 23–34, 2009.
48. H. Holden and R. Rada, "Understanding the influence of perceived usability and technology self-efficacy on teachers' technology acceptance," Journal of Research on Technology in Education, vol. 43, no. 4, pp. 343–367, 2011.
49. L. Faulkner and D. Wick, "Cross-user analysis: Benefits of skill level comparison in usability testing," Interacting with Computers, vol. 17, no. 6, pp. 773–786, 2005.
50. F. Sauret, V. Emin-Martinez, G. Loup et al., "REARTH un exemple de Jeu Épistémique Numérique, de la conception à lexpérimentation," in CETSIS 2017, Le Mans , France, 2017.

Chapter

7

RoboTable: An Infrastructure for Intuitive Interaction with Mobile Robots in a Mixed-Reality Environment

Haipeng Mi[1] , Aleksander Krzywinski[2] , Tomoki Fujita[1] , and Masanori Sugimoto[1]

[1]Interaction Technology Laboratory, Department of Electrical Engineering and Information Systems, University of Tokyo, 7-3-1 Hongo, Bunkyo-ku, 113-8656 Tokyo, Japan

[2]The Interaction Research Group, Department of Information Science and Media Studies, University of Bergen, Fosswinckelsgate 6, 5020 Bergen, Norway

ABSTRACT

This paper presents the design, development, and testing of a tabletop interface called RoboTable, which is an infrastructure supporting intuitive

Citation: Haipeng Mi, Aleksander Krzywinski, Tomoki Fujita, and Masanori Sugimoto, "RoboTable: An Infrastructure for Intuitive Interaction with Mobile Robots in a Mixed-Reality Environment," Advances in Human-Computer Interaction, vol. 2012, Article ID 301608.

interaction with both mobile robots and virtual components in a mixed-reality environment. With a flexible software toolkit and specifically developed robots, the platform enables various modes of interaction with mobile robots. Using this platform, prototype applications are developed for two different application domains: RoboPong investigates the efficiency of the RoboTable system in game applications, and ExploreRobot explores the possibility of using robots and intuitive interaction to enhance learning.

INTRODUCTION

In the past few years, much development has taken place in the research field of human-computer interaction. Several research approaches in this field, including tabletop interaction, tangible user interfaces (TUIs), augmented reality, and mixed-reality, show great promise for bringing new interaction styles to other related research domains. The research presented in this paper is an attempt to integrate several research approaches to create a mixed reality environment for novel human-robot interaction (HRI).

Because the horizontal surface of a table permits the placement of objects, and its large surface area enables spreading, piling, and organization of the items, digital tabletop user interfaces are becoming increasingly popular for supporting natural and intuitive interaction [1–3].

A TUI is a user interface in which a person interacts with digital information via the physical environment. It gives a physical form to digital information and computation, facilitating the direct manipulation of bits [4]. Such physical interactions are very natural and intuitive for human beings, because they enable two-handed input and can provide spatial and haptic feedback [5].

In this paper, we present RoboTable, an infrastructure that combines tabletop interaction with TUIs to support intuitive interaction with mobile robots. This framework can create a mixed-reality environment in which interaction with real robots and virtual objects can be combined seamlessly. This capability also extends the robot entity into the virtual world, enabling rich and complex HRIs to be supported in various applications.

Based on the RoboTable framework, we have developed two prototype applications for proof-of-concept purposes. RoboPong is a tabletop game in which a robot player also participates. This game supports touch input for virtual objects and graspable interaction with robots simultaneously. ExploreRobot is designed for educational purposes. It enables users to interact with the robot at a behavioral level, enabling the robot to be reconfigured easily for different tasks.

An important motivation for this research is to explore new possibilities for HRI in a tabletop mixed-reality environment. We believe that with these new interaction styles, the RoboTable system will enable us to build attractive games and playful educational applications, which will give instant and intuitive feedback to the user, further facilitating the entertainment or learning experience.

RELATED WORK

In the past decade, several applications for HRI using mobile robots have been discussed in the literature. As an alternative solution to traditional HRI, TUIs have been developed in various forms. TUIs bridge the physical world and the digital world to enable users to manipulate information in a natural way [4]. Recent researchers are trying to develop HRI methods that are more intuitive, such as finger-touch control [6] and tangible-object control [7, 8].

Curlybot is an early example of enabling graspable manipulation for interaction with a mobile robot [9]. The curlybot robot has encoders for its motors by which robot movements corresponding to user manipulations can be recorded in the microcontroller. The recorded robot trajectory can be replayed after user definition.

Kato et al. developed a multitouch interface for controlling multiple robots [6]. This system utilizes ceiling-mounted cameras to track the mobile robots on the ground. A multitouch table enables users to control the robots by manipulating the corresponding image of each robot on the table.

Guo et al. discussed a manipulation method using TUIs [7, 8]. In this system, physical toys are used as indicators of robots on a table. Two multicamera systems are used to track the robot space and the toy-indicator space so that a mapping from the toy-indicator space to the robot space can be created. Users can manipulate toys on the table to move the corresponding remote robot to a desired position. A shortcoming of this system is that users and robots are insulated from each other, preventing the perception of physical feedback.

Other projects have investigated the intuitive control and programming of a mobile robot. Furthermore, other researchers have attempted to give users not only an intuitive control experience but also intuitive feedback during their interaction with mobile robots.

The Augmented Coliseum developed by Kojima et al. creates an environment in which a physical robot can be augmented by projection [10]. The robot has light sensors mounted on its top to enable tracking of a specifically designed light pattern projected onto the table. The robot will track and move to follow the projected image's translation and rotation. This configuration scheme realized robot control and its augmentation using only one projector. However, there was neither direct interaction between users and the robot nor between users and the environment.

IncreTable, developed by Leitner et al. [11] is another project utilizing projection-augmented robots. This system uses the same robots as those in the Augmented Coliseum project. Compared with the Augmented Coliseum project, IncreTable has improved user interaction. In this application, a special pen is used, with which the user can create virtual objects on the table. In addition, the system also enables interaction between physical and virtual objects. This system is an effective attempt at implementing a mixed-reality environment on a tabletop platform. However, because of the limitations of the robots, graspable manipulation with the robots was not supported. Moreover, "placing" virtual objects with a pen cannot be considered intuitive.

Other recent projects have extended the capabilities of tabletop HRI applications. Robot Arena, developed by Calife et al. [12], is an augmented-reality platform for game development. This system utilizes camera tracking and Bluetooth (BT) communication for the robot to make the robot more flexible. This wireless communication enables users to control the robot remotely, and it can be extended to a multirobot system. Because the camera only tracks specifically designed color markers on the robot, and is not sensitive to hand manipulations, users cannot interact directly with the virtual world.

In reviewing these related projects, we found that no project creates a mixed-reality environment in which users can both directly interact with either real robots or virtual objects using familiar techniques and perceive all objects as cosituated in the same space. This consideration inspired and motivated us to develop the RoboTable system. This work tries to go beyond existing projects to explore a mixed-reality tabletop environment in which novel and intuitive HRI is enabled.

ROBOTABLE IMPLEMENTATION

Table

To achieve the research goal of creating a tabletop that supports both robot tracking and multitouch input, we implemented a combination of two different tracking techniques: frustrated total internal reflection (FTIR) [13] and diffused illumination (DI) [14].

Figure 1 shows the hardware setup for our table. A piece of 10 mm clear acrylic board is applied as the table surface. An infrared (IR) LED stripe is placed at the side of the acrylic board to generate the necessary light for FTIR. On top of this surface, we applied two thin layers of silicone-coated plastic film to form a compliant surface and a separate piece of tracing paper to act as a diffuser. Four IR illuminators fixed on the bottom of the baseplate create a light field inside the table for DI tracking. The combination of the two techniques, where DI helped the tracking of objects and FTIR enhanced finger-touch recognition, enables both tracking goals to be achieved.

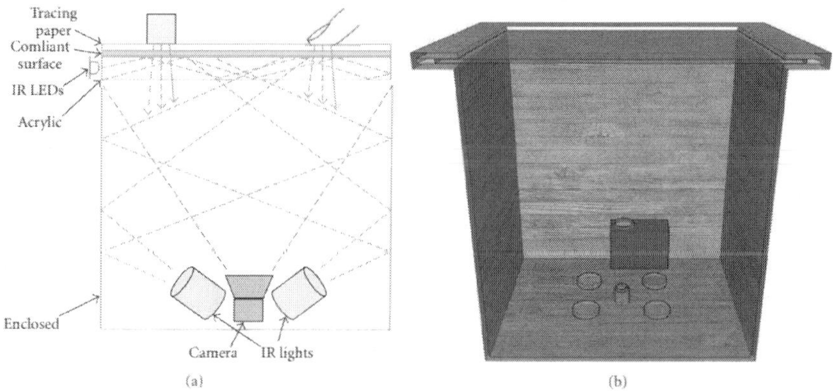

Figure 1: Tabletop setup.

A short-throw projector (Benq MP522T) is mounted underneath the surface. A piece of IR-block filter is applied to the projector lens to reduce hot spots introduced by the projector lamp. The projection area is 870 mm × 652 mm. A Firefly MV B/W camera (640 × 480 @ 60 fps) is mounted at the center of the baseplate with a piece of IR band-pass filter. In combination with particular tracking software, this table achieves a tracking resolution of 1.36 mm/pixel for both fingers and objects.

Robot

The definitions of "robot" range widely. For the RoboTable project, the robot is a simple mobile robot. Its microcontroller covers low-level motion control, whereas higher-level strategy and path planning take place in the remote console of the RoboTable system. Therefore, the robot used in this project can be classified as a nonautonomous mobile robot.

The robot is designed and developed using five design principles.(1) It must have a small footprint because of the relatively small size of the table.(2)It must be highly maneuverable.(3)Its baseplate has to be as close to the table as possible because of the DI tracking.(4)It must be able to communicate with the table system.(5)It must be aesthetically pleasing and "touchable".

Actuation

The robot is a simple two-wheel design, with each wheel being actuated by an independent DC motor and gearbox unit to enable differential steering. With this arrangement, the robot can move forward or backward and turn with a zero-radius turning circle. The speed of the DC motor is controlled by the microcontroller via power width modulation (PWM).

Tracking

Each robot has a ReacTIVision [14] fiducial marker carved into the baseplate, creating a durable, high-contrast symbol that is easily tracked by the camera (Figure 2(a) left). The ReacTIVision fiducial markers are specifically designed and optimized for rapid and high-precision recognition of both position and direction in the tabletop system. The white dots in the fiducial marker have a minimum diameter of 5 mm, and the distance from the marker to the surface is only 0.5 mm. This design ensures stable tracking; the robot can move at high speed without tracking failure. The maximum speed for stable tracking is about 120 mm/sec.

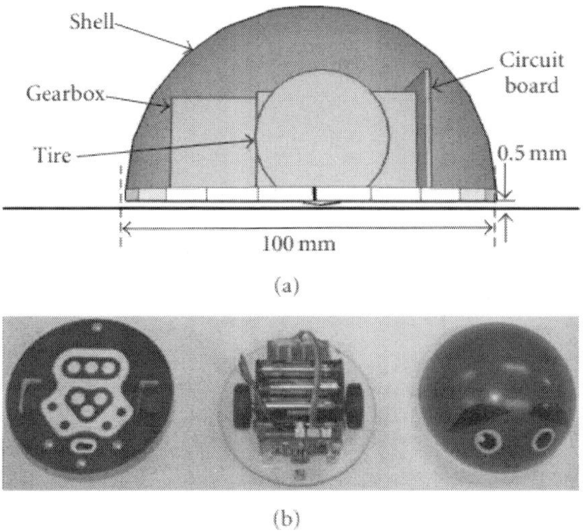

Figure 2: Robot.

Communication

We have chosen BT technology to connect the robot and the server in the RoboTable system, which gives us a communication channel that has relatively low power consumption, readily available hardware, and software libraries and is easily able to accommodate several units simultaneously. However, most BT devices require manual setup before the connection can be established. For this project, a manual connection setup would significantly reduce the smoothness of the interaction because a robot unit may be introduced into the environment or be removed from the environment by users at any time. To solve this problem, we introduced an automatic connection-setup mechanism.

As shown in Figure 3, when a working robot is put on the surface, the system will recognize the fiducial marker of the robot and will look up the BT address of that particular robot. If the address is found, the system negotiates a connection with that address automatically. The connection will be established seamlessly within seconds of placing the robot on the surface.

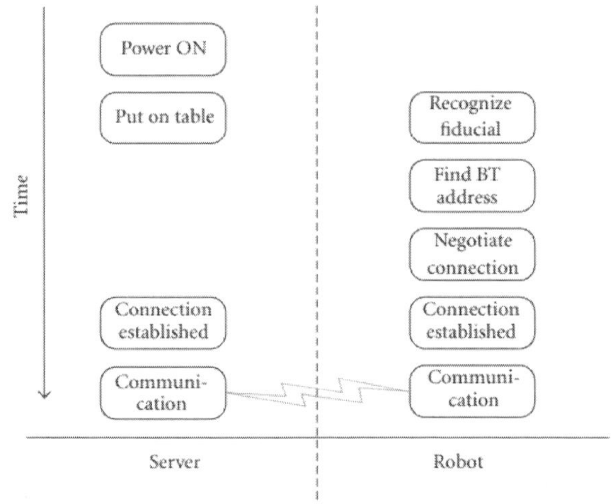

Figure 3: Robot connection flow chart.

Control

The robot uses a microcontroller (PIC16F886) as the main control unit, which receives commands from, and sends responses to, the server and drives each motor according to the received commands.

In addition, another important task of the microcontroller is to manage the differential steering. Because mechanical tolerances exist for each driving unit (DC motor, gearbox, wheel, and tire), there is always some imbalance between the wheels. To compensate for the deviation angle introduced by the imbalance in differential steering, a gyroscope sensor is also implemented to monitor the angular velocity of the robot in real time.

Figure 4 illustrates the feedback control diagram for the robot using a gyroscope sensor. v_y and ω_z are the desired robot speed and rotation parameters, respectively. A transformation matrix A transforms v_y and ω_z to left and right motor speeds V_L and V_R, which are then sent to the PWM drivers for the two motors. The actual rotation is observed by the gyroscope, and a control algorithm will correct the motion error.

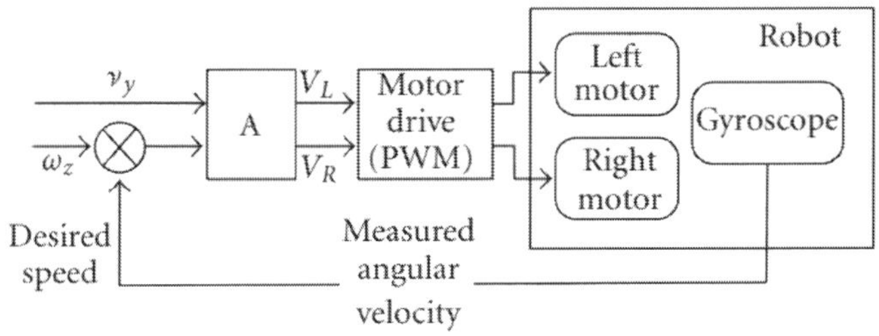

Figure 4: Motion control diagram.

Integration

All components of the robot sit on the baseplate, whose diameter is 100 mm (Figure 2(b) center). A hemispherical acrylic shell, which is painted and decorated, covers all components. The compact design fits snugly in a user's palm (Figure 2(b) right).

Software Implementation

All the RoboTable software components are developed in Java. We used several open-source tools in the project, developing specific drivers and application-programmer interfaces (APIs) for mixed-reality applications based on the RoboTable platform.

Software Architecture

The RoboTable API was implemented as a layer above the supporting layer, which comprised several libraries. These toolkits support event-handling and rendering functions, physical simulations and wireless communications. An independent tracking engine delivers a stream of input events via a TUIO protocol. Figure 5 illustrates the software architecture of the developed infrastructure.

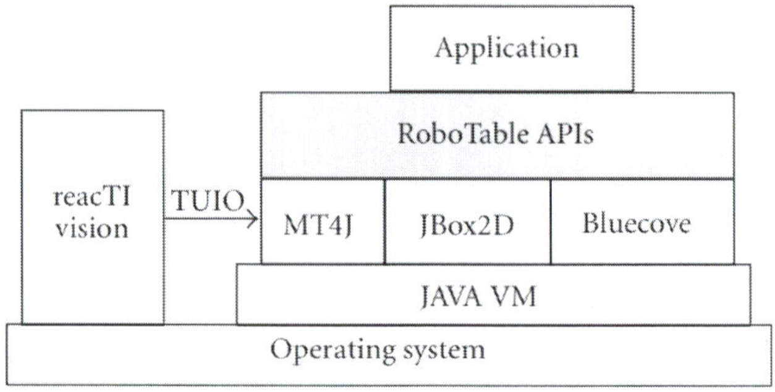

Figure 5: Software architecture.

Tracking

The main tracking engine in our system was that used in the reacTIVision project. The reacTIVision engine [14] handles the segmentation, fiducial marker, touch recognition and tracking, and delivers a stream of TUIO-based data to a specific network address and port. Usually, the address is that of a local interface, but configurations where the workload is divided amongst several computers are easily implemented. Therefore, the TUIO stream provides simple add, update and remove events for both cursors (i.e., touches) and objects (i.e., tangibles with fiducial markers).

Physical Simulation

To accommodate mixed-reality applications, we must ensure that both the robots and the virtual objects on the screen behave in a way that is intuitive for users, being based on human experience of the real world. Otherwise, users will find it difficult to understand the interaction with the virtual objects on the table, and any advantage in usability leveraged by the familiarity of the user with everyday physical objects is lost. For the flat, horizontal surface of a table, it is most appropriate to simulate the interaction of bodies on a plane. Therefore, we used a 2D physics simulation framework provided by the JBox2D project [15]. (Simulating a third dimension normal to the surface is superfluous, justifying the limitation to two dimensions.) The chosen framework has powerful APIs for defining the properties of physical objects and their interaction with each other when set in motion, enabling us to create rapidly a world in which the objects on the screen collide and exert forces on each other.

Event Handling and Rendering

Another open-source framework, MultiTouch for Java (MT4J) [16], is included in the software toolkit for handling events, managing a canvas and rendering objects on a screen. MT4J is a powerful tool that handles all TUIO events, including both touches and objects. It also provides a rendering engine based on OpenGL technology that supports both 2D and 3D rendering. The MT4J framework has predefined many common gestures such as drag, rotate and zoom. By providing rich APIs, MT4J offers easy extension to different application areas.

Communications

We have chosen the Bluecove library [17] for BT communication to handle all the wireless communications between the robots and the RoboTable server.

The RoboTable API

For the RoboTable project, the mixed-reality application environment requires seamless management of both on-screen objects and physical robots. For example, an on-screen object will collide with another object if contact is made, whether on-screen or in the real world. In other words, both virtual objects and physical robots should have the same abstraction in the mixed-reality world. The RoboTable API provides such features to upper-layer application development, enabling a specific application with intuitive HRI to be developed easily via the RoboTable infrastructure.

INTERACTION

An important feature of the RoboTable system's interaction is that users can interact with both real and virtual objects in an intuitive way. Because the RoboTable system leverages the strong points of multitouch interfaces and TUIs, users can interact seamlessly with all objects involved in RoboTable applications in a mixed-reality environment.

Multitouch

The RoboTable system supports the most popular multitouch and gesture interactions. Users can manipulate on-screen objects simply, in ways they are familiar with. The multitouch interaction feature can be used in many tabletop applications.

Robot

The requirements for interaction with robots depend on the application. Interaction with robots in the RoboTable project falls mainly into two classes, namely, direct interaction and interaction at the behavioral level. These specialized HRIs enable the development of flexible game and learning-assistant applications involving mobile robots.

Direct Interaction

The robot used in the RoboTable system is, to some extent, a specific TUI. It has a physical form of input as an ordinary TUI that can be used as a physical token for manipulating virtual information. In addition, the robot also has the ability to transform responses from the virtual world back into the physical world. In RoboTable applications, the robot can be used as a normal TUI, enabling users to manipulate it via everyday actions such as pick up, move or put down. The robot will also respond to any change in the virtual environment (e.g., collision) by changing its physical properties such as position and movement accordingly.

Interaction at the Behavioral Level

The robots also have their own natural properties regarding specific behaviors. A robot with a certain behavior can be used in a variety of applications involving simulation tools, games and learning applications. However, in most of these applications, users expect the robot behavior to be changed easily. In other words, the robot behavior is like an attribution of this special object. Based on this consideration, we argue that if one can interact with the robot at the behavioral level, such as by changing the robot's behavior in a simple way, it can benefit several applications.

The robots used in the RoboTable project are capable of a certain level of autonomous action, and we introduce a behavior arbitration structure for them. The robot has a set of real sensors and actuators, and an additional range of virtual sensors (virtual actuators are also possible, such as those for controlling a virtual robot arm) that can report data about the virtual world in which the robot is cosituated. By being able to attach and detach various virtual sensors easily, the robot becomes reconfigurable. In addition, by having a simple robot behavior-definition feature, the reconfigurable robot can also be redefined (reprogrammed) with a different behavior.

APPLICATION PROTOTYPES

As proof-of-concept tests for the platform, two application prototypes were developed to explore the characteristics of the RoboTable. The first, RoboPong, is a tabletop game that explores the basic interactions in a mixed-reality gaming environment. The second is ExploreRobot, a learning assistant application for school students and programming beginners. This application explores the features of interaction with robots at a behavioral level.

RoboPong

The goal of the development of the RoboPong game prototype was to explore basic interactions in a mixed-reality gaming environment.

The RoboPong game was developed from the classical arcade game of "Pong". The basic version of RoboPong enables two players to play together. Each player uses two fingers to create a paddle on the player's own side of the table, trying to place this paddle where the ball will hit it and bounce back to the opponent's side, hopefully scoring a point in the process.

Ball

The ball can be created simply by touching the center ring. Only one ball can be created at a time. Once created, the ball will move in a random direction at a certain speed. If the ball collides with the boundary or a paddle, it will rebound like an actual collision in a real environment.

Paddle

A paddle can be created if a player touches the player's own defense area with two fingers. The created paddle is a straight bar whose endpoints are the player's touch points. (The player can only create a paddle of up to 130 mm in length.) Only one paddle for each player can be created at a time. If a new paddle is created, the old paddle is removed immediately.

Score

If the ball reaches the baseline of a player, the player's opponent scores one point. A game will end with the winning player being the first to score five points.

The most important difference between RoboPong and classical Pong is the participation of the robot player. Various behaviors for the robot player were implemented, enabling the robot to influence the game in different ways. Figure 6 illustrates two game modes of RoboPong for which the robot is deployed differently.

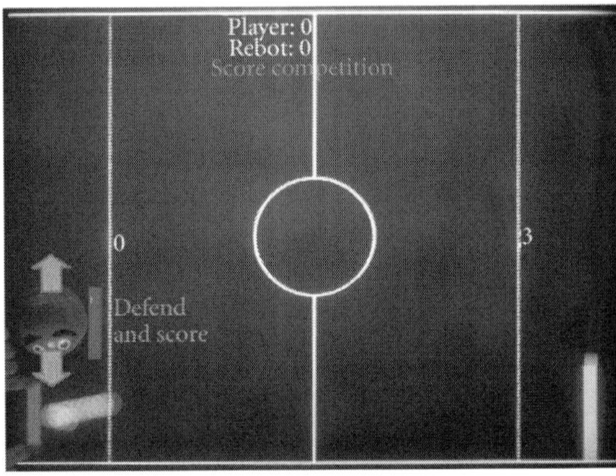

(a)

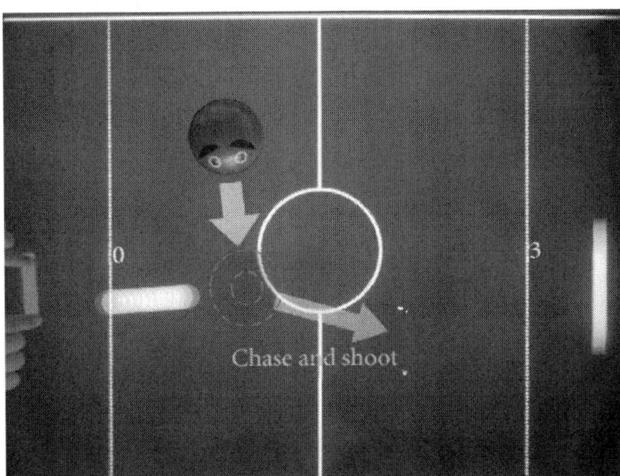

(b)

Figure 6: RoboPong game: competitive robot (a) and cooperative robot (b).

Competitive Mode

In the competitive mode, a human player plays against a robot player. The robot carries a paddle and moves across the defense area to return the incoming ball. The robot will find the best defending position and automatically move to that position. In this mode, the human player competes with the robot player, aiming to achieve the higher score (Figure 6(a)).

Cooperative Mode

In the cooperative mode, two (human) players play with up to two robots. A robot joins one side as a member of that human player's team. The robot tries to chase the ball and return it to the opponent's side. The human player can pick up the robot and place it appropriately whenever necessary. In this mode, the robot effectively cooperates with the human player in playing the game (Figure 6(b)).

ExploreRobot

The goal of the development of the ExploreRobot application was to explore the features of interaction with robots at a behavioral level.

ExploreRobot was a learning assistant application targeting school students and programming beginners. The aim of this application was to help users understand the basic concepts of robot programming. A robot equipped with virtual radar is placed in a virtual maze. An acrylic plate is placed somewhere on the table to indicate the goal of the robot explorer.

The robot has virtual radar that can detect obstacles and the goal. The radar will report the approximate direction of a detected object as left, right, or front. A programming mechanism is introduced that involves radar detection and a simple behavior-definition method for users. As shown in Figure 7(a), the player can move the robot directly on the table to define a motion path. The recorded motion path can be assigned as a default behavior or a special behavior responding to a specific event.

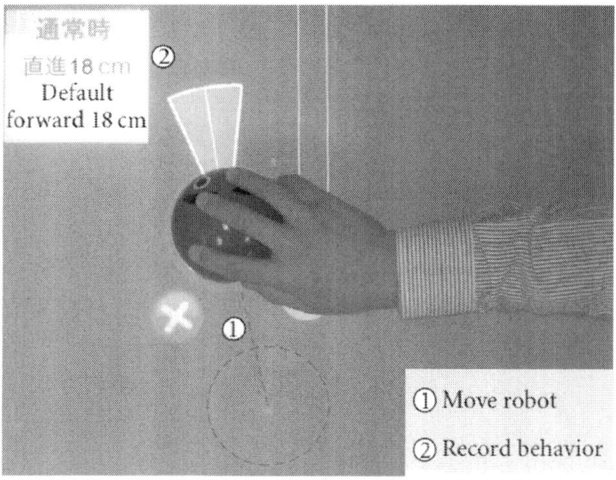

(a)

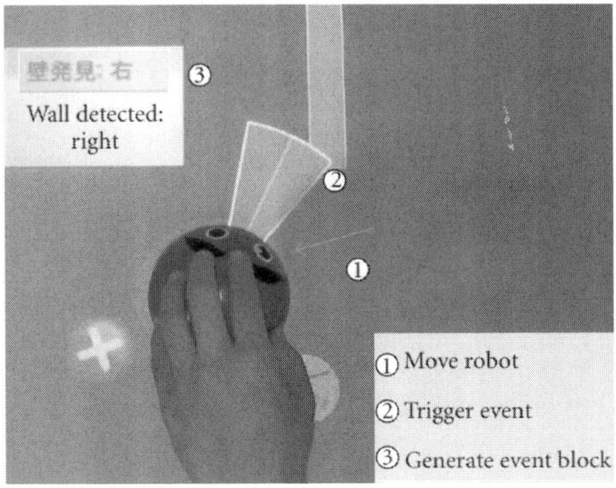

(b)

Figure 7: ExploreRobot: definition of motion path (a) and definition of event (b).

Figure 7(b) illustrates how to assign a motion behavior to a specific event. As the robot is moved to a certain place involving particular radar events, the robot will enter the behavior-defining state and players can then assign the corresponding motion behavior to that specific event using the same method as described above.

After defining the default behavior and response behavior for various cases, the robot-programming phase is completed, with all definitions being stored and organized automatically. When the player puts the robot into executing mode, the robot will start exploring the maze to find the goal, driven by the program created by the player. If the robot reaches the goal successfully, the player wins the game. Alternatively, the player can stop the execution and revise the robot's behavior by simply recalling the stored behaviors and redefining them.

Figure 8 is an example program for the simple maze-explorer robot. While no objects are detected, the default action will be executed repeatedly. If an event occurs that is caused by radar detection, the corresponding action will be executed immediately as an interrupt.

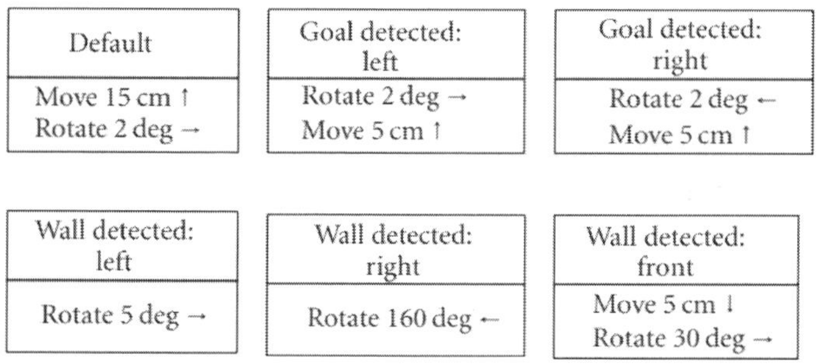

Figure 8: A simple program for the maze explorer.

Exploratory Evaluation

As one of the research goal, RoboTable infrastructure is expected to improve users' experience by introducing real robots to create a mixed-reality environment. In order to better understand users' perception playing with real robots in mixed-reality applications compared to traditional graphical applications, we have carried out a preliminary evaluation experiment.

We have modified the RoboPong game as the test-bench which has two different setups. These two setups were almost the same except the robot deployed in the game. Either a real robot or a virtual robot was deployed for each setup. In order to reduce effects caused by robot appearance and behavior, the virtual robot was presented with a photograph of the real robot and behaved exactly the same as the real robot so that the two robots look quite similar. In other words, one setup was a mixed-reality version of RoboPong game and the other setup was a traditional graphical version.

A number of participants were recruited to experience this game. Each participant was asked to play the game under two different setups. During the experiment, we have taken video record and memos of special dialogues or actions. After a video analysis and memo summary, we have found some interesting episodes from the evaluation experiment.

(1) Episode 1

Participant A was playing with a real robot, but could not defeat against the robot opponent. A heavily patted the robot with anger.

(2) Episode 2

Participant B was playing with a real robot, and got scored with the robot's help. B gently patted the robot with happiness.

(3) Episode 3

Participant C was playing with a real robot. C had a dialogue with the Experimenter (E): (During the game)

C: What's the name of this guy?
E: It has no name yet.
C: Tom? How about Tom?
E: You gave a name to the robot?
C: Yes! It's Tom!
(After the game)
C: May I come to play again? With Tom!

It is a remarkable fact that these episodes were all observed when participants were playing with the real robot. We did not find any special episode in the case of playing with the virtual robot. Because the real robot is cosituated in the same space with players, it is possible for players to express their emotion by direct gestures such as push, pull, or pat. In addition, the dialogue happened in Episode 3 implies a fact that players may treat the real robot as an anthropomorphic co-player.

This result has an implication that mixed-reality games with real robot provide a higher social engagement to players compared to graphical games with virtual robot.

Analysis of Results

In terms of the goals set for this infrastructure, the results were satisfactory and promising, with respect to the techniques implemented in the system. The combination configuration of RoboTable provided stable tracking of both finger touches and objects simultaneously. Using the integrated calibration feature of ReacTIVision, the projection coordinates and the tracking coordinates coincided perfectly, enabling interaction with both virtual objects and the robot to be carried out seamlessly during the application. The robot's flexible maneuverability and rapid response enabled different levels of interaction. In addition, multiple robots worked together simultaneously and successfully. These basic tests of the configuration of the RoboTable infrastructure show great promise for supporting various applications that involve intuitive interaction with mobile robots in a mixed-reality environment.

The RoboPong prototype aimed to test direct interaction with mobile robots in games. As observed in the test, the robot interacts very well with the virtual world. It can interact not only with virtual objects (e.g., return the incoming ball), but can also respond to virtual environment changes (e.g., move according to the opponent's action). Interactions between virtual objects and the physical robot were successful. The impression that both robot and virtual objects were colocated in the same environment could be perceived.

The ExploreRobot prototype aimed to test interaction at a behavioral level. As observed in the test, a simple reconfigurable robot was achieved successfully. The redefinition method for robot-motion paths was simple and robust. In addition, virtual sensors can work very well with the real robot, and the addition of complexity to the behavior programming was tested successfully.

However, the two applications met problems in some special situations. RoboPong is a fast-paced game. The robot has only a few seconds to move to the desired position for defense against the opponent's action. However, the robot we implemented was not omnidirectional, having only the ability to move in a direction parallel to the wheels. In other words, to move to a desired position, the robot must first rotate to a specific direction and then move forward or backward. This maneuverability problem was sometimes the cause of the robot failing to defend against the incoming ball.

In a later prototype, the robot explorer met the problem of accumulated error. Here, the overall robot behavior can be decomposed into a sequence of motion actions, where each action is a user-defined motion path. However, with every execution of a motion action, a motion error is generated. Although a single error is not significant, repeated motions can generate a significant accumulated error, which can result in uncertain behavior by the robot. For example, if the robot is placed initially at exactly the same position with the same direction, and the program is executed several times, the final position of the robot will be variable. Although this problem was not serious in the ExploreRobot application, it could be a major problem for other applications with more stringent requirements.

Although some problems for robot control and maneuverability still exist, the RoboTable system has performed well overall. As one of the most important research issue, the result of exploratory evaluation implies that real robot and mixed-reality environment provide higher social engagement to users. The feature of integrating interactions with both real and virtual objects shows a great possibility of RoboTable infrastructure to develop several kinds of attractive and interactive applications.

DISCUSSION

Interactions

Exploring interactions is the main objective of this work. In the RoboTable prototype applications, we uncovered some interesting issues concerning interaction.

Multitouch interaction extends traditional HRI to a mixed-reality environment. In aiming to manipulate virtual objects attached to the robot directly, the robot entity spreads to the virtual world. This enables the user to interact with the robot in new ways, such as moving the robot a little and then adjusting the parameters of the virtual components, or even performing these actions in an arbitrary order, which enables the perception of manipulating a unified entity, rather than separate objects.

Another interesting issue is related to interaction at a behavioral level. RoboTable applications have the capability for users to reconfigure a robot directly as well as via its behavior. The simple interaction by which the user grasps and moves a robot to define a motion path as a segment of a behavior sequence ensures a direct and intuitive perception of a user wanting to reconfigure the robot. Even though this kind of "programming" is not precise, enabling only approximate definitions, we would argue that this intuitive programming method is suited to games and educational contexts because of its intuitiveness and tangibility.

Although the RoboTable infrastructure is only a combination of existing interaction techniques, we found new possibilities for HRI when we connected the real world and the virtual world, and enabled seamless interaction with all objects involved in the mixed-reality environment. We believe that the RoboTable system can offer users a new experience of HRI.

Application Domain

The RoboTable system creates a mixed-reality environment in which users can interact with mobile robots in an intuitive way. One main consideration is the range of application domains that can benefit from this kind of system.

In general, the tabletop mixed-reality environment has three main strong points: a collaborative workspace, interaction with both physical and virtual objects, and reconfigurable robots.

The RoboTable system utilizes a tabletop interface, which offers the advantages of tabletop interaction such as face-to-face communication and a collaborative workspace. These advantages can benefit applications involving games, discussions and collaborative work and learning.

In addition, the mixed-reality environment created by the RoboTable system enables rich interaction with both virtual and real objects. By successfully implementing interactions between the real world and virtual world, all objects involved in RoboTable applications are perceived as colocated in the same environment. Interactions across the mixed-reality environment can be performed seamlessly.

Last but not least, the virtual components extend the capability of the robot by converting it into a reconfigurable robot. This feature widens the range of application domains for the RoboTable system.

With these advantages for the RoboTable system, we believe that the platform offers great benefits in the creation of applications for games, entertainment, and collaborative learning. Other possible application domains would include museum exhibitions and tactical simulation.

Games and Entertainment

The RoboTable platform is suited to the creation of a mixed-reality environment for face-to-face gaming. The physical robot as a game protagonist will enhance the attraction of the game, and the visual effects and virtual components greatly extend the boundaries of the physical gaming environment.

Collaborative Learning

As reported in some research articles [18], the TUI has benefits for some learning activities because of its physicality. In our experimental configuration of ExploreRobot, the intuitive interaction that helped users create a direct mapping between the program and the behavior of the robot showed great benefit for this specific learning activity. Moreover, collaborative learning can be implemented easily on the tabletop platform, further enhancing learning activities in some situations. In addition to programming-learning applications, the storytelling application domain [19] would be another possibility for collaborative learning.

Robot Maneuverability

Maneuverability is one of the most important characteristics of the mobile robot. The requirements for robot maneuverability depend on the application. Based on the experimental results for our prototype applications, two main issues related to robot maneuverability should be considered carefully.

The first issue concerns the robot architecture. In the RoboTable system, we implemented the robot using a simple two-wheel architecture, which only has maneuverability in two directions. Although a differential steering mechanism is implemented to realize zero-radius rotations, the additional rotation time will limit the robot's capability whenever the robot is expected to move rapidly to a desired position. A possible solution to this problem is to make the robot omnidirectional. However, this method will result in higher cost and greater complexity. Therefore, we consider that an omnidirectional robot should be used only if the application has stringent requirements for the timing of robot movements.

The second issue concerns robot control. Because we implemented the robot using only simple DC motors, the robot lacked a precise control capability. To improve the precision of the robot motion, there are two possible options. The first involves upgrading the motor systems to servomotors with a control unit, enabling the robot to move with a higher level of precision. The second option is to create a global observation and calibration unit from the software side. Because the RoboTable system can track the robot across the whole table-surface area, a prediction mechanism could be used to reduce the accumulated error of motion and calibrate the robot position dynamically. For most RoboTable applications, the latter solution is considered better because of its easy implementation and good performance. It is expected that it will be included in future developments of the system.

CONCLUSIONS

This work has two main achievements. First, we have created a complete framework that can create a mixed-reality environment involving mobile robots and that enables seamless interaction with both physical and virtual objects. The second contribution involves new possibilities for interaction styles.

To accommodate the goal of seamless interaction with different kinds of objects, we have developed the RoboTable framework by incorporating two approaches. First, we have successfully integrated existing interaction technologies to create an environment in which both robot tracking and finger-touch input could be used simultaneously and with a high degree of responsiveness. In this way, hand manipulation, such as touching and gesturing, for virtual objects is enabled, extending HRI from the real world to the virtual world. The extended robot entity, which now includes physical and virtual components, enables rich and complex interaction between the user and the robot. In addition, the physical simulation enables users to utilize their knowledge of the real world for interaction in the mixed-reality environment. The RoboTable system ensures that users perceive a unified world containing cosituated objects that interact in ways that fit the users' experience and common sense.

The framework provides three main interaction styles for users in the mixed-reality environment. The multitouch feature allows users to interact directly with virtual objects via touching and common gestures. In addition, interaction with the robot bridges the real world and the virtual world, with the robot responding not only to the user's direct physical interaction but also to interactions from the virtual world. Lastly, the robot has the capability of reconfiguration according to user requirements, where the behavior of the robot can be defined easily, using simple gestures.

For proof-of-concept purposes, we have developed two prototype applications. RoboPong is a simple game based on a classical arcade game. A human player uses touch to create a paddle, which can return an incoming ball in competition with an opponent. The robot is deployed in the game as a player with different behaviors. In competition mode, the robot can automatically move a virtual paddle to compete with a human player. In cooperation mode, the robot becomes a team member alongside one of the human players. The second application, ExploreRobot, is a learning-assistant application for school students and programming beginners. It provides simple sensors and programming mechanisms that enable users to redefine a robot's behavior, aiming to reach the goal in a virtual maze.

Robots have played an important role in education for many years, and their presence has proved stimulating for students [20]. The framework presented in this paper enables the creation of an intuitive and powerful interface that enables users to program robots easily for different tasks. Via programming and playful interaction with robots on a tabletop, students can learn concepts and principles in different disciplines such as mathematics and physics at different educational levels while also learning to think creatively, reason systematically, and work collaboratively. The prototype applications demonstrate the possibility of developing interactive applications to support student learning, using the RoboTable framework. In addition, the advantages of the RoboTable system lead to prospects for several other application domains.

Future Work

The first task we will focus on is the improvement of global robot control. As discussed above, the current system has an accumulated error problem, which will affect applications that have stringent requirements for precise robot control. Compared with the hardware solution of upgrading the motors and control units inside the robot, the global tracking and calibration method is a more cost-effective solution. We will implement a predictor unit for the robot and a global control module that can correct the robot motion dynamically to enable its arrival at the required position.

Another promising direction for the RoboTable system is the investigation of its possible use in other serious application domains such as transportation simulation and urban planning. Because the robot provides a TUI in addition to physical forms of feedback, it is capable of representing a simulation target in some applications. The intuitive manipulation and physical representation of a simulation process might have benefits in some specific areas.

We will also consider another interesting direction of development for the RoboTable system, namely, implementing remote interaction between two tabletop systems. Because the robots can be treated as both input and output devices, they are capable of connecting two or more remote environments in which users can manipulate the robot as well as perceive physical outputs according to other users' manipulations. Remote interaction has great benefits for games and collaborative workspace applications.

Conducting serious user studies is a further objective, enabling the evaluation of different applications for different target users. Particularly for educational purposes, we hope to analyze the efficiency of the applications as teaching tools, and to collect user feedback that will help us improve the RoboTable system and applications further.

REFERENCES

1. E. Hornecker, "'I don't understand it either, but it is cool'—visitor interactions with a multi-touch table in a museum," in Proceedings of the IEEE International Workshop on Horizontal Interactive Human Computer System (IEEE TABLETOP '08), pp. 113–120, Amsterdam, The Netherlands, October 2008.
2. A. Mahmud, O. Mubin, J. R. Octavia et al., "Affective tabletop game: a new gaming experience for children," in Proceedings of the 2nd IEEE International Workshop on Horizontal Interactive Human-Computer Systems (IEEE TABLETOP '07), pp. 44–51, Newport, RI, USA, October 2007.
3. M. R. Morris, A. M. Piper, A. Cassanego, A. Huang, A. Paepcke, and T. Winograd, "Mediating group dynamics through tabletop interface design," IEEE Computer Graphics and Applications, vol. 26, no. 5, pp. 65–73, 2006.
4. H. Ishii, "Tangible bits: beyond pixels," in Proceedings of the 2nd International Conference on Tangible and Embedded Interaction (ACM TEI '08), pp. 15–25, Bonn, Germany, February 2008.
5. D. Rosenfeld, M. Zawadzki, J. Sudol, and K. Perlin, "Physical objects as bidirectional user interface elements," IEEE Computer Graphics and Applications, vol. 24, no. 1, pp. 44–49, 2004.
6. J. Kato, D. Sakamoto, M. Inami, and T. Igarashi, "Multi-touch interface for controlling multiple mobile robots," in Proceedings of the 27th International Conference Extended Abstracts on Human Factors in Computing Systems (ACM CHI '09), pp. 3443–3448, Boston, Mass, USA, April 2009.
7. C. Guo, J. E. Young, and E. Sharlin, "Touch and toys: new techniques for interaction with a remote group of robots," in Proceedings of the 27th International Conference Extended Abstracts on Human Factors in Computing Systems (ACM CHI '09), pp. 491–500, Boston, Mass, USA, April 2009.
8. C. Guo and E. Sharlin, "Utilizing physical objects and metaphors for human robot interaction," in Proceedings of the Artificial Intelligence and the Simulation of Behaviour Convention (AISB '08), AISB Press, Aberdeen, UK, April 2008.
9. P. Frei, V. Su, B. Mikhak, and H. Ishii, "Curlybot: designing a new class of computational toys," in Proceedings of the Conference on Human

Factors in Computing Systems 'The Future is Here' (ACM CHI '20), pp. 129–136, The Hague, The Netherlands, April 2000.

10. M. Kojima, M. Sugimoto, A. Nakamura, M. Tomita, H. N II, and M. Inami, "Augmented coliseum: an augmented game environment with small vehicles," in Proceedings of the 1st IEEE International Workshop on Horizontal Interactive Human-Computer Systems (IEEE TABLETOP '06), pp. 3–8, Adelaide, Australia, January 2006.
11. J. Leitner, M. Haller, K. Yun, W. Woo, M. Sugimoto, and M. Inami, "IncreTable, a mixed reality tabletop game experience," in Proceedings of the International Conference on Advances in Computer Entertainment Technology (ACM ACE '08), pp. 9–16, Yokohama, Japan, December 2008.
12. D. Calife, J. L. Bernardes, and R. Tori, "Robot arena: an augmented reality platform for game development," Computers in Entertainment, vol. 7, no. 1, Article ID 11, 2009.
13. J. Y. Han, "Low-cost multi-touch sensing through frustrated total internal reflection," in Proceedings of the 18th Annual Symposium on User Interface Software and Technology (ACM UIST '05), pp. 115–118, Seattle, Wash, USA, 2005.
14. M. Kaltenbrunner and R. Bencina, "ReacTIVision: a computer-vision framework for table-based tangible interaction," in Proceedings of the 1st ACM International Conference on Tangible and Embedded Interaction (ACM TEI '07), pp. 69–74, Baton Rouge, La, USA, 2007.
15. http://www.jbox2d.org.
16. http://www.mt4j.org/mediawiki/index.php/Main_Page.
17. http://bluecove.org.
18. P. Marshall, "Do tangible interfaces enhance learning," in Proceedings of the First International Conference on Tangible and Embedded Interaction (ACM TEI '07), pp. 163–170, Baton Rouge, La, USA, 2007.
19. H. Mi, A. Krzywinski, and M. Sugimoto, "RoboStory: a tabletop mixed reality framework for children's role play storytelling," in Proceedings of the 1st International Workshop on Interactive Storytelling for Children (ACM IDC '10), Association for Computing Machinery, Barcelona, Spain, June 2010.
20. T. Fong, I. Nourbakhsh, and K. Dautenhahn, "A survey of socially interactive robots," Robotics and Autonomous Systems, vol. 42, no. 3-4, pp. 143–166, 2003.

Chapter 8

A Novel Training System of Lathe Works on Virtual Operating Platform

Hui-Chin Chang

Department of Mechanical Engineering, De Lin Institute of Technology, Taipei, Taiwan, China

ABSTRACT

In recent years virtual reality technology has been extensively applied to the areas relating to manufacturing, such as factory layout planning, manufacturing planning, operation training, system testing, and process control, etc. Most of the studies made in the past focused on the simulation and monitoring of the entire manufacturing system, or the simulation of

Citation: "A Novel Training System of Lathe Works on Virtual Operating Platform" written by Hui-Chin Chang, published by Journal of Software Engineering and Applications, Vol.3 No.3, 2010.

working schedule implementation. There was no complete research result on the most basic processing unit of manufacturing system—the operation training for the lathe works. However, these skills of operating methods are the basic skills and particularly emphasized in the practical operation during instruction. As observed from the past experience, after workers had learned the operating process of lathe works, they could achieve very good results in the written examination of the basic knowledge about the operation of different works. However, when they faced the actual operation in front of machine, they were always at a loss. The reason behind this was that when the workers had to face the possible collision and damage during actual operation of machine, since they did not have performed many times of simulated computer rehearsal designed for them to get familiar with the entire operating process, fear and nervous psychology were naturally derived from them. In view of this, the paper uses EON Studio software to integrate virtual reality technology with the application of 3D solid model to simulate a virtual operation of the various operating steps and virtual machining of lathe works during practical operation of lathe machine. The simulation enables users to learn in the simulated environment without scruple. After the accumulation of learning experience, it can be applied in the actual environment to accomplish the mission of operation.

Keywords: Virtual Reality, Lathe Machine

INTRODUCTION

Computer graphics technology was originally developed from the traditional 2D cartographic technology, which was then developed to be 2.5D, and then the 3D solid object and animation production. In recent years, virtual reality (VR) technology gradually becomes mature. Man and computer have been brought to a communication interface of "going into the environment". The scenes appeared in computer are no longer the single stiff images, but the continuous, vivid and animated images. VR is an operation environment composed of "intelligent objects" with different particular attributes. Currently, VR has been extensively applied to medical science, education, military, entertainment, engineering, machines, marketing, etc.

The so-called "virtual reality" (VR) technology mainly uses computer to simulate a real or virtual environment, enabling users to have a feeling of being in the environment. The environment not only gives a three-dimensional and layered look, but also lets users learn in the simulated environment. After they have accumulated their learning experience, they can apply it in the real environment to accomplish their missions.

Presently, VR technology has been adopted in many areas. For example, in the area of medical science, M. Tavakoli et al. [1] and Chen E. et al. [2] used haptic interface for the computer-integrated endoscopic surgery system. Through force feedback device, user could interact with the virtual scene in computer to perform more effective training of surgical and medical operation. The intravenous injection simulation system of Shoaw [3] concretely provided a training course that met the requirements for the learning of intravenous injection technique by nursing students. The system decreased the happening of accidents and the sliding of syringe during intravenous injection, and raised the quality of nursing and clinical services. The palpation simulation system of M. Dinsmore et al. [4] was applied by doctors to the simulation of looking for tumors from patients. It could train doctors to diagnose the tumor of subcutaneous tissue accurately through palpation by fingertips.

As to the engineering and mechanical domain, Korves and Loftus [5] and Sly [6] imported VR technology to the outlay and planning of manufacturing system for factories. The system could more intuitively and efficiently use the computer digitalized virtual prototype. Through the simulated prototype, before the design of a product and the actual prototype or manufacturing system appears, the designer was able to experience and feel the performance of the future product or the status of the manufacturing system. Immediately, the designer could discover the mistakes and defects that were not considered in the process of product design, and then make amendments accordingly. Hence, more perspective decisions could be made, and more excellent implementation projects could be implemented to guarantee the quality and quantity of product.

Dewar et al. [7] indicated that in the process of product assembly, since it always involved such problems as product design and assembly, it had to rely on professional knowledge and the actual assembly by experienced experts so as to formulate standard assembly procedures. Therefore, in order to decrease effectively the time spent on the assembly procedures of product, VR technology is up to now a technology most frequently applied. As to the studies in this aspect, they mainly included two directions: one was undergone directly by using VR technology to assist assembly training [8–10]; and the other was the application of VR, together with the related technologies like CAD/CAM, etc., to preserve many significant concepts, procedures or experience in the assembly process by digitalized (visualized) or formalized ways (steps) [11–13]. There was one thing worthy of mentioning that the visual assembly design environment (VADE) system developed by Jayaram et al. [14] emphasized the integration of VADE and CAD system. On the one hand, VADE information was acquired from CAD system; and on the other, the design performed by VADE or assembly information could be transmitted back to CAD system for further application. At the same time, after VADE system was added with detection of collision and simulation of physical nature, the application area of VR technology was tremendously enlarged.

Regarding VR instruction and training, the related application and research are very extensive. There were studies on the benefits of haptic feedback in virtual reality environment in terms of the shortening of completion time and the improvement of perceptual motor capabilities of human operator [15,16]. Wu Y. L. et al. [17] established a virtual network laboratory. Students can do physical experiment in the virtual laboratory on the internet. The laboratory can protect students from encountering possible danger when doing physical experiments. Eder Arroyo et al. [18] established a virtual control and operation system of apparatuses, providing staff with the training on control and operation procedures of the apparatuses and equipments in factory, and assisting staff in becoming competent for their jobs within a short period of time. Lei Li et al. [19] proposed an immersive virtual reality system called ERT-VR, in which the instructors assigned a specific training scenario to the trainees by using the scenario creator. Trainees took on the role of the characters in the training scenario, and controlled their actions and ultimately the scenario outcome.

Lathe machine is one of the working machines with the widest range of usage in machinery factories, and lathe works are also the basic skill for their workers. Lathe works use cutter to machining raw material to form the shapes of facing, external turning, internal turning, knurling, grooving, drilling, taper turning, contour turning, threading, etc. Therefore, this paper firstly uses VR application software to integrate the 3D models of lathe machines. After that, through step-by-step use of function nodes provided by EON studio software, the operation features for the driving function of each operating handwheel of lathe machine are constructed. At the same time through the connection with external program, it is available to simulate the virtual machining actions. In this way, users are able to learn the operation of lathe machine in the simulated environment. After they have accumulated their learning experience, they can apply it in the real environment, thus decreasing the damage of mechanical operation, and saving the time for education and training.

DEVELOPMENT OF VIRTUAL LATHE MACHINE

This paper mainly applies the combination of VR technology and 3D solid model to simulate the virtual operation of the practical operating process of lathe machine, and virtual machining operation of the lathe works. The simulation reduces the worker' fear aroused when facing the large-sized machine in the learning process of lathe works. It not only improves the learning effects of workers, but also decreases the damage of machine caused by the wrong operation of workers for their unfamiliarity or nervousness. The main task of this section includes:

- Construction of 3D models of virtual lathe machine;
- Development of the virtual operation platform of lathe machine.

Construction of 3D Models of Virtual Lathe Machine

The paper adopts Pro/Engineer software, which has the characteristics of 3D solid model, single database, feature-based design and parametric design, as the operation tool for establishing the 3D model of the various parts of lathe machine and for setting the relationship among their mutual positions. Therefore, besides the main fixed bed the 3D model required to be constructed still needs to Figure 2. build up the components of transmitting mechanism, such as the axle, variable-speed mechanism, auto-feed mechanism, machining feed bench, tool post, power clutch, and tailstock assembly and dead center, etc. As shown in Figure 1.

Principles for Establishment of Virtual Operation Platform of Lathe Machine

To the entire lathe machine, the overall operation functions are: 1) Operation for the action of tool change of tool post; 2) Automatic and manual operation for longitudinal/transverse feed control; 3) Control of CW and CCW rotation of axle, operation of braking, and simulation of its axle rotation inertia. Here using (1) Operation for the action of tool changes of tool post function as example to explain its construction process.

Principles for Action Control of Tool Change of Tool Post

1) Requirements of system

- When carriage clamping lever is locked, there is a position limit of locking;
- Only when carriage clamping lever is at loosening position, the tool change of tool post can be implemented.
- Tool post should be able to rotate in CW and CCW direction, and there is no position limit.

The tool change of tool post mechanism is shown in Figure 2.

2) Principles of construction

- Initial condition is carriage clamping lever to be in sensing status, and transmit its orientation into orientation judgment program;
- When carriage clamping lever is active (mouse left button or mouse right button be clicked), then carriage clamping lever rotate in CW or CCW direction, and transmit action signal into orientation judgment program;
- To judge whether carriage clamping lever is situated at the position of locked limit by means of orientation judgment program;
- If carriage clamping lever has been at the locked position, it is required to disable the sensing of both the right button of carriage clamping lever and tool post rotation;
- If carriage clamping lever has been deviated from the locked position, it is required to active the sensing of both the right button of carriage clamping lever and tool post rotation.

The flow chart of tool change of tool post control as shown in Figure 3.

3) Software construction techniques

- Use the right (left) button sensing of "ClickSensor" function node (symbol of "tool post open" ("tool post lock") icon depicted in Figure 4) to detect whether the mouse right (left) button be clicked on the object of carriage clamping lever or not;

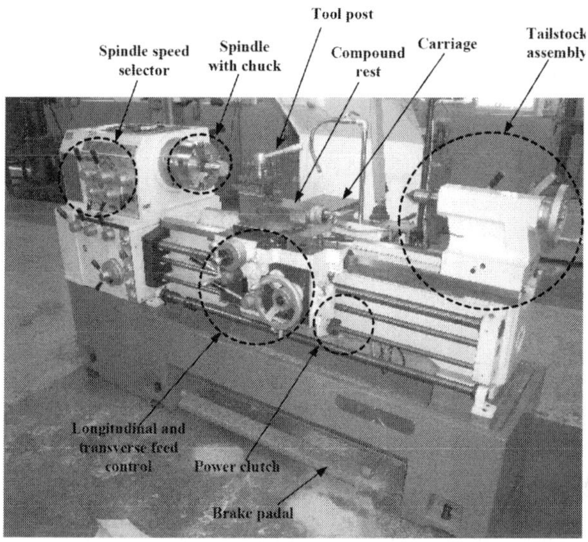

Figure 1: Lathe machine (WH 1000G-Win Ho Technology Industrial Co., Ltd. Manufacturing).

- Use the "Place" function node (symbol of "tool post open act" ("tool post lock act") icon depicted in Figure 4) to control the object of carriage clamping lever action. i.e. when the mouse right (left) button be clicked on the object of carriage clamping lever, the "ClickSensor" function node will receive the "OnButtonDownTrue" signal, and then it will send out the "SetRun" signal (as the Table 1 listed) to drive the object of carriage clamping lever action;
- Use the "Frame" function node (symbol of "tool post handle-1" icon depicted in Figure 4) to transmit the object of carriage clamping lever's orientation ("World Orientation" as the Table 1 listed) into orientation judgment program (symbol of "Script" icon depicted in Figure 4);
- To judge whether carriage clamping lever is situated at the position of locked limit by means of orientation judgment program (as the Figure 5 depicted);
- If carriage clamping lever has been at the locked position, the orientation judgment program will send out the "statussign" and "statussign1" (as the Table 1 listed) signals to "Place" function node (symbol of "tool post left turn" and "tool post right turn"

icons depicted in Figure 4).

At this time, the value of "statussign" and "statussign1" signals both are "0", in other words, it will disable the action of "Place" function node, and then the object of tool post can not rotate;

- In contrast, if carriage clamping lever has been at the loosened position, the orientation judgment program will send out the signal value "1" to the "Place" function node, that is say, it will active the "Place" function node, and then the object of tool post can rotate in CW and CCW direction.

The control process and script function of orientation judgment program of tool change of tool post as shown in Figures 4–5, and their interactive relationship between each function nodes are listed in Table 1.

Requirements for Automatic and Manual Operation of Longitudinal/Transverse Feed Control

Requirements of system:

- The longitudinal/transverse feed selection lever should possess the functions of upper/lower limit position, and central neutral position.
- When the longitudinal/transverse feed selection lever is situated at the central neutral position, it can be used for longitudinal and transverse manual feed operation.
- During the CCW (CW) rotation of axle, and when the longitudinal/transverse feed selection lever is situated at the lower limit position, then after the automatic feed control lever is pulled down and geared, the apron shall implement automatic feed movement towards (staying away from) the chuck direction.
- During the CCW (CW) rotation of axle, and when the longitudinal/transverse feed selection lever is situated at the upper limit position, then after the automatic feed control lever is pulled down and geared, the carriage shall implement automatic feed movement staying away from (towards) the worker direction.
- When implementing longitudinal or transverse automatic feed process, if the automatic feed control lever is pulled back to manual position, the apron or carriage shall immediately stop the feeding movement.

The longitudinal and transverse feed control mechanism is shown in Figure 6.

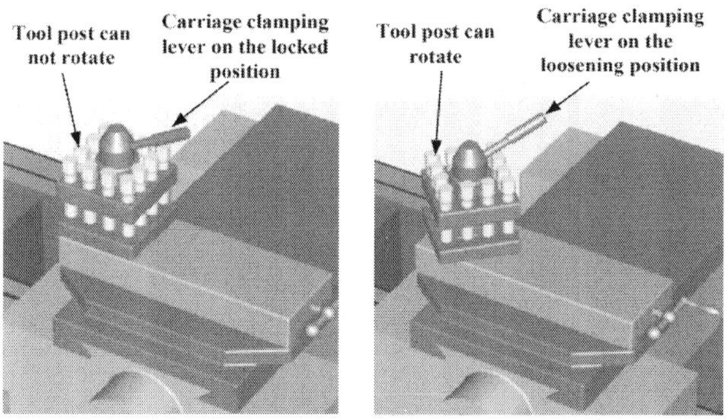

Figure 2: Tool change of tool post mechanis.

Table 1: The software control skill of tool change of tool post

Output node	Output signal	Receive node	Receive signal	comment
Tool post handle 「Frame」	WorldOrientation	Script 「Script」	posvalue	
Tool post left 「ClickSensor」	OnButtonDownTrue	Script 「Script」	Mousein1	
Tool post right 「ClickSensor」	OnButtonDownTrue	Script 「Script」	Mousein	Recording and judging the carriage clamping lever orientation
Script 「Script」	statussign	Tool post left turn 「Place」	SetRun	
Script 「Script」	Statussign1	Tool post right turn 「Place」	SetRun	

Principles of Control for CW and CCW Rotation and Inertia Action of Axle

Requirements of system:

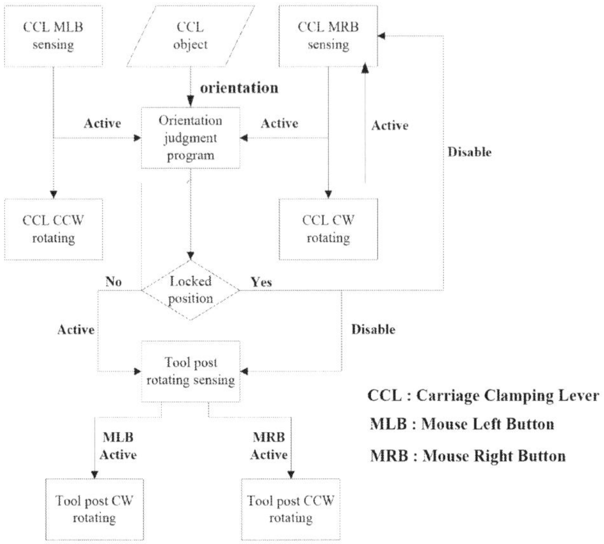

Figure 3: Flow chart of tool change of tool post control.

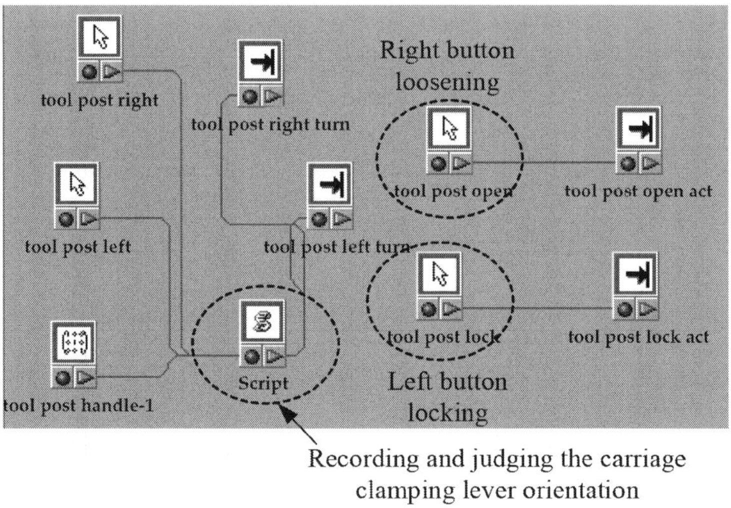

Figure 4: Control process of tool change of tool post.

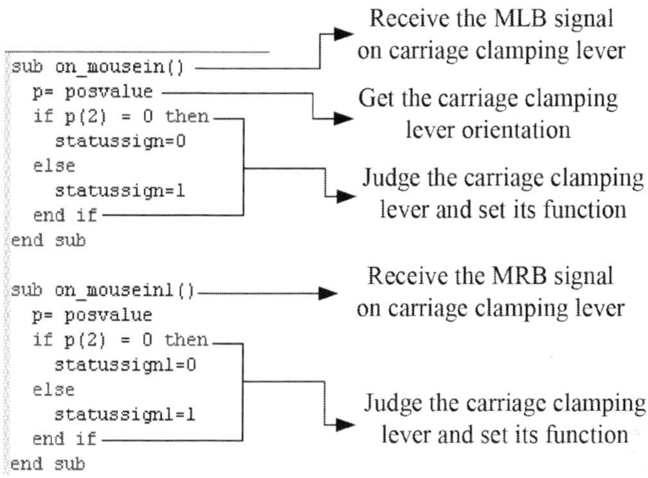

Figure 5: Script function of orientation judgment program.

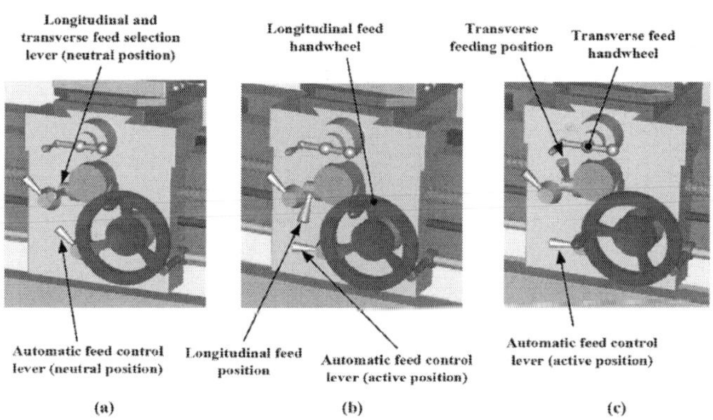

Figure 6: Longitudinal and transverse feed control mechanism.

- Power clutch has to possess the function of being at upper/lower limit position;
- When power clutch is at the upper (lower) limit position, the axle rotates in CW (CCW) direction at specified speed;

After the axle is turned on, when power clutch resumes to the neutral position, the axle gradually stops rotating at a constantly decreasing speed;

- When the brake pedal is stepped down, the axle has to be able to stop rotating immediately. Meanwhile, the brake pedal should be able to resume to the original position actively.

The axle rotating control with power clutch mechanism is shown in Figure 7.

PRINCIPLES FOR ESTABLISHMENT OF VIRTUAL MACHINING PLATFORM

To the entire lathe works, the overall operation functions are:

- External straight turning;
- Internal straight turning;
- Facing;
- Necking;
- External threading;
- Taper turning.

Simulated Theorem of External Straight Turning

We utilize an assembly operation of outer-annular hollow part and solid mandrel workpiece to simulate unmachined raw material and at the same time, we adjust the scaled rotation origin "O" of outer-annular hollow part to its left-sided shaft center shown in Figure 8. While simulating cutting operation, if the collision occurs between the cutter and the outer-annular hollow part, it triggers the outer-annular hollow part to induce scaled operation and the scale proportion, i.e., $SCALE_{external}$ along the X direction can be expressed as the follows.

$$SCALE_{external} = \frac{L - tv}{L - (t-1)v} \qquad t = 1, 2, 3 \tag{1}$$

L denotes the original length of outer-annular hollow part, v is the cutting speed along the X direction, and t is the time to be a unit of second.

Simulated Theorem of Internal Straight Turning

We utilize an assembly operation of outer-annular hollow part and solid mandrel workpiece to simulate unmachined raw material and at the same time, we adjust the scaled rotation origin "O" of outer-annular hollow part to itsleft-sided shaft center shown in Figure 9. While simulating cutting operation, if the collision occurs between the cutter and the solid mandrel workpiece, it triggers the solid mandrel workpiece to induce scaled operation and the scale proportion, i.e., $SCALE_{inner}$ along the X direction can be expressed as the follows.

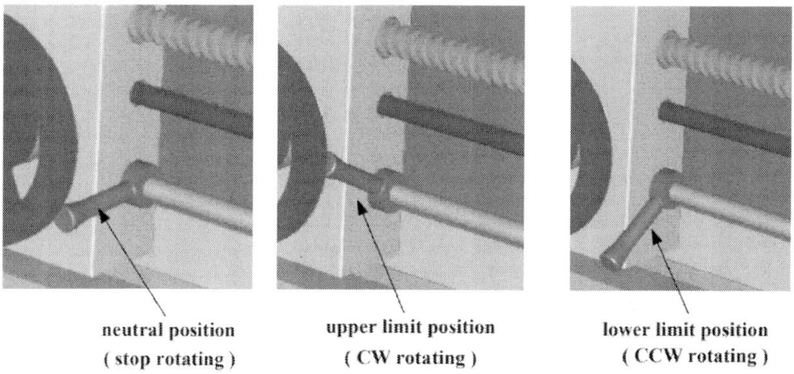

Figure 7: Axle rotating control with power clutch mechanism.

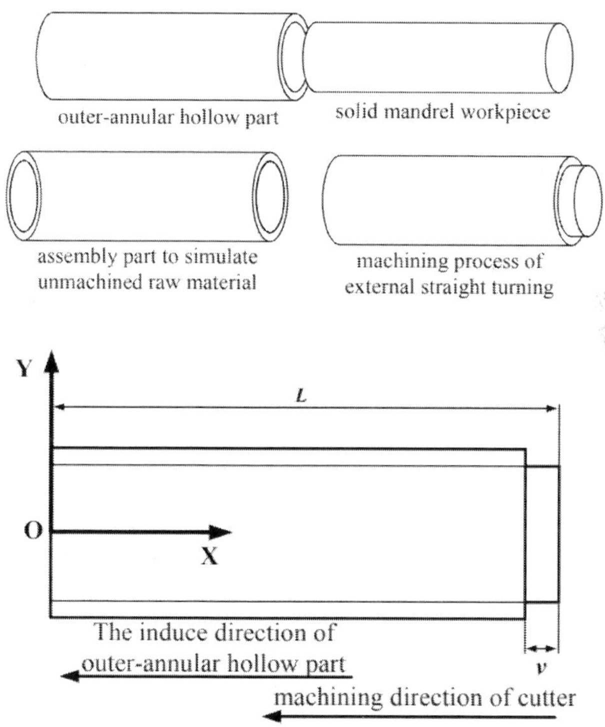

Figure 8: Simulated theorem of external straight turning.

$$SCALE_{inner} = \frac{L - tv}{L - (t-1)v} \qquad t = 1,\ 2,\ 3 \tag{2}$$

L denotes the original length of outer-annular hollow part, v is the cutting speed along the X direction, and t is the time to be a unit of second.

Simulated Theorem of Facing

We utilize an assembly operation of finished part and solid cutting-ring workpiece to simulate unmachined raw material and at the same time, we adjust the scaled rotation origin "O" of solid cutting-ring workpiece to its left-sided shaft center shown in Figure 10. While simulating cutting operation, if the collision occurs between the cutter and solid cutting-ring workpiece, it triggers the solid cutting-ring workpiece to induce scaled operation and the scale proportion, i.e., $SCALE_{face}$ along the YZ plane di- rection can be expressed as the follows.

$$SCALE_{face} = \frac{D-2tv}{D[1+2(t-1)v]} \quad t = 1, 2, 3 \tag{3}$$

D denotes the original diameter of solid cutting-ring workpiece, v is the cutting speed along the Z direction, and t is the time to be a unit of second.

Simulated Theorem of Necking

As the facing simulation, we also utilize an assembly operation of finished part and solid cutting-ring workpiece to simulate unmachined raw material and at the same time, we adjust the scaled rotation origin "O" of solid cutting-ring workpiece to its left-sided shaft center shown in Figure 11. While simulating cutting operation, if the collision occurs between the cutter and solid cutting-ring workpiece, it triggers the solid cutting-ring workpiece to induce scaled operation and the scale proportion, i.e., $SCALE_{groove}$ along the YZ plane direction can be expressed as the follows.

$$SCALE_{groove} = \frac{D-2tv}{D[1+2(t-1)v]} \quad t = 1, 2, 3 \tag{4}$$

D denotes the original diameter of solid cutting-ring workpiece, v is the cutting speed along the Z direction, and t is the time to be a unit of second.

Simulated Theorem of External Threading

As the external straight turning simulation, we also utilize an assembly operation of cutting workpiece and finish part to simulate unmachined raw material and at the same time, we adjust the scaled rotation origin "O" of cutting workpiece to its left-sided shaft center shown in Figure 12.

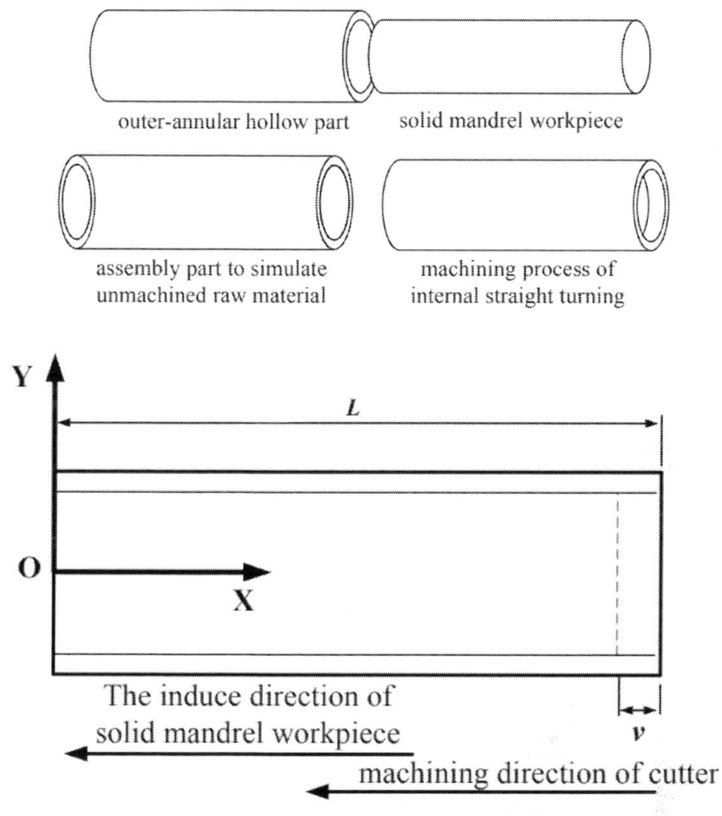

Figure 9: Simulated theorem of internal straight turning.

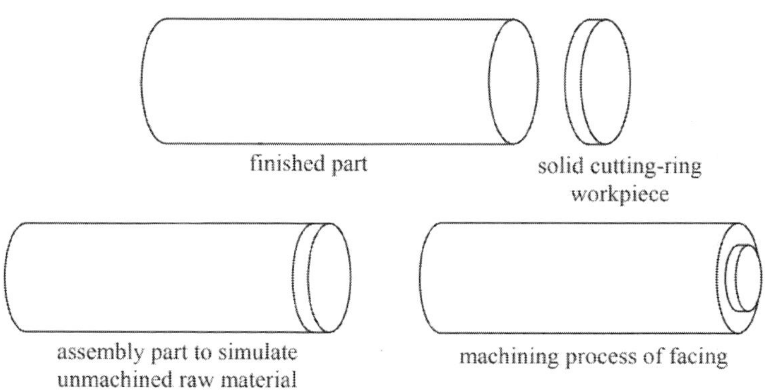

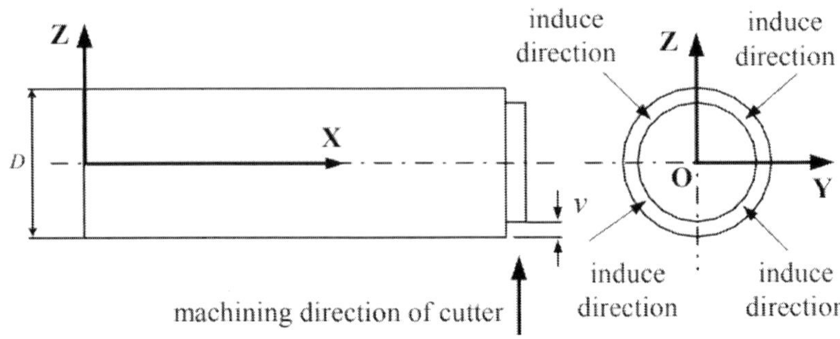

Figure 10: Simulated theorem of facing.

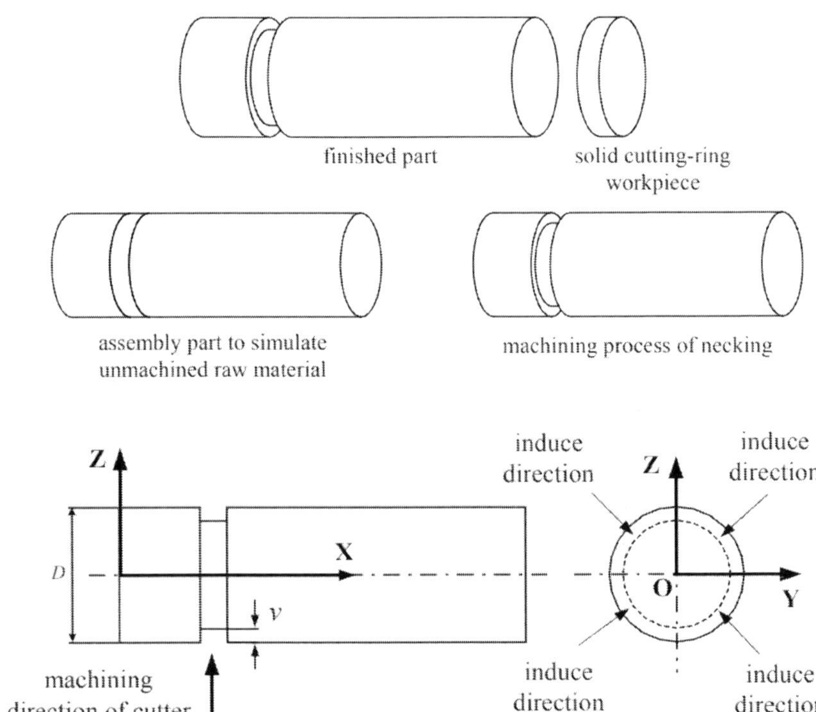

Figure 11: Simulated theorem of necking.

While simulating cutting operation, if the collision occurs between the cutter and the cutting workpiece, it triggers the cutting workpiece to induce scaled operation and the scale proportion, i.e., $SCALE_{thread}$ along the X direction can be expressed as the follows.

$$SCALE_{thread} = \frac{L - tv}{L - (t-1)v} \quad t = 1, 2, 3 \tag{5}$$

L denotes the original length of outer-annular hollow part, v is the cutting speed along the X direction, and t is the time to be a unit of second.

Simulated Theorem of External Taper Turning

As the external straight turning simulation, we also utilize an assembly operation of outer-annular hollow part andfinish part to simulate unmachined raw material and at the same time, we adjust the scaled rotation origin "O" of outer-annular hollow part to its left-sided shaft center shown in Figure 13. While simulating cutting operation, if the collision occurs between the cutter and the outer-annular hollow part, it triggers the outer-annular hollow part to induce scaled operation and the scale proportion, i.e., $SCALE_{taper}$ along the X direction can be expressed as the follows.

$$SCALE_{taper} = \frac{L - tv\cos(\tan^{-1}(\frac{D-d}{2L}))}{L - (t-1)v\cos(\tan^{-1}(\frac{D-d}{2L}))} \quad t = 1, 2, 3 \tag{6}$$

D denotes large diameter, d is small diameter, L is the length of taper, v is the cutting speed along the X direction, and t is the time to be a unit of second.

Constructed Technique of Virtual Machining System

This paper utilizes the reducible feature and mutual collision detection functions of function node, and then by means of programmable function to carry out the induced proportion, to achieve the virtual machining simulation. Here uses the external straight turning as example to show the constructed technique of virtual cutting system.

1) Requirements of system

- When "S" key has been pushed down, the cutter shall implement automatic feed movement towards the part;
- When the cutter collided with the outer-annular hollow part, the length of outer-annular hollow part must be induced, and the induced speed is the same as cutter moving feed.

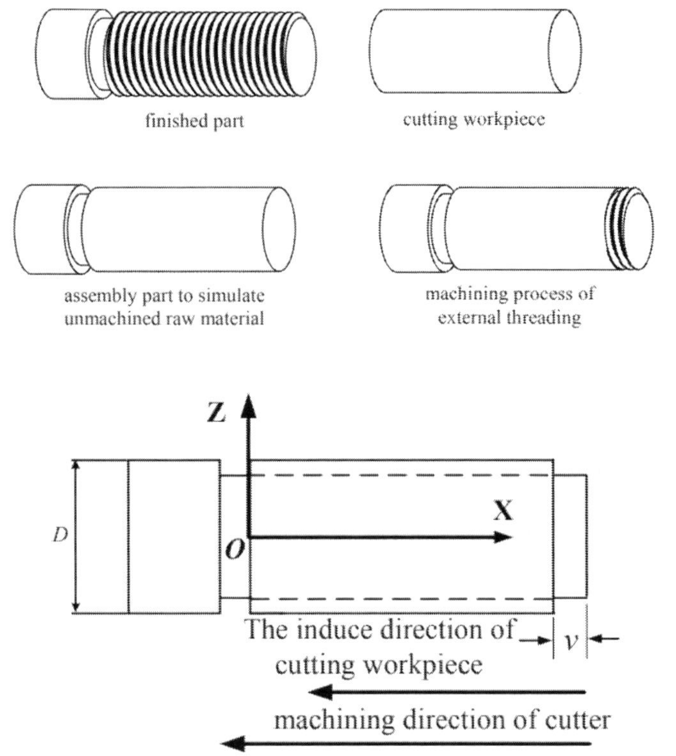

Figure 12: Simulated theorem of external threading.

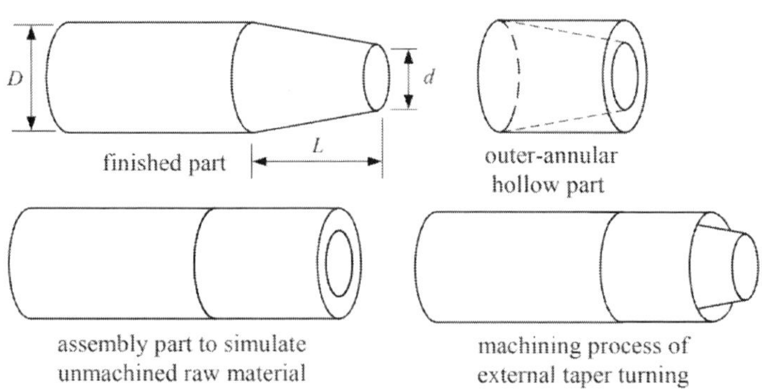

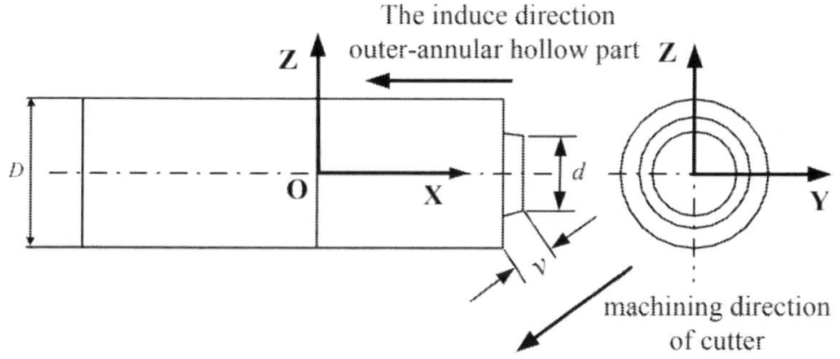

Figure 13: Simulated theorem of external taper turning.

2) Constructed technique of software

- Use the "ClickSensor" function node to detect the condition that whether "S" key has been pushed down or not;
- Use the "Place" function node to control the cutter moving feed.
- Use "Script" function node to receive, record, judge and output the induced proportion of length of outer-annular hollow part, so as to control the induced speed is the same as cutter moving feed.

The model tree, routes, and parameters of script node are shown in Figure 14.

PRACTICAL OPERATION CASES

This paper makes a comparison between the situations before and after the operating process of the overall transmitting control function and machining function of lathe works, and takes it as an implementation example of virtual lathe machine operating and machining for lathe works.

Figure 15 shows the virtual lathe machine platform for this paper. Figure 16 presents the results after the forward and backward movements of apron caused in the longitudinal feed operating process. Figure 17 shows the results after the forward and backward movements of carriage caused in the transverse feed operating process. Figure 18 shows the results after the forward and backward movements of compound rest caused in compound rest operating process. Figure 19 presents the initial and results during external straight turning process. Figure 20 shows the initial and results during internal straight turning process. Figure 21 shows the initial and results during facing process. Figure 22 shows the initial and results during necking process. Figure 23 shows the initial and results during external threading process. Figure 24 shows the initial and results during external taper turning process.

CONCLUSIONS AND RESULTS

The paper integrates virtual reality technology with the application of 3D solid model to complete a virtual operation platform based on the transmitting principles of lathe machine during practical operation. At the same time, the paper has completed the virtual machining for various lathe works. Users are able to learn in the simulated environment without scruple, increasing the effects of training. After the accumulation of learning experience, it can be applied by users in the actual environment to accomplish the mission of operation.

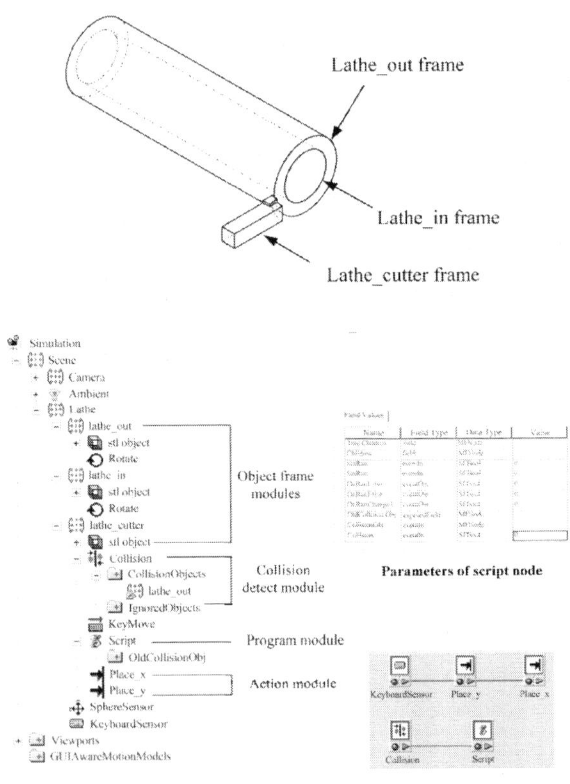

Figure 14: Relative data.

Figure 15: Virtual lathe machine.

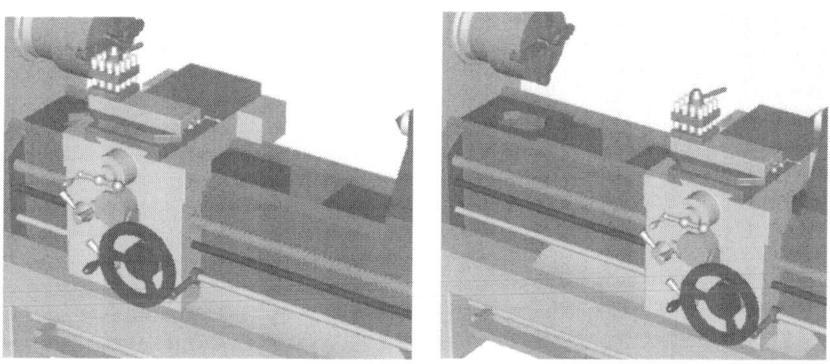

Figure 16: Longitudinal feed operating process.

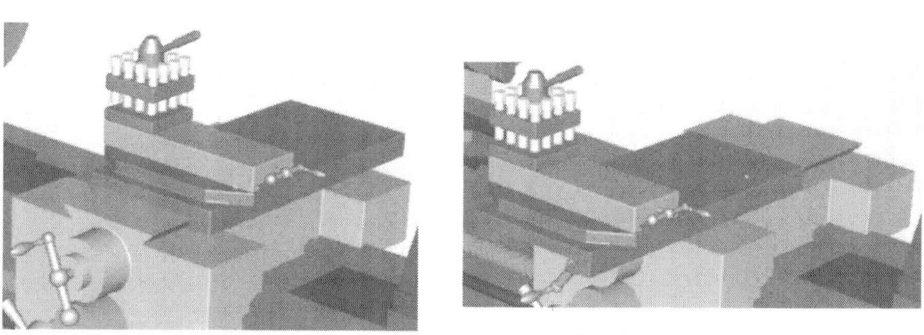

Figure 17: Transverse feed operating process.

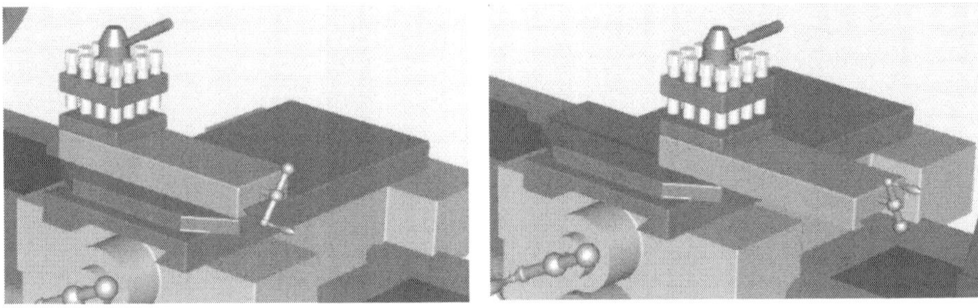

Compound rest forward moving **Compound rest backward moving**

Figure 18: Compound rest operating process.

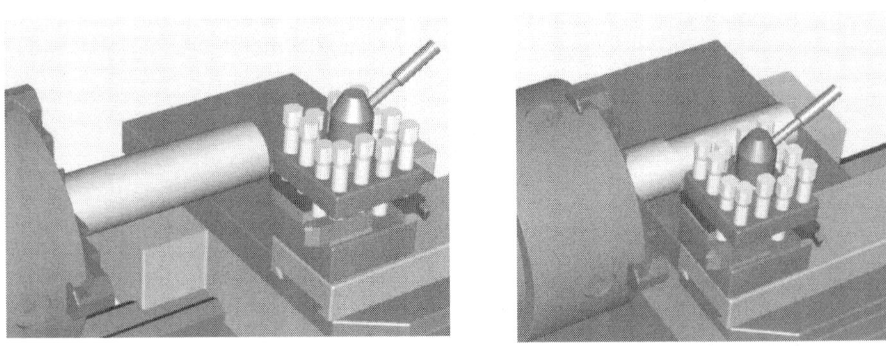

(a) Initial condition **(b) During external straight turning process**

Figure 19: External straight turning process.

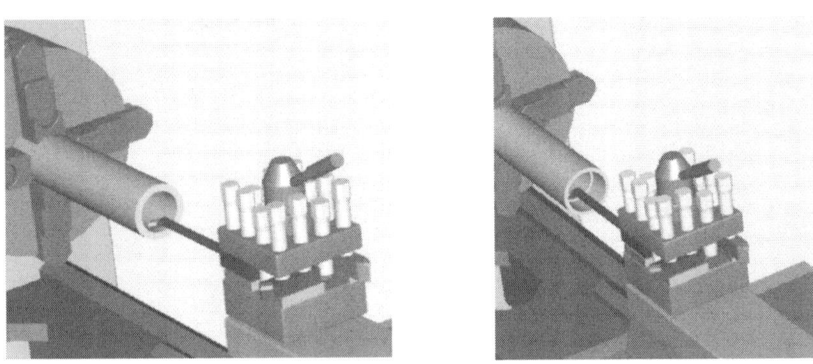

(a) Initial condition **(b) During internal straight turning process**

Figure 20: Internal straight turning process.

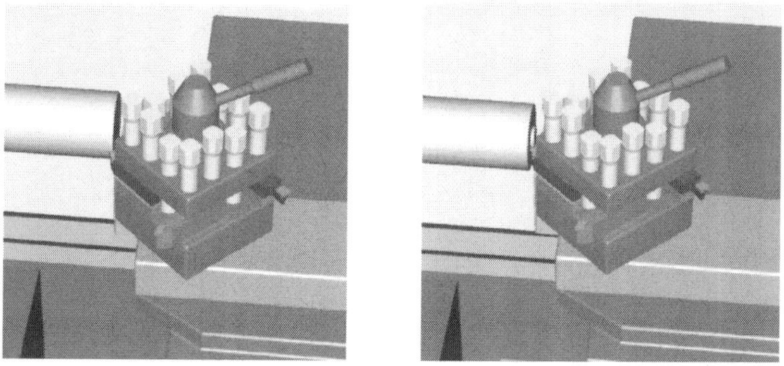

(a) Initial condition (b) During facing process

Figure 21: Facing process.

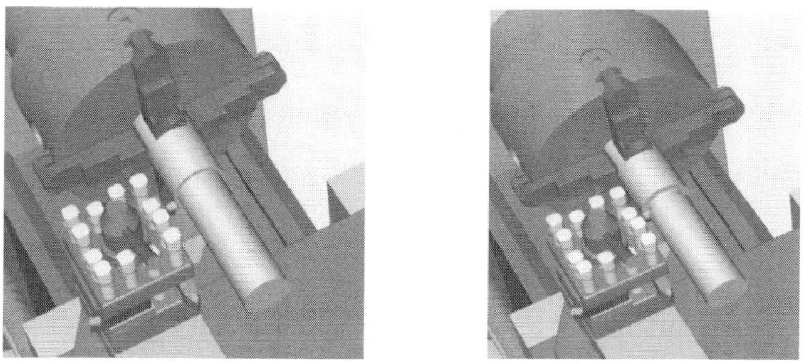

(a) Initial condition (b) During necking process

Figure 22: Necking process.

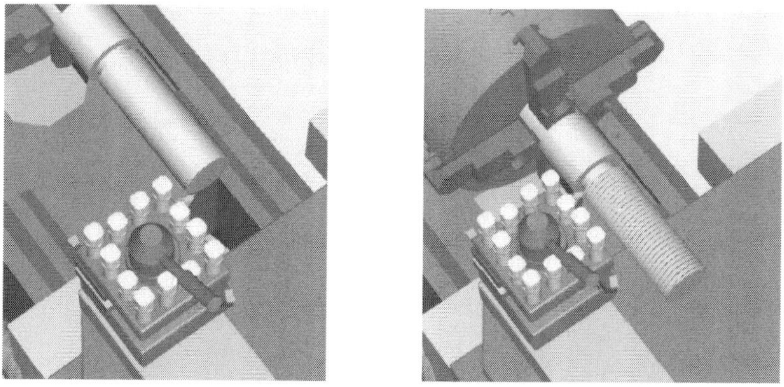

(a) Initial condition (b) During external threading process

Figure 23: External threading process.

(a) Initial condition

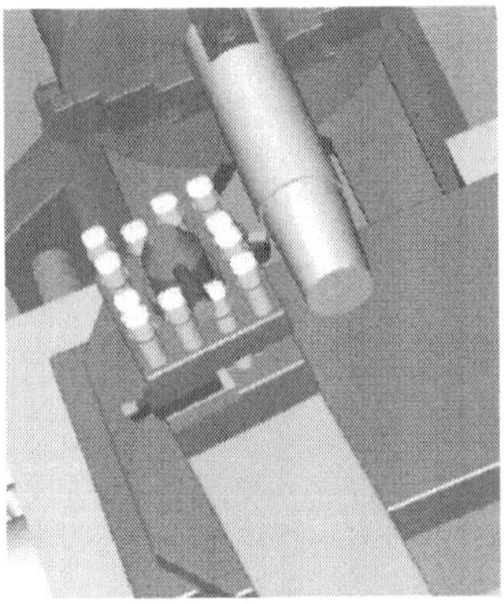

(b) During external taper turning process

Figure 24: External taper turning process.

ACKNOWLEDGEMENTS

It is gratefully acknowledged that this research was supported by the National Science Council under contract No. NSC 95-2520-S-237-001.

REFERENCES

1. M. Tavakoli, R. V. Patel, and M. Moallem, "A haptic interface for computer-integrated endoscopic surgery and training," Virtual Reality, Vol. 9, No. 2–3, pp. 160–176, 2006.
2. E. Chen and B. Marcus, "Force feedback for surgical simulation," Proceedings of the IEEE, Vol. 86, No. 3, pp. 524–530, 1998.
3. C. G. Shoaw, "The simulation system of virtual reality of intravenous injection," Master Thesis, National Central University, 2001.
4. M. Dinsmore, N. Langrana, G. Burdea, and J. Ladeji, "Virtual reality training simulation for palpation of subsurface tumors," Proceedings of the 1997 Virtual Reality Annual International Symposium, Albuquerque, pp. 54–60, 1–5 March 1997.
5. B. Korves and M. Loftus, "The application of immersive virtual reality for layout planning of manufacturing cells," Proceedings of the Institution of Mechanical Engineers, Part B: Journal of Engineering Manufacture, Vol. 213, No. 1, pp. 87–91, 1999.
6. D. P. Sly, "A systematic approach to factory layout and design with factoryplan, factoryopt, and factoryflow," Proceedings of the 28th conference on Winter simulation, San Diego, pp. 584–587, 8–11 December 1996.
7. R. G. Dewar, I. D. Carpenter, J. M. Ritchie, and J. E. Simmons, "Assembly planning in a virtual environment," Proceedings of Portland International Center for Management of Engineering and Technology, Portland, 27–31 July 1997.
8. J. E. Brough, M. Schwartz, S. K. Gupta, D. K. Anand, R. Kavetsky, and R. Pettersen, "Towards the development of a virtual environment-based training system for mechanical assembly operations," Virtual Reality, Vol. 11, pp. 189–206, 2007.
9. A. C. Boud, D. J. Haniff, C. Baber, and S. J. Steiner, "Virtual reality and augmented reality as a training tool for assembly tasks," 3rd International Conference on Information Visualization, London, pp. 32–36, 14–16 July 1999.
10. S. Feiner, B. MacIntyre, and D. Seligmann, "Knowledge based augmented reality," Communications of the ACM, Vol. 36, No. 7, pp. 53–62, 1993.
11. M. Billinghurst, S. Weghorts, and T. Furness, "Shared space: An augmented reality approach for computer support collaborative work,"

Virtual Reality, Vol. 3, pp. 25–26, 1998.

12. N. Ye, P. Banerjee, A. Banerjee, and F. Dech, "A comparative study of assembly planning in traditional and virtual environments," IEEE Transactions on System, Man and Cybernetics, Part C: Application and Reviews, Vol. 29, No. 4, pp. 546–555, 1999.
13. J. M. Ritchie, R. G. Dewar, and J. E. L. Simmons, "The generation and practical use of plans for manual assembly using immersive virtual reality," Proceedings of the Institution of Mechanical Engineers, Part B: Journal of Engineering Manufacture, Vol. 213, No. 5, pp. 461–474, 1999.
14. S. Jayaram, U. Jayaram, Y. Wang, H. Tirumali, K. Lyons, and P. Hart, "VADE: A virtual assembly design environment," IEEE Computer Graphic and Application, Vol. 19, No. 6, pp. 44–50, 1999.
15. R. Gupta, T. Sheridan, and D. Whitney, "Experiments using multi-modal virtual environments in design for assembly analysis," Presence: Teleoperators and Virtual Environments, Vol. 6, No. 3, pp. 318–338, 1997.
16. Y. Hurmuzlu, A. Ephanov, and D. Stoianovici, "Effect of a pneumatically driven haptic interface on the perceptional capabilities of human operators," Presence: Teleoperators and Virtual Environments, Vol. 7, No. 3, pp. 290–307, 1998.
17. Y. L. Wu, T. Chan, B. S. Jong, C. Yuan, and T. W. Lin, "A web-based virtual reality physics laboratory," Proceedings of the 3rd IEEE International Conference on Advanced Learning Technologies, Athens, 9–11 July 2003.
18. E. Arroyo and J. Luis, "SRV: A virtual reality application to electrical substations operation training," IEEE International Conference on Multimedia Computing and System, Vol. 1, 7–11 June 1999.
19. L. Li, M. J. Zhang, F. J. Xu, and S. H. Liu, "ERT-VR: An immersive virtual reality system for emergency rescue training," Virtual Reality, Vol. 8, pp. 194–197, 2005.

SECTION III - MEDICAL APPLICATIONS OF THE VR

Chapter 9

Virtual Reality Surgical Training in Ear, Nose and Throat Surgery

Patorn Piromchai[1,2]

[1]Department of Otolaryngology, Royal Victorian Eye and Ear Hospital, University of Melbourne, East Melbourne, Australia

[2]Department of Otorhinolaryngology, Faculty of Medicine, Khon Kaen University, Khon Kaen, Thailand

ABSTRACT

Virtual reality has been introduced to the medical field and it is now used in medical education as an alternative high fidelity simulator. The major components to successful learning that has contributed to the efficacy of the virtual reality system are the ability to provide repetitive practice under controlled environment, self-directed learning and proved construct validity.

Citation: Piromchai, P. (2014) Virtual Reality Surgical Training in Ear, Nose and Throat Surgery. International Journal of Clinical Medicine, 5, 558-566.

This review evaluated the validity and the efficacy of current virtual reality systems in ear, nose and throat surgery.

Keywords: Virtual Reality, Otolaryngology, Surgery

INTRODUCTION

Virtual reality simulation uses computer-generated imagery to present a training environment. It aims to increase educational outcomes over traditional methodologies [1] , to enable surgical education to occur before entering theatre, and to provide a more flexible way to teach adult learners. Several potential roles have been identified for simulation in medical or surgical education, which include: 1) improved educational outcomes over traditional methodologies [1] ; 2) enabling surgical education to occur before entering the operating theatre; and 3) more flexible ways to teach adult learners. Kolb [2] has suggested that knowledge is created through experience. By simulating scenarios for students, experience can be imparted to facilitate learning [3] . Simulations allow scenarios to be conducted in an arena where failure is allowed, and students can learn from these mistakes without causing harm to the actual patients [4] . This capacity to learn surgical procedures requires actual experience and a period of reflection to consolidate the students' understanding [5] , and an accumulation of surgical experience provides an increase in performance and confidence regardless if it is simulated or real [6] .

In current ear, nose and throat residency surgical training programs, residents learn by observing their mentors and practicing under their supervision. For the safety of the patients, the mentors have to ensure that residents have the capability to practice on patients prior to the surgery. Many ear, nose and throat simulator training courses were developed to facilitate the learning process for the residents. These courses range from low fidelity (e.g. rubber model for suture practice) to high fidelity (e.g. temporal bone dissection).

Many studies have found that virtual reality simulators improved trainees' operative performance. The major components to successful learning that has contributed to the efficacy of the virtual reality system are the ability to provide repetitive practice under controlled environment, self-directed learning and proved construct validity. In the early stages of learning, the simulator can be used to augment conventional training methods such as anatomical understanding, disease pathology and treatment. For the later stages of learning that require the use of clinical skills, simulators are proved to be better than conventional training techniques [7] [8] . Virtual reality simulation has been shown to improve cadaveric temporal bone dissection compared to traditional teaching methods [7] [9] . The capacity of virtual reality simulators to provide self-directed learning allows teaching to occur outside and alongside operative hours, making learning more flexible for both trainers and trainees [10] [11] .

The purpose of this review was to evaluate the validity and the efficacy of current virtual reality systems in ear, nose and throat surgery.

VIRTUAL REALITY IN EAR SURGERY

Temporal Bone Dissection

Cadaveric temporal bone dissection is the main activity for residents that is used as simulation training for temporal bone surgery. Most temporal bone surgical dissection courses provide training on the principles of temporal bone and skull base surgery for practicing surgeons. The course usually emphasizes the common procedures for ear diseases. Mastoidectomy is one of the common procedures that the residents need to familiarize themselves with and have the confidence to practice without causing harm to the patient. However, there are a few setbacks associated with cadaveric dissection training. For example, the reduction in the availability of cadavers as caused by the Alder Hey controversy, together with an increased number of residency training positions, the bones have to be discarded after drilling and cannot be reused. Another concern is that illnesses may be transmitted through contact with diseased tissues and/or bodily fluids.

Many authors have addressed these problems and proposed the use of alternative simulators that can replace or augment training for cadaveric temporal bone dissection. Some authors have developed bony models to practice temporal bone dissection surgery [12] , but the majority prefers to use virtual reality systems. Beside of temporal bone dissection simulators, some authors have also developed the middle ear surgery simulator for myringotomy [13] [14] and benign paroxysmal positional vertigo treatment [15] .

Current Systems

The VOXEL-MAN Tempo Surgery Simulator is the first commercially available temporal bone virtual reality simulator [16] . Volumetric high-resolution computed tomography images of the temporal bone are used to produce a 3-dimensional representation. The surgical site is displayed in stereoscopic mode, which the user views through shutter glasses. Vital structures are color-coded. The station houses a computer with software that is linked to a force-feedback hand stylus. This stylus serves as a virtual drill, which is activated by the foot pedal to alter the appearance of the virtual temporal bone. The drill responds with forces according to the contact situation visible on screen, allowing the user to experience changes in pressure. The computer records its location, direction in space, and a number of performance measures such as excessive force or injuries relating to vital structures. The user is able to alter the surgical orientation, drill size, type, and rotation speed.

Another commercial model of temporal bone dissection simulator is the Mediseus Surgical Simulator (CSIRO/University of Melbourne Temporal Bone Simulator). This simulator consists of a simulated operating microscope. The user interacts with a 3-D volumetric virtual rendering of a cadaver temporal bone, which is controlled by the surgeon using two haptic motorized 3-D pointing devices. These devices allow the computer to track the exact movement of the tool relative to the virtual bone model. The bone model was given color and hardness properties to provide visual and tactile cues that helped to simulate real operating conditions. The coloring of the bone also changes as the bone is progressively thinned over the critical structures such as the sigmoid sinus, dura, and facial nerve. Physiological functions, such as bleeding from the sigmoid sinus and facial nerve monitoring with auditory and visual feedback were also built into the simulator [9] .

Many ear surgery simulators are currently under development [17] -[20] . They mostly share common features of haptic feedback. Some of them also work with acoustic feedback (Table 1).

Efficacy of Simulator on Skills Improvement

The VOXEL-MAN Tempo Surgery Simulator trial [21] conducted a before-after investigation and found that some surgical skills that were evaluated based on the Objective Structured Assessment of Technical Skills (OSATS) rubric experienced a significant improvement after practices were conducted by using the VR temporal bone simulator system. The OSAT scores were improved for both tegmen task from 2.125 to 3.1 ($P = 0.026$) and sigmoid task from 2 to 2.75 (P = 0.0098). The time to complete the tasks also decreased from 8.37 to 5.39 minutes (P = 0.018) for tegmen task and from 8.99 to 8.68 minutes (P = 0.594) for sigmoid task.

The Mediseus Surgical Simulator did further research on the improvement in the users' skills by conducting controlled trials comparing the simulator training with the conventional textbook based training and found that the participants trained on the simulator performed significantly better than the participants trained using conventional training methods [7] [8] . The experts were invited to review the participant's task through a sequence of actions (procedural score). They found that the virtual reality group was performed better than conventional training group (Table 2).

In additional to procedural skill evaluation, the authors [7] [8] also inspected the dissection results by evaluating the end-product temporal bones. The end-product score represents the combination of anatomical knowledge, procedural skill and psychomotor behavior. They found that the virtual reality group performed better than conventional training group but there was no statistically significance difference (Table 3).

The virtual simulation for temporal bone dissection [22] [23] also conducted a controlled trial comparing the virtual reality temporal bone dissection training simulator with the temporal bone dissection training. Two studies involving 92 participants used the 35-item Welling scale to determine end-product scores for the virtual reality group and cadaveric temporal bone dissection training group. There was no statistically significance difference between virtual reality group and cadaveric temporal bone dissection training group (Table 4).

The results from these studies showed that the virtual reality temporal bone dissection training is more effective than traditional training methods and as effective as cadaveric temporal bones as assessed by summative end-product score.

Table 1: Virtual reality temporal bone dissection systems

Simulators	Characteristics	Validation	Efficacy
VOXEL-MAN Tempo Surgery	Stereoscopic display, haptic drill, foot pedal	Yes [16]	· Pre-post study · Significantly improved OSATs score
Mediseus surgical simulator	Stereoscopic display, haptic drill, haptic suction, auditory and visual feedback	Yes [9]	· RCTs · Significantly improved procedural score

Virtual simulation for temporal bone dissection	Stereoscopic display, haptic feedback	Yes [19]	· RCTs · Comparable to cadaveric temporal bone dissection training
Virtual surgical training system for middle ear surgery	Stereoscopic display, haptic feedback, visual feedback	Yes [17]	· Not available
Virtual reality temporal bone dissection simulator	Haptic feedback [18]	No	· Not available

Table 2: Comparing the procedural score of the Mediseus virtual reality temporal bone dissection training with conventional training

Studies	VR[a] Mean (S.D.)	Control Mean (S.D.)	Mean difference (95% CI)
Zhao 2011a [7]	3.54 (0.82)	2.51 (0.97)	1.03 (0.24 to 1.82)
Zhao 2011b [8]	3.56 (1.79)	2.97 (1.72)	0.59 (−0.95 to 2.13)

a. VR = virtual reality.

Table 3: Comparing end-product score of the Mediseus virtual reality temporal bone dissection training with conventional training

Studies	VR[a] Mean (S.D.)	Control Mean (S.D.)	Mean difference (95% CI)
Zhao 2011a [7]	2.79 (0.79)	1.98 (1.12)	0.81 (−0.04 to 1.66)
Zhao 2011b [8]	3.48 (1.87)	2.64 (1.46)	0.84 (−0.63 to 2.31)

a. VR = virtual reality.

Table 4: Comparing the end-product score of virtual reality temporal bone dissection training with temporal bone dissection training

Studies	VR[a] Mean (S.D.)	Control Mean (S.D.)	Mean difference (95% CI)
Wiet 2009 [22]	23 (8.6)	17 (8.5)	6.00 (−3.68 to 15.68)
Wiet 2012 [23]	2.2 (0.54)	2.14 (0.56)	0.06 (−0.21 to 0.33)

a. VR = virtual reality.

Myringotomy

Myringotomy is the most common pediatric surgery procedure [24] , which perforates the ear drum to equilibrate the pressure in the middle ear. This procedure can be conducted with or without the insertion of a tube. As there is a steep learning curve associated with the development of technical skills for middle ear surgery, there are inherent risks that patients have to face during the skills acquisition phase. The benefits of simulation training for acquiring surgical skills have also been demonstrated with previous low-fidelity models [13] .

Cadavers and physical models of the tympanic membranes in the ear are the most common methods to train otolaryngology trainees in performing this operation. Neither the cadaveric nor the physical models allow for automated metrics to quantify the progress of the trainees or provide any feedback. Tactile sensation is an important feedback mechanism in middle ear surgery, hence a three-dimensional virtual reality myringotomy simulator with haptic feedback was developed [14] .

A virtual reality myringotomy simulator was developed at the Auditory Biophysics Laboratory (ABL) at the University of Western Ontario (UWO) [25] . The system includes a standard 3-D gaming visor for display and a PHANTOM Omni haptic arm (SensAble Technologies, Woburn, MA) for user input and force feedback. The visor is mounted on a stand that simulates the surgical microscope. The haptic device controls a virtual blade in the scene and provides force feedback to the trainee if they collide with the ear canal, malleus, or promontory.

From the face-validation questionnaire, the virtual reality myringotomy simulator with the first to integrate a real-time deformable tympanic membrane appears to be validated for simulation. The Delaunay cutting algorithm was found to be the most realistic algorithm representing the incision during myringotomy ($P < 0.05$) [25] .

Benign Paroxysmal Positional Vertigo

Benign paroxysmal positional vertigo (BPPV) is the most common cause of dizziness that physicians usually encounter in out-patient department settings. BPPV is a clinical syndrome that is characterized by short bursts of severe vertigo associated with changes in head orientation. The treatments for this syndrome include canalith repositioning maneuver (Epley), the Brandt-Dar off exercise, and the liberatory maneuver of Semont.

Steiner et al. [15] scanned the human membranous labyrinth at a thickness of 20 μm and selected areas were segmented using the AMIRA® 4.1 program. The stereoscopic representation of the inner ear was positioned according to anatomic norms. Artificial spherical surfaces representing otoliths can be loaded in the labyrinth. The model allows a basic orientation for the novice surgeons as well as complex clinical hypothesis testing for the experts.

The current virtual reality system for BPPV demonstrated how the canalith was positioned in the larynrinth by rotating the 3-D model using the mouse. The next potential step is to incorporate the mannequin that the trainee can practice the canalith repositioning maneuver on and simultaneously demonstrate the position of the canalith in the labyrinth on screen.

Cochlear Implantation

Cochlear implantation inserts a cochlear prosthetic implant into the cochlea to stimulate the cochlear nerve for a patient experiencing a severe hearing impairment for mimicking the natural hearing function of the inner ear. The procedure includes a temporal bone drilling (mastoidectomy) to access the middle ear through the facial recess. The round window was identified before cochleostomy was done to access the basal turn of the cochlear. The surgeon then inserted the cochlear implant at full insertion depth. Connection tissue was placed around the cochleostomy site to seal it.

During the cochlear implant insertion, the implant disappears out of the surgeon's view soon after the initial advancement past the cochleostomy site, around the region of the basal turn. The surgeon then relies on a sense of touch for the rest of the insertion. Excess pressure after the first point of resistance may lead to induced trauma to the cochlear partition. Force feedback is required during this intricate process to minimize the risk of avoidable damage to the cochlea. Force rendering is therefore vital to accurately relay information associated with device/structure interactions for this surgical procedure.

Todd et al. [26] created a prototype simulator for prosthetic insertion. The simulator provides the ear, nose and throat surgeon with real-time visual and haptic responses during virtual cochlear implantation into a 3D model of the human scala tympani. The simulator provides the user with real-time, quantitative insertion force information and associated electrode positions as the user inserts the virtual implant into the model.

VIRTUAL REALITY IN NOSE SURGERY

Functional Endoscopic Sinus Surgery

While endoscopic sinus surgery is quickly becoming popular, external approaches for nasal surgery is reserved for more complicated cases. The endoscopic approach was introduced into the rhinology field not more than

30 years ago. The efficacy of this approach is similar to the external approach but is more desirable cosmetically. Endoscopic sinus surgery training workshops are very popular among rhinologists today. The workshop usually consists of a full day of lectures and a hands-on practice to acquire the skills for endoscopic sinus surgery [27] . Functional endoscopic sinus surgery (FESS) procedure is conducted by inserting the endoscopes through the nostrils to illuminate the inside of the nasal cavity and the sinuses. The instruments can be inserted through the same nostril using another hand to manipulate the structure to get rid of diseased mucosa and maintain normal sinus drainage.

Endoscopic sinus surgery simulator was the majority in this field. Some authors also developed intranasal models and nasal packing simulators for treating epistaxis. The endoscopic sinus surgery system comprised an endoscope for the left hand and a tool manipulator for the right hand. The participants performed the surgery on the nasal model or mannequin. The endoscopic sinus surgery system has been shown to improve the performance of the participants when conducting real surgeries in operating theatre [28] [29] . However, most of the models that are used are prototypes.

Current Systems

The Lapsim® virtual reality simulator uses the Virtual Laparoscopic Interface non-haptic-enhanced hardware platform (Immersion Inc., San Jose, CA), which includes two endoscopic handles. The interface includes a 2600 MHz hyper-threading processor Pentium IV computer running Windows XP and is equipped with a 256 MB RAM GeForce graphic card and an 18-inch TFT monitor. The system used the Lapsim Basic Skills 3.0 software (Surgical Science Ltd., Goteburg, Sweden).

The endoscopic sinus surgical simulator (ES3) was developed by Lockheed Martin, Inc. (Akron, Ohio) with a team from the University of Washington Human Interface Technology Laboratory (Seattle), the Ohio Supercomputer Center (Columbus), and Immersion Corp (San Jose, CA). The hardware comprises 4 principal components: 1) an SGI Octane workstation (Silicon Graphics Inc., Mountain View, CA), which serves as the simulation host platform; 2) a personal computer-based haptic controller, providing control and coordination between a universal physical instrument handle and a set of virtual surgical instruments; 3) a personal computer-based voice recognition-enabled instructor, which operates the simulator by responding to spoken commands; 4) an electromechanical platform, which serves as the human interaction interface, with a replica of an endoscope, a surgical tool handle, and a rubber-headed mannequin.

The VOXEL-MAN Sinus Surgery Simulator was adopted from their previously developed VOXEL-MAN Tempo Surgery Simulator for temporal bone surgery [30] . A 3-D model was created based on a high-resolution computed tomography. The model may be manipulated with virtual surgical tools controlled with a low-cost haptic device, which is also used to adjust microscope or endoscopic views. Visualization, haptic rendering, and tissue removal are represented with sub-voxel resolution (Table 5).

Efficacy of Simulator on Skills Improvement

For the physical coordination providing precise movement (psychomotor) skill, Edmond et al. assessed the efficacy of the ES3 for improving the operating room performance by evaluating the following sub-skills: navigation, injection, uncinectomy, anterior ethmoidectomy, maxillary antrostomy, orientation of image, image-task alignment, proper depth of image, tool manipulation, tool selection, tool-tool dexterity, tissue respect, surgical confidence, and case difficulty using 10 point scales [31] . Fried et al. evaluated surgical confidence and instrument manipulation performance in the operating room using scales from 1 to 10 [28] . The results showed a statistically significant difference improvement in psychomotor score for ES3 virtual reality training group in the recent study (Table 6).

For procedural skills, Fried et al. reported procedural scores using the time taken to complete the task [28] . There was a statistically significant difference in the time taken to complete task (MD 5.50 minutes, 95% CI 1.03 to 9.97).

For knowledge of specific anatomical structures, Solyar et al. [32] showed that the ES3 virtual endoscopy group had a significantly higher anatomical identification score (MD 4.3, 95% CI 2.31 to 6.29).

VIRTUAL REALITY IN THROAT SURGERY

Throat examination is the first step in diagnostic and treatment of the diseases. Ruthenbeck et al. [33] developed a virtual reality throat examination simulator that was capable of representing a range of throat pathologies. The computer interface employs haptic feedback to allow students to interact naturally with the software. For the otolaryngologist, phonosurgery is one of the main procedures in this field. Surgeons require precise movements to maneuver around vocal cords under microscopy. To prevent any complications, students can first be trained using the high-fidelity vocal cord model simulator. The vocal cord in the simulator is usually made from animal tissues or synthetic materials. One study developed a complete model for laryngeal surgery. The system comprised microscopes and micro-instruments for laryngeal surgery. The results found that the physicians who were training with this simulator performed significantly better in the operating room [34] .

Cricothyroidotomy is an emergency procedure that is performed when the patient's airway is blocked and less invasive attempts to clear it have failed. Cricothyroidotomy has been identified as an essential skill for military readiness. This training is relevant to more than 40,000 U.S. military medics and thousands of civilian health care providers. Current training methods use animals, cadavers and plastic mannequins. Liu et al. [35] developed the prototype of the virtual cricothyroidotomy simulator to address the problem from other simulators e.g. animal models do not have the correct anatomy and cadavers do not have the correct physiology. Mannequins do not adequately cover the full range of anatomical variations.

Table 5: Virtual reality endoscopic sinus surgery systems

Simulators	Characteristics	Validation	Efficacy
ES3	Stereoscopic display, haptic devices, voice recognition	Yes [29]	· RCTs · Significantly improved psychomotor, procedural and anatomical score
VOXEL-MAN Sinus Surgery	Stereoscopic display, haptic devices	Yes [30]	· Not available
Lapsim	Stereoscopic display, haptic devices	Yes [36]	· Not available

Table 6: Comparing the psychomotor scores of ES3 virtual reality endoscopic sinus surgery training with conventional training

Studies	VR Mean (S.D.)	Control Mean (S.D.)	Mean difference (95% CI)
Edmond 2002 [32]	6.68 (1.09)	6.68 (0.07)	0.00 (−1.51 to 1.51)
Fried 2010 [28]	6.65 (2.53)	2.73 (1.89)	3.92 (2.16 to 5.68)

Another field in laryngology is bronchoscopic surgery. The simulators in this field ranged from mannequin to virtual models. One study also developed an online virtual bronchoscopy simulator [37] . A commercial model of fiber optic bronchoscopy was the Endoscopy VR Simulator by CAE Healthcare, USA. The simulator consists of an anatomic model of the face, with an opening in one nare for nasal insertion of the fiber optic bronchoscope. The anatomic model is attached to a long compartment that houses the motion sensor system. As the user inserts and manipulates the bronchoscope, the simulator senses the movements and adjusts the screen images in real time. The simulation begins with a brief review of teaching objectives, which is followed by a patient history and relevant history and physical exam results. If X-rays or CAT scans were performed, those images are available for review. The trainee is then required to perform the selected procedure. Feedback is given during the procedure (such as an audible patient cough if topical anesthetic is insufficient) as well as after the procedure is complete. Some of the feedback is related to patient care (including how much lidocaine was administered and how many lesions were found and captured on video) [38].

CONCLUSION

Patorn Piromchai, Virtual reality surgical training in ear, nose and throat surgery is more effective than conventional training methods and could supplement standard surgical apprenticeship training to improve their technical skills before entering operating room.

REFERENCES

1. Rafiq, A., Tamariz, F., Boanca, C., Lavrentyev, V. and Merrell, R.C. (2008) Objective Assessment of Training Surgical Skills Using Simulated Tissue Interface with Real-Time Feedback. Journal of Surgical Education, 65, 270-274. http://dx.doi.org/10.1016/j.jsurg.2008.05.012
2. Kolb, D.A. (1984) Experiential Learning: Experience as the Source of Learning and Development. Prentice-Hall, Englewood Cliffs.
3. George, A.P. and De, R. (2010) Review of Temporal Bone Dissection Teaching: How It Was, Is and Will Be. The Journal of Laryngology & Otology, 124, 119-125.http://dx.doi.org/10.1017/S0022215109991617
4. Satava, R.M. (2008) Historical Review of Surgical Simulation—A Personal Perspective. World Journal of Surgery, 32, 141-148. http://dx.doi.org/10.1007/s00268-007-9374-y
5. Rourke, L., Schmidt, M. and Garga, N. (2010) Theory-Based Research of High Fidelity Simulation Use in Nursing Education: A Review of the Literature. International Journal of Nursing Education Scholarship, 7, Article 11.
6. Morgan, P.J., Cleave-Hogg, D., McIlroy, J. and Devitt, J.H. (2002) Simulation Technology: A Comparison of Experiential and Visual Learning for Undergraduate Medical Students. Anesthesiology, 96, 10-16. http://dx.doi.org/10.1097/00000542-200201000-00008
7. Zhao, Y.C., Kennedy, G., Yukawa, K., Pyman, B. and O'Leary, S. (2011) Improving Temporal Bone Dissection Using Self-Directed Virtual Reality Simulation: Results of a Randomized Blinded Control Trial. Otolaryngology Head Neck Surgery, 144, 357-364.http://dx.doi.org/10.1177/0194599810391624
8. Zhao, Y.C., Kennedy, G., Yukawa, K., Pyman, B. and O'Leary, S. (2011) Can Virtual Reality Simulator be Used as a Training Aid to Improve Cadaver Temporal Bone Dissection? Results of a Randomized Blinded Control Trial. Laryngoscope, 121, 831-837. http://dx.doi.org/10.1002/lary.21287
9. Zhao, Y.C., Kennedy, G., Hall, R. and O'Leary, S. (2010) Differentiating Levels of Surgical Experience on a Virtual Reality Temporal Bone Simulator. Otolaryngology—Head and Neck Surgery, 143, S30-S35. http://dx.doi.org/10.1016/j.otohns.2010.03.008
10. Sedlack, R.E., Kolars, J.C. and Alexander, J.A. (2004) Computer

Simulation Training Enhances Patient Comfort during Endoscopy. Clinical Gastroenterology and Hepatology: The Official Clinical Practice Journal of the American Gastroenterological Association, 2, 348-352.

11. Sedlack, R.E. and Kolars, J.C. (2004) Computer Simulator Training Enhances the Competency of Gastroenterology Fellows at Colonoscopy: Results of a Pilot Study. The American Journal of Gastroenterology, 99, 33-37. http://dx.doi.org/10.1111/j.1572-0241.2004.04007.x
12. Varadarajan, V., Verma, R. and Auccott, W. (2010) The Portable Temporal Bone Lab—A Useful Training Adjunct for the ENT Trainee. Clinical Otolaryngology, 35, 449-450.http://dx.doi.org/10.1111/j.1749-4486.2010.02203.x
13. Sowerby, L.J., Rehal, G., Husein, M., Doyle, P.C., Agrawal, S. and Ladak, H.M. (2010) Development and Face Validity Testing of a Three-Dimensional Myringotomy Simulator with Haptic Feedback. Journal of Otolaryngology—Head & Neck Surgery, 39, 122-129.
14. Wheeler, B., Doyle, P.C., Chandarana, S., Agrawal, S., Husein, M. and Ladak, H.M. (2010) Interactive Computer-Based Simulator for Training in Blade Navigation and Targeting in Myringotomy. Computer Methods and Programs in Biomedicine, 98, 130-139. http://dx.doi.org/10.1016/j.cmpb.2009.09.010
15. Steiner, K.V., Teixido, M., Kung, B., Sorensen, M., Forstrom, R. and Coller, P. (2007) A Virtual-Reality Approach for the Treatment of Benign Paroxysmal Positional Vertigo. Studies in Health Technology and Informatics, 125, 451-453.
16. Arora, A., Khemani, S., Tolley, N., Singh, A., Budge, J., Varela, D.A., Francis, H.W., Darzi, A. and Bhatti, N.I. (2012) Face and Content Validation of a Virtual Reality Temporal Bone Simulator. Otolaryngology—Head and Neck Surgery, 146, 497-503. http://dx.doi.org/10.1177/0194599811427385
17. Agus, M., Giachetti, A., Gobbetti, E., Zanetti, G., Zorcolo, A., Picasso, B. and Franceschini, S.S. (2003) A Haptic Model of a Bone-Cutting Burr. Studies in Health Technology and Informatics, 94, 4-10.
18. Kuppersmith, R.B., Johnston, R., Moreau, D., Loftin, R.B. and Jenkins, H. (1997) Building a Virtual Reality Temporal Bone Dissection Simulator. Studies in Health Technology and Informatics, 39, 180-186.
19. Stredney, D., Wiet, G.J., Bryan, J., Sessanna, D., Murakami, J.,

Schmalbrock, P., Powell, K. and Welling, B. (2002) Temporal Bone Dissection Simulation—An Update. Studies in Health Technology and Informatics, 85, 507-513.

20. Agus, M., Giachetti, A., Gobbetti, E., Zanetti, G., Zorcolo, A., John, N.W. and Stone, R.J. (2002) Mastoidectomy Simulation with Combined Visual and Haptic Feedback. Studies in Health Technology and Informatics, 85, 17-23.
21. Francis, H.W., Malik, M.U., Varela, D.A.D.V., Barffour, M.A., Chien, W.W., Carey, J.P., Niparko, J.K. and Bhatti, N.I. (2012) Technical Skills Improve after Practice on Virtual-Reality Temporal Bone Simulator. The Laryngoscope, 122, 1385-1391.http://dx.doi.org/10.1002/lary.22378
22. Wiet, G.J., Rastatter, J.C., Bapna, S., Packer, M., Stredney, D. and Welling, D.B. (2009) Training Otologic Surgical Skills through Simulation-Moving toward Validation: A Pilot Study and Lessons Learned. Journal of Graduate Medical Education, 1, 61-66.http://dx.doi.org/10.4300/01.01.0010
23. Wiet, G.J., Stredney, D., Kerwin, T., Hittle, B., Fernandez, S.A., Abdel-Rasoul, M. and Welling, D.B. (2012) Virtual Temporal Bone Dissection System: OSU Virtual Temporal Bone System: Development and Testing. The Laryngoscope, 122, S1-S12. http://dx.doi.org/10.1002/lary.22499
24. McIsaac, W.J., Coyte, P.C., Croxford, R., Asche, C.V., Friedberg, J. and Feldman, W. (2000) Otolaryngologists' Perceptions of the Indications for Tympanostomy Tube Insertion in Children. Canadian Medical Association or Its Licensor, 162, 1285-1288.
25. Ho, A.K., Alsaffar, H., Doyle, P.C., Ladak, H.M. and Agrawal, S.K. (2012) Virtual Reality Myringotomy Simulation with Real-Time Deformation: Development and Validity Testing. The Laryngoscope, 122, 1844-1851. http://dx.doi.org/10.1002/lary.23361
26. Todd, C. (2011) Real-Time Haptic Modeling and Simulation for Prosthetic Insertion. World Academy of Science, Engineering and Technology, 49, 343-351.
27. Arora, H., Uribe, J., Ralph, W., Zeltsan, M., Cuellar, H., Gallagher, A. and Fried, M.P. (2005) Assessment of Construct Validity of the Endoscopic Sinus Surgery Simulator. Archives of Otolaryngology—Head and Neck Surgery, 131, 217- 221.http://dx.doi.org/10.1001/archotol.131.3.217

28. Fried, M.P., Sadoughi, B., Gibber, M.J., Jacobs, J.B., Lebowitz, R.A., Ross, D.A., Bent 3rd, J.P., Parikh, S.R., Sasaki, C.T. and Schaefer, S.D. (2010) From Virtual Reality to the Operating Room: The Endoscopic Sinus Surgery Simulator Experiment. Otolaryngology—Head and Neck Surgery, 142, 202-207. http://dx.doi.org/10.1016/j.otohns.2009.11.023
29. Fried, M.P., Sadoughi, B., Weghorst, S.J., Zeltsan, M., Cuellar, H., Uribe, J.I., Sasaki, C.T., Ross, D.A., Jacobs, J.B., Lebowitz, R.A., et al. (2007) Construct Validity of the Endoscopic Sinus Surgery Simulator: II. Assessment of Discriminant Validity and Expert Benchmarking. Archives of Otolaryngology—Head & Neck Surgery, 133, 350-357. http://dx.doi.org/10.1001/archotol.133.4.350
30. Tolsdorff, B., Pommert, A., Hohne, K.H., Petersik, A., Pflesser, B., Tiede, U. and Leuwer, R. (2010) Virtual Reality: A New Paranasal Sinus Surgery Simulator. The Laryngoscope, 120, 420-426.
31. Edmond Jr., C.V. (2002) Impact of the Endoscopic Sinus Surgical Simulator on Operating Room Performance. The Laryngoscope, 112, 1148-1158. http://dx.doi.org/10.1097/00005537-200207000-00002
32. Solyar, A., Cuellar, H., Sadoughi, B., Olson, T.R. and Fried, M.P. (2008) Endoscopic Sinus Surgery Simulator as a Teaching Tool for Anatomy Education. The American Journal of Surgery, 196, 120-124. http://dx.doi.org/10.1016/j.amjsurg.2007.06.026
33. Ruthenbeck, G.S., Owen, H. and Reynolds, K.J. (2008) A Virtual Reality Throat Examination Simulation. Studies in Health Technology and Informatics, 132, 433-435.
34. Contag, S.P., Klein, A.M., Blount, A.C. and Johns III, M.M. (2009) Validation of a Laryngeal Dissection Module for Phonomicrosurgical Training. The Laryngoscope, 119, 211-215. http://dx.doi.org/10.1002/lary.20018
35. Liu, A., Bhasin, Y. and Bowyer, M. (2005) A Haptic-Enabled Simulator for Cricothyroidotomy. Studies in Health Technology and Informatics, 111, 308-313.
36. van Dongen, K.W., Ahlberg, G., Bonavina, L., Carter, F.J., Grantcharov, T.P., Hyltander, A., Schijven, M.P., Stefani, A., van der Zee, D.C. and Broeders, I.A. (2011) European Consensus on a Competency-Based Virtual Reality Training Program for Basic Endoscopic Surgical Psychomotor Skills. Surgical Endoscopy, 25, 166-171.http://dx.doi.org/10.1007/s00464-010-1151-6

37. Duffy, C. and Myles, P.S. (2008) Review: Thoracic-Anesthesia.com. Journal of Cardiothoracic and Vascular Anesthesia, 22, 644. http://dx.doi.org/10.1053/j.jvca.2007.09.005
38. Dalal, P.G., Dalal, G.B., Pott, L., Bezinover, D., Prozesky, J. and Murray, W.B. (2011) Learning Curves of Novice Anesthesiology Residents Performing Simulated Fibreoptic Upper Airway Endoscopy. Canadian Journal of Anesthesia/Journal Canadien d'Anesthésie, 58, 802-809. http://dx.doi.org/10.1007/s12630-011-9542-2

Chapter 10

Development of a Medical Training System with Integration of Users' Skills Assessment

Ronei M. Moraes and Liliane S. Machado

Federal University of Paraíba Brazil

INTRODUCTION

Virtual Reality (VR) joins several areas to produce environments that contain elements with realistic behaviour. The real-time processing of users interactions is a mandatory requirement and one or more user senses can be explored in VR systems. Machado & Moraes (2010) presented the multidisciplinary aspect of the VR systems and pointed out their importance for training. Particularly, the training of medical procedures can be improved by VR systems. It occurs due to the fact that traditional training in medicine is frequently performed with cadavers or guinea pigs, which do not present

Citation: Ronei M. Moraes and Liliane S. Machado (January 8th 2011). Development of a Medical Training System with Integration of Users' Assessment, Virtual Reality, Jae-Jin Kim, IntechOpen, DOI: 10.5772/13521. Available from: https://www.intechopen.com/books/virtual-reality/development-of-a-medical-training-system-with-integration-of-users-assessment.

the same characteristics of live bodies. Practice supervised by a tutor, with real patients, is another usual situation used for training. Both cases present problems: dead bodies, besides the degradation along the time, cannot be reused if cuts or punctures were done and need to be discarded after some manipulation; and supervised training can be risky or even uncomfortable for patients. Additionally, supervised training depends directly on the cases attended, what could not represent the variability and diversity of cases that students must learn. These observations make VR powerful to improve training, since it can rebuild digitally the same components of real procedures and can present virtual bodies with similar features of live bodies. Moreover, it can allow realistic and interactive simulation, in safe conditions, for users and patients; can provide variability of cases and offers reusability of the structures.

A very important aspect related to VR for medical simulation is the possibility of monitoring users' actions. Since VR systems are computational applications, all input and output data can be stored and used to assess users. This feature allows users to know their skills and to identify the points that must be improved in the execution of the procedure. This is particularly important in blind procedures in which a videotape of the execution cannot give possibilities of assessment by an expert. However, only recently this resource has been explored (Machado et al., 2000; Machado & Moraes, 2010).

This chapter will present the development process of a medical training system for bone marrow harvest procedure, a minimally invasive procedure. The problem approached will be described in order to identify the senses involved in the real procedure. Then, difficulties to assess trainees' skills and problems present in a real procedure, such as risks for donors, will be discussed allowing the identification of key points in the conception of a simulator based on VR. Those key points, the project budget and technological limitations will help to define the main features to be included in the computational architecture of the simulator.

The use of a framework that integrates several tools and methods will be introduced to demonstrate how this kind of software can decrease implementation time and standardize the development of this kind of application.

DEVELOPMENT DIFFICULTIES

There are four aspects related to the development of simulations for medical training: know the procedure, presence of a multidisciplinary team, presence of methods to assess the quality of training performed in the simulator and knowledge of computational tools and technologies for programming the application. It makes challenging the activities of the researchers to produce advances that could benefit all areas involved, without duplicity of efforts.

Know the procedure refers to obtain a detailed description about all elements involved in it: objects, structures, tools, anatomical parts, ways to perform the procedure and its variations, senses included (sight, touch, hearing, smell), range of expected time necessary to perform the procedure, and other aspects necessary to have a complete description. That information should be analysed according to the project budget and the technology available and can demand changes in the approach to be adopted. However, any decision must be discussed among the team: computer scientists and engineers will point out the technological possibilities and physicians will evaluate the approaches proposed, as example. The method to be used to assess users in the simulator must also be discussed according to the simulator subject. The detailed description will provide information that will allow identifying the type of variables included in the procedure. It must be discussed with a statistician or mathematician to define an adequate and good assessment method capable to deal with input and output data of simulator. During the implementation and after it, the development team will continuously refine and correct the approach adopted. Finally, the physicians must do the validation of the simulator.

A simulator based on VR must contain the same steps present in a real procedure and can use volumetric models, stereoscopic visualization, haptic systems, deformation methods and interactive cut. The use of all those features requires a lot of processing and can compromise the real-time performance. Thus, a VR simulator for medicine is defined and developed to deal with specific parts of the human body and present some limitations: according to the procedure requirements, some VR techniques are more explored than others. The architecture components could present educational aspects beyond training. Educational contents include explanations of the procedure, models with transparent view, attach, detach and other 3D manipulation tools, that only can be present by a VR application, to help users to solve some doubts about the procedure. Additionally, data collected during interaction in a VR-based simulation can be used to assess users' performance in training and to allow them to identify mistakes and improve their skills. An online assessment tool coupled to the simulator can do it.

A difficulty related to the development of simulators, which explore more than one human sense, is the integration of the tasks related to each sense and their synchronization. Most of the simulators found in literature were developed through the implementation and integration of all routines necessary. Because there are several devices and specific APIs (Application Programming Interface) dedicated to their programming, a programmer with experience to deal with each device or API is necessary to develop the VR simulators. Methods for collision detection, deformation, and stereoscopic visualization also need to be completely implemented each time an application is developed. Besides, the several methods need to deal with the same models and interaction devices. Then, all this information and all application tasks must be synchronized to avoid delays or inconsistencies that can compromise the realism. Figure 1 presents a diagram with some tasks that can be present in a simulator for medical training: the tasks can depend on process from other tasks. Finally, there isn't any guarantee of compatibility among simulators and codes are not usually shared among groups, fact that causes constant duplicity of efforts and recoding of the same tasks.

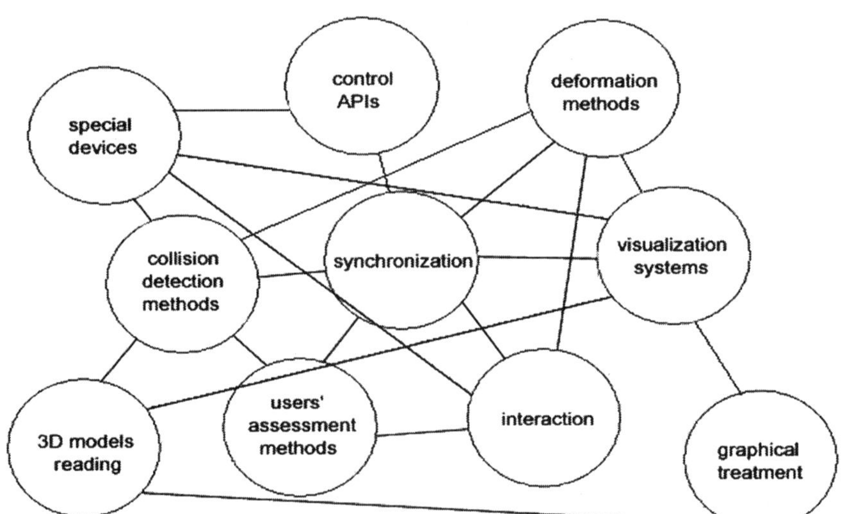

Figure 1: Tasks that could compose medical simulators based on VR and their relation.

The Framework CyberMed

To programming a simulator it is necessary to know a set of methods and tools: the method for generation of stereoscopic images and their adequacy to the visualization device chosen must be considered; the haptic device has specific API for programming; there are different methods for collision detection between objects in virtual environments; deformation methods depends on collision detection and can be more or less complex, depending on the one chosen; assessment is related to the type of input data (interaction) and demand the knowledge of mathematical or statistical concepts; the models must be readable; and, finally, all processes must be synchronized.

The use of frameworks was recently adopted to minimize duplicity of efforts, to make interoperable the simulators and to allow fast development. It means that the stage of implementation can be accelerated if programmers do not need to learn and develop all methods and tools related to each task. Examples of frameworks for the development of medical simulators are the GiPSi, Spring, SOFA, SSVE, Chai3D, ViMeT, and CyberMed (Machado et al., 2009; Correa et al., 2009). In Table 1 is possible to observe that most of them are open source, feature that augments the possibilities of discussion and code exchange among programmers. Support to haptics is also an important component since it allows including routines that provide sense of touch and force feedback for users. However, only the CyberMed presents support to assessment and can be pointed as a framework for the development of training simulator capable to provide feedback about users' skills.

Table 1: Comparison among frameworks for medical development based on VR

Framework	Open Source	Free License	Support to haptics	Support to assessment
GiPSi	X	X	X	
SSVE				
Spring	X		X	
SOFA	X	X		
CHAI3D	X	X	X	
ViMeT	X	X	X	
CyberMed	X	X	X	X

CyberMed is a framework to the development of VR simulators based on VR for commodity computers (Souza et al., 2007). It is composed by a set of open and free libraries that allows integrating new methods or supporting new devices. It also supports low cost devices as much as high-end devices, depending on the budget of the project. This flexibility permits to attend a large group of applications and programmers can select the resources available according to the goal and public of the final system. It allows programming in high-level but permit expanding its functionalities in a low-level programming. It is available for download at http:/ / cybermed. sourceforge.net/ . Figure 2 presents CyberMed layers and their disposition inside the system.

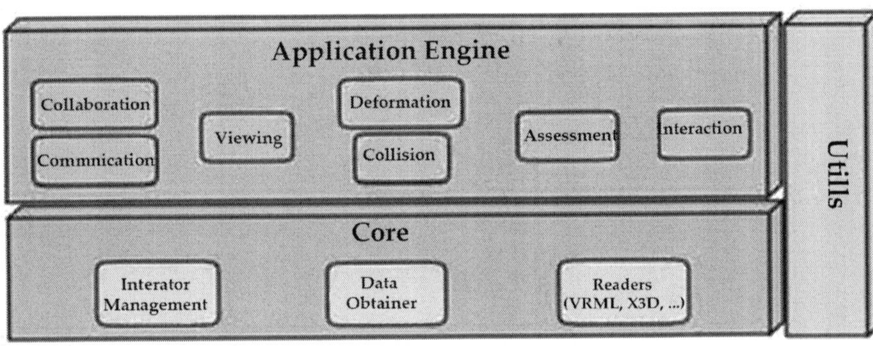

Figure 2: CyberMed architecture.

The architecture of CyberMed is based on the object-oriented paradigm and follows some pattern designs to guarantee software reuse and agile development. Then, singleton and Abstract Factory were patterns applied in CyberMed development: singleton offers a single instance of a class to allow singleness of information; and Abstract Factory allows the creation of interfaces to make new objects with common operations.

The framework is composed by a set of layers that provide services for its users. Each layer abstracts several concepts to facilitate the development of VR applications. Nowadays, CyberMed offers support to: three different modes of stereoscopy, mass-spring deformation, two collision detection modes, import 3D meshes, optical and magnetic tracking, haptics, network collaboration, synchronization, and three different assessment methods.

DESIGN OF THE SIMULATOR

The design of the simulator starts with the complete description of the procedure. The bone marrow transplant is a minimally invasive medical procedure to treat recently considered incurable diseases, as some specific occurrences of cancer. It is used to replace the cells of the immune system, mainly after chemotherapy or radiotherapy sessions. To obtain bone marrow it is necessary to extract it through many material aspirations from the iliac crest bone marrow (sometimes it includes the sternum bone also) of a donator under general anaesthesia. The harvest is executed blindly without any visual feedback except the external view of the donor's body. So, the physician needs to touch patient's body and identify the position of the iliac crest. After, he will insert a needle from this position to reach the bone marrow. In order to do that, he must apply adequate force and feel the tissue layers pierced by the needle.

The knowledge of the anatomic structures of the pelvic region, as well as the physician ability to find the iliac crest under the skin and the perception of the tissues pierced by the needle are essential to perform the bone marrow harvest procedure. Thus, it is possible to observe that the sense of touch is essential to perform the procedure and will be from it that the physician will decide the correct position to insert the needle and when to stop doing it. The dexterity of the physician will determine his skills.

The process of learning the bone marrow harvest procedure can be divided in three stages: understand the anatomy of the pelvis, learn how to identify the iliac crest and acquire dexterity to insert the needle, with correct force and precision, to reach the bone marrow. The elements necessary to compose these stages are: anatomical models of structures of the iliac region; needle for harvest; hand or fingers for palpation; hardness and elasticity properties of tissues from each structure; colour of structures.

Factors that determine a correct execution are related to the time of harvest, correctness of place in needle insertion, and adequate application of forces during the piercing. This information can be used for decision making about users dexterity and their skill level.

Assessment Methodologies

The research area on training assessment for simulators based on VR is recent (Burdea & Coiffet, 2003). The early works in that area probably were proposed by Dinsmore et al. (1996; 1997) (Langrana et al., 1997) that used a quiz to assess users of a VR environment to identify subcutaneous tumors. The quiz contained questions related to the diagnosis and hardness of tumor. Similarly, Wilson et al. (1997) created a minimally invasive system (MIST) in which each task could be programmed for different difficulty levels. Performance data of each user could be saved to post analysis (offline) by an expert or statistical methods.

In parallel, methods to assess surgical skills have been developed by several research groups. Some of them use statistical models to do that offline (Derossis et al., 1998) and others use statistical methods to show that through VR based systems is possible to discriminate between expert and novice physicians (Taffinfer et al., 1998; Gallagher et al., 2001). It was showed also that surgeons trained in VR systems could obtain better results (Gallagher et al., 1999) when compared to others trained by traditional methods. Additionally, the assessment of psychomotor skills in VR systems that include haptic devices can quantify surgical dexterity with objective metrics (Darzi et al., 1999). Thus, VR systems for training can be used to provide metrics to a proficiency criterion of learning (Darzi et al., 1999; Gallagher et al., 2005). Due to those reasons, McCloy & Stone (2001) pointed out the assessment of psychomotor skills as the future of medical teaching and training.

The first proposal for online training assessment in VR systems was presented by (Burdea et al., 1998) and was based on a boolean logic that compared diagnoses provided by users with correct ones stored in the simulator. However, ordinary computers of that generation were not able to run simultaneously virtual reality environments/ simulators and online assessment systems if several interaction variables were monitored. After that, more sophisticated assessment methods were proposed for several training systems (McBeth et al., 2002; Huang et al., 2005; Mackel et al., 2006; Kumagai et al., 2007; Farber et al., 2008).

Apart from methods for evaluating a user, have also been proposed methodologies for evaluation of multiple users interacting in the same VR environment (Moraes & Machado, 2007). It is important to note that there are evaluations systems for training systems based on Web (Moraes & Machado, 2005b; 2006; Machado & Moraes, 2006). Some methodologies, which cannot be able to run in real time in commodity computers, can be implemented using embedded systems, coupled to them (Moraes & Machado, 2008).

The choice of an assessment methodology is strongly related to the procedure itself. For example, in a procedure in which information can be obtained from procedures performed in simulators based on VR are fully quantitative, numerical methods based on probability distributions can be most appropriate (Machado & Moraes, 2006). However, one should take into consideration what types of such information specialists are able to interpret. In cases where such information coming from specialists are imprecise or vague, modelling from fuzzy sets (Moraes & Machado, 2009a) or hybrid modelling can be good choices (Moraes & Machado, 2010). Can still be used in knowledge-based modelling, such as rule-based expert systems (classical or fuzzy) (Machado et al., 2000). Approaches based on models for discrete variables or statistical models based on binomial or multinomial distributions are not indicated, since the need for changes on the original variables that can cause loss of information (Moraes & Machado, 2009b). In cases where information is qualitative, the use of expert systems can be a good solution (Machado et al., 2008). Other approaches based on multinomial probability models (Moraes & Machado, 2009a; 2009b) can also be used for these cases. There are still cases in which information is obtained from both qualitative and quantitative variables. In these cases, evaluation method to be used should take into consideration these aspects and be able to analyse the two types variables simultaneously (Machado & Moraes, 2009).

Because users can have forgotten some decisions and actions done during the training, the main problem in this kind of evaluation is the interval between training and evaluation. Additionally, some performances cannot be classified as good or bad due to procedure complexity. Thus, the existence of an evaluation system coupled to a simulation allows fast feedback that can be used improve user performance. However, it demands low computational complexity in order to not compromise the simulation performance and high accuracy to do not compromise the quality of evaluation. Figure 3 shows the independence between simulator and evaluation systems in spite of their simultaneous action. Theoretically, the system can collect any information related to position, forces, torque, resistance, velocity, acceleration, temperature, angle of visualization, sound, smells, temperature, velocity and shape. Spatial position can be captured by tracking devices attached to some part of users' body or to an object manipulated by them. Those devices can collect movements in three or more degrees of freedom in constant intervals of time. Such information allows VR system to calculate object position in the virtual scene, the velocity of the movement and its acceleration. In a similar way, haptic devices (Burdea & Coiffet, 2003) also can do the same, but in a limited physical space. In both examples, sampling rates vary according to the device chosen. The positioning of objects manipulated by users can allow the identification of collision with other objects of the virtual scene, besides the direction of contact and its intensity. In order to achieve this, position vectors with last and present position are used to determine the collision velocity and intensity.

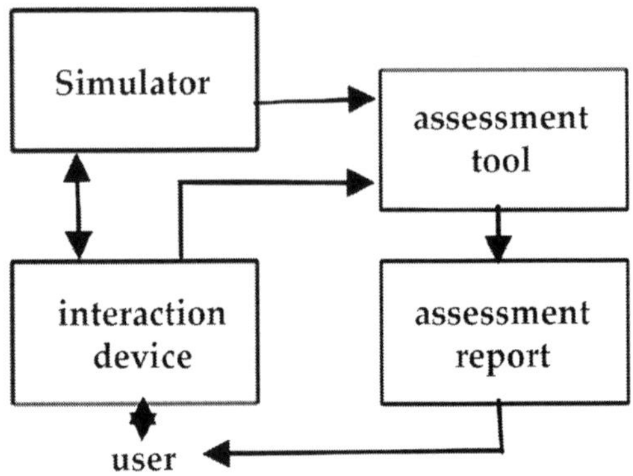

Figure 3: Assessment and its relation with VR simulator.

Reactions from data processing collected from interaction can be send to users as force feedback, a new point of view of the scene, deformation of objects, sound, increase or decrease of temperature, change of objects (as cuts or divisions) and smells. The intensity of feedback will depend on device capabilities. However, the continuity of reaction is an important factor in the levels of immersion.

a. Maximum Likelihood

Maximum Likelihood decision rule is the most common statistical technique used in data classification. Its application for training evaluation based on VR was presented by Moraes & Machado (2005a). Formally, the classes of performance for an user are done by: w_i , i=1,...,M, where M is the total number of classes of performance. It is possible to determine the most probable class of a vector of training data X, by conditional probabilities (Johnson & Wichern, 2001):

$$P(w_i \mid X), \text{ where } i=1,...,M. \qquad (1)$$

The probability done by (1) gives the likelihood that for a data vector X, the correct class is w_i. Classification rule is performed according to

$$X \in w_i \text{ if } P(w_i \mid X) > P(w_j \mid X) \text{ for all } i \neq j. \qquad (2)$$

However, all the probabilities done by (1) are unknown. So, probabilities denoted by $P(X \mid w_i)$ can be estimated if there is sufficient information available for each class of performance. Using the Bayes Theorem:

$$P(w_i \mid X) = [P(X \mid w_i)\, P(w_i)] \,/ P(X), \qquad (3)$$

where $P(X) = \sum^{M}_{i=1} P(X \mid w_i)\, P(w_i)]$.

As P(X) is the same for all classes w_i, then it is not relevant for data classification. In Bayesian theory, $P(w_i)$ is called a priori probability for w_i and $P(w_i \mid X)$ is a posteriori probability for w_i where X is known. Then, the classification rule done by (2) is modified:

$$X \in w_i \text{ if } P(w_i \mid X)\, P(w_i) > P(w_j \mid X)\, P(w_j) \text{ for all } i \neq j. \tag{4}$$

Equation (4) is known as the maximum likelihood decision rule or maximum likelihood classification. However, it can be convenient to use (Johnson & Wichern, 2001):

$$g(X) = \ln\,[P(X \mid w_i)\, P(w_i)] = \ln\,[P(X \mid w_i)] + \ln\,[P(w_i)] \tag{5}$$

where g(X) is known as the log-likelihood function and it is known as discriminant function. Equation (5) can be used to modify the formulation done by (4):

$$X \in w_i \text{ if } g_i(X) > g_j(X) \text{ for all } i \neq j. \tag{6}$$

It is important to note that if statistical distribution of training data can assume multivariate Gaussian distribution, the use of (6) has interesting computational properties (Johnson & Wichern, 2001). If training data cannot assume that distribution, (6) can provide a significant reduction of computational cost of implementation. Thus, the user's interactions with the system are monitored and the information is sent to the evaluation system, where Maximim Likelihood is in its kernel. This method can produce good results even with small bases calibration. However it is necessary that these data are able to translate the scope of the problem addressed.

For the calibration of the evaluation system, an expert executes several times the procedure, labelling each one into a class of performance among M classes available. For each one, the vectors of each variable are storage. At the end of calibration, the information of variability about each one procedure class is acquired by calculate the mean vector and covariance matrix. These parameters are sufficient to characterize the multivariate Gaussian distribution for each class of performance. When it is done, the evaluation system is ready to run.

The users perform their training in the VR simulator and the Evaluation Tool based on Maximum Likelihood collects the data from that manipulation. All probabilities of data for each class of performance are calculated by evaluation tool and a wj class of performance is assigned to the user at the end of simulation, according (4) or (6), which is reported to the trainee.

b. General Bayesian Network (GBN)

A Bayesian network is a probabilistic model that can represent a set of probabilities distributions from all variables in a complex process and also establish their relationships (Neapolitan, 2003). Formally, a Bayesian network is defined as directed acyclic graphs, denoted by G and a probabilistic distribution denoted by P. The graph G is a set of nodes and oriented arcs, where nodes represent variables in process and oriented arcs encode conditional dependencies between variables (Neapolitan, 2003). The dependencies are modeled by specific conditional probabilistic distributions (Krause, 1998).

Cheng & Greiner (2001) proposed a classification for Bayesian networks, according to their graph structure, in five classes: Naive-Bayes, Tree Augmented Naive-Bayes, Augmented Naive-Bayes, Bayesian Multi-net nets e General Bayesian Networks (GBNs). The choice of a specific structure to knowledge representation depends on dependencies relationship between variables, which describe that process. That choice is critical, because it changes the final results. The GBN is a generalized form of Bayesian networks, which allows nodes to form an arbitrary graph, rather than just a tree. Another important characteristic is that each child node cannot be connected to the final classes of evaluation.

The General Bayesian Network is convenient to serve as base for a training evaluation due to its generality. In that network, the dependencies between nodes can adjust itself to real dependencies. Thus, it is possible to verify dependencies between variables during network modelling and put them in structure nodes of GBN, which did not occur in other structures. Formally, let the classes of performance be in space of decision Ω with M classes of performance. Let be w_j, $j \in \Omega$ the class of performance for a user and X_i, $1 \leq i \leq n$, represents a node in GBN with n as the number of nodes in a graph. The joint probability distribution in GBN for an event is done by:

$$P(X_1, X_2, \ldots, X_n) = \prod^{n}_{i=1} \; P(X_n \mid X_{n-1}, X_{n-2}, \ldots, X_1) \tag{7}$$

where $P(X_1, X_2, \ldots, X_n)$ is the joint probability distribution and $P(X_n \mid X_{n-1}, X_{n-2}, \ldots, X_1)$ is the conditional probability of X_n conditioned by its predecessor nodes $X_{n-1}, X_{n-2}, \ldots, X_1$.

If the conditional independence between variables is verified, this permits simplifications in (7). Then,

$$P(X_1, X_2, \ldots, X_n) = P(X_1 \mid w_j)\, P(X_2 \mid w_j)\, P(X_3 \mid w_j) \tag{8}$$

The node probabilities are associated to probability distribution. For example, a node A can have a Gaussian distribution and a node B, which depends on A, can have a bivariate Gaussian distribution, with a mean vector and a covariance matrix (Johnson & Wichern, 2001).

The structure of GBN is learned from data, as well as the parameters of conditional probabilities. By the use of probabilities calculus is possible to find dependencies among nodes in a Bayesian network. If those dependencies are founding and, if is possible to assume Gaussian distribution for nodes, dependencies can be estimated using multivariate linear regression (Neapolitan, 2003). Scores are used to help the estimation of the final structure of GBN for each class of assessment. In a first moment, a network is created with all independent nodes and an initial score is calculated. Following, all combinations are searched and an arc is designed between two nodes to obtain an increment of initial score. Then, the parameters for that nodes set are re-estimated using linear regression. This cycle is repeated until the total network score could be less than a predetermined value or a fixed number of cycles. This methodology has the ability to obtain better results for larger calibration databases.

Previously, an expert calibrates the system, according M classes of performance. The information of variability about these procedures is acquired using GBN based method (Moraes et al., 2009). The users perform their training in the VR simulator and the Assessment Tool based on GBN collects the data from that manipulation. All probabilities of data for each class of performance are calculated by GBN and a w_j class of performance is assigned to the user at the end of simulation, according to (7) or (8), depending on the particular case. At the end of the training, the assessment system reports the classification to the trainee.

For the calibration of the evaluation system, an expert executes several times the procedure, labeling each one into a class of performance among M classes available. For each one, the vectors of each variable are storage. At the end of calibration, the structure of GBN is learned from data, as well as the parameters of conditional probabilities for each class of performance. Using probabilities calculus is possible to find dependencies among nodes in a Bayesian network. If those dependencies are founding and, if is possible to assume Gaussian distribution for nodes, dependencies can be estimated using multivariate linear regression (Neapolitan, 2003). Scores are used to help estimate the final structure of GBN for each class of assessment. In a first moment a network is created with all independent nodes and an initial score is calculated. Next, all combinations are searched and an arc is designed between two nodes for which an increment of initial score is obtained. Then, the parameters for that nodes set are re-estimated using linear regression. This cycle is repeated until total network score is less than a predetermined value or a fixed number of cycles.

The users perform their training in the VR simulator and the Evaluation Tool based on GBN collects the data from that manipulation. All probabilities of data for each class of performance are calculated by evaluation tool and a w_j class of performance is assigned to the user at the end of simulation, according (7) or (8), which is reported to the trainee.

c. Expert system based on Fuzzy Rules

As it is possible that some variables in the training system do not present an exactly correspondence to the real world, some measures cannot be exact. Then we must use fuzzy sets to measure those variables (Dubois & Prade, 1980).

In classical set theory a set A of a universe X can be expressed by means of a membership function $\mu_A(x)$, with $\mu_A: X \rightarrow \{0,1\}$, where for a given a ∈ A, $\mu_A(a)=1$ and $\mu_A(a)=0$ respectively express the presence and absence of a in A. Mathematically:

$$\mu_A(x) = \begin{cases} 1, & \text{if } x \in A \\ 0, & \text{if } x \notin A \end{cases} \tag{9}$$

\(9)

Zadeh (1965) introduced the fuzzy set theory in 1965. A fuzzy set or fuzzy subset is used to model an ill-known quantity. A fuzzy set A on X is characterized by its membership function $\mu_A: X \rightarrow [0,1]$. We say that a fuzzy set A of X is "precise" when $\exists\, c^* \in X$ such that $\mu_A(c^*)=1$ and $\forall c \neq c^*$, $\mu_A(c)=0$. A fuzzy set A will be said to be "crisp", when $\forall\, c \in X$, $\mu_A(c) \in \{0,1\}$.

The intersection and union of two fuzzy sets are performed trough the use of t-norm and tconorm operators respectively, which are commutative, associative and monotonic mappings from $[0,1] \rightarrow [0,1]$. Moreover, a t-norm Γ (respec. t-conorm $\perp$) has 1 (respec. 0) as neutral element (e. g.: Γ=min, $\perp$=max) (Dubois & Prade, 1988). Thus, we can define intersection and union of two fuzzy sets as:

The intersection of two fuzzy sets A and B, with membership functions $\mu_A(x)$ e $\mu_B(x)$ is a fuzzy set C with membership function given by:

$$C = A \cap B \Leftrightarrow \mu_C(x) = \Gamma\{\mu_A(x), \mu_B(x)\},\ \forall\, x \in X. \tag{10}$$

The union of two fuzzy sets A and B, with membership functions $\mu_A(x)$ e $\mu_B(x)$ is a fuzzy set C with membership function given by:

$$C = A \cup B \Leftrightarrow \mu_C(x) = \perp\{\mu_A(x), \mu_B(x)\}, \ \forall x \in X. \quad (11)$$

The complement of a fuzzy set A in X, denoted by ¬A is defined by:

$$\mu_{\neg A}(x) = n(\mu_A(x)), \ \forall x \in X. \quad (12)$$

where: n: [0,1]→[0,1] is a negation operator which satisfies the following properties:

- n(0)=1 and n(1)=0
- n(a) ≤ n(b) if a>b
- n(n(a))=a, ∀ x∈ [0,1]

and a negation is a strict negation if it is continuous and satisfies

- n(a)< n(b) if a>b.

The main negation operator which satisfies these four conditions is n(a) = 1-a.

The implication function between two fuzzy sets A and B, with membership functions $\mu_A(x)$ e $\mu_B(x)$, is a fuzzy set C with membership function given by:

$$C = A \Rightarrow B \Leftrightarrow \mu_C(x,y) = \nabla\{\mu_A(x), \mu_B(y)\}, \ \forall x \in X, \ \forall y \in Y \quad (13)$$

where ∇: $[0,1]^2 \rightarrow [0,1]$ is an implication operator which obeys the following properties: ∀ a, a', b, b' ∈ [0,1]:

- If b ≤ b' then ∇ (a,b) ≤ ∇ (a,b');
- ∇ (0,b)=1;
- ∇ (1,b)=b.

The pure implications obeys too:

- If a ≤ a' then ∇ (a,b) ≥ ∇ (a',b);
- ∇ (a, ∇ (b,c))= ∇ (b, ∇ (a,c)).

Expert systems (Rich & Knight, 1993) use the knowledge of an expert in a given specific domain to answer non-trivial questions about that domain. For example, an expert system for image classification would use knowledge about the characteristics of the classes present in a given region of the image to classify a pixel of that region. This knowledge also includes the "how to do" methods used by the human expert. Usually, the knowledge in an expert system is represented by rules in the form:

IF <condition> THEN <conclusion>.

Most rule-based expert systems allow the use of connectives AND or OR in the premise of a rule and of connective AND in the conclusion. From rules and facts, new facts will be obtained through an inference process.

In several cases, we do not have precise information about conditions or conclusions, then the knowledge in the rules cannot be expressed in a precise manner. Thus, it can be interesting to use a fuzzy rule-based expert system (Zadeh, 1988). However, it is important to emphasize that obtaining rules from an expert can be a long process and eventually must be done in several stages. This is the major limitation of this methodology.

For example, using a fuzzy expert system coupled to a surgical simulator based on virtual reality, experts can define, in an imprecise way, regions of tissue and bones in where is possible to find bone marrow harvest. To evaluate a user, values of variables are collected by a haptic device and sent to expert system for evaluation. The system must analyse each step performed by users and classify users, at the end of training, according to predefined performance classes. Machado et al. (2000) used five performance classes, described by the following fuzzy sets: you need much more training, you need more training, you need training, your training is good or your training is excellent, to identify if more training of bone marrow harvest procedure is or not necessary. The fuzzy rules of expert system are modelled by membership functions according to specifications of experts. Several types of membership functions can be used as trapezoidal, triangular and pi-functions and the fuzzy inference system used is Mamdani-type (Mamdani & Assilian, 1975). An example of rule for this expert system is:

IF Position_x is left_center AND Position_y is up_center

AND Position_needle is acceptable AND Marrow_harvest is yes

THEN Trainee_class is you_need_training

where: Position_x, Position_y are coordinates which the needle touch the patient body; Position_needle is the angle of needle input to body of patient; Marrow_harvest shows the success or failure of trainee to harvest bone marrow and Trainee_class is the classification of trainee.

In a different way from previous methods, the calibration of an expert system based on fuzzy rules is made by extraction of knowledge from one or several experts. In general, the experts explain the procedure and which variables must be taking in account in evaluation process. From those variables is necessary to know their parameters (which translate by fuzzy numbers) and as they are related with evaluation process to create rules to express each one of the M classes of performance. The number of rules depends on the complexity of procedure. When users perform their training, the Evaluation Tool based on Expert System collects the data from that manipulation. All rules are applied over data and, according to the expert system, one class of performance w_j is assigned to the user at the end of simulation, which is reported to the user.

IMPLEMENTATION

A simulator based on VR must contain the same steps present in a real procedure and can use volumetric models, stereoscopic visualization, haptic systems, deformation methods and interactive cut. The use of all those features requires a lot of processing and can compromise the real-time performance. Thus, a VR simulator for medicine is defined and developed to deal with specific parts of the human body and present some limitations: according to the procedure requirements, some VR techniques are more explored than others. The architecture components could present educational aspects beyond training. Educational contents include explanations of the procedure, models with transparent view, attach, detach and other 3D manipulation tools, that only can be present by a VR application, to help users to solve some doubts about the procedure. Additionally, data collected during interaction in a VR-based simulation can be used to assess users' performance in training and to allow them to identify mistakes and improve their skills. An online assessment tool coupled to the simulator can do it.

In order to deal with the main points of the learning of bone marrow harvest (BMH), the three stages described in the design were considered. It was also decided that learning and practice should be treated in different moments, and the simulator was conceived to present these two possibilities. When is learning the anatomy and understanding the procedure, the user should be able to view internally the virtual body and become familiarized with the tools and tissues properties. However, the practice should reproduce exactly the reality of the procedure and the user must be assessed in this process. Figure 4 presents how the different moments were approached in the simulator and the tasks related to each one.

Sight and touch are the two senses identified as fundamental in the procedure. The touch is necessary for the palpation of the virtual body and for the puncture with the needle. In this case, the use of a haptic device is mandatory to simulate the tissues properties and provide touch feedback for users. Haptic devices are special devices that incorporate sensors and actuators to capture user actions and provide touch and force feedback.

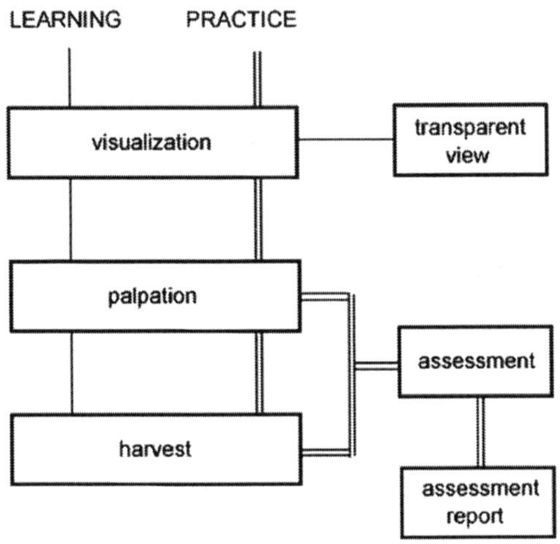

Figure 4: Learning (I) and practice (II) tasks defined for the bone marrow harvest simulator.

The perception of touch allows identifying texture of objects and force feedback allows feeling sense of position and movement associated to the interaction with objects. Haptic devices with 6DOF1 permit spatial movements and are the type of device necessary to the simulator for BMH. If the manipulation will occur in three dimensions, the visualization must follow the same principle and stereoscopic visualization will also be necessary. Figure 5 presents the haptic and visualization devices selected for BMH simulator.

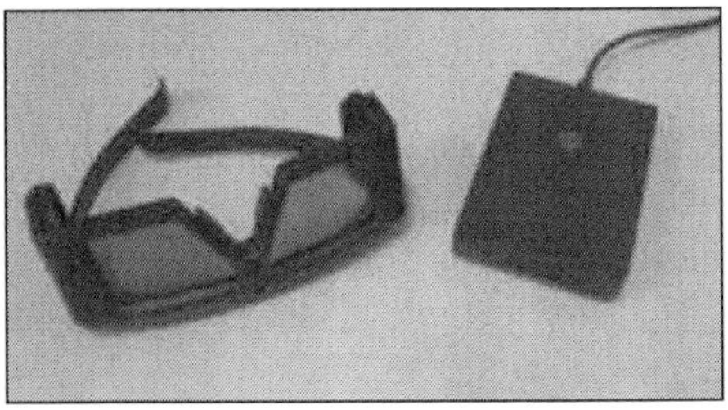

Figure 5: 6DOF haptic device (left) and shutter glasses for stereoscopic visualization (right).

Five models compose the application: three for the human body structures and two for the interaction object. The interaction objects, finger and needle, were modelled with the Blender package and saved in VRML 2.0 format.

The models of human body structure were obtained from a previous work (Machado, 2003) and represent the skin of the pelvic region, the iliac bone and the bone marrow (Figure 6).

The tissues properties are important information for the simulator. They are used to give to models the same properties of the real tissues. In this case, textures can be acquired or designed, and colours must be defined. Touch properties, as hardness, elasticity and roughness must also be acquired. Because several tissues do not have a numerical value to describe their properties, it is common to acquire them from physicians' impressions. A haptic calibrator was used to do that (Figure 7). Then, some virtual spheres were presented to physicians and they could select and refine their properties according to what they feel when manipulate the real tissues: first they do for it for skin, after for bone and, finally, for bone marrow. The properties they could calibrate were: hardness, roughness, friction and viscosity.

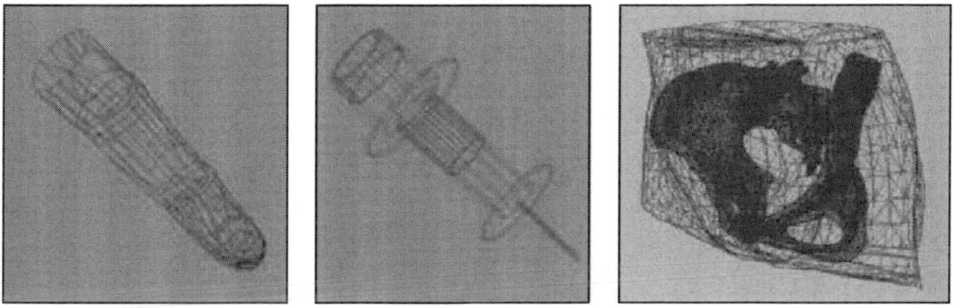

Figure 6: Models conceived to represent the interaction device and pelvic structures (skin, iliac bone and bone marrow).

Figure 7: Tool for calibration of material properties from physicians' impressions.

There is a last information necessary to make the simulator and it refers to the correct and wrong ways to perform the bone marrow harvest. However, describe it in natural language with details is not an easy tasks, even for physicians. Thus, the best way to do that will be making the physicians use the simulator and perform the procedure in several ways labelling what is correct and what is not correct. In this case, their interactions can be saved and used to construct models for users' assessment.

Coding with CyberMed

The application was implemented using the follow CyberMed classes: CybView, CybMouse, CybParameters, OF, CybInterator, CybHaptics and CybAssess. These classes offer the functionalities, respectively: visualization, mouse interaction, storage and management of 3D models, interaction control, haptic control and online user's assessment.

The five tasks defined in the design process were implemented. The CybView class allowed choosing the visualization mode of the application. In spite of CyberMed support four different view modes, the simulator was defined to provide only the monoscopic and temporal multiplexing visualization modes (using shutter glasses). With this class two light sources were defined and an illumination model was enable to the visual scene and its objects. The menu entries were also made in the CybView. The objects used in the visualization are obtained from the OF and CybParameters classes which store the models topology, the model used to represent the interaction device and the transformation matrixes of the scene. The CybInterator class was used to choose the interaction object. The CybAssess will access in realtime the transformation matrixes and CybInterator to the user's assessment. In order to reach that, it was used the CybAssess with an assessment method based on Maximum Likelihood. The CybHaptics class allowed setting the material properties of the models and enabling the haptic device. This class provided an abstract layer for several API used to programming haptic devices and did not demand knowledge about the device API.

Figure 8 shows parts of the implementation with the CyberMed used to read the models and set the material properties for the haptic interaction. In that figure, it is possible to observe the reading of five VRML models in lines 1 to 8. The lines 10 to 16 define the properties of the first layer, the skin, as being touchable and pierceable. Observe that there isn't any mention of the haptic device in use. It is done in a single way with the class CybInterator and is independent of device manufacturer.

The visualization mode chosen does not need any special programming and the only thing necessary is instance the view mode and start it:

```
/* instance view mode for shutter glasses */
   CybViewShutter view;
/* Initialize visualization*/
   view.init();
```

```
int numLayer = 5;

// read the models
char *arqname[30] = {"1.wrl","2.wrl","3.wrl","4.wrl", "5.wrl"};
ofMesh<cybTraits> malha[numLayer];
CybDataObtainer<cybTraits> data(numLayer);
ofWrlReader<cybTraits> entrada;
CybParameters cybCore;

// set haptic material properties for the skin
interator.hapticDevice.createHapticLayers(0,true);
interator.hapticDevice.createMaterialPropertyContext(numLayer, true);
interator.hapticDevice.setMaterialPropertyValue(0, POPTHROUGH, 1.0f);
interator.hapticDevice.setMaterialFace(0, POPTHROUGH, FRONT);
interator.hapticDevice.setMaterialPropertyValue(0, DYNAMIC_FRICTION, 0.6f);
interator.hapticDevice.setMaterialFace(0, DYNAMIC_FRICTION, FRONT);

// set haptic material properties for the bone
interator.hapticDevice.createHapticLayers(1,true);

// association of the contact point to a model point
interator.setObjectType(0, -0.020913, 0.078050, -10.034132);

//  enable material property for haptics
interator.hapticDevice.enableHapticMaterialProperty();
```

Figure 8: Code of the BMH simulator using CyberMed 1.2.

The menu was implemented to be dynamically modified, according to user choices. A visual exploration is enable in the Study module and the user can choose which structures he wants to see and set their transparency. Figure 9 shows the Study module and the menu options available. The user can also modify the position and orientation of the structures through mouse interaction. If shutter glasses were available, it is possible to start the stereoscopy visualization.

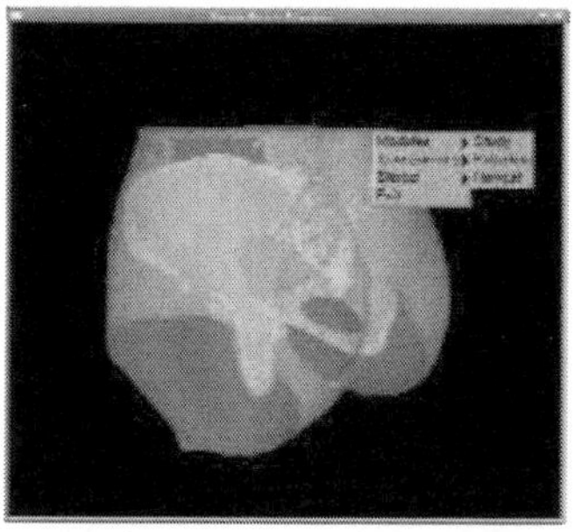

Figure 9: Screenshot of the transparent view task and menu options available.

The second module available is the Palpation module. For this step of the training, all interaction with the objects was disabled and the position of the objects was fixed. In fact, the only visualization possible is from the backside of the skin model. Because the visualization of the bone and bone marrow models is not allowed, these models were disable and will not be rendered. However, they can be identified by touch since the user starts the haptic interaction (Figure 10). With the haptic device the user will be able to feel the different material properties throughout the skin and identify a hardest area, located under the iliac crest (not visible). In this module, the finger model was related to the haptic device and the point of contact is located on its tip.

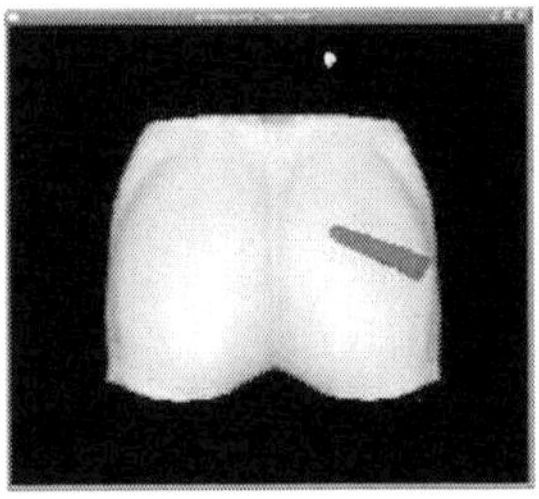

Figure 10: Palpation tasks and the representation of the haptic device by a finger.

In the last module, the Harvest, the user can practice how to harvest the bone marrow. As in the Palpation module, movements with the body models are not allowed and a needle represents the haptic device. In this module is possible to penetrate into the models with the haptic device and all body structures - skin, bone and bone marrow - are haptically displayed. It allows reaching the bone marrow under the skin and inside the bone.

To the online user's assessment the simulation had to be executed several times to calibrate the assessment tool. This stage allows acquiring the assessment parameters to be used in the on-line assessment. In order to reach that, an expert executes several times the training and at the end of that, he/she labels each one into M classes of performance (M=5 in the Figure 8: "Well Qualified", "Qualified", "Need Some Training", "Need More Training" and "Novice"). This procedure is necessary to measure the statistical variability for each class of performance and improve the accuracy of the assessment method. It was used the Maximum Likelihood based method (Moraes & Machado, 2005a). Figure 11 shows the calibration stage of the simulator in the harvest module. The only difference between the calibration procedure for training assessment and the final training application is the presence of calibration options in the menu. In the calibration procedure, these options will be selected by an expert to label the class of performance for each calibration procedure. In the final application this menu option is replaced by an assessment option which can be selected by the user to receive his assessment report at the end of the simulation.

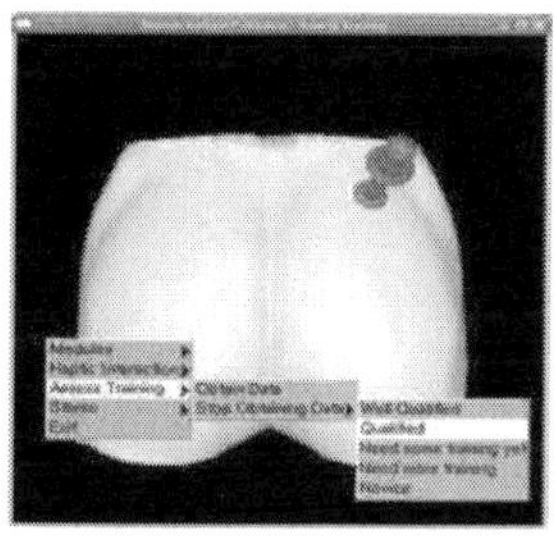

Figure 11: Assess of training: acquisition of the assessment parameters.

RESULTS

The bone marrow harvest simulator was designed and developed by Machado (2003). The present work used the same models and material property parameters of the previous work to develop a new application, with the same training goal but using a framework in its development. To compare the applications, the previous simulator will be called BMHSimulator and the new application CybBMH. Table 2 shows the main differences between BMHSimulator and CybBMH.

The CybBMH was developed only using free tools: GNU C++ language and the CyberMed system. The modeling package used to model the needle and the finger was the Blender, also free. Because the CyberMed integrates and synchronizes visual and haptic routines, it was not necessary the use of other tools for the development of the CybBMH. In opposite, the BMHSimulator required the use of several tools that must to be integrated, besides the necessity of synchronization of the visual and haptic tasks. The use of a single class to store the models topology allows utilizing the same three objects for visual and haptic scenes in the CybBMH. Additionally, two models were used to represent the haptic device in the visual scene. The illumination treatment offered by the CyberMed also allows providing a better visual quality. The visual quality of the simulators can be observed in the Figure 12. The BMHSimulator used three models for the visual scene and other three models for the haptic scene. Due to performance reasons, the haptic models were simplified and the number of vertexes was reduced. Then, visual and haptic scenes did not share the same object and was necessary to use six different models in the past simulator. The representation of the haptic device was done through textures applied on crossed plans. In spite of optimizing the rendering process, this approach presented graphic imperfections.

Table 2: Main differences between the simulator previously developed and the new simulator

	BMHSimulator	CybBMH
Operational system	Windows™	Linux
programming tools	- Visual C++ - OpenGL - Ghost API - Microsoft Foundation Classes	- GNU C++ - CyberMed
Haptic device	Phantom Desktop	any Phantom family device
Stereoscopy method	temporal multiplexing	temporal multiplexing
Number of models	6	5
Time for application development	~1 year	~2 months

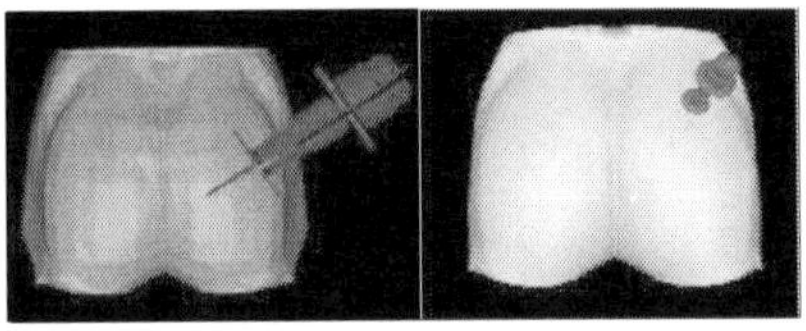

Figure 12: Visual results of a previous application (left) and of the simulator developed with the CyberMed (right).

Both simulators support the use of shutter glasses and haptic devices. However, in the BMHSimulator the use of this hardware required a previous study of OpenGL functions to implement the routines for stereoscopic images generation. The same effort was necessary to integrate the haptic device and its routines to the application through the device API. In that simulator, the application window and menus were defined using the Visual C++ IDE (Integrated Development Environment) and the Microsoft Foundation Classes. The efforts needed to learn how to use all the tools mentioned above and to the implement the application demanded approximately one year for the complete development of the simulator. The CybBMH also demanded efforts to its development. However, it was focused in the use of the CyberMed classes. By the definition of objects and by the access to their of methods, it was possible to use methods, already integrated, ready to deal with stereoscopy, haptic devices and menus. It allowed reducing the time of development of the simulator to approximately two months. Additionally, the CyberMed classes provided an on-line assessment method to assess user's performance. This functionality offers a performance feedback to the user and can be used to know his ability level.

The sequence of the steps of the simulation is the same in both applications. The dissection and the transparency settings available in the Study module can be equally performed through menus. However the illumination model provided by the CyberMed classes allowed to offer better graphic results in the CybBMH, especially in the Study module, due to the presence of three models composed by thousands of points (skin, bone and bone marrow).

Two haptic devices of the Phantom family (Sensable, 2010) were tested and used with the CybBMH: the Omni and the Phantom Desktop. The exchange of the haptic devices did not require any change in the final code of the application. The main differences between the two devices are the size of the workspace, the precision and the amount of force which can be exerted.

The time consumed in the development of the BMHSimulator and the CybBMH did not include the acquisition of the simulation parameters or the design of models used in the application.

Assessment of Users

The framework CyberMed presents a higher level of abstraction, is dedicated to the development of medical applications and presents methods for on-line assess users' performance. In the version 2.0 of CyberMed, three evaluation methods are available: Maximum Likelihood, General Bayesian Network and Expert system based on Fuzzy Rules, which were described early. All of them can be applied to bone marrow harvest simulator.

When a training system based on VR is implemented, always need to involve experts in the area object of the system, not only in the design and calibration properties, but also to assess the final version of the system. The ideal way to evaluate is to perform procedures under various specific conditions in which the system is able to allow. So, the experts through questionnaires record their impressions about the system. Another option is doing usability tests with the experts. At this stage, some problems still can be detected and should be fixed, after which another round of evaluation is performed. Once the experts qualify the system, it really becomes useful for the medical community that will use it.

In the case of development of the bone marrow harvest system, experts followed its conception from the Children Hospital of the University of São Paulo (Brazil). They calibrated the system properties and tested them. At the end of development, system qualification tests were performed (Machado, 2003). When redesigning the system using CyberMed framework, these experiences have been incorporated and the configuration parameters were reused from the previous system (Souza et al., 2007).

For the problem of bone marrow harvest, it is possible to choose any one of three methods of assessment in CyberMed. However, in this case was chosen the method of maximum likelihood, due to limitation of other methods on the size of the database and the expert knowledge.

To verify performance of the method of maximum likelihood and for reasons of general performance of the VR simulator, the following variables were chosen to be monitored: spatial position, velocities, forces and time on each layer. Previously, an expert, according to M classes of performance defined by him, calibrated the system. The calibration process consists in to execute several times the procedure and to classify each one according to classes of performance. The number of classes of performance was defined as M=3: 1) correct procedures, 2) acceptable procedures, 3) badly executed procedures. So, the classes of performance for a trainee could be: "you are well qualified", "you need some training yet", "you need more training". Sixty samples of training (twenty of each class of performance) were used for calibration of evaluation system. After that, users performed 150 procedures. The information of variability about these procedures was acquired using the maximum likelihood method. In our case, we assume that the source of information for w_j classes is the vector of the sample data D. The user makes his/ her training in the virtual reality simulator and the evaluation tool collects data from his/ her manipulation. All probabilities of data for each class of performance are calculated and at the end the user is assigned to a w_j class of performance. So, when a trainee uses the system, their performance is compared with each expert's class of performance and the assessment tool assigns the most appropriated class, according to the trainee's performance. At the end of the training, the assessment system reports the classification to the trainee.

The Cohen's Kappa Coefficient was used to perform the comparison of the classification agreement, as recommended in the literature (Duda et al., 2000) because it is known to be over conservative. The classification matrix obtained for the method is presented in the Table 3. The Kappa coefficient was K=81.0% with variance 1.6×10^{-3} %. In 19 cases, the evaluation tool made mistakes and at least one classification was made incorrectly in all classes. That performance is good and shows that maximum likelihood method is a competitive approach in the solution of assessment problems.

Table 3: Classification Matrix for the Evaluation Tool based on Maximum Likelihood

Class of performance according to experts	Class of performance according to Evaluation Tool		
	1	2	3
1	46	0	4
2	1	49	0
3	8	6	36

In statistical terms, the performance of maximum likelihood method is acceptable. About computational performance the average of CPU time consumed was 0.0160 seconds, showing the method is qualified as online.

CONCLUSION

The development of applications based on VR for medical training involves knowledge of several areas and demands a multidisciplinary team. The union of ideas is important in all stages of the development as: definition of scope, design, modelling, definition of assessment method, implementation, tests and validation.

A simulator based on VR must contain the same steps present in a real procedure and can use volumetric models, stereoscopic visualization, haptic systems, deformation methods and interactive cut. The use of all those features requires a lot of processing and can compromise the real-time performance. Usually, the development team defines the most important features to integrate the simulator. It will also depend on the budget available.

Several systems were developed to the design and implementation of VR applications. Some of them are not free and demands specific non-free platforms. There are also, free systems to allow the development, integration and synchronization of tasks and tools in VR systems. In particular, the framework CyberMed presents a higher level of abstraction, is dedicated to the development of medical applications and presents methods for on-line assess users' performance.

A bone marrow harvest simulator was developed with CyberMed, explaining their facilities when compared to the full implementation of techniques and devices support routines. Thus, this Chapter showed the challenges and possible solutions related to the development of VR-based simulators for training. Particularly, was presented the importance of a user assessment included in the system to allow identifying mistakes and points for improvement. In this context, CyberMed is the only framework that provides assessment methods ready for use.

In particular, an assessment tool can, in real-time, to modify simulation aspects, as variables and functions responsible for feedback. Besides, this information can also be utilized to verify the degree of accuracy of users when performing the simulation. In the bone marrow harvest simulator implementation was used an assessment tool based on maximum likelihood, which achieved good results in a performance test.

Nowadays, there are other simulators been developed with CyberMed. The inclusion of new classes and methods already allow the development of tutoring applications over Internet. However, the framework has been expanded with new functionalities for synchronous collaboration (Sales et al., 2010).

As future works, is intended to make tests and statistical comparisons among the others assessment methodologies presented in this Chapter, as well as, to make a statistical comparison between trainees that use the VR system in their training and other trainees that do not use.

REFERENCES

1. Burdea, G.; Patounakis, G.; Popescu, V.; Weiss, R.E. (1998) Virtual Reality Training for the Diagnosis of Prostate Cancer. Proc. IEEE Virtual Reality Annual Int. Symposium (VRAIS'98), pp. 190-197.
2. Burdea, G & Coiffet, P. (2003) Virtual Reality Technology. Wiley Interscience.
3. Cheng, J. & Greiner, R. (2001) Learning Bayesian Belief Network Classifiers: Algorithms and System, Proc. 40th Canadian Conference on Artificial Intelligence.
4. Correa, C.G.; Nunes, F.L.S.; Bezerra, A. (2009) Evaluation of VR Medical Training Applications under the Focus of Professionals of the Health Area. Proc. ACM-SAC Symposium on Applied Computer, pp. 821, Hawaii, ACM, Honolulu.
5. Darzi, A.; Smith, S.; Taffinder, N. (1999) Assessing operative skills. British Medical Journal, v.318, n.7188, pp.887-888.
6. Derossis, A.M. et al. (1998) Development of a model for training and evaluation of laparoscopic skills. American Journal of Surgery, v. 175, n.6, pp. 482-487.
7. Dinsmore, M. (1996) Virtual reality simulation: training for palpation of subsurface tumors. Master's Thesis, Department of Mechanical and Aerospace Engineering, Rutgers University, October.
8. Dinsmore, M.; Langrana, N.; Burdea, G.; Ladeji, J. (1997) Virtual Reality Training Simulation for Palpation of Subsurface Tumors. Proc. IEEE VRAIS 1997, pp. 54-60.
9. Dubois, D. & Prade, H. (1980) Fuzzy sets and systems - theory and applications. New York: Academic Press.
10. Dubois, D. & Prade, H. (1988) Possibility theory: An approach to computerized processing of uncertainty. Plenum Press.
11. Duda, R.O.; Hart, P.E.; Stork, D.G. (2000) Pattern Classification. 2nd ed. Wiley.
12. Färber, M. et al. (2008) Heinz Handels Training and evaluation of lumbar punctures in a VRenvironment using a 6DOF haptic device, Studies in Health Technology and Informatics v.132, p.112-114.
13. Gallagher, A. G. et al. (1999) Virtual Reality training in laparoscopic surgery: A preliminary assessment of minimally invasive Surgical trainer Virtual Reality (MIST VR). Endoscopy, v.31, n.4, pp. 310-313.

14. Gallagher, A. G. et al. (2001) Objective psychomotor skills assessment of experienced, junior, and novice laparoscopists with virtual reality. World Journal of Surgery, v.25, n.11, pp. 1478-1483.
15. Gallagher, A. G. et al. (2005) Virtual Reality Simulation for the Operating Room: ProficiencyBased Training as a Paradigm Shift in Surgical Skills Training. Annals of Surgery, v.241, n.2, pp. 364-372.
16. Huang, J.; Payandeh, S.; Doris, P.; Hajshirmohammadi, I. (2005) Fuzzy Classification: Towards Evaluating Performance on a Surgical Simulator. Studies in Health Technology and Informatics v.111, pp. 194-200.
17. Johnson, R.A. & Wichern, D.W. (2001) Applied Multivariate Statistical Analysis, Prentice Hall, 5 edition.
18. Kumagai, K.; Yamashita, J.; Morikawa, O.; Yokoyama, K. (2007) A New Force-Based Objective Assessment of Technical Skills in Endoscopic Sinus Surgery. Studies in Health Technology and Informatics v.125, pp. 235-237.
19. Krause, P. J. (1998) Learning Probabilistic Networks, Knowledge Engineering Review, vol. 13, pp. 321-351.
20. Langrana, N.; Burdea, G.; Ladeji, J.; Dinsmore, M. (1997) Human Performance Using Virtual Reality Tumor Palpation Simulation. Computer & Graphics, v.21, n.4, pp.451-458.
21. Machado, L.S. (2003) Virtual Reality to Modeling and Simulation of Invasive Procedures for Pediatrics Oncology: A Case Study in Bone Marrow Transplant. PhD Thesis. Dept. of Electrical Engineering, University of Sao Paulo. (In Portuguese)
22. Machado, L.S. & Moraes, R.M. (2006). Evaluation of Training Executed by Web Using Multilayer Perceptron Based Systems. Proceedings of World Congress on Computer Science, Engineering and Technology Education (WCCSETE'2006). March, Santos, Brasil, p. 228-232.
23. Machado, L.S. & Moraes, R.M. (2009). Qualitative and Quantitative Assessment for a VRBased Simulator. Studies in Health Technology and Informatics, v. 142, p. 168-173.
24. Machado, L.S. & Moraes, R.M. (2010) Intelligent Decision Making in Training Based on Virtual Reality. In: Da Ruan. (Org.) Computational Intelligence in Complex Decision Systems, Chapter 4. Atlantis Press, 9789078677277 , Paris.
25. Machado, L. S.; Moraes, R. M.; Zuffo, M. K. (2000)A Fuzzy Rule-

Based Evaluation for a Haptic and Stereo Simulator for Boné Marrow Harvest for Transplant. In: Annals of Phantom Users Group. Aspen.

26. Machado, L. S.; Valdek, M. C. O.; Moraes, R. M. (2008) On-Line Assessment System for a Training System with Multiple Stages Based on Virtual Reality. Journal of MultipleValued Logic and Soft Computing, v.14, n.3-5, p.511-524.
27. Machado, L.S.; Moraes, R.M.; Souza, D.F.L; Souza, L.C.; Cunha, I.L.L. (2009) A Framework for Development of Virtual Reality-Based Training Simulators. Studies in Health Technology and Informatics, v. 142, pp. 174-176. IOSPress.
28. Mackel, T.; Rosen, J.; Pugh, C. (2006) Data Mining of the E-Pelvis Simulator Database: A Quest for a Generalized Algorithm for Objectively Assessing Medical Skill, Studies in Health Technology and Informatics 119, 355-360.
29. Mamdani, E.H. & Assilan, S. (1975) An experiment in linguistic synthesis with a fuzzy logic controller. International Journal of Man-Machine Studies, v. 7, no. 1, pp.1–13, 1975.
30. McBeth, P.B. et al. (2002) Quantitative Methodology of Evaluating Surgeon Performance in Laparoscopic Surgery. Studies in Health Technology and Informatics v. 85. 2002, pp. 280-286.
31. McCloy, R. & Stone, R. (2001) Science, medicine, and the future: Virtual reality in surgery. British Medical Journal, v.323, n.7318, p. 912–915.
32. Moraes, R.M. & Machado, L.S. (2005a) Maximum Likelihood for On-line Evaluation of Training Based on Virtual Reality. Proc. Global Congress on Engineering and Technology Education (GCETE'2005). March, Santos, Brasil, p.299-302.
33. Moraes, R.M. & Machado, L.S. (2005b) Evaluation of Training Executed by Web Using Fuzzy Rule Based Expert Systems. Proc. Global Congress on Engineering and Technology Education (GCETE'2005). March, Santos, Brasil, p.857-860.
34. Moraes, R.M. & Machado, L.S. (2006) Continuous Evaluation in Training Systems Based on Web. Proceedings of World Congress on Computer Science, Engineering and Technology Education (WCCSETE'2006). Março, Santos, Brasil, p. 223-227.
35. Moraes, R.M. & Machado, L.S. (2007) Multiple Assessment for Multiple Users in Virtual Reality Training Environments. Lecture

Notes in Computer Science. Berlim. v. 4756, p. 950-956. Springer.

36. Moraes, R.M. & Machado, L.S. (2008) Using Embedded Systems to Improve Performance of Assessment in Virtual Reality Training Environments. Proc. Int. Conference on Engineering and Technology Education 2008 (Intertech'2008). March, Santos, Brasil, p. 140-144.
37. Moraes, R.M. & Machado, L.S. (2009a) Online Training Evaluation in Virtual Reality Simulators Using Possibilistic Networks. Proc. Safety Health and Environmental World Congress 2009 (SHEWC'2009). July, Mongaguá, Brasil, p. 67-71.
38. Moraes, R.M. & Machado, L.S. (2009b) Another Approach for Fuzzy Naive Bayes Applied on Online Training Assessment in Virtual Reality Simulators. Proc. Safety Health and Environmental World Congress 2009 (SHEWC'2009). July, Mongaguá, Brazil, p. 62-66.
39. Moraes, R.M. & Machado, L.S. (2010). Fuzzy Gaussian Naive Bayes Applied to Online Assessment in Virtual Reality Simulators. Proc. 9th Int. FLINS Conf. Foundations and Applications of Computational Intelligence (FLINS'2010). August, Chengdu, China, p. 243-248.
40. Moraes, R.M.; Machado, L.S.; Souza, L.C. (2009) Online Assessment of Training in Virtual Reality Simulators Based on General Bayesian Networks. In: Proc. VI International Conference on Engineering and Computer Education (ICECE 2009). Mongaguá, Brazil. CDROM.
41. Neapolitan, R.E. (2003) Learning Bayesian Networks, Prentice Hall. Series in Artificial Intelligence.
42. Rich, E. & Knight, K. (1993) Artificial Intelligence. McGraw Hill.
43. Sales, B.R.A.; Machado, L.S.; Moraes, R.M. (2010) Interactive Collaboration for Virtual Reality Systems related to Medical Education and Training. In: Proc. 6th Int. Conference on Technology and Medical Sciences (TMSi), Porto, Portugal. CDROM. Sensable Technologies – Haptic Devices. Online: http:/ / www.sensable.com/ productshaptic-devices.htm. Access in July, 2010.
44. Souza, D.F.L.; Cunha, I.L.L.; Souza, L.C.; Moraes, R.M.; Machado, L.S. (2007) Development of a VR Simulator for Medical Training Using Free Tools: A Case Study. In: Proc. of Symp. Virtual and Augmented Reality (SVR2007), p. 100-105, Brazil, SBC.
45. Taffinder, N. et al. (1998) Validation of virtual reality to teach and assess psychomotor skills in laparoscopic surgery: results from randomised controlled studies using the MIST VR laparoscopic simulator. Medicine

Meets Virtual Reality. Amsterdam: IOS Press, p. 124-130.

46. Wilson, M.S.; et al. (1997) MIST VR: a virtual reality trainer for surgery assesses performance. Annals of the Royal College of Surgeons of England, v.79, p. 403-404.
47. Zadeh, L.A. (1965) Fuzzy Sets. Information Control. n 8., pp. 338-353.
48. Zadeh, L.A. (1988) Fuzzy Logic. Computer, v. 1. pp.83-93.

Chapter 11

On the Development of Virtual Reality Scenarios for Computer-Assisted Biomedical Applications

Eder H. Govea-Valladares[1] , Hugo I. Medellin-Castillo[1] , Jorge Ballesteros[2] , and Miguel A. Rodriguez-Florido[2]

[1]Facultad de Ingeniería, Universidad Autónoma de San Luis Potosí, 78290, San Luis Potosí, Mexico
[2]Instituto Tecnológico de Canarias, Playa Pozo Izquierdo s/n, 35119, Las Palmas, Islas Canarias, Spain

ABSTRACT

The modelling of virtual environments and scenarios is an important area of research for the development of new computer-assisted systems in the areas of engineering and medicine, particularly in the area of biomechanics and biomedical engineering. One of the main issues while designing a virtual environment is the level of realism, which depends on the computing capacity

Citation: Eder H. Govea-Valladares, Hugo I. Medellin-Castillo, Jorge Ballesteros, and Miguel A. Rodriguez-Florido, "On the Development of Virtual Reality Scenarios for Computer-Assisted Biomedical Applications," Journal of Healthcare Engineering, vol. 2018, Article ID 1930357.

and the level of accuracy and usefulness of the generated data. Thus, the dilemma is between the aesthetic realism and the information utility. This paper proposes a methodology to develop low-cost and high-quality virtual environments and scenarios for computer-aided biomedical applications. The proposed methodology is based on the open-source software Blender and the Visualization Toolkit libraries (VTK). In order to demonstrate the usability of the proposed methodology, the design and development of a computer-assisted biomedical application is presented and analysed.

INTRODUCTION

In the early days, scientific research was based on observations of natural and physical phenomena. However, in the last years, the research scope has included the modelling and simulation of physical phenomena by means of computer technologies. The sight has been the most developed sense in computer simulations and virtual environments, leading to the origin of the scientific visualization concept [1]. By means of scientific visualization, it is possible to transform mathematical data into 2D or 3D images or vice versa [2], allowing the communication and understanding of large amount of information efficiently. It also allows the visualization of physical phenomena that are not possible to visualize by common methods, such as experimental observations. Moreover, the representation of reality is also possible by means of animations, modelling, and graphic renderings.

Virtual reality (VR) can be described as a set of technologies that enable people to interact with a virtual environment beyond reality [3]. VR takes advantage of the computer technological development and scientific visualization to create a virtual world [4]. The use of VR has become very popular because it offers a high level of realism and immersion but requires advanced computing technologies capable of processing large amounts of scientific data and graphics [5]. VR has been used in different areas such as engineering, medicine, education, entertainment, astronomy, archaeology, and arts. In the area of medicine, virtual environments are created to enable the interaction with the human body anatomy [6]. The practice of medicine is a complex decision-making process that requires knowledge, experience, and manual abilities [7]; practitioner abilities are gained by training and experience, which is a slow process that may take several years. In order to get experience and abilities, a medical apprentice must be the protagonist of his/her training but considering as the main priority the avoidance of risks and unnecessary inconveniences for the patient [8]. Consequently, the use of VR and computer technologies in medicine has become an important tool for students and practitioners to understand and confirm concepts and to improve surgical skills and for experienced surgeons to make more precise diagnosis and plan the surgery [9–11]. One of the main applications of VR and computer technologies in medicine has been the development of computer-assisted surgery and simulation systems [12, 13].

In the area of engineering, VR applications include the design and evaluation of components and prototypes before construction [14–16], the manufacturing planning of components [12, 17–19], and assembly training [20]. On the other hand, VR applications in the area of art include virtual sculpting [21], reconstruction and preservation of buildings [22, 23], and development of environments, structures, and scenarios for the film industry [24].

A main issue of VR and computer-assisted applications is the design and development of the virtual environment (VE), which comprises the modelling of virtual objects, including their geometry and surface characteristics such as colours and textures. However, the amount of data to be processed by the VR application increases as the level of realism of the virtual environment increases, affecting the performance of the application. Thus, the dilemma is between the largest amount of data to increase the quality of the results, and the minimum use of computer resources with an acceptable level of realism.

This work presents a methodology to design and develop high-quality virtual scenarios with a high degree of realism for medical applications. The methodology is based on the open-source software Blender and VTK, leading to a low-cost development. The proposed approach is intended to be used in the development of computer-assisted biomedical applications, such as surgery planning, simulation, and training.

LITERATURE REVIEW

The solid modelling developed in the mid-1970s [25] is a set of mathematical principles for modelling objects, such as solid or hollow shapes delimited by a mesh, using computational methods [26], that is, creating digital models of physical objects of the real world. The main feature of solid modelling is that it is focused on the surface characteristics of the object. The constructive solid geometry (CSG) considers the modelling of solid objects using Boolean operations, which is useful for tasks requiring mathematical precision [27, 28]. On the other hand, Boundary Representation (B-Rep)

[29] connects vertices with lines to create faces, allowing the generation of complex geometries where the level of accuracy depends on the amount of elements in the mesh [27, 28].

Several applications of solid modelling in the area of medicine can be found in the literature, for instance, the 3D modelling of a femur by using the software called 3ds Max [30]. One example of designing virtual scenarios for surgical planning was presented by Domínguez-Quintana et al. [31]. Snyder et al. [32] presented an investigation to compare the impact of training with or without supervision using a virtual reality surgical simulator of laparoscopy and endoscopy. Debes et al. [33] compared the training effectiveness between a virtual simulator and a training video in laparoscopic surgery. A successful virtual environment requires that virtual parts behave as the parts in the real world [34].

Virtual reality (VR) technologies can be used to enhance the performance of surgical simulators by providing a virtual environment where users can get the feeling of immersion in a real environment, in addition to more intuitive cues such as collisions between virtual objects, collisions with obstacles, friction, inertia, restitution, 3D rendering, and sound [35]. Moreover, virtual environments can be improved by incorporating haptic technologies to provide the user with the sense of touch. Haptics allows natural manipulation of virtual objects by enabling the user with the feeling of collisions, forces, weight, and inertia of virtual objects. In this way, haptic-enabled computer-assisted medical applications are more intuitive, accurate, and efficient than conventional computer-aided systems in medicine [11].

In general, a VR application in medicine comprises five main modules:

- model reconstruction module, to generate 3D models from medical data such as CT and MRI images,
- visualization module, responsible for the graphics rendering of the virtual environment,
- manipulation module, to provide the interaction between the user and the virtual environment,
- simulation module, responsible for the physical based behaviour of the virtual environment and objects, and
- data module, responsible for processing, analysing, and exporting the medical data.

There have been several research works reported in the literature focusing on the development and analysis of computer-aided VR applications in medicine. However, few works have addressed the development of virtual environments for such applications [10]. A virtual environment has a great impact on the performance of the application; therefore, its importance is high. Sometimes, it is necessary to sacrifice the level of realism to prioritize the data processing and time response of the system. Nowadays, there are several tools such as modelling software, computers with high computing power, and measurement devices, to develop virtual scenarios. However, these tools can be very expensive and limited to those users with financial capability to such tools. In addition, very few works in the literature have focused on reducing the costs of developing virtual environments.

METHODOLOGY

A new methodology to create virtual reality scenarios (environments) is proposed as shown in Figure 1. This methodology has been implemented using the open-source software Blender 2.49, the Visualization Toolkit VTK 5.6, and the Python 2.7 programming language in Windows operating system.

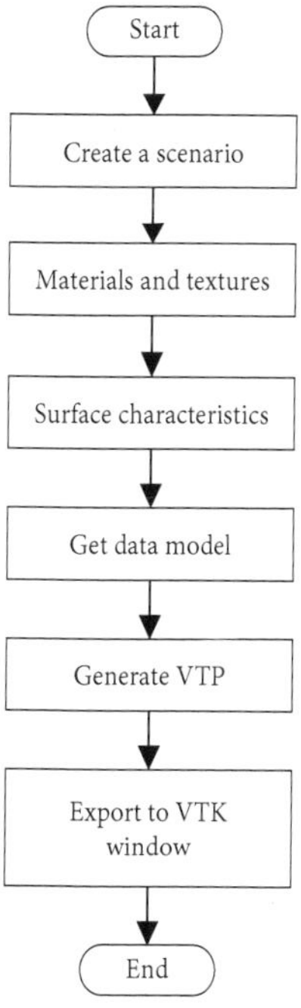

Figure 1: Methodology to create virtual reality scenarios.

The main steps of the proposed methodology are as follows:

- Create scene. Modelling starts in Blender and the first step is to generate the virtual models to be placed on the stage. 3D models can be imported or created using the commands, primitive objects, and Boolean operations of Blender.
- Materials and textures. Textures are then assigned to each element of the models. The texture corresponds to the type of material and the visual aspect that they have in the real world. This process of adding textures is done by using standard images or by assigning colour to each part in Blender.

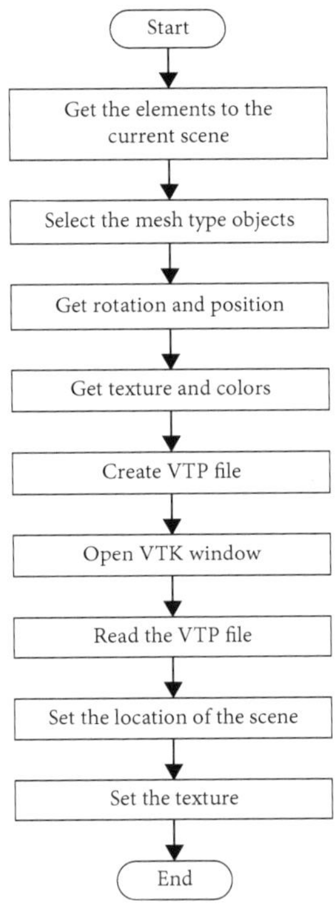

Figure 2: Algorithm to export the Blender scene to a VTK application.

- Surface characteristics. To boost realism, it is necessary to provide the VE with visual features like lighting, shadows, reflections, transparencies, and more. This process can be carried out in Blender.
- Get data model. Once the scene has been completed, the next step is to extract the information corresponding to orientation,

rotation, and location of each object in the scene.

- Generate VTP. In this step, the virtual scenario is converted into a VTP file. The VTP (VTK Polygonal Data) is a VTK file that contains the polygonal data of the 3D model.

Export to VTK window. Finally, the VTP file is used to import all the elements of the scene into a VTK window in the external application being developed. The algorithm to export the Blender scene to a VTK window of the external application is shown in Figure 2. In order to show the level of realism that can be obtained using the proposed methodology, two virtual scenarios were developed. These scenarios are described in the next paragraphs.

Jaw Articulator

The first medical virtual scenario corresponds to a jaw articulator, which is a mechanical device that represents the human jaw joints, and that is used to simulate and adjust the motion of the jaw physical models. The jaw articulator is used for oral and maxillofacial surgery planning. Figure 3(a) shows the real-world articulator used as reference. Each part of the articulator was created using primitive objects and Boolean operations in Blender 2.49. Texture characteristics such as colour and visualization properties such as transparency level, reflection, shadows, and so on were also added to the different parts of the virtual model, Figure 3(b). A 3D model of a human jaw was obtained from medical image reconstruction and imported into the virtual scenario where the articulator was created. Also an image type texture was added to simulate the real bone texture. Finally, a smoothing filter was applied to obtain a smooth surface free of imperfections due to the mesh. Figure 3(c)shows the virtual jaw articulator and the final virtual scenario corresponding to a hospital.

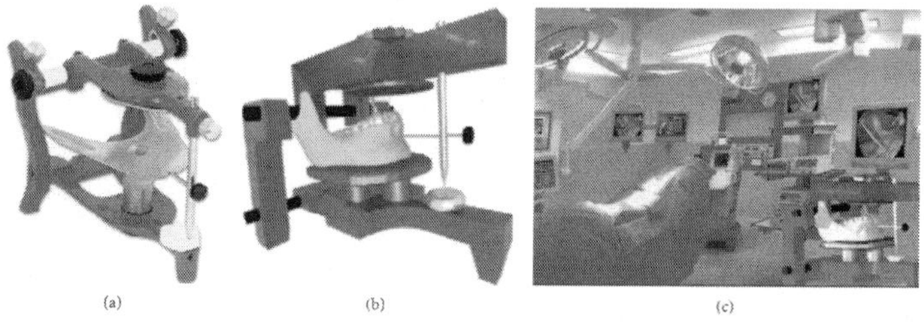

Figure 3: Jaw articulator. (a) Real articulator. (b) Virtual articulator. (c) Virtual scenario.

From Figure 3, it can be observed the lighting effects on the elements' surface, the texture applied to the mandible, and some surface properties to simulate the light reflection. It can also be observed that there are some elements that simulate different types of materials, such as plastics and metals, resulting in objects with transparency and very high gloss. Moreover, metallic elements give a more realistic visualization.

Surgical Simulator

Biomedical engineering makes use of virtual environments to develop surgical simulators for planning and training various clinical procedures. Thus, the second virtual scenario corresponds to an orthognathic surgery simulator to perform dental surgeries or procedures in a virtual dental office environment. Figure 4(a) shows the virtual scene corresponding to a dental room with a patient sitting in a dental unit.

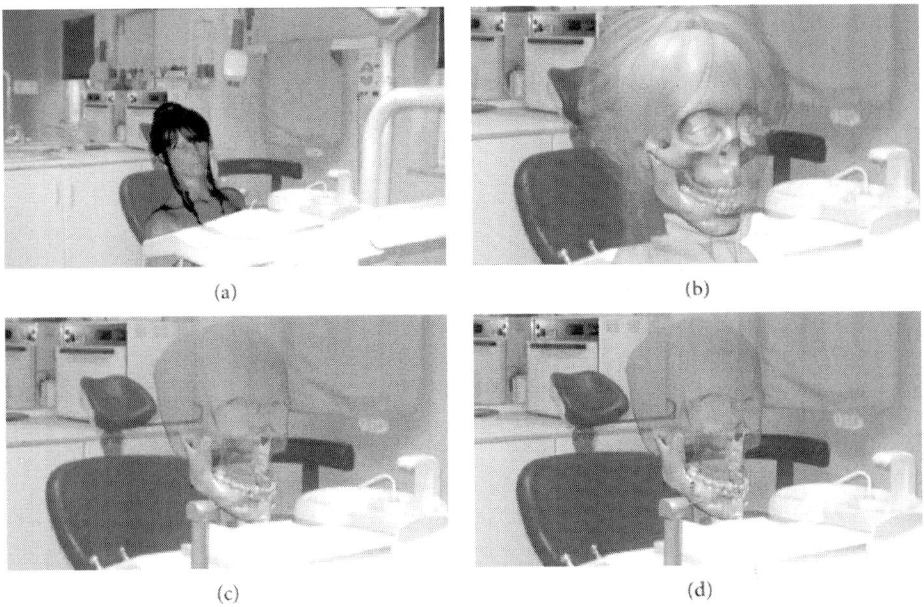

Figure 4: Medical surgical simulator. (a) Dental room. (b) Transparent layers of virtual patient. (c) Virtual tool for bone cutting. (d) Results of virtual bone cutting.

Textures, lights, and images can be used to increase the level of realism. Transparency can be also used to observe internal details such as the bone structure, Figure 4(b). Dental surgical tools, such as mills or drills, can be modelled and added to the virtual scenario to perform virtual cuts on the patient jaw bone, Figure 4(c). The advantage of this type of virtual scenarios is that the practitioner can perform the surgical procedures as many times as necessary in order to practice or to plan the real surgery procedure. Figure 4(d) shows the footprint of the virtual cut performed on the virtual mandible.

CASE STUDY

In order to show the details and usability of the proposed methodology for the development of VR scenarios for computer-aided biomedical applications, a Virtual Osteotomy Simulator System (VOSS) for 3D osteotomy simulation and training was developed and evaluated.

System Description

The VOSS general architecture is shown in Figure 5 and comprises four main modules:

- Visualization module, responsible for carrying out the graphic rendering of virtual objects, tools, and virtual environments
- Osteotomy module, responsible for computing bone cuts and enabling virtual osteotomies
- Manipulation module, to allow the 3D free-form movement and manipulation of virtual objects and surgical tools
- Data exportation module, to export any information regarding the osteotomy simulation (e.g., STL models)

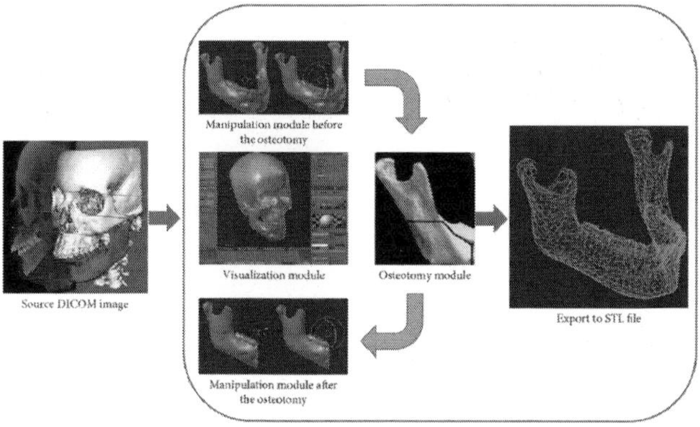

Figure 5: VOSS architecture.

The VOSS was implemented using Python 2.7 and Blender 2.59 in a Workstation with a dual-core AMD processor (3.0 GHz/dual core), 4 GB of RAM, and a NVIDIA Quadro FX3500 PCI Express graphics card. The main capabilities of the VOSS are as follows:

- Virtual reality environment and real-time response
- 3D visualization of anatomical models and tools, including textures and transparency
- 3D free manipulation and interaction of virtual cutting tools, bones, and bone fragments
- Simulation of single and multiple osteotomies
- Free-form cutting path to perform osteotomies
- Free camera manipulation
- Automatic scaling of models.

The GUI of the VOSS is shown in Figure 6. The biomodels can be imported into VOSS as STL or 3DS file formats, which can be generated from medical images (e.g., DICOM images) or 3D scanning.

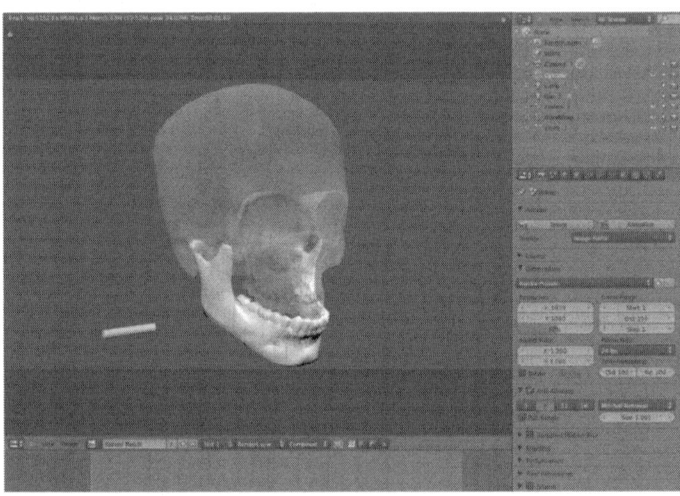

Figure 6: VOSS graphic user interface (GUI).

Virtual Scenario

Figure 7 shows the particular methodology used to define the virtual reality environment of the VOSS. This methodology comprises the following steps in Blender:

- Create a scenario. Generate the virtual environment (lights, cameras, and background image)
- Load skull and jaw biomodels. Import the skull and jaw models as STL or 3DS file formats
- Add texture to bone. Add texture to the skull and jaw bones by means of images. Since the skull is used only as reference and visual support, its texture can be set as transparent
- Model cutting tools. Create the surgical cutting tools (saw and drill) in Blender or import them as STL or 3DS file formats
- Add texture to tools. In order to reproduce the real appearance of surgical cutting tools, provide them with texture
- Create sensors. Generate sensors for the user to control and manipulate objects in the virtual environment by means of the keyboard and/or mouse buttons
- Create controllers. Generate controllers to specify the action to be executed after the activation of a sensor
- Create actuators. Generate actuators to perform the movement or manipulation of the virtual objects according to the sensors. Movements can be either linear or rotational.

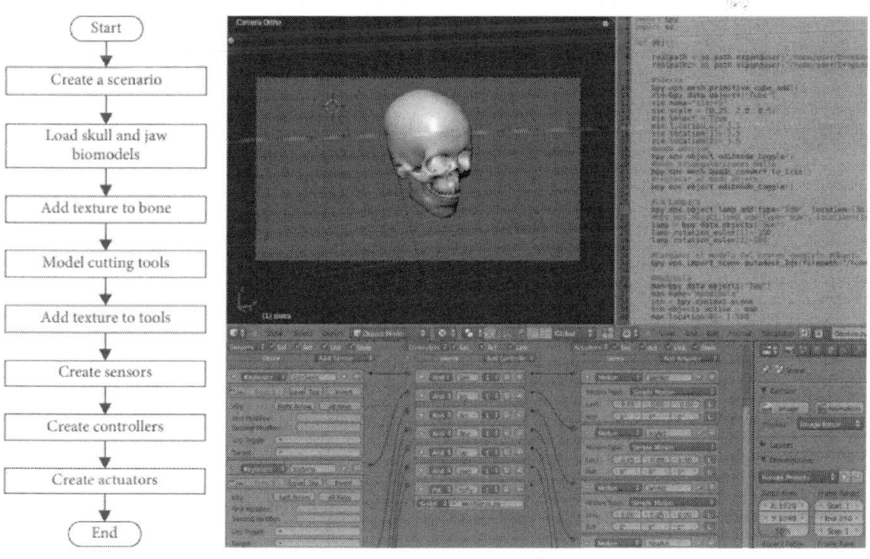

Figure 7: VOSS virtual reality environment. (a) Methodology. (b) Implementation.

The addition of textures to biomodels or tools can be made by means of images with standard file formats (e.g., bmp, jpg, jpeg, and png). The movement and manipulation of virtual models in VOSS is made by means of a numeric keypad, an alphanumeric keypad, a standard computer mouse, or a 3D computer mouse. These movements are defined by sensors, controllers, and actuators, which are created in the Logic mode of the Game Engine in Blender. A sensor is a function for the user to control objects in the virtual environment by means of the keyboard and/or mouse buttons. On the other hand, a controller is a function used to define the action to be executed after the activation of a sensor. Finally, an actuator executes the movements of the virtual objects according to the sensors.

Virtual Osteotomy

The virtual osteotomy procedure implemented in the VOSS corresponds to a Bilateral Sagittal Split Osteotomy Ramus Mandibular (BSSROM) of a human mandible. The aim is to perform bone cutting operations on virtual models of human jaws, that is, to simulate the work of a maxillofacial surgeon when correcting bone malformations. Figure 8 shows the general virtual osteotomy procedure in VOSS.

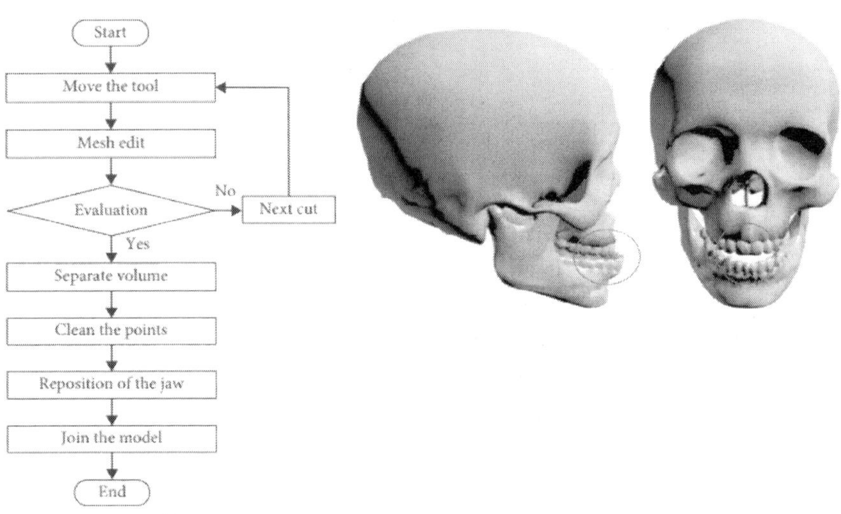

Figure 8: Virtual osteotomy. (a) Procedure. (b) Virtual model with malformation.

The osteotomy procedure begins by selecting a cutting tool and placing it at the position where the first cut is meant to be made, Figure 9. Once the tool is positioned, the cut is performed and it can be repeated as many times as necessary to make a longitudinal cut along the jaw. The user is able to freely move the tool in any 3D path while performing the cut. Figure 10(a) shows the simulation of a vertical cut using a drill, while Figure 10(b) shows the simulation of a cut operation using a sagittal saw. Similar to the real procedure, the virtual jaw can be separated into two fragments (jaw 1 and jaw 2), which can be moved or manipulated independently. Figure 11 shows the bone fragments after the bone separation. The virtual cutting and separation of biomodels are performed by means of the Boolean operations in Blender.

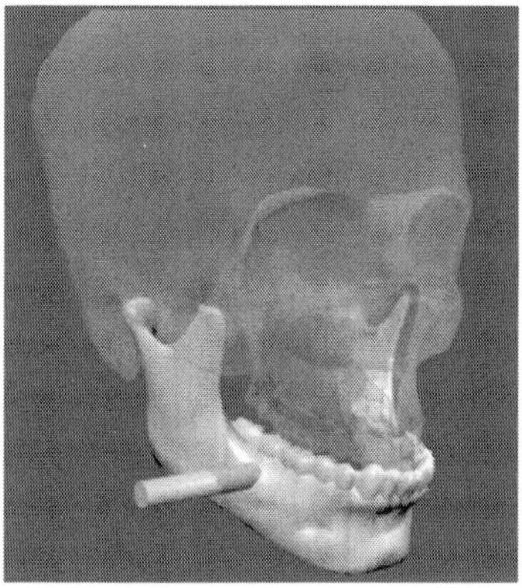

Figure 9: Initial positioning of the tool.

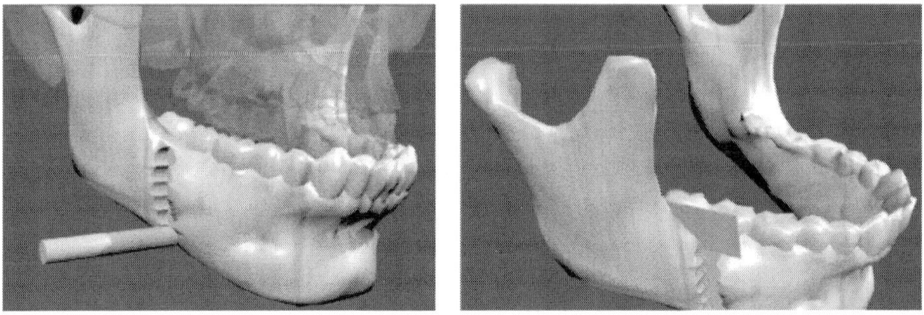

(a) (b)

Figure 10: Cutting process. (a) Drilling. (b) Sawing.

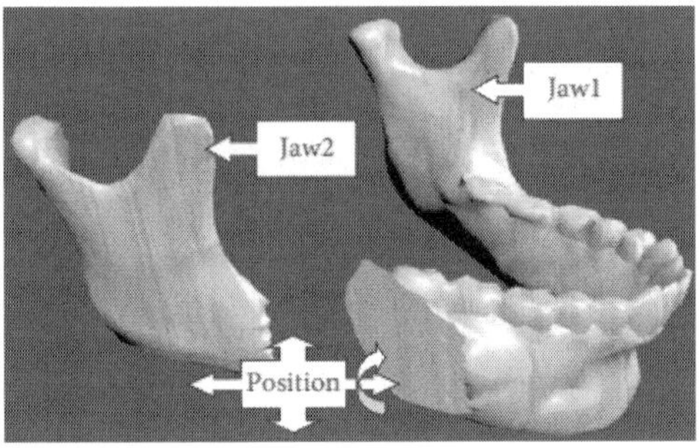

Figure 11: Repositioning of mandible fragments, jaw 1 and jaw 2.

After the mandible splitting, the user is able to manipulate and relocate the jaw fragments in order to reduce or eliminate the bone defect or malformation. Once the mandible fragments are relocated at the correct position, a Boolean operation is carried out to join the jaw fragments. Figure 12 shows the last movement and final relocation of the mandible.

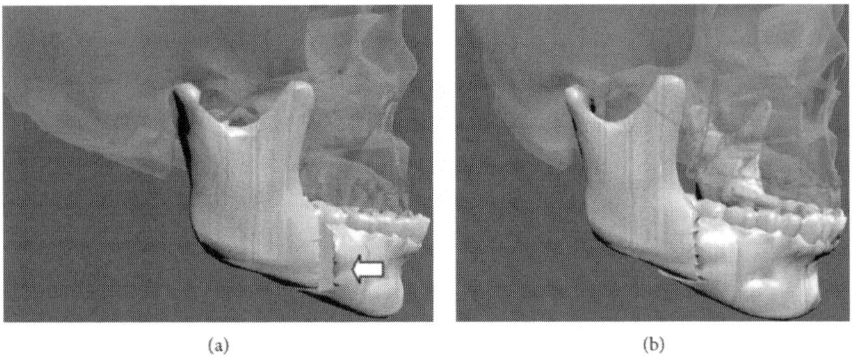

Figure 12: Final step of the virtual osteotomy. (a) Relocation of mandible fragments. (b) Joining of the mandible.

Virtual Osteotomy Training

A biomedical application to evaluate the proposed virtual osteotomy approach as a training tool was developed in the programming language C++ using the Microsoft Foundation Classes (MFC) of Visual Studio 2010, the Visualization Toolkit libraries (VTK) for graphics rendering, and the H3DAPI haptic rendering software development platform for the manipulation of virtual objects. The application provides the user with force feedback by means of a haptic device. Additionally, the application supports different types of haptic devices, including the Phantom Omni from Sensable and the Falcon from Novint. The overall experimental methodology used to evaluate the virtual osteotomy training is shown in Figure 13. A total of nine students of the Oral and Maxillofacial Surgery Postgraduate Program of the "Hospital Central Dr. Ignacio Morones Prieto" in San Luis Potosi, Mexico, were selected. These participants were selected because previous knowledge of the maxillofacial surgical procedures was required. The nine participants were divided into three groups with three persons in each group:(i)Group I. No virtual training. This group of participants carried out the real osteotomy procedure without previous virtual training. (ii)Group II. Virtual training without force feedback. Before carrying out the real osteotomy procedure, this group of participants undertook virtual training but with no force feedback.(iii)Group III. Virtual training with force feedback. Before carrying out the real osteotomy procedure, this group of participants undertook virtual training with force feedback.

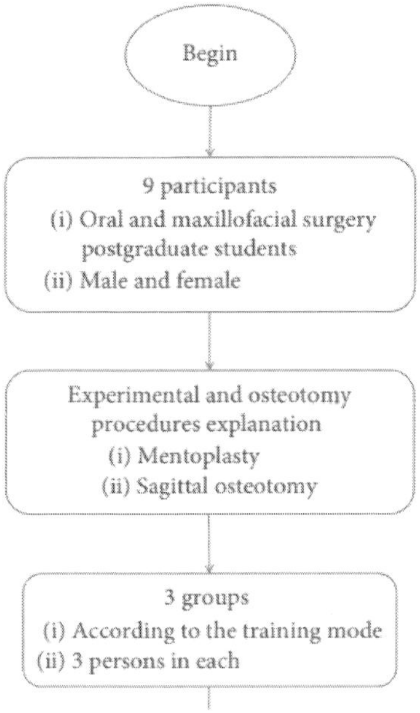

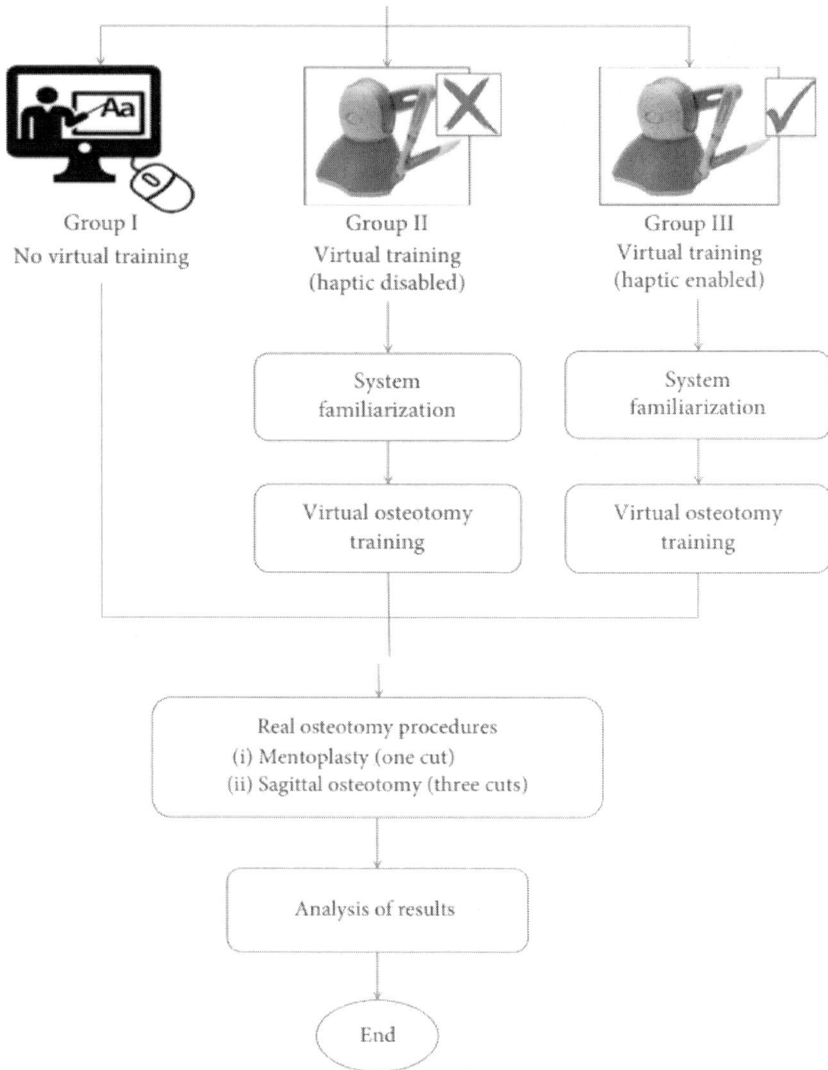

Figure 13: Experimental methodology to evaluate the virtual osteotomy training.

Two different osteotomy procedures were considered in the evaluation: mentoplasty (or chin cut) and sagittal osteotomy (or branch cut) of a human mandible. The mentoplasty procedure comprises one main cut on the chin, while the sagittal osteotomy procedure comprises three cuts: sagittal exterior, sagittal superior, and sagittal interior. Figure 14 shows these four cuts marked by an experienced maxillofacial surgeon on a real human mandible. These cutting trajectories were used as reference for evaluating the usability of virtual training.

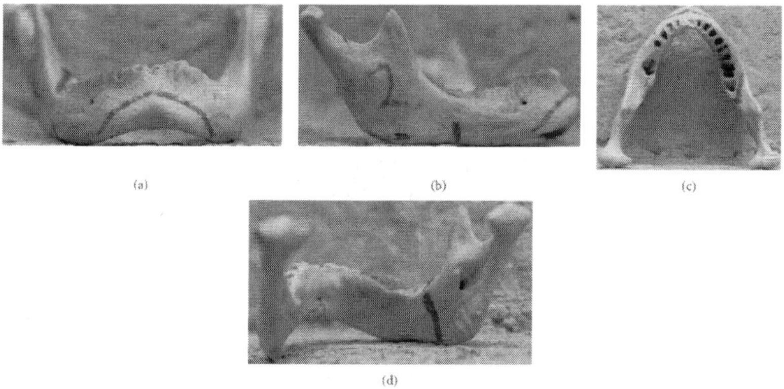

Figure 14: Osteotomy procedures marked by an expert on a real human mandible. (a) Mentoplasty. (b) Sagittal exterior. (c) Sagittal superior. (d) Sagittal interior.

At the beginning, all participants were informed about the general background related to the experiments, the conditions in which they would be working, and the experimental procedure. Then, all participants received a verbal explanation about the osteotomy procedures under consideration and the cuts required, allowing them to ask questions and receive further explanation. Participants of Groups II and III were instructed on the use of the virtual system and the virtual osteotomy procedure, given them the opportunity to familiarise themselves with the system for twenty minutes before undertaking virtual training.

Virtual osteotomy training for participants of Groups II and III consisted in the realization of the two osteotomy procedures in the virtual environment. Participants of Group II were able to manipulate the virtual surgical tools by means of the haptic device but without receiving force feedback, whereas participants of Group III did receive force feedback during the manipulation of the virtual surgical tools.

Virtual training was carried out on virtual models in the virtual environment by means of a Phantom Omni haptic device. On the other hand, the real osteotomy procedures were carried out on physical 3D prototypes, made of PLA in a 3DTouch printer from 3D systems®, and using a conventional high-speed milling tool, as shown in Figure 15.

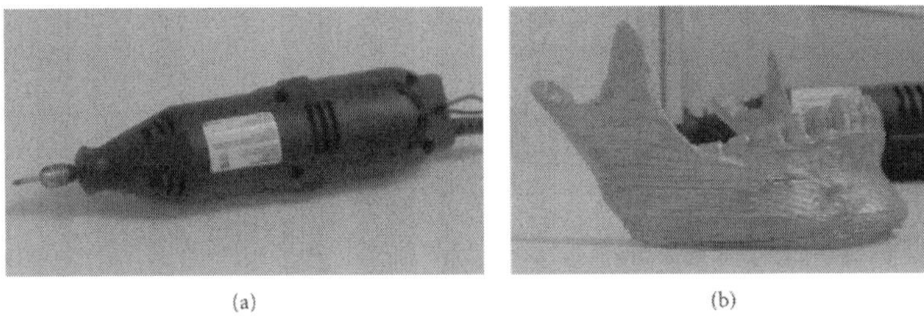

Figure 15: Real osteotomy implements. (a) Manual high-speed milling tool. (b) Physical jaw.

Results and Discussion

Figure 16 shows the results of the four virtual osteotomies performed by one participant of Group II. On the other hand, Figure 17 shows the real osteotomy procedure being performed by one participant of Group I.

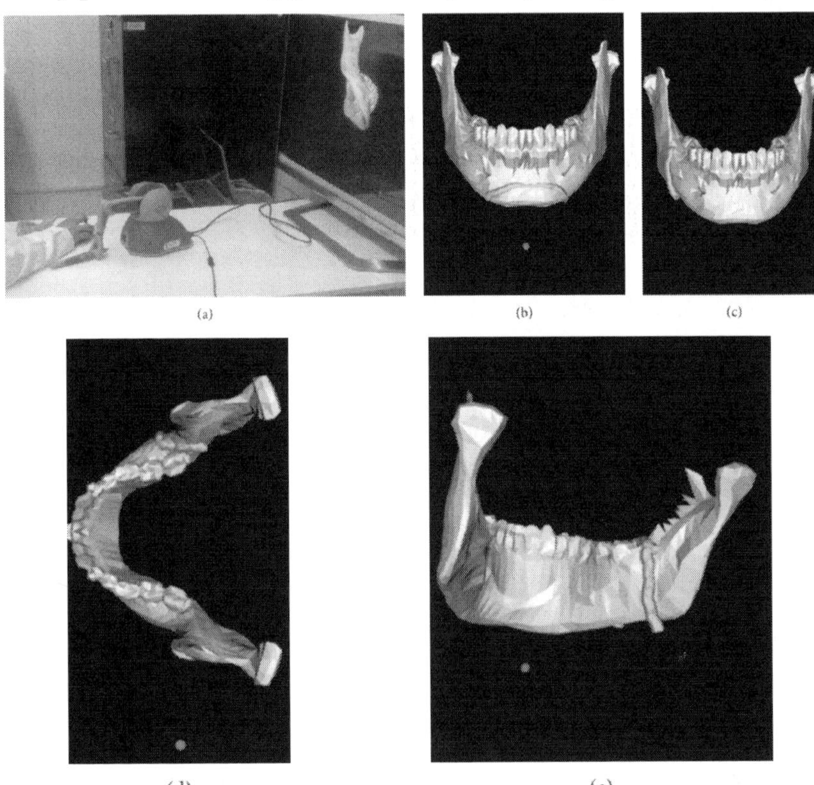

Figure 16: Virtual osteotomy training. (a) Participant. (b) Mentoplasty. (c) Sagittal exterior. (d) Sagittal superior. (e) Sagittal interior.

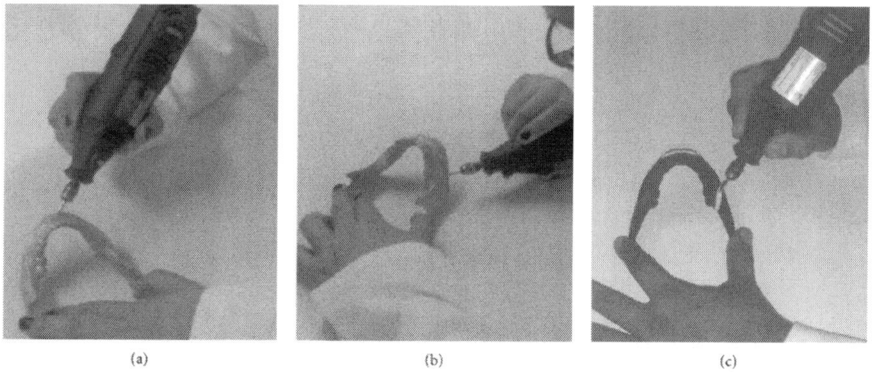

Figure 17: Real osteotomy procedure. (a) Mentoplasty. (b) Sagittal exterior. (c) Sagittal superior.

To evaluate the effectiveness of virtual training, all participants of Groups I, II, and III were observed during the real osteotomy procedure executions, and the time to complete the task was measured for all participants. The cutting error was also evaluated by comparing the cutting trajectory performed by each user, with the "ideal" cutting trajectory performed by an experienced maxillofacial surgeon, as shown in Figure 18(a). The cutting error was defined as the difference between the two trajectories, red area of Figure 18(b). This error was quantified in a CAD software.

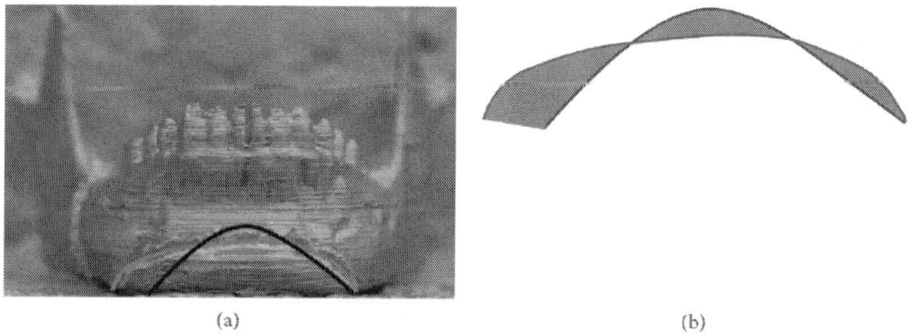

Figure 18: Error evaluation (black line: ideal trajectory, blue line: participant trajectory). (a) Front picture. (b) Error measurement (red area).

Table 1 summarizes the results obtained for Groups I, II, and III during the real osteotomy procedures. The values reported in this table correspond to the average values obtained by each group of participants. From these results, it is observed that participants of Group I showed average task completion times of 432 s and 389 s for the mentoplasty and sagittal real osteotomy procedures, respectively. On the other hand, participants of

Group II performed these procedures in 308 s and 317 s, respectively, and participants of Group III carried out these real tasks in 120 s and 241 s, respectively. These results suggest that participants that undertook virtual training first (Groups II and III) had superior performance, in terms of time, than those who did not train (Group I). In other words, participants who trained virtually completed the real osteotomy procedures faster than those who did not train. Moreover, participants who virtually trained with haptic force feedback (Group III) completed the real osteotomy procedures faster than those who virtually trained but without force feedback.

Table 1: Time and error results of the real osteotomy procedures

	Mentoplasty		Sagittal	
Participants	RO time (seconds)	Cutting error (%)	RO time (seconds)	Cutting error (%)
Group I	432	24.2	389	27.7
Group II	308	14.6	317	21.2
Group III	120	6.4	241	4.9

RO: Real Osteotomy.

Regarding the cutting error, participants of Group I exhibited an average cutting error of 24.2% and 27.7% for the mentoplasty and sagittal real osteotomy procedures, respectively, whereas participants of Group II exhibited an average cutting error of 14.6% and 21.2%, respectively, and participants of Group III obtained an average cutting error of 6.4% and 4.9%, respectively. These results clearly evidence than participants of Group II and Group III, who undertook a virtual training period first, achieved a more accurate mandible cutting during the real osteotomy procedure than those who did not train first (Group I). Furthermore, participants of Group III who trained with force feedback exhibited smaller cutting errors than participant of Group II who trained but without force feedback.

Therefore, it can be said that the proposed virtual osteotomy training procedure is a feasible approach to improve the performance and skills of the participants. A faster and more accurate osteotomy procedure was achieved by subjects who undertook virtual training first than those who did not train virtually first. Additionally, the use of haptic force feedback during virtual training has showed to enhance the virtual training procedure; a better performance is achieved by subjects that train with haptic force feedback than subjects that train with no haptic force feedback. Thus, the usability of the proposed methodology to design and develop virtual scenarios for biomedical applications has been demonstrated.

CONCLUSIONS

A new methodology to develop virtual reality environments for biomedical applications has been presented in this paper. This methodology represents a low-cost solution for the development of virtual environments with a high level of realism and with physical characteristics very close to the real devices. A case study corresponding to a virtual osteotomy simulator was developed using the proposed methodology. The results of this virtual osteotomy training biomedical application have demonstrated the effectiveness of the virtual system; users increased their abilities and skills to perform real osteotomy procedures. Therefore, the usability of the proposed methodology and approach has been validated. Future work considers a more comprehensive analysis of the effect of biomedical virtual training on the performance of subjects. This analysis will include a larger number of participants, modelling and rendering of real cutting forces, and comparison with traditional training.

ACKNOWLEDGMENTS

The authors acknowledge the financial support from CONACYT (National Science and Technology Council of Mexico), research grant CB-2010-01-154430, and from Secretariat of Public Education (SEP) of Mexico. They also thank the Instituto Tecnológico de Canarias ITC for the support provided to this research.

REFERENCES

1. C. Wang and H. W. Shen, "Information theory in scientific visualization," Entropy, vol. 13, no. 1, pp. 254–273, 2001.
2. P. Du, W. Li, S. Sang, L. Wang, and X. Zhou, "Application of 3D visualization concept layer model for coal–bed methane indez system," Procedia Earth and Planetary Science, vol. 1, no. 1, pp. 977–981, 2009.
3. P. BergLeif and M. VanceJudy, "Industry use of virtual reality in product design and manufacturing: a survey," Virtual Reality, vol. 21, no. 1, pp. 1–17, 2016.
4. I. Kartiko, M. Kavakli, and K. Cheng, "Learning science in a virtual reality application: the impacts of animated-virtual actors visual complexity," Computers and Education, vol. 55, no. 2, pp. 881–891, 2010.
5. O. Rübel, S. Ahern, E. W. Bethel et al., "Coupling visualization and data analysis for knowledge discovery from multi-dimensional scientific data," Procedia Computer Science, vol. 1, no. 1, pp. 1757–1764, 2010.
6. C. A. Ruiz, F. Montagut, J. Yeison, and E. Heidenreich, "Algorithm for virtual modeling of organs by medical images," Vector, vol. 4, pp. 14–26, 2009.
7. G. Vázquez-Mata, "Realidad virtual y simulación en el entrenamiento de los estudiantes de medicina," Educación Médica, vol. 11, no. 1, pp. 29–31, 2008.
8. G. Subhas, A. Gupta, and V. K. Mittal, "Necessity for improvement in endoscopy training during surgical residency," The American Journal of Surgery, vol. 199, no. 3, pp. 331–335, 2010.
9. L. Hanna, "Simulated surgery: the virtual reality of surgical training," Surgery, vol. 28, no. 9, pp. 463–468, 2010.
10. E. Govea and H. I. Medellín-Castillo, "Design and development of virtual reality environments for biomedical and engineering applications," in Proceedings of ASME International Mechanical Engineering Congress and Exposition, Volume 14: Emerging Technologies; Safety Engineering and Risk Analysis; Materials: Genetics to Structures, Houston, TX, USA, November, 2015.
11. H. I. Medellín-Castillo, E. H. Govea-Valladares, C. N. Pérez-Guerrero, J. Gil-Valladares, T. Lim, and M. Ritchie James, "The evaluation of a novel haptic-enabled virtual reality approach for computer-aided

cephalometry," Computer Methods and Programs in Biomedicine, vol. 130, pp. 46–53, 2016.

12. S. Girod, E. Keeve, and B. Girod, "Advances in interactive craniofacial surgery planning by 3D simulation and visualization," International Journal of Oral and Maxillofacial Surgery, vol. 24, no. 1, pp. 120–125, 1995.
13. V. N. Palter and T. P. Grantcharov, "Virtual reality in surgical skills training," Surgical Clinics of North America, vol. 90, no. 3, pp. 605–617, 2010.
14. J. D. Cardona, M. A. Hidalgo, H. Castán, F. Rojas, D. Borro, and H. Jaramillo, Realidad Virtual y Procesos de Manufactura, Programa Editorial Universidad Autonoma de Occidente, Rosemead, CA 91770, USA, 1st edition, 2007.
15. AA. Kadir, X. Xu, and E. Hammerle, "Virtual machine tools and virtual machining—a technological," Robotics and Computer-Integrated Manufacturing, vol. 27, no. 3, pp. 494–508, 2011.
16. J. Nomura and K. Sawada, "Virtual reality technology and its industrial applications," Annual Reviews in Control, vol. 25, pp. 99–109, 2001.
17. G. Gonzalez-Badillo, H. Medellin-Castillo, T. Lim, J. Ritchie, and S. Garbaya, "The development of a physics and constraint-based haptic virtual assembly system," Assembly Automation, vol. 34, no. 1, pp. 41–55, 2014.
18. S. Jayaram, H. I. Connacher, and K. W. Lyons, "Virtual assembly using virtual reality techniques," Computer Aided Design, vol. 29, no. 8, pp. 575–584, 1997.
19. A. Pérez and L. A. Sanz, "Virtual reality simulation applied to a numerical control milling machine," International Journal on Interactive Design and Manufacturing (IJIDeM), vol. 1, no. 3, pp. 143–154, 2007.
20. E. Gallegos-Nieto, H. I. Medellín-Castillo, G. González-Badillo, T. Lim, and J. Ritchie, "The analysis and evaluation of the influence of haptic-enabled virtual assembly training on real assembly performance," The International Journal of Advanced Manufacturing Technology, vol. 89, no. 1, pp. 581–598, 2017.
21. L. Stanculescu, R. Chaine, and M. P. Cani, "Freestyle: sculpting meses with self-adaptive topology," Computers and Graphics, vol. 35, pp. 614–622, 2011.
22. F. Bellotti, R. Berta, R. Cardona, and A. De Gloria, "An architectural

approach to efficient 3D urban modeling," Computers and Graphics, vol. 35, no. 5, pp. 1001–1012, 2011.

23. D. A. Guttentag, "Virtual reality: applications and implications for tourism tourism management," Tourism Management, vol. 31, no. 5, pp. 637–651, 2010.
24. D. Di Sorte, M. Femminella, and G. Reali, "QoS-enabled multicast for delivering live events in a digital cinema scenario," Journal of Network and Computer Applications, vol. 32, pp. 314–344, 2009.
25. G. Farin, J. Hoschek, and M. S. Kim, "Solid modeling. Handbook of computer aided geometric design," Elsevier, North Holland, Netherlands, 2001, Tech. Rep. 2.
26. G. Elber, N. Patrikalakis, and P. Burnet, "Solid modeling theory and applications," Graphical Models, vol. 67, no. 5, pp. 371-372, 2005.
27. A. A. G. Requicha, "Representations for rigid solids: theory, methods, and systems," ACM Computing Surveys, vol. 12, p. 4, 1980.
28. A. Thakur, A. G. Banerjee, and S. K. Gupta, "A survey of CAD model simplification techniques for physics-based simulation applications," Computer-Aided Design, vol. 41, no. 2, pp. 65–80, 2009.
29. R. V. Fleisig and A. D. Spence, "Techniques for accelerating B-rep based parallel machining simulation," Computer-Aided Design, vol. 37, no. 12, pp. 1229–1240, 2005.
30. S. Filippi, B. Motyl, and C. Bandera, "Analysis of existing methods for 3D modelling of femurs starting from two orthogonal images and development of a script for a commercial software package," Computer Methods and Programs in Biomedicine, vol. 89, no. 1, pp. 76–82, 2008.
31. L. Domínguez-Quintana, M. A. Rodríguez-Florido, J. Ruiz-Alzola, and D. Sosa, "Modelado 3D de escenarios virtuales realistas para simuladores quirúrgicos aplicados a la funduplicatura de nissen," Revista Científica de la Sociedad Española de Informatica y Salud, vol. 48, pp. 14–20, 2004.
32. C. W. Snyder, M. J. Vandromme, S. L. Tyra, and M. T. Hawn, "Proficiency–based laparoscopic and endoscopic training with virtual reality simulators: a comparison of protored and independent approaches," Journal of Surgical Education, vol. 66, pp. 201–206, 2009.
33. A. J. Debes, R. Aggarwal, I. Balasundaram, and M. B. Jacobsen, "A tale of two trainers: virtual reality versus a video trainer for acquisition

of basic laparoscopic skills," The American Journal of Surgery, vol. 199, pp. 840–845, 2010.

34. B. M. Howard and J. M. Vance, "Desktop haptic virtual assembly using physically based modeling," Virtual Reality, vol. 11, no. 4, pp. 207–215, 2007.
35. T. Gutierrez, J. I. Barbero, M. Aizpitarte, A. R. Carrillo, and A. Eguidazu, "Assembly simulation through haptic virtual prototypes," in Proceedings of the Third PHANTOM Users Group Workshop, Cambridge, MA, USA, December 1998.

SECTION IV- BRAIN AND NEURAL APPLICATIONS OF THE VR

Chapter 12

Augmented Reality: A Brand New Challenge for the Assessment and Treatment of Psychological Disorders

Irene Alice Chicchi Giglioli[1] , Federica Pallavicini[1] , Elisa Pedroli[1] , Silvia Serino[1] , and Giuseppe Riva[1,2]

[1]Applied Technology for Neuro-Psychology Lab, IRCCS Istituto Auxologico Italiano, 20145 Milan, Italy

[2]Department of Psychology, Catholic University of Milan, 20123 Milan, Italy

ABSTRACT

Augmented Reality is a new technological system that allows introducing virtual contents in the real world in order to run in the same representation and, in real time, enhancing the user's sensory perception of reality. From another point of view, Augmented Reality can be defined as a set of techniques and tools that add information to the physical reality. To date, Augmented Reality has been used in many fields, such as medicine, entertainment, maintenance,

Citation: Irene Alice Chicchi Giglioli, Federica Pallavicini, Elisa Pedroli, Silvia Serino, and Giuseppe Riva, "Augmented Reality: A Brand New Challenge for the Assessment and Treatment of Psychological Disorders," Computational and Mathematical Methods in Medicine, vol. 2015, Article ID 862942

architecture, education, and cognitive and motor rehabilitation but very few studies and applications of AR exist in clinical psychology. In the treatment of psychological disorders, Augmented Reality has given preliminary evidence to be a useful tool due to its adaptability to the patient needs and therapeutic purposes and interactivity. Another relevant factor is the quality of the user's experience in the Augmented Reality system determined from emotional engagement and sense of presence. This experience could increase the AR ecological validity in the treatment of psychological disorders. This paper reviews the recent studies on the use of Augmented Reality in the evaluation and treatment of psychological disorders, focusing on current uses of this technology and on the specific features that delineate Augmented Reality a new technique useful for psychology.

INTRODUCTION

Augmented Reality (AR) is a new technological system that allows inserting virtual contents in the real world in order to run in the same representation and, in real time, enhancing the user's sensory perception of reality [1]. Compared to a virtual reality system characterized by a computer-generated environment that elicits a strong user's experience of "presence" [2, 3], an AR system applies virtual and real elements in a real scene augmenting the user's perception of the world.

More precisely, Azuma et al. [4, 5] defined an AR platform as a system that [6](i)combines real and virtual objects in a real environment,(ii)runs interactively and in real time,(iii)registers real and virtual objects with each other.

Furthermore, according to Milgram et al. [7, 8], AR places between reality (real environment) and virtuality (virtual environment) on the reality-virtuality continuum (see Figure 1).

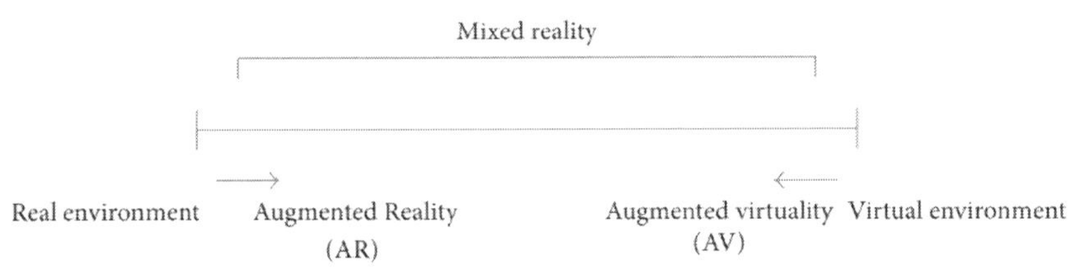

Figure 1: It shows a continuum between reality and virtual reality. Mixed reality is located between them and includes Augmented Reality (AR) and augmented virtuality (AV). AR is placed closer to real enviroment than virtual environment.

In an AR system, users see an image made up of a real image and virtual elements that are superimposed over it. The addition of virtual elements may also inhibit the perception of real elements by overimposing the virtual elements on the real elements. Nevertheless, the most important aspect in AR is that the virtual elements provide the real world with remarkable and valuable information. The addiction of virtual elements may involve not only the view but also the hearing, smell, and touch [9].

From the point of view of technology devices, AR can be defined as a set of techniques and tools that allow adding information to the physical reality. Various technologies are used in AR rendering including handheld devices, display system worn on one's user (nonhandheld devices), and projection displays.

Modern handheld mobile computing like smartphones and tablets contain these elements, which include a camera and sensors such as accelerometer, Global Positioning System (GPS), and solid-state compass, making them a suitable AR platform. The smartphone or tablet take in real time the surrounding environment and the virtual elements are superimposed to the real world.

An example of nonhandled device is the head mounted display (HMD), a display system worn on one user's head such as a helmet or glasses. HMD systems are characterized by sensors that receive input information about the environment by the user's head movements adding at a later stage various virtual contents.

As regards the projection displays, the virtual elements are projected on the real objects in order to be augmented. The projection occurs with a single room-mounted projector without any display system worn on one user's head. The projector generates a virtual image on the room surface using an automated calibration procedure that takes into account the structure of the surface overlapping the virtual image.

Furthermore, an AR platform requires a software application able to augment the real world by using one or more hardware devices. Marker-based and markerless systems are the two main software applications used in AR system. The AR marker-based systems are stylized pictures in black and white that are recognized by the computer webcam and which are superimposed in real time multimedia contents: video, audio, 3D objects, and so forth. Instead, in the markerless [10] AR system the software application catches the user's positional and orientation data through GPS and compass device adding the virtual contents in an accurate position on or in the real environment.

To date, AR has been used in medicine [11], entertainment [12], maintenance [13], architecture [14], education [15, 16], and cognitive [17, 18] and motor rehabilitation [19–24] but very few applications of AR exist in clinical psychology and, in particular, it is still underused in the treatment of psychological disorders [25].

Starting from these premises, the aim of this paper is to review the recent studies on the use of AR in the evaluation and treatment of psychological disorders, focusing on current uses of AR in psychology and the various factors that make a new technique useful for the treatment of psychological disorders, expanding the possible fields of use of AR.

MATERIALS AND METHODS

We followed the Preferred Reporting Items for Systematic Reviews and Meta-Analysis (PRISMA) guidelines [26].

Search Strategy

A computer-based search in several databases was performed for relevant publications describing the use of AR in psychology. Databases used for the search were PsycINFO, PubMed/Medline, and Web of Science (Web of Knowledge). We searched using the string "Augmented Reality" AND (psychology* OR assessment OR treatment). We excluded articles where the full text was not available or where the abstract lacked basic information for review. The first search was performed for publications in the English language, and then we decided to clean the results, considering only publications for the last ten years, from 2004 forward and eventually updated the search results through December 2014. Expert colleagues in the field were contacted for suggestion on further studies not considered in our search.

Selection Criteria

We have included articles on AR used for psychological settings in assessment or treatment studies. Excluded from the analysis were studies that omitted the inclusion criteria, non-English published studies, review articles, case reports, letters to the editor, research protocols, patents, and editorials. We tried to contact corresponding authors of the included studies with the intent of obtaining incomplete or supplementary data.

Quality Assessment and Data Abstraction

To assess a risk of bias, PRISMA recommendations for systematic literature analysis have been strictly followed. Three authors (Irene Alice Chicchi Giglioli, Federica Pallavicini, and Silvia Serino) independently selected paper abstracts and titles and analyzed the full papers that met the inclusion criteria, resolving disagreements through consensus.

The data extracted from each included study were sample type, study design, sample size, type of therapy or assessment, and selected findings.

RESULTS AND DISCUSSION

Systematic Review Flow

The flow chart of the systematic review is shown in Figure 2. Our initial search yielded 918 nonduplicate citations screened via PsycINFO, PubMed/Medline, Web of Science (Web of Knowledge), and other sources: more information is available in Search Strategy and supplement. After the application of inclusion/exclusion criteria, papers have been reduced to 301 articles. A more in-depth investigation of the full papers resulted in an exclusion of 286 articles. During the data extraction procedure, 2 additional full papers were excluded. In the end, 13 studies met full criteria and were included in this review (see Table 1).

Table 1: Detailed search strategy

	"Augmented Reality" and psycholog*	Assessment	Treatment	Other sources	Total
Medline	23	56	267		346
PsycINFO	133	21	28		182
Web of Science (Web of Knowledge)	69	145	164		378
Total	225	222	459	12	918
Nonduplicated	191	203	378	12	784
Excluded (after reading title and abstract)					483

Retrieved					301
Excluded (after applying inclusion criteria)					286
Excluded (missing experimental data)					2
Included					13

*is a Jolly characters that means that the search strategy included terms as psychology and/or psychological.

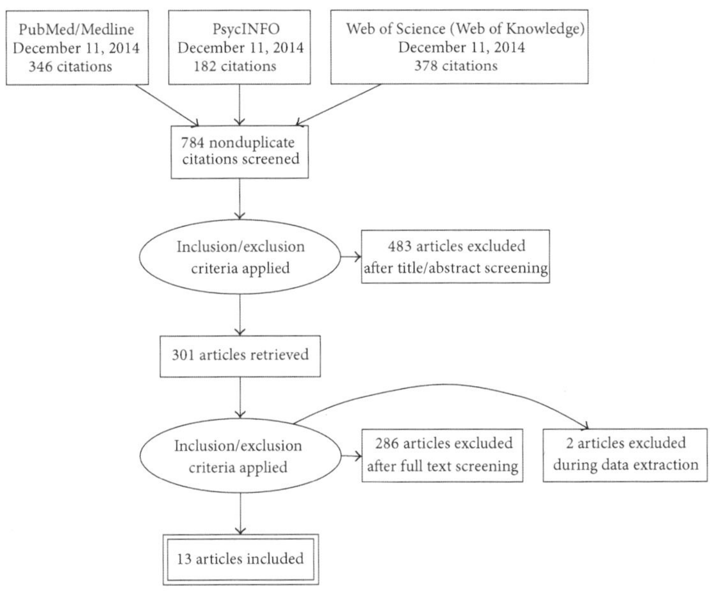

Figure 2: Flow diagram of study selection.

Selected Studies on Augmented Reality

Despite a large volume of studies on AR, little has been done specifically to psychological assessment or treatment. In the current review we present a broad range of experimental and clinical studies.

Results

In the area of clinical psychology, a few but remarkable studies have met the DSM-IV-TR criteria [27], showing the usefulness of AR in the treatment of a specific phobia. More specifically, the review of the literature showed that the phobia of small animals (cockroaches and spiders) and the acrophobia [28–38] are the current areas that used AR in the assessment and treatment of specific psychological disorders. For the readability of the contents, we have divided the results section in two paragraphs based on specific phobia's typology. The studies are presented in chronological order for showing the developments and advancements that occurred in the use of AR in this area. In addition, the selected final studies can be found in Tables 2 and 3. Each of them is described below.

Table 2: Information about the selected studies on the assessment and treatment of specific phobia for small animals using an AR system

Authors	Year	Sample	Conditions	Dependent variables	AR device	Results
Juan et al. [39]	2004	1 patient with cockroach phobia	Case study with AR	Anxiety	HMD with AR-tags	Decrease of anxiety level after treatment
Botella et al. [35, 40]	2005	1 patient with cockroach phobia	Case study with AR	Avoidance behaviour Degree of belief in catastrophic thought Anxiety Target behaviour Presence Reality judgment	HMD with AR-tags	Decrease of anxiety, fear, and avoidance after treatment High level of presence and judgment of reality
Juan et al. [31]	2005	9 patients with cockroach and spider phobia	AR	Anxiety Fear Avoidance behaviours Presence Reality judgment	HMD with AR-tags	Decrease of anxiety, fear, and avoidance after treatment High level of presence and judgment of reality
Botella et al. [34]	2010	6 patients with cockroach phobia	AR	Anxiety Target behaviour Behavioural avoidance	HMD with AR-tags	Decrease of anxiety, fear, and avoidance after treatment and maintained at follow-up periods (three, six, and twelve months follow-up)
Bretón-López et al. [32]	2010	6 patients with cockroach phobia	AR	Anxiety Presence Reality judgment	HMD with AR-tags	Decrease of anxiety. High levels of presence and reality judgment
Botella et al. [33]	2011	1 patient with cockroach phobia	Case Study with AR	Anxiety Target behaviours Behavioural avoidance	Mobile phone marker less versus HMD AR-tags	Decrease of anxiety, fear, and avoidance behaviours in both conditions.

Juan and Calatrava [37]	2011	24 healthy volunteers	AR-OST HMD AR-VST	Anxiety Presence	AR-OST HMD versus AR-VST	The AR-VST induced grater sense of presence than AR-OST. Significant anxiety in both conditions
Juand and Joele [38]	2011	24 healthy volunteers	AR marker-based versus invisible AR-tags	Anxiety Presence	HMD with visible AR-tags versus invisible AR-tags	The invisible AR-tags induced a higher sense of presence and anxiety than the visible AR-tags
Wrzesien et al. [29]	2011a	22 patients with cockroach and spider phobia	In vivo versus AR	Anxiety, behavioural avoidance Belief in negative thoughts	HMD with AR-tags	Decrease of anxiety, fear, avoidance behaviours, and belief in negative thoughts
Wrzesien et al. [28]	2011b	22 patients with cockroach and spider phobia	AR	Anxiety, behavioural avoidance Belief in negative thoughts	HMD with AR-tags	Decrease of anxiety, fear, avoidance behaviours, and belief in negative thoughts
Wrzesien et al. [30]	2013	26 healthy volunteers	AR	Anxiety Avoidance	Therapeutic lamp (TL)	Decrease of anxiety

Table 3: Information about the selected studies on the assessment of acrophobia using an AR system

Authors	Year	Sample	Conditions	Dependent variables	AR device	Results
Juan et al. [43]	2006	41 healthy volunteers	Real environment versus AR environment	Sense of presence	AR-HMD	High sense of presence in the AR environment
Juan and Prez [36]	2010	20 healthy volunteers	AR system versus VR system	Sense of presence Anxiety	HMD-AR with tags VR-HMD	In regard to sense of presence and anxiety levels, AR is effective as VR

AR and Specific Phobia for Small Animals

In the studies, the AR exposure therapy was based on Öst et al.'s "one-session treatment" guidelines [41, 42]. Individuals make one single intensive exposure session that lasts up to three hours.

The first analysed study that used an AR system to assess and treat specific phobias was conducted by Juan et al. (2004) [39]. A single individual with cockroach phobia [27] was assessed using an HMD-AR system. The AR device used was an HMD system connected with a camera and a PC. The camera, placed on the HMD, recognized the marker through the movement of the subject's head, projecting the virtual cockroaches in front of the subject. The AR single exposure session consisted progressively in seeing, touching, and finally killing one or more virtual cockroaches. The therapist chose in any moment how many cockroaches had to appear on the scene, their size, and if they had to move or not. During the treatment, the augmented cockroaches were able to arouse anxiety in patient that decreased after an hour of exposure. More specifically, before, during, and after treatment, the patient ranked her level of anxiety on a 10-point scale (where 0 represents no anxiety and 10 very high anxiety) using the Subjective Units of Discomfort Scale (SUDS) [44]. The data showed a decrease in anxiety score after exposure (with a score of 10 on SUDS at the beginning of the session and a score of 0 after the session) and clinical improvements regarding patient's phobia. In particular, after exposure, the patient was able to approach, interact, and kill real cockroaches.

Botella et al. (2005) [35] assessed a cockroach phobia case study [27] using an HMD-AR system developed for this specific disorder. The AR device used was an HMD system connected with a camera and a PC. The camera, placed on the HMD, recognized the marker through the movement of the subject's head, projecting the virtual cockroaches in front of the subject. The AR system included the possibility for the therapist to choose the number of cockroaches, their size, and movements and for the patient to kill one or more cockroaches using two different instruments, a fly swatter or a cockroach killer. Depending on the selected tool the system played a sound analogous to the real one. In order to assess the intensity of the phobia, the behaviour avoidance test (BAT) [42], degree of belief in catastrophic thought (assessed daily on scale from 0% to 100%), Fear and Avoidance Scales [45], Fear of Spiders Questionnaire (FSQ) [46], Spider Phobia Beliefs Questionnaire (SPBQ) [47], and Subjective Units of Discomfort Scale (SUDS) [44] were used. Furthermore, in order to assess the degree of presence and reality judgment experienced in the AR session, the authors created specifically for this study one ad hoc questionnaire composed by two questions related to presence: "To what degree have you felt present in the situation?" and "To what degree have you felt that you were in the place where the cockroaches appeared?" and one question for the reality judgment: "To what degree did the cockroaches appear to be real?" After AR exposure, the participant was asked to evaluate these features on a scale from 0 (no degree of being in a place/being real) to 10 (very high degree of being in a place/being real). The results showed that, before the exposure, patient exhibited a considerable fear and avoidance behaviours and after exposure not only were there important decreases in the fear and avoidance scores, but also the patient was able to approach, interact, and kill cockroaches with a high degree of presence and reality judgment. Similarly, at the beginning of the experiment, virtual cockroach induced anxiety in patient but after one hour of exposure the anxiety was significantly declined. Finally, the treatment gains were maintained in a follow-up conducted two months after the end of the treatment, showing decreases in the various scales of the BAT [42].

Juan et al. (2005) [31], for the first time, evaluated the effectiveness of an AR system not in one single case but in a sample of nine patients with cockroach and spider phobia [27]. The AR system was the same used in the Botella et al. study [35], described previously. The AR exposure involved the gradual appearance of one or more spiders/cockroaches and the possibility for the patients to approach them with hands, to look in boxes in order to simulate when you are searching for a small animal in your house, and to beat and throw away them. With respect to psychological measures, anxiety, fear, and avoidance behaviours were assessed using Fear and Avoidance Scales [45] and SUDS [44]. The degree of presence and reality judgment experienced by the users in the AR system were assessed using three ad hoc questions, created specifically for this study. The three questions were "To what degree have you felt present in the situation?" "To what degree have you felt that you were in a place in which spiders/cockroaches appeared?" And "To what degree did you think the spiders/cockroaches were real?" Participants were asked to evaluate these features in a scale from 0 to 10 (where 0 represents the lowest degree of being in a place/being real and 10 the highest degree of being in a place/being real). The results showed that the treatment produced a decrease in the patient's fear and avoidance behaviours [45] when they had to face with the target spider/cockroach. Furthermore, as in the study of Botella et al. [35], during the exposure, the participant's anxiety scores (SUDS) [44] were high, but they diminished at the end of the treatment.

In Botella et al. (2010) [34] an AR system was tested in the short and long term (three-, six-, and twelve-month follow-up) on a sample of six individuals suffering from cockroaches phobia [27]. The AR system was the same as that used in the preceding studies [31, 35]. Before, during, and after the AR exposure, participants were asked to fill out questionnaires, including SUDS [44] to evaluate anxiety levels, BAT [42], FSQ [46], and SPBQ [47] to assess fear and avoidance behaviours. AR exposure has been led in a single extended session lasting up to three hours. Each participant faced with various scenarios, progressing from the easiest to the most difficult situation. For example, at the beginning of the exposure, the program exhibited one cockroach to the participants, and more animals were added progressively. The purpose of the exposure was to interact with many cockroaches repeatedly, touch them, kill them, and remain in the situations until they experienced a considerable decrease in anxiety. As above in Botella et al. (2005), the results showed that AR was effective in treating cockroach phobia, improving significantly in all outcome measures after treatment. More specifically, the AR system, at the beginning of the exposure, was able to induce anxiety in the participants and after treatment produced a significant decrease in the level of fear and avoidance behaviours in all participants. In accordance with the BAT's scores [42], before treatment, none of the participants were able to interact with a real cockroach, while after treatment all participants could approach it. At the same time, also the self-report scores of FSQ [46] and SPBQ [47] improved significantly after treatment. Furthermore, the treatment gains were maintained at three-, six-, and twelve-month follow-up periods. Unlike the study conducted in 2005 by Botella et al. [35], measures related experience has not been recorded.

Bretón-López et al. (2010) [32] evaluated the ability of an AR system to raise anxiety and, secondly, to elicit sense of presence and reality judgment in six participants suffering from cockroach phobia [27]. In the single AR exposure session, participants were exposed to various stimuli, based on each individual's hierarchy of fears (from one static insect to the one in movement, from more static insects to ones in movement, and from insects next to personal belongings to those next to hands). Moreover, the AR system included the possibility to vary the numbers of cockroaches on the scene and the movement and the size of cockroaches. During and after the AR exposure, patients' level of anxiety was evaluated through the SUDS on a scale of 0 (no anxiety) to 10 (very high anxiety) [44], and the degree of presence through the Presence and Reality Judgment Questionnaire (PRJQ) [48]. The data showed that, at the start of AR immersion, the anxiety levels, measured through the SUDS questionnaire [44], ranged from 9 to 10 (the highest levels of the scale) but they decreased progressively during the exposure. The levels and the duration of exposure needed for anxiety reduction were based on initial levels of fear and on the severity of the phobia. Furthermore, patients showed high scores in the PRJQ [48], representing high levels of presence and reality judgment experienced during the AR exposure.

In 2011, Botella et al. [33] assessed a single cockroach phobia case study [27] testing an AR system using a mobile phone and creating a mobile game, "Cockroach Game" [33] for the treatment of this phobia. The subject conducted three therapeutic phases. In the first phase, the participant was asked to play, as much as she wanted, "Cokroach Game" for nine days and to record her levels of fears, avoidance, and belief in the catastrophic thought using the BAT [42] and FSQ [46]. In the second phase, the participant received the AR exposure treatment, assessing again the psychological measures. In the third phase, the participant was asked to play again the "Cockroach Game" for another period of nine days and recorded the same questionnaire. In this study the experiential measures of presence and reality judgment have not been taken into account. The data showed that before and after the first phase a slight improvement is obtained in performance, fear, and avoidance, whereas there was an increased in the belief in the catastrophic thought. After the AR exposure there were improvements in all BAT measures [42]: performance, fear, avoidance, and belief. After the third phase a significant decrease was obtained in all psychological measures, maintaining them at one, three-, six-, and twelve-month follow-up periods.

In 2011, Juan and Calatrava [37] compared an AR optical see-through (OST) system with a video see-through (VST) for the treatment of spiders and cockroaches phobia in twenty-four nonphobic participants. Individuals were divided in low and high fear subject's group according to scores in the fear and avoidance of cockroach and spider questionnaires [46] and underwent both experimental conditions. Before, during, and after exposure subjects were asked to rate their level of anxiety from 0 (no anxiety) to 10 (very high anxiety). Presence experienced by participants was assessed using an adapted version of the Slater et al.'s (1994) questionnaire [49]. The six question were "Please rate your sense of being in a room where there are cockroaches/spiders." "To what extent were there times during the experiment when the cockroaches/spiders were real for you?" "When you think back to your experience, do you think of cockroaches/spiders more as images that you saw (a movie, a picture), or more as cockroaches/spiders that were in the same room as you were?" "During the experiment which was strongest on the whole: your sense of being in the room where there were cockroaches/spiders, or your sense of being in a room without cockroaches/spiders?" "Think about your memory of being in a room where there were cockroaches/spiders. How similar is this memory to your memories of other places where there were these animals?" And "During the experiment, did you often think that you were actually in a room where there were cockroaches/spiders?" The scoring was on a scale of 1–7 (where 0 corresponds to not being in a place and 7 represents the normal experience of being in a place). Results showed that the VST system induced a higher sense of presence than the OST system and the two systems produced similar and significant anxiety before treatment that decreased after exposure.

Juan and Joele (2011) [38] compared an AR visible marker-based system with an AR invisible marker system in twenty-four healthy subjects. Participants rated their intensity of anxiety level from 0 (no anxiety) to 10 (very high anxiety) at eight different moments during the AR exposure. As in the previous study, after each AR exposure, individuals were asked to fill out an adapted Slater et al.'s (1994) questionnaire (SUS) [49] to rate the subjective feelings of presence experienced. Results showed that the AR invisible marker system elicited a higher sense of presence compared to the AR visible marker system. Furthermore, at the beginning of the treatment, the AR invisible marker system provokes a higher level of anxiety that decreases significantly during and at the end of the AR exposure.

Wrzesien et al. (2001a; 2011b) [28, 29] conducted two studies to evaluate the level of anxiety, avoidance, behavioural avoidance, and belief in negative thoughts in patients with small animal phobia [27].

The first study [29] compared the in vivo exposure therapy with the AR exposure therapy in twenty-two individuals with specific phobia for spiders and cockroaches [27]. The patients were randomly allocated to one of two groups. Before and after the exposure session, the participants were asked to fill out the behaviour avoidance test (BAT) [42]. The data showed that both in vivo and AR exposure are therapeutically effective in reducing anxiety, avoidance, and behavioural avoidance. In particular, the analysis of the pre- and posttest BAT scores showed no statistically significant differences between the in vivo group and the AR exposure group. Furthermore, an intragroup analysis showed a statistically significant decline in the severity of avoidance under both conditions, suggesting that both exposures are effective in the reduction of avoidance behaviours after treatment.

In the second study [28], five patients were assessed and treated using only an AR therapeutic exposure [27]. Before, during, and after the exposure session, the participants were asked to rank their level of anxiety on a scale of 0 (no anxiety) to 10 (very high anxiety), avoidance on a scale of 0 (low degree of avoidance) to 10 (high degree of avoidance), behavioural avoidance on a scale of 0 (low degree of behavioural avoidance) to 13 (very high degree of behavioural avoidance), and belief in catastrophic thoughts on a scale of 0 (low degree of belief) to 10 (high degree of belief). The results showed a posttreatment decrease in level of anxiety, avoidance, and belief in negative thoughts. More precisely, if, before the therapy, patients were unable to get close to live cockroaches, after the treatment they were able to interact with real cockroaches into a terrarium.

In a further study, Wrzesien et al. (2013) [30] experimented with an innovative technological AR system named therapeutic lamp (TL). The TL is an AR display projector created for the treatment of small animals' phobia. The trial included twenty-six healthy volunteers and consisted of one single exposure session composed by twelve exercises progressed from those who induced less anxiety to the ones that elicited more anxiety. For example, at the beginning of the exposure, participants observed three dead and three paralyzed animals and, at the end, they had to kill 30 animals with the flyswatter. In order to measure the participants' experience during the exposure, four clinical instruments were used. The Spider and Cockroach Anxiety and Avoidance Questionnaire was assessed before the session on a scale of 0 (no degree of fear and avoidance) to 7 (high degree of fear and avoidance). The Self-Efficacy Belief Questionnaire was used before and after the exposure session on a scale of 0 (no degree of belief that the participant could confront a real cockroach or spider) to 7 (high degree of belief). The Subjective Units of Discomfort Scale (SUDS) [44] was assessed at the beginning and end of each exercise in the session on a scale to 0 (no anxiety) to 10 (very high anxiety). The Presence and Reality Judgment Questionnaire (PRJQ) [48] was tested at each exercise's start on a scale of 0 (no degree of being in a place/being real) to 10 (high degree of being in a place/being real). The data showed that the participants' anxiety scores, measured by SUDS [44], were high at each exercise's beginning but decreased after the exercise session. In addition, the participant's belief in their capacity to face with the small animals improved significantly after the session. Finally, the PRJQ [48] scores showed that the participants felt the virtual animals' presence relatively well and considered them to be rather real. Therefore, the authors concluded that the AR-TL could be a good and helpful treatment's tool for psychological disorders even if the system has to be validated with patients in future studies.

All these studies represent new potentiality and possibility of assessment and treatment in the area of psychological disorders. However, they disclose some limitations. The majority of the disclosed studies [28, 29, 31–35] include a too small sample for the experimental validity characterized by patients with specific phobias. Instead, one study [30] focused on testing an innovative AR system with healthy volunteers in order to verify the efficacy, usability, and quality of user's experience of the new platform. Related to the previous consideration, the presented studies [28, 30–35] have not included control groups, experimental controls, or randomized controlled studies. Only one study conducted by Wrzesien et al. (2011a) [29] has performed a randomized controlled study, comparing the in vivo exposure therapy with the AR exposure therapy.

AR and Acrophobia

In 2006, Juan et al. [43] advanced the use of immersive photography in an AR system to treat acrophobia. For evaluating this system, forty-one healthy volunteers walked around at the top of a staircase in a real environment and using the immersive photography environment. After their experience, the participants filled out the SUS questionnaire [49] to assess their subjective sense of presence. The data showed that the AR condition induced a sense of presence equal to the one experienced by the subjects in the real world.

Another study, conducted by Juan and Prez (2010) [36], compared an acrophobic virtual reality (VR) and AR environment assessing differences in the sense of presence and anxiety elicited by the two systems. Twenty healthy participants underwent both experimental conditions and after using each system (AR or VR), they completed an adapted SUS questionnaire [49]. Moreover, at six different moments during the two experiences, the participants were also asked to rate their anxiety level from 0 (no anxiety) to 10 (very high anxiety). Regarding the sense of presence, the results showed no differences between the two systems. Moreover, data revealed that anxiety levels decrease after the exposure.

DISCUSSION

In the current scientific scenario, AR is a relevant issue and offers a viable alternative to traditional methods as the in vivo exposure therapy. This paper is the first systematic review that explores studies in the literature that use AR as a tool in the treatment of psychological disorders.

To date, the analysis of the literature suggested that AR has been mainly used in the evaluation and treatment of specific phobias such as phobias for small animals (cockroaches and spiders) and acrophobia. Regarding the assessment and treatment of specific phobias, from the literature analysis, it has been observed that thirteen studies have used an AR system in order to reduce anxiety, fear, and avoidance behaviours. Specifically, eleven studies concerned the evaluation and treatment of cockroaches and spiders phobia, while two studies affected the acrophobia.

As regards the cockroaches and spiders phobia, nine studies applied an AR-HMD system connected with a camera and a computer [28, 29, 31, 32, 34, 35, 37–40]. The camera was placed on the HMD helmet and connected with a USB to the computer where the AR system ran. The camera, recognizing the marker through the movement of the subject's head, projected the virtual images and objects in front of the subject. Among these studies, two [37, 38] compared different AR systems in order to evaluate their efficacy. In particular, Juan and Calatrava (2011) [37] compared an AR optical see-through (OST) system with a video see-through (VST), and Juan and Joele (2011) [38] contrasted an AR visible marker-based system with an AR invisible marker system.

The last studies have tested two innovative technological AR systems [30, 33]. In 2011, Botella et al. [33] have experimented with a new AR-mobile phone system and have created a mobile game, "Cockroach Game" [33] for the treatment of the cockroach phobia. The Cockroach Game is a puzzle game characterized by different levels of fear stimuli divided in two situations allowing players to progress in the game. The first included the possibility to see animals on various virtual situations inside the mobile phone. The second one allowed seeing them on real environment such as on the hands. In a further study, Wrzesien et al. [30] experiment with an innovative technological AR system, named therapeutic lamp (TL). The TL is an AR display projector created for the treatment of small animals' phobia.

As mentioned above, the majority of the studies concerned the assessment and the treatment of small animals phobias: five studies have focused on patients with cockroaches' phobia [32–35, 39, 40] and three on the cockroaches and spiders phobia [28, 29, 31] according the DSM-IV [27] criteria. Instead, three studies [30, 37, 38] have included healthy volunteers without any diagnosis of psychological and medical problems. In most of the studies [28, 29, 31–35], the AR exposure therapy was applied using the "one-session treatment" guidelines developed by Öst [41, 42].

A remarkable feature refers to the number of subjects included in these studies and the psychological and experiential measures in the assessment of the AR exposure therapy. Three studies experimented with one case study [33, 35, 39], two studies tested the AR system on six patients [32, 34], and one study assessed nine patients [31]. The remaining five studies have experimented with a higher number of subjects [28–30, 37, 38]. In 2011, Juan et al. [37, 38] assessed twenty-four healthy volunteers, while Wrzesien et al. (2011a; 2011b; 2013) [28–30], in the first two studies [28, 29], assessed twenty-two patients and, in the third study [30], they tested twenty-six healthy subjects.

Furthermore, all these studies considered anxiety as psychological measure showing that AR elicits anxiety as soon as the stimulus appeared that decreased during the time of exposure [28–35, 37–39]. Among these studies, seven of them also considered fear and avoidance behaviours showing that AR was able to reduce significantly fear and avoidance behaviours after the stimuli exposure [28–31, 33–35]. Finally, as regards the quality of user's experience, five studies measured presence [31, 32, 35, 37, 38] and three of them evaluated reality judgment [31, 32, 35] showing a high sense of presence in the AR system and reality judgment of the small animals.

Taking the two acrophobia studies [36, 43] into account, both applied an AR-HMD system to evaluate its efficacy comparing, in the first study, the AR-HMD system with a real environment [43] and, in the second study, the AR-HMD system with a VR- HMD system [36].

Regarding the number of subjects, both of the studies included healthy volunteers and, specifically, in 2006, Juan et al. [43] assessed forty-one participants, while in 2010 they evaluated twenty [36].

Among these studies, just Juan and Prez (2010) [36] considered anxiety as psychological measure showing that AR is effective as VR to induce anxiety when the stimulus appeared, which decreased during the exposure. In conclusion, both studies assessed the sense of presence showing, in the study of 2006 [43], a higher sense of presence in the AR environment than the real environment and in the study of 2010 [36] no difference between the AR and the VR environment.

The studies mentioned above suggest that AR offers many advantages such as the possibility to reproduce real objects in the environment (ecological validity), controlled situations, and ad hoc environments and objects in order to tailor the situations on the subject's needs and therapeutic purposes. However, the discussed studies are mostly preliminary researches that disclose some limitations due to the fact that AR exposure has only been recently tested for the evaluation and treatment of psychological disorders. The majority of the disclosed studies [28, 29, 31–35, 39] include a too small individual's sample and only one [29] of them is based on a randomized controlled design.

Instead, the reaming studies focused on testing the AR system on healthy subjects in order to verify the efficacy, usability, and the quality of user's experience of the new platform using randomized controlled studies

[30, 36–38, 43]. Apart from these studies, the literature is lacking studies of AR on the treatments of other several psychological disorders.

Currently, other technological devices have proven effective in the evaluation and treatment of psychological disorders. In particular, VR has been demonstrated to be a very useful tool for the treatment of several psychological problems such as eating disorders and anxiety disorders [50–54]. The traditional treatment for these psychological disorders is the in vivo exposure therapy. As the term implies, the in vivo exposure therapy allows subjects to experience their fears under the close supervision of a physician or a therapist. However, not all patients benefit from this treatment and, according to Jefferey et al. (2000) [55] and Mann et al. (2007) [56], some patients do not improve after treatment and others relapse in the long term.

In the last few years many studies have showed the efficacy of VR environments as therapeutic tool [50–53, 57–60]. A VR environment is a completely simulated three-dimensional environment modelled by a computer that allows, through the simulation, coping with critical and fear situation in a safe condition without losing sensory experience and physical presence.

A feature that makes VR a useful tool for evaluation and treatment of psychological disorders is to elicit emotional responses commensurate with the real ones.

The emotional engagement in virtual exposure depends on a number of factors such as the sense of presence. The sense of presence in virtual exposure is defined as the degree of "being there" in the virtual environment [61] and is marked by the sense of immersion and a sense of interaction. The sense of immersion is the result of the technological tools used such as the use of the HMD device that allows an immersive 3D experience to subjects. Instead, the sense of interaction is defined as the degree of interaction and manipulation for individuals of the virtual content or environment. Therefore, a high sense of presence in a virtual environment provides a greater realistic perception of the experience and consequently a strong and deep emotional engagement. This experience increases the ecological validity of the instrument of VR in the treatment of psychological disorders ensuring, through a simulated environment, a similar experience to the real one. At the same time, the user, feeling "present" in the simulated environment, perceives it as real and tends to transfer the expected skills from the virtual world to the real one in a nearly automatic manner. Recent studies have shown that virtual exposure is as effective as in vivo exposure [62–64] and, in particular, the exposure to virtual environments has produced emotional and behavioural responses similar to those that occurred in the real world.

In the studies of Ferrer-García and Gutiérrez-Maldonado [62, 63] six virtual environments emotionally relevant and significant to subjects with eating disorders (ED) have been realized. Before and after exposure to each virtual environment, they estimated the state of anxiety and depression levels and the data showed that the virtual exposure is effective in causing and provoking relevant emotional responses to subjects.

Gorini et al. [64] started from the two previous studies but compared the virtual stimuli with the real ones and with their correspondent pictures to test the psychological (measuring the level of anxiety and sense of presence) and physiological (measuring the heart and respiration rate and the skin conductance) reactions to food in a sample of ED patients and healthy controls. After each experimental condition, in order to estimate the psychological variations, the subjects carried out two states of anxiety tests (STAI-S and VAS-A) and then the virtual exposure completed the presence questionnaire. The data showed that virtual stimuli are effective as the real one and more than photographs in eliciting emotional responses in ED patients and, more generally, the use of VR instead of real stimuli may simplify the framework of very specific contexts to help patients to cope with their conditions through a very controlled stimulation.

Finally, regarding the sense of presence, the results showed a significant degree of presence on the level of state anxiety in VR and real exposure conditions. As mentioned above, the VR gives the possibility of the subject to manipulate and interact with the environment and contents as in the real world.

Similarly, AR could be considered a useful tool in the evaluation and treatment of psychological disorders providing a number of advantages as the VR. Indeed, the AR, as VR simulation, can be seen as an experiential process, and the experience is an essential component in dealing with critical situations. Furthermore, this experience could allow exploring environments and situations hard to reproduce in reality and, as the VR, the feeling of presence in the AR system could permit the user to assign the learned behaviours from the AR world to the real one.

The AR simulation, therefore, could be considered an efficient method to act on real behaviours avoiding the risks and complications typical of real environments.

CONCLUSIONS

The aim of this paper was to review the recent studies on the use of AR in the evaluation and treatment of psychological disorders, focusing on current uses of AR in psychology and the various factors that make a new technique useful for the treatment of psychological disorders, expanding the possible fields of use of AR.

In general, the presented studies show that the AR seems to be a promising and useful tool for intervention in the treatment of specific phobias. Nevertheless, the small sample of subjects examined and the lack of control group and randomized controlled studies necessitate more randomized controlled experiments for exploring the AR efficacy in the clinical treatments. Despite these limitations, AR is proving to be a new technique useful to patients to experiment with technologically different and severe situations, as the exposure to fear or phobic stimuli, in a safe environment under the control of the therapist. Indeed, an AR system extends interactivity for assessing and supervising patient's reactions in real time and adaptability for creating controlled exposure settings based on the patient's needs or therapeutic purposes. Furthermore, it is to be noted that AR allows subjects/patients to manipulate and control the virtual elements, interacting with virtual objects placed in the real world in real time.

As a consequence, the experience to amplify the physical world with virtual contents can improve the ecological validity of the "mixed reality" [7] on environment, augmenting the sense of presence and engagement of the subject/patient. Indeed, studies of VR have shown that virtual stimuli are comparable to the real stimuli with regard to emotional responses [62–64]. Finally a strong and deep sense of presence and engagement can, also, improve the adherence to treatment.

Overall, AR may represent a new challenge for the assessment and treatment of different kinds of psychological disorders, such as eating and anxiety disorders performing new studies based on systematic measures of psychological and neurophysiological effects.

AUTHORS' CONTRIBUTION

Irene Alice Chicchi Giglioli, Federica Pallavicini, and Silvia Serino independently selected paper abstracts and titles and analyzed the full papers that met the inclusion criteria, resolving disagreements through consensus. Irene Alice Chicchi Giglioli, Federica Pallavicini, Elisa Pedroli, and Silvia

Serino participated in the study design and wrote the paper. Elisa Pedroli, Silvia Serino, and Giuseppe Riva conceived the study and participated in its drafting, design, and coordination. All authors read and approved the final paper.

ACKNOWLEDGMENT

This work was supported by the Italian funded project "VRehab. Virtual Reality in the Assessment and TeleRehabilitation of Parkinson's Disease and Post-Stroke Disabilities" (RF-2009-1472190).

REFERENCES

1. O. Hugues, P. Fuchs, and O. Nannipieri, New Augmented Reality Taxonomy: Technologies and Features of Augmented Environment, Springer, New York, NY, USA, 2011.
2. G. Riva, F. Davide, and W. A. IJsselsteijn, Eds., Being There: Concepts, Effects and Measurements of User Presence in Synthetic Environment, Studies in New Technologies and Practices in Communication, IOS Press, Amsterdam, The Netherlands, 2003.
3. G. Riva, J. A. Waterworth, and E. L. Waterworth, "The layers of presence: a bio-cultural approach to understanding presence in natural and mediated environments," Cyberpsychology and Behavior, vol. 7, no. 4, pp. 402–416, 2004.
4. R. T. Azuma, "A survey of augmented reality," Presence: Teleoperators and Virtual Environments, vol. 6, no. 4, pp. 355–385, 1997.
5. R. Azuma, Y. Baillot, R. Behringer, S. Feiner, S. Julier, and B. MacIntyre, "Recent advances in augmented reality," IEEE Computer Graphics and Applications, vol. 21, no. 6, pp. 34–47, 2001.
6. F. Zhou, H. B.-L. Dun, and M. Billinghurst, "Trends in augmented reality tracking, interaction and display: a review of ten years of ISMAR," in Proceedings of the 7th IEEE/ACM International Symposium on Mixed and Augmented Reality (ISMAR '08), pp. 193–202, IEEE, Cambridge, UK, September 2008.
7. P. Milgram and F. Kishino, "A taxonomy of mixed reality visual displays," IEICE Transactions on Information and Systems D, vol. 77, pp. 1321–1329, 1994.
8. P. Milgram, T. Haruo, U. Akira, and K. Fumio, "Augmented reality: a class of displays on the reality-virtuality continuum," in Telemanipulator and Telepresence Technologies, pp. 282–292, 1994.
9. D. Yu, J. S. Jin, S. Luo, and W. Lai, "A useful visualization technique: a literature review for augmented reality and its application, limitation & future direction," in Visual Information Communication, M. L. Huang, Q. V. Nguyen, and K. Zhang, Eds., pp. 311–337, Springer, New York, NY, USA, 2010.
10. Y. Genc, S. Riedel, F. Souvannavong, C. Akinlar, and N. Navab, "Marker-less tracking for AR: a learning-based approach," in Proceedings of the International Symposium on Mixed And Augmented Reality (ISMAR '02), pp. 295–304, IEEE Computer Society, Darmstadt, Germany,

2002.

11. S. de Buck, F. Maes, J. Ector et al., "An augmented reality system for patient-specific guidance of cardiac catheter ablation procedures," IEEE Transactions on Medical Imaging, vol. 24, no. 11, pp. 1512–1524, 2005.
12. C. S. Özbek, B. Giesler, and R. Dillmann, "Jedi training: playful evaluation of head-mounted augmented reality display systems," in The Conference Medical Imaging, Proceedings of SPIE, San Diego, Calif, USA, May 2004.
13. B. Schwald and B. Laval, "An augmented reality system for training and assistance to maintenance in the industrial context," in Proceedings of the International Conference in Central Europe on Computer Graphics, Visualization and Computer Vision, pp. 425–432, University of West Bohemia, Plzen, Czech Republic, 2003.
14. R. Grasset, X. Decoret, and J. D. Gascuel, "Augmented reality collaborative environment: calibration and interactive science editing," in Proceedings of the Virtual Reality International Conference (VRIC '01), Laval Virtual, 2001.
15. T. N. Arvanitis, A. Petrou, J. F. Knight et al., "Human factors and qualitative pedagogical evaluation of a mobile augmented reality system for science education used by learners with physical disabilities," Personal and Ubiquitous Computing, vol. 13, no. 3, pp. 243–250, 2009.
16. L. Kerawalla, R. Luckin, S. Seljeflot, and A. Woolard, "'Making it real': exploring the potential of augmented reality for teaching primary school science," Virtual Reality, vol. 10, no. 3-4, pp. 163–174, 2006.
17. Y.-J. Chang, Y.-S. Kang, and P.-C. Huang, "An augmented reality (AR)-based vocational task prompting system for people with cognitive impairments," Research in Developmental Disabilities, vol. 34, no. 10, pp. 3049–3056, 2013.
18. R. Hervás, J. Bravo, and J. Fontecha, "An assistive navigation system based on augmented reality and context awareness for people with mild cognitive impairments," IEEE Journal of Biomedical and Health Informatics, vol. 18, no. 1, pp. 368–374, 2014.
19. G. A. Assis, A. G. Corrêa, M. B. R. Martins, W. G. Pedrozo, and R. D. Lopes, "An augmented reality system for upper-limb post-stroke motor rehabilitation: a feasibility study," Disability and Rehabilitation:

Assistive Technology, vol. 4, pp. 1–8, 2014.

20. A. J. Espay, Y. Baram, A. K. Dwivedi et al., "At-home training with closed-loop augmented-reality cueing device for improving gait in patients with Parkinson disease," Journal of Rehabilitation Research and Development, vol. 47, no. 6, pp. 573–582, 2010.
21. X. Luo, T. Kline, H. C. Fischer, K. A. Stubblefield, R. V. Kenyon, and D. G. Kamper, "Integration of augmented reality and assistive devices for post-stroke hand opening rehabilitation," in Proceedings of the 27th Annual International Conference of the Engineering in Medicine and Biology Society (EMBS '05), pp. 6855–6858, IEEE, September 2005.
22. M. Markovic, S. Dosen, C. Cipriani, D. Popovic, and D. Farina, "Stereovision and augmented reality for closed-loop control of grasping in hand prostheses," Journal of Neural Engineering, vol. 11, no. 4, Article ID 046001, 2014.
23. M. Khademi, H. M. Hondori, L. Dodakian, S. Cramer, and C. V. Lopes, "Comparing 'pick and place' task in spatial augmented reality versus non-immersive virtual reality for rehabilitation setting," in Proceedings of the 35th Annual International Conference of the IEEE Engineering in Medicine and Biology Society (EMBC '13), pp. 4613–4616, 2013.
24. H. M. Hondori, M. Khademi, L. Dodakian, S. C. Cramer, and C. V. Lopes, "A Spatial Augmented Reality rehab system for post-stroke hand rehabilitation," Studies in Health Technology and Informatics, vol. 184, pp. 279–285, 2013.
25. O. Baus and S. Bouchard, "Moving from virtual reality exposure-based therapy to augmented reality exposure-based therapy: a review," Frontiers in Human Neuroscience, vol. 8, article 112, 2014.
26. D. Moher, A. Liberati, J. Tetzlaff, D. G. Altman, and P. Grp, "Preferred reporting items for systematic reviews and meta-analyses: the PRISMA statement," PLoS Medicine, vol. 6, no. 7, Article ID e1000097, 2009.
27. A. P. Association, Diagnostic and Statistical Manual for Mental Disorders (DSM-IV-TR), American Psychiatric Association, American Occupational Therapy, Washington, DC, USA, 4th edition, 2000.
28. M. Wrzesien, J.-M. Burkhardt, M. A. Raya, and C. Botella, "Mixing psychology and HCI in evaluation of augmented reality mental health technology," in Proceedings of the 29th Annual CHI Conference on Human Factors in Computing Systems (CHI '11), pp. 2119–2124, Vancouver, Canada, May 2011.

29. M. Wrzesien, J.-M. Burkhardt, M. Alcañiz, and C. Botella, "How technology influences the therapeutic process: a comparative field evaluation of augmented reality and in vivo exposure therapy for phobia of small animals," in Proceedings of the Human-Computer Interaction (INTERACT '11), pp. 523–540, Lisbon, Portugal, 2011.
30. M. Wrzesien, M. Alcañiz, C. Botella et al., "The therapeutic lamp: treating small-animal phobias," IEEE Computer Graphics and Applications, vol. 33, no. 1, pp. 80–86, 2013.
31. M. C. Juan, M. Alcañiz, C. Monserrat, C. Botella, R. M. Baños, and B. Guerrero, "Using augmented reality to treat phobias," IEEE Computer Graphics and Applications, vol. 25, no. 6, pp. 31–37, 2005.
32. J. Breton-López, S. Quero, C. Botella, A. García-Palacios, R. M. Baños, and M. Alcañiz, "An augmented reality system validation for the treatment of cockroach phobia," Cyberpsychology, Behavior, and Social Networking, vol. 13, pp. 705–710, 2010.
33. C. Botella, J. Breton-López, S. Quero et al., "Treating cockroach phobia using a serious game on a mobile phone and augmented reality exposure: a single case study," Computers in Human Behavior, vol. 27, no. 1, pp. 217–227, 2011.
34. C. Botella, J. Bretón-López, S. Quero, R. Baños, and A. García-Palacios, "Treating cockroach phobia with augmented reality," Behavior Therapy, vol. 41, no. 3, pp. 401–413, 2010.
35. C. Botella, R. Banos, B. Guerrero, M. Juan, and M. Alcañiz, "Mixing realities? An augmented reality system for the treatment of cockroach phobia," CyberPsychology & Behavior, vol. 8, pp. 305–306, 2005.
36. M. C. Juan and D. Prez, "Using augmented and virtual reality for the development of acrophobic scenarios. Comparison of the levels of presence and anxiety," Computers and Graphics, vol. 34, no. 6, pp. 756–766, 2010.
37. M. C. Juan and J. Calatrava, "An augmented reality system for the treatment of phobia to small animals viewed via an optical see-through HMD. Comparison with a similar system viewed via a video see-through HMD," International Journal of Human-Computer Interaction, vol. 27, no. 5, pp. 436–449, 2011.
38. M. C. Juan and D. Joele, "A comparative study of the sense of presence and anxiety in an invisible marker versus a marker augmented reality system for the treatment of phobia towards small animals," International

Journal of Human Computer Studies, vol. 69, no. 6, pp. 440–453, 2011.

39. M. C. Juan, C. Botella, M. Alcañiz et al., "An augmented reality system for treating psychological disorders: application to phobia to cockroaches," in Proceedings of the 3rd IEEE/ACM International Symposium on Mixed and Augmented Reality (ISMAR '04), pp. 256–257, IEEE, November 2004.
40. C. M. Botella, M. C. Juan, R. M. Baños, M. Alcañiz, V. Guillén, and B. Rey, "Mixing realities? An application of augmented reality for the treatment of cockroach phobia," Cyberpsychology & Behavior, vol. 8, no. 2, pp. 162–171, 2005.
41. L.-G. Ost, P. M. Salkovskis, and K. Hellstrom, "One-session therapist-directed exposure vs. self-exposure in the treatment of spider phobia," Behavior Therapy, vol. 22, no. 3, pp. 407–422, 1991.
42. L. G. Öst, Rapid Treatment of Specific Phobias, John Wiley & Sons, New York, NY, USA, 2000.
43. M. C. Juan, R. Baños, C. Botella, D. Pérez, M. Alcañiz, and C. Monserrat, "An augmented reality system for the treatment of acrophobia: the sense of presence using immersive photography," Presence: Teleoperators and Virtual Environments, vol. 15, no. 4, pp. 393–402, 2006.
44. J. Wolpe, The Practice of Behavior Therapy, Pergamon Press, New York, NY, USA, 1969.
45. I. M. Marks and A. M. Mathews, "Case histories and shorter communication," Behaviour Research and Therapy, vol. 17, pp. 263–267, 1979.
46. J. Szymanski and W. J. O'Donohue, "Fear of spiders questionnaire," Journal of Behavior Therapy and Experimental Psychiatry, vol. 26, no. 1, pp. 31–34, 1995.
47. A. Arntz, E. Lavy, G. van Den Berg, and S. van Rijsoort, "Negative beliefs of spider phobics: a psychometric evaluation of the spider phobia beliefs questionnaire," Advances in Behaviour Research and Therapy, vol. 15, no. 4, pp. 257–277, 1993.
48. R. M. Baños, S. Quero, S. Salvador, and C. Botella, The Role of Presence and Reality Judgement in Virtual Environments in Clinical Psychology, Verlag Integrative Psychiatrie, Innsbruck, Austria, 2005.
49. M. Slater, M. Usoh, and A. Steed, "Depth of presence in virtual environments," Presence: Teleoperators and Virtual Environments, vol. 3, pp. 130–144, 1994.

50. A. Gorini and G. Riva, "The potential of Virtual Reality as anxiety management tool: a randomized controlled study in a sample of patients affected by generalized anxiety disorder," Trials, vol. 9, article 25, 2008.
51. T. D. Parsons and A. A. Rizzo, "Affective outcomes of virtual reality exposure therapy for anxiety and specific phobias: a meta-analysis," Journal of Behavior Therapy and Experimental Psychiatry, vol. 39, no. 3, pp. 250–261, 2008.
52. G. Riva, "Virtual reality in eating disorders and obesity: state of the art and future directions," CyberPsychology & Behavior, vol. 8, p. 351, 2005.
53. G. Riva, M. Bacchetta, M. Baruffi, and E. Molinari, "Virtual reality-based multidimensional therapy for the treatment of body image disturbances in obesity: a controlled study," Cyberpsychology and Behavior, vol. 4, no. 4, pp. 511–526, 2001.
54. A. Rizzo, J. C. Buckwalter, and C. Van der Zaag, "Virtual environment applications in clinical neuropsychology," in The Handbook of Virtual Environments, K. M. Stanney, Ed., pp. 1027–1064, Erlbaum, New York, NY, USA, 2002.
55. R. W. Jeffery, L. H. Epstein, G. T. Wilson et al., "Long-term maintenance of weight loss: current status," Health Psychology, vol. 19, no. 1, pp. 5–16, 2000.
56. T. Mann, A. J. Tomiyama, E. Westling, A.-M. Lew, B. Samuels, and J. Chatman, "Medicare's search for effective obesity treatments. Diets are not the answer," American Psychologist, vol. 62, no. 3, pp. 220–233, 2007.
57. G. M. Manzoni, G. L. Cesa, D. Villani, G. Castelnuovo, E. Molinari, and G. Riva, "VR-enhanced treatment of anxiety in obese subjects: a follow-up study on trait-anxiety, psychological symptornatology, and generalized self-efficacy," CyberPsychology & Behavior, vol. 9, pp. 699–700, 2006.
58. S. Côté and S. Bouchard, "Virtual reality exposure for phobias: a critical review," Journal of Cyber Therapy & Rehabilitation, vol. 1, no. 1, pp. 75–91, 2008.
59. F. Pallavicini, A. Gaggioli, S. Raspelli et al., "Interreality for the management and training of psychological stress: study protocol for a randomized controlled trial," Trials, vol. 14, no. 1, article 191, 2013.

60. A. Gaggioli, G. Pioggia, G. Tartarisco et al., "A system for automatic detection of momentary stress in naturalistic settings," Studies in Health Technology and Informatics, vol. 181, pp. 182–186, 2012.
61. W. Barfield, D. Zeltzer, T. B. Sheridan, and M. Slater, Virtual Environments and Advanced Interface Design, Oxford University Press, Oxford, UK, 1995.
62. M. Ferrer-García, J. Gutiérrez-Maldonado, A. Caqueo-Urízar, and E. Moreno, "The validity of virtual environments for eliciting emotional responses in patients with eating disorders and in controls," Behavior Modification, vol. 33, no. 6, pp. 830–854, 2009.
63. J. Gutiérrez-Maldonado, M. Ferrer-García, A. Caqueo-Urízar, and A. Letosa-Porta, "Assessment of emotional reactivity produced by exposure to virtual environments in patients with eating disorders," Cyberpsychology and Behavior, vol. 9, no. 5, pp. 507–513, 2006.
64. A. Gorini, E. Griez, A. Petrova, and G. Riva, "Assessment of the emotional responses produced by exposure to real food, virtual food and photographs of food in patients affected by eating disorders," Annals of General Psychiatry, vol. 9, article 30, 2010.

Chapter 13

Reducing the Schizophrenia Stigma: A New Approach Based on Augmented Reality

Rafael D. de C. Silva[1] , Saulo G. C. Albuquerque[2,3] , Artur de V. Muniz[2] , Pedro P. Rebouças Filho[4] ,Sidarta Ribeiro[5] , Plácido Rogerio Pinheiro[1] , and Victor Hugo C. Albuquerque[1]

[1]Programa de Pós-Graduação em Informática Aplicada, Laboratório de Bioinformática, Universidade de Fortaleza, Fortaleza, CE, Brazil

[2]Hospital de Saúde Mental de Messejana, Fortaleza, CE, Brazil

[3]Internato em Saúde Coletiva e Mental, Universidade de Fortaleza, Fortaleza, CE, Brazil

[4]Laboratório de Processamento de Imagens e Simulação Computacional, Instituto Federal de Educação, Ciência e Tecnologia do Ceará, Maracanaú, CE, Brazil

[5]Instituto do Cérebro, Universidade Federal do Rio Grande do Norte, Natal, RN, Brazil

ABSTRACT

Schizophrenia is a chronic mental disease that usually manifests psychotic

---

Citation: Rafael D. de C. Silva, Saulo G. C. Albuquerque, Artur de V. Muniz, et al., "Reducing the Schizophrenia Stigma: A New Approach Based on Augmented Reality," Computational Intelligence and Neuroscience, vol. 2017, Article ID 2721846.

symptoms and affects an individual's functionality. The stigma related to this disease is a serious obstacle for an adequate approach to its treatment. Stigma can, for example, delay the start of treatment, and it creates difficulties in interpersonal and professional relationships. This work proposes a new tool based on augmented reality to reduce the stigma related to schizophrenia. The tool is capable of simulating the psychotic symptoms typical of schizophrenia and simulates sense perception changes in order to create an immersive experience capable of generating pathological experiences of a patient with schizophrenia. The integration into the proposed environment occurs through immersion glasses and an embedded camera. Audio and visual effects can also be applied in real time. To validate the proposed environment, medical students experienced the virtual environment and then answered three questionnaires to assess (i) stigmas related to schizophrenia, (ii) the efficiency and effectiveness of the tool, and, finally (iii) stigma after simulation. The analysis of the questionnaires showed that the proposed model is a robust tool and quite realistic and, thus, very promising in reducing stigma associated with schizophrenia by instilling in the observer a greater comprehension of any person during an schizophrenic outbreak, whether a patient or a family member.

INTRODUCTION

The World Health Organization (WHO) describes schizophrenia as one of the most serious and challenging psychiatric diseases nowadays, which still demands strong efforts in order to acquire a more solid knowledge on the pathology. It is a complex disease categorized by distortions of thought, self-perception, and external reality, as well as inadequacy and dullness of affection [1]. Schizophrenia affects more than 21 million people worldwide, and one in every two schizophrenia-afflicted subjects does not receive care for the disease [2], despite the fact that there are effective schizophrenia symptom-mitigation treatments and affected people can lead a productive life and be inserted into society [3].

Amongst the main schizophrenia manifestations the positive symptoms stand out, ordinarily termed psychotic symptoms, which include hallucinations and delusions, typifying the loss of the patient's contact with reality. Negative symptoms (mostly impairment of motivation, reduction of spontaneous speech, and social isolation) and cognitive impairment are also considered key features of this illness [4]. Hallucinations can be defined as the perception of an object, such as voice, noise, or image, without it being present, that is, without the respective sensorial stimulus [5]. They are experiences comparable to perception that occur without an external stimulus; it means that the patient experiences the behavior as not being under voluntary control [6]. In schizophrenia, hallucinations concerning visual, somatic, tactile, and olfactory modalities may take place, but the auditory ones are the most frequent indicators [7].

Over the past years, a greater access to technology has allowed the use of tools such as virtual reality (VR) in medicine. VR is an instrument capable of inserting the user into an interactive three-dimensional virtual world, using a computer that can generate images and a display that presents sensory information. Over the last few decades, the use of VR in psychotic disorders, such as schizophrenia, has been a promising candidate, for example, for a clearer understanding of symptoms, for training of instrumental and social skills, and for the treatment of the disease, as an adjuvant technique [8, 9]. With reference to the stigma, VR has been shown to be useful for diminishing negative stereotypes [10] and as a supporting device to increase empathy and positive impressions towards schizophrenic people [11] amongst other applications [12–24].

In addition to the severe symptoms of the disease, patients afflicted with schizophrenia face another key trouble: the stigma. Discrimination against these patients can be perceived when they try to make or maintain friendships, look for a job, or maintain intimate or sexual relations. Moreover, discrimination often comes from members of their own family [25]. In a study conducted in the United Kingdom, it was observed that more than 70% of the general public classified schizophrenia-afflicted people as dangerous or unpredictable [26].

One aspect to fight the stigma is intervention in specific groups of the population, such as police authorities and health providers. There are studies showing that training of police forces to recognize mental disorders could decrease the number of arrests and unnecessary force used against people with mental illnesses, as well as increase the adequate referral to psychiatric institutions [27].

Even though the effects of the stigma on the evolution of schizophrenia are still scarcely addressed by patients families and health practitioners, they have been observed in a number of studies. In recent times, it has been demonstrated, for instance, that stress instigated by stigma may be related to the transition to schizophrenia in young people at risk of psychosis [28]. Habitually, the patient feels downgraded. The disorder itself often leads to a condition of hypobulia and decreased motivation, which culminates with impaired physical conditioning. Environment-generated stimuli maybe cannot induce severe side effects, as there are no literary reports of serious symptoms generation (e.g., convulsive crisis) [29].

A number of approaches have been developed aiming at reducing the public stigma of mental illness and the damage it causes to the patient's life. For example, virtual environments to educate patients with schizophrenia of the hallucinations they suffer [30]. Amongst these approaches, social protest or activism, education of the public, and contact with mentally handicapped people stand out, while the latter two show positive results in the stigma reduction. Educational strategies comprise public messages, books, pamphlets, films, videos, web pages, virtual reality, and other audiovisual tools [31].

A healthy sample of the population submitted to the demonstration of the proposed environment can reduce interrelated obstacles, for example, to the delay in the beginning of the treatment and difficulties in interpersonal and professional relationships to have a proper approach to the conditions of people afflicted this serious mental illness.

The development of a VR-based tool capable of reducing the stigma related to schizophrenia is of utmost importance to treat this disease. To fill this gap, we propose a new augmented-reality-based tool capable of simulating the typical psychotic symptoms of schizophrenia and analyzing its effectiveness, the influence of the tool on stigmas reduction, emotional impact on users, and its validation by specialists and students of the medicine course by use and application of a questionnaire. The proposed system can interact, in real time, with a healthy sample of the population, medical students, simulating the psychotic symptoms typical of schizophrenia. The environment was developed with the support of a psychiatry specialist team.

Appraisal of the tool effectiveness is performed by Mental Health specialists through three questionnaires: schizophrenia-related stigma evaluation, environment simulation evaluation, and stigma evaluation after augmented-reality simulation. In the questionnaire assessing the schizophrenia-related stigma, volunteers' personal data, family experience in cases of schizophrenia-diagnosed persons, and a fictional history of a schizophrenia-afflicted individual were made. For the simulation evaluation, inquiries related to the performance of the AR environment were made. In the last questionnaire, the reassessment was made after an environment simulation of how the volunteer turned out to perceive the person from the fictional story about schizophrenia.

Environment-generated stimuli should not be able to trigger serious side effects, as there are no literature reports about serious symptoms induction (e.g., convulsive crises). Simulations can be applied in educational environments (school groups, colleges, and technical training) in professional settings such as hospitals and clinics, and in training and awareness-raising groups that may interact with psychosis-afflicted people, such as police officers, municipal guards, and family members of disease carriers.

By applying such virtual systems, connected with clinical purposes, they can play an important role in the healthcare area, as they are easily handled by the specialist as well as by the patient, being such a reassuring feature for the treatment continuousness [32]. For example, [9] presented a pilot study to investigate the feasibility and potential negative side effects of exposure to different virtual social risk environments in patients with first episode psychosis and in healthy controls.

DEVELOPMENT OF THE PROPOSED VIRTUAL ENVIRONMENT

Virtual and augmented reality are technological tools that use virtual elements that can be inserted in realistic scenarios, becoming an alternative and complementary approach to the treatments and diagnoses, being a very promising method to be adopted definitively in the health area [33].

Virtual reality is an advanced interface for computational applications in which users can navigate and interact with a three-dimensional computer-generated environment through multisensory devices. This technology establishes the relationship between the user and the created environment, allowing real-time integration with controlled virtual objects, and can simulate touch-screen monitors, mount-head goggles, mouse, and data glove and explore virtually freely, without real constraints like gravity, according to the immersion scenario and controls in which the user is interacting. In it, the individual has the sensation, in real time, of interacting with the virtual world manipulating objects around it [34].

Augmented reality is a type of advanced virtual reality interface that allows the user to experience sensations through stimuli to see, hear, feel, and interact with information and virtual elements inserted in the real environment [35]. In this work, the voices and figures were generated from the narrative of three schizophrenic patients treated at the NUEsq Schizophrenia outpatient clinic of Frota Pinto Mental Hospital in Fortaleza, Ceará. The data collection was qualitatively focused, based on the patients' verbal description of their psychotic experiences focusing on sensory perception alterations (auditory hallucinations and visual pseudohallucinations). The evaluation was led by a psychiatrist heading the clinical follow-up of the patients under discussion.

The tool consists of a software that reproduces some schizophrenia typical psychotic symptoms in an augmented-reality environment so that healthy people can undergo a simulation and thus provides a reality immersion for a patient carrying such ailment. In the environment, a 3-minute duration simulation was set, as it could become tiring over an extended period of time.

At the beginning, in the tool created in the Unity 3D program, a software that is used to create games and animations, an environment that could simulate what would be the reality was produced; namely, it was able to produce an immersion to the user as close to the reality as possible. To achieve this, a GameObject, named Cubo1 was designed, aimed at conveying with its texture a camera, so that when the operator used the environment he/she could visualize the real scenario in which he/she was inserted.

After the creation of the object that would use the camera to visualize the real-time environment, pictures that would make the process of simulation of the appearances of figures (common visual pseudohallucinations, referred by carriers) were inserted, with 2D sprites being used as scene GameObject, which could have their humanoid or geometric shapes a little rounded, and in them a blur effect was applied (blurred feature). The human-shaped figure has its animation modeled with fade-in and fade-out effects, causing it to appear or disappear at a particular point in time according to its program design, while its total four-second appearance is the most common. The geometric figure generally features the same outline when its animation is programmed similarly to the humanoid version, but in some cases the animation suffers the spawn effect (when the GameObject undergoes a transformation on the x-axis from one particular point to another), causing the GameObject to move from side to side, with a speed script being added. Additionally, the problem of the GameObject being "spawned" though never disappearing became evident, causing a future memory error. In consequence, a script was inserted so that it destroyed itself at a given time.

In the facial detection phase, a Unity plugin called OpenCV for Unity, which is a plugin that makes Unity recognize OpenCV scripts used in facial detection, was used. In the development of the facial modification a sprite (2D animated image) of a blurred spot was used to cause a somber effect in the interviewees' gaze. The effect of the facial modification lasted about 1 second, running twice during the three minutes.

The voices heard in the simulation via headphones were digitally recorded by two actors from a script prepared by the psychiatrist who piloted the interview with the volunteer patients. The audio plays a generic content, usually heard by patients with auditory hallucinations: whispers, threatening and commanding speech, laughter, and offending content phrases. Two voices were chosen, one male and one female, based on recurrent schizophrenia hallucinatory phenomena involving voices of different characteristics that often talk to each other. The choice of actors and nonrobotic voices was aimed at promoting authenticity and naturalness, which are distinctive of true hallucinations. All students gave their informed consent to the procedure, which was approved by the Ethics Committee of Escola de Saúde Pública do Ceará, Ceará, Brazil (permit 1.569.510, June 1, 2016).

SYSTEM ARCHITECTURE

The implementation of the proposed system is based on the use of Unity as an engine of the augmented-reality environment, being used as 2D sprites scene objects produced in an image editing software. The HMZ-T2, Sony Glasses, responsible for transmitting the image processor, coupled with a LifeCam Studio Microsoft is placed in the user's head with a Panasonic RP-BTGS10 phone shown in Figure 1, which uses the bone to convey sound vibrations to the nervous system, transporting the sound of the environment and not interfering in the interviewer's voice. Figure 2 shows the integration of the devices in the system.

Figure 1: Panasonic phone RP-BTGS10.

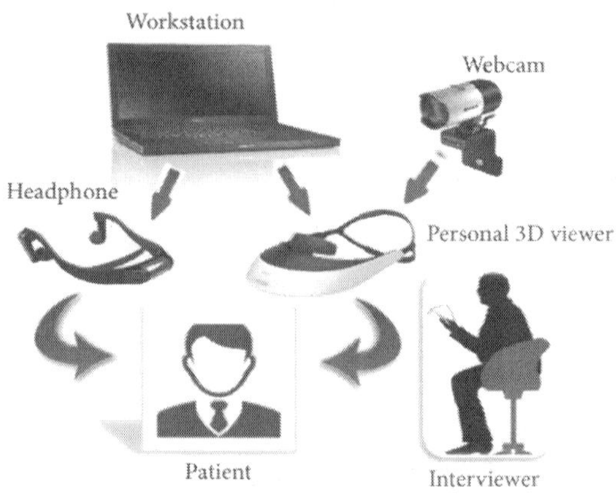

Figure 2: Device integration.

Environment Integration with the Equipment

As the purpose of this paper was to convey the psychotic symptoms to a healthy sample of the population, it demanded a good interaction of the tool with the equipment employed. The tool consists of software that can be installed on any computer that has Windows operating system with versions from Win 7. It already has a simple interface that was created by the graphic engine Unity 3D itself, being easily accessible to any user.

Modeling and Animation

Modeling and Audio Animation

Sound hallucinations were created by means of sound editing software and recorded with a microphone that was emitted by a headset. In creating the audio hallucinatory phrases noises, whispers and provocations, like "you aren't worth a thing" type were implemented. Some order phrases with "he will kill you" or "get out of here" were used in the environment audio. While developing the audio some pauses were made. In order to give more immersion as if a person were whispering in the ear, the procedure was applied in each and every phrase or any sound emitted by the environment, by using a sound channel coming out separately on each side of the headset. In the environment, the user of the glasses should listen to the voice of the interviewer who would make questions to the user while he/she listened to the sound effects.

Modeling and Figure Animation

The figure, modeled on an imaging software and animated in Unity, plays a major role in the augmented-reality environment, because it simulates one of the typical schizophrenia psychotic symptoms. This is the case when a patient has hallucinations in his/her vision that cause a perception of something nonexistent, but that is a subjective impression that it is something real without external stimulus. Consistent with reports from patients the figure may have a human appearance or a blur. To develop the figure images of a man silhouette and a flattened circumference were used, and then the blur effect was applied so that the image provided an impression of an image with twisted visual focus. Figure 3 shows model types made of figures for the environment with man silhouette, where there are more blur in Figure 3(a), less blur in Figure 3(b), and medium blur Figure 3(c). Figure 4 illustrates the model of a circumference flattened by the sides. The animations were constructed so that there was some relation with what was being heard with the audio mentioned. The figure underwent a transformation of position on the x-axis corresponding to the camera and appeared in parts demarcated by the studies. The other figures, which are the man silhouette, appeared in the extreme part of the camera view, while the fade effect was applied by varying the fade-in and fade-out time according to the sound effects.

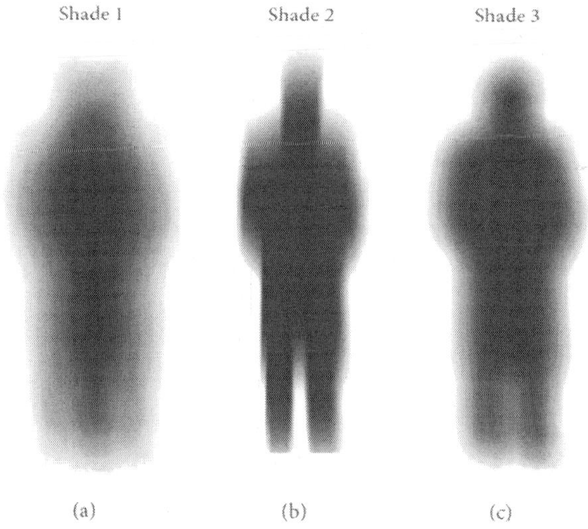

Figure 3: Models of figures with man silhouette: (a) more blur; (b) less blur; (c) middle blur.

Figure 4: Flat circumference figure model.

Modeling and Animation of Facial Transformation Effect

In facial modification, the OpenCV plugin for Unity available in the Unity Asset Store was used. Plugins function to include the use of OpenCV in Unity. As this package is an OpenCV Java clone, we can use the same API with OpenCV Java 3.1.0. It works with Unity free and pro with iOS, Android, Windows Store Apps 8.1 support, Windows Phone 8.1, Windows 10 UWP support (beta), Support Win, Mac, and Linux Standalone Support for Editor viewing. Its image processing is in real time using the Drive WebCamTexture capabilities (real-time face detection works flawlessly on iPhone 5). Version 1.9.0 of the plugin was used. With this plugin, we can proceed with the facial recognition and thus apply deformation and facial modification effects. In this work, to perform the facial modification, a dark circumference, see Figure 4, was placed over the eyes, accompanying the movements of the user's face through a 2D sprite provided by Unity Technologies for use in prototyping of games.

The process is aimed at simulating psychopathological changes experienced by the schizophrenia-afflicted individuals during their psychotic symptoms. Some patients report illusions involving the face of interlocutors, who may appear to patients as gloomy or even monstrous. As such, the simulated effect causes discomfort and estrangement feelings, rendering the experience more threatening.

RESULTS

As a result of this work, a simulator was developed in an augmented-reality environment called "Schizophrenia Simulator" originally designed as the proposal in this work, so that the environment could be evaluated as to the possibility of being used as a tool to help reducing the stigma with reference to schizophrenia.

In this work, the analysis was made through observations and analysis of the questionnaire based on multiple comparison to evaluate the significance of the changes in the observed parameters.

Screenshots of the Developed Environment and Testing Used

Figure 5(a) shows the use of an environment simulation tool by a medical student, analyzing his behavior during his interaction with the augmented-reality environment through virtual reality glasses, as well as the usability of the tool for possible adjustments for difficulties presented by users. From this test, it was acknowledged that initially the user had difficulties adjusting the glasses on his head, because in some cases the device did not fit properly because of its size. The infrastructure used for this test was a doctor's office of Frota Pinto Mental Hospital. A medical consultation was performed using a simulator, in which the volunteer (medical student) would answer some questions in a personal, professional, and logical reasoning scheme at a time when the schizophrenia psychotic-symptom simulating environment was running. Figure 5(b) shows how the medical student (patient) sees the visual-effect simulating figures of a schizophrenia psychotic symptom. Figure 5(c) shows the facial modification effect applied in the environment visualized by the medical student (patient) in real time.

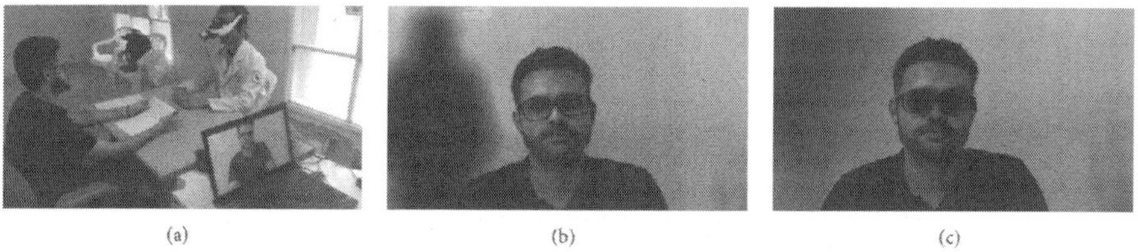

Figure 5: (a) Environment simulation with the medical student; (b) visualization in the simulation; (c) visualization of the facial modification in the simulation.

Evaluation of the Virtual Environment

In order to validate the augmented-reality environment, medical students at Mental Hospital Frota Pinto were invited to take part in a simulation of augmented-reality environment using virtual reality glasses. They had the opportunity to use it to explore their possibilities and to analyze the feasibility of this augmented-reality environment as an alternative to help in decreasing the schizophrenia-related stigma. Twenty-one students from three universities in the state of Ceará were present for the environment trial. After using the augmented-reality environment, the medical students were submitted to three questionnaires: evaluation of the schizophrenia-related stigma, evaluation of the environment simulation, and evaluation of stigma after an augmented-reality simulation. According to Pfleeger (1994) and Wohlin et al. (2000), a questionnaire should be applied to analyze quantitative data before and/or after application of an approach.

The aim of the questionnaires was to be used as a prestudy in order to certify that important issues related to the study were anticipated, as well as to depict expectations, perceptions, and opportunities related to the possibility of the actual use of an augmented-reality environment in users as a complementary tool for understanding, stigma reduction, and prejudice. The questionnaire to assess the schizophrenia-related stigma consisted of 9 questions; the last one was related to José's story, a fictitious schizophrenic patient, in his first contact with the user, and the other 8 questions have a personal nature and asked whether there are cases of family members diagnosed with schizophrenia. The other questionnaires (Table 1 to Table 4) correspond to the evaluation of the proposed virtual environment on stigma reduction related to schizophrenia. In the last questionnaire evaluating the stigma after an augmented-reality simulation, questions related to José's story with a postsimulation feature were made.

Table 1: Questions and analysis of the medical students' responses on the proposed augmented-reality environment

Objective questions made	Extremely [%]			Little [%]	
	5	4	3	2	1
(1) Does the proposed environment ensure realism in the execution of its sound effects?	42.85	42.85	14.30	—	—
(2) Does the proposed environment ensure realism in the execution of its visual effects?	23.80	47.60	14.20	14.20	—

(3) Does the proposed environment create a sensation of immersion in reality (feeling of belonging to reality)?	9.50	57.15	28.60	4.75	—
(4) Was the simulation educational about schizophrenia symptoms?	80.95	19.05	—	—	—
(5) Should simulation make users more empathetic towards people with schizophrenia?	71.40	19.05	4.75	4.75	—

Analyzing the results of the questionnaires application, see Table 1, it was found that in the questionnaire related to the environment simulation evaluation, on a 1–5 scale, of not at all to extremely, 42.85% of medical students chose the value 5, 42.85% of the students considered 4, and 14.30% chose 3, regarding the realism of the proposed environment in the execution of its sound effects; 23.80% of the medical students considered on a 1–5 scale, of not at all to extremely, value 5 and 47.60% considered 4, 14.20% of the medical students chose 3, and the same value chose 2, regarding the realism of the proposed environment in the execution of its visual effects. With regard to the augmented-reality environment proposed, there is the sensation of reality immersion (feeling of belonging to reality): 9.50% of the medical students considered on a 1–5 scale, of not at all to extremely, the value 5, while 57.15% considered 4 and 28.60% of the medical students chose 3 and 4.75% chose 2. On the other hand, 80.95% and 19.05% of the medical students, on a 1–5 scale, of not at all to extremely, chose 5 and 4, respectively, if the simulation was educational concerning the schizophrenia symptoms. Regarding whether the simulation should make users more empathetic towards schizophrenia-afflicted individuals, on a 1–5 scale, of not at all to extremely, 71.40% considered the value 5, 19.05% considered 4, 4.75% indicated 3, and the same value, 4.75%, chose 2. Table 1 shows the results quantitatively found with the objective questions of the questionnaire.

Questions on the environment simulation evaluation questionnaire related to the symptoms experienced during or shortly after the simulation reported that 19.05% of the medical students had a general malady (a general sensation of discomfort and uneasiness), fatigue, and "heavy headache" (due to the equipment weight); 4.76% said that they had problems with headache, dizziness with open eyes, and abdominal discomfort (stomachache). On the other hand, 38.10% reported they had a tired eye and blurred vision. It was found that 71.40% of the medical students had difficulty maintaining focus and concentration (seeing clearly and getting confused with the voices of the environment). 9.52% of the users reported sweating problems (perspiration or sweating) and nausea (an uncomfortable stomach feeling) and 14.30%

reported dizziness with open eyes. Table 2 shows the analysis of the medical students' answers about the symptoms felt during or shortly after the simulation.

Table 2: Analysis of medical students' answers about the symptoms felt during or shortly after the simulation

Questions related to symptoms	Reports [%]
(1) General malady	19.05
(2) Weariness	19.05
(3) Headache	4.76
(4) Eyestrain	38.10
(5) Difficulty to maintain focus	71.40
(6) Increased salivation	—
(7) Sweating	9.52
(8) Nausea	9.52
(9) Difficulty to concentrate	71.40
(10) "Heavy head"	19.05
(11) Blurry vision	38.10
(12) Dizziness with open eyes	14.30
(13) Dizziness with closed eyes	4.76
(14) Vertigo	—
(15) Abdominal discomfort	4.76
(16) Belch	—

Regarding the subjective questions, the medical students emphasize that the proposed environment stands out.

Positive Points. Positive points are as follows: being educational for health professionals and others, simulation in a suitable place rendering realistic effects, experience in understanding a psychotic patient's mind, reducing stigma and prejudice, showing the reality experienced by a schizophrenic, understanding the disease symptoms, interactivity being more attractive than the conventional information practice, and empathy with the schizophrenia symptoms.

Negative Points. Negative points were as follows: difficulty in putting glasses on the head, discomfort using the device, simulating in a more restless setting, difficulties in viewing for glasses users, voice-audio synchronization improvement, and possibility of causing uneasiness for some individuals.

Possibilities for Improvement. Possibilities for improvement include improving the external environment lighting, use of VR glasses with a better and more comfortable fitting and better closing of vision, adding real people in simulations, and figure-audio synchronization improvement.

In order to evaluate the impacts on the schizophrenia-related stigma, a questionnaire that evaluated questions about a fictional patient called "José" was applied, and these same questions were applied after using an augmented-reality environment, assessing the result changes. Appendix 2 of the questionnaire tells José's story. Questions and inquiries in the questionnaire comprised the following: "Would I feel sorry for José?," "How dangerous do you think José is?," "How scared would you feel with José?," "I think José is guilty of his present condition," "I think it would be better for José's community that he be admitted to a psychiatric hospital," "How angry would you feel about José?," "How likely is it that you will help José?," "I would try to stay away from José," and "Do you think José should be forced to take medical treatment, even against his will?" on a 1–9 scale, in which 1 corresponds to "no or nothing" and 9 corresponds to "very or completely."

During the results analysis of the application of the questionnaire related to the evaluation of the medical students' responses (Table 3) on the schizophrenia-related stigma, on a 1–9 scale of no/nothing and very/completely, 28.57% of the medical students gave value of 9; 23.80% considered 8; 14.28% chose 7; 6. 9.52% indicated value 5; 4.6% picked 4 and 3 for item "I would feel sorry for José," 4.76% of the medical students on a 1–9 scale of no/nothing and very/completely considered value 8, while 9.52% indicated 7; 14.20% recorded 6; 23.80% chose 5; 9.52% took 4 and 19.04% selected items 3 and 2 on the scale for item "How dangerous do you think José is?" Concerning the "How scared would you feel with José?" item, on a 1–9 scale of no/nothing and very/completely, 9.52% of the medical students scored values of 8, 6, 5, and 4; 4.76% indicated 7; 23.80% picked value 3; 14.28% chose value 2; and 19.04% scored 1. 9.52% of the medical students on a 1–9 scale of no/nothing and very/completely, item "I think José is guilty of his present condition" chose value of 3, and 90.47% picked value 1. Regarding item "I think it would be better for José's community that he be admitted to a psychiatric hospital" on a 1–9 scale of no/nothing and very/completely, 4.76% of the medical students pointed out values of 9, 7, 6, and 3. 9.52%, 19.04%, and 53.38% chose 5, 2, and 1, respectively. 4.76% of the medical students on a 1–9 scale of no/nothing and very/completely chose values 4 and 3, 28.57% selected 2, and 61.90% marked value 1 concerning item "How angry would you feel about José?"

Values 9 and 5 were marked by 9.52% each. 28.57% selected value 8. 33.33% chose 7, 14.28% considered 6 and 4.76% scored 4 on a 1–9 scale of no/nothing and very/completely of item "How likely is it that you will help José?" In regard to "I would try to stay away from José," on a 1–9 scale of no/nothing and very/completely, 14.20% chose 7, while 19.04% selected 6 and 2; 4.76% considered 4. 9.52% chose 3 and 33.33% picked 1. On a 1–9 scale of no/nothing and very/completely relative to item "Do you think José should be forced to take medical treatment, even against his will?" 14.28% of the medical students considered values 9, 8, and 1, 4.76% selected 7, 6, and 2, 23.80% marked 5, and 19.04% pointed out 4. Table 3 shows the analysis of the medical students' responses about the schizophrenia-related stigma evaluation.

Table 3: Questions and analysis of medical students' responses about the schizophrenia-related stigma evaluation

Question/statement	No/nothing [%]					Very/completely [%]			
	1	2	3	4	5	6	7	8	9
I would feel sorry for José.	—	—	4.76	4.76	9.52	14.28	14.28	23.80	28.57
How dangerous do you think José is?	—	19.04	19.04	9.52	23.80	4.28	9.52	4.76	—
How scared would you feel with José?	19.04	14.28	23.80	9.52	9.52	9.52	4.76	9.52	—
I think José is guilty of his present condition.	90.47	—	9.52	—	—	—	—	—	—
I think it would be better for José's community that he be admitted to a psychiatric hospital.	52.38	19.04	4.76	—	9.52	4.76	4.76		4.76
How angry would you feel about José?	61.90	28.57	4.76	4.76	—	—	—	—	—
How likely is it that you will help José?	—	—	—	4.76	9.52	14.28	33.33	28.57	9.52
I would try to stay away from José.	33.33	19.04	9.52	4.76	—	19.04	14.28	—	—
Do you think José should be forced to take medical treatment, even against his will?	14.28	4.76	—	19.04	23.80	4.76	4.76	14.28	14.28

Table 4: Questions and analysis of medical students' answers on the evaluation of stigma after augmented-reality simulation

Question/statement	No/nothing [%]					Very/completely [%]			
	1	2	3	4	5	6	7	8	9
I would feel sorry for José.	—	—	—	—	9.52	9.52	9.52	4.76	66.66
How dangerous do you think José is?	4.76	14.28	14.28	9.52	9.52	9.52	19.04	19.04	—
How scared would you feel with José?	9.52	14.28	23.80	9.52	9.52	4.76	14.28	4.76	9.52
I think José is guilty of his present condition.	90.47	4.76	—	—	4.76	—	—	—	—
I think it would be better for José's community that he be admitted to a psychiatric hospital.	33.33	14.28	4.76	4.76	14.28	9.52	—	—	19.04
How angry would you feel about José?	76.19	4.76	14.28	4.76	—	—	—	—	—
How likely is it that you will help José?	—	—	—	—	9.52	14.28	14.28	9.52	52.38
I would try to stay away from José.	38.09	19.04	4.76	14.28	14.28	4.76	—	4.76	—
Do you think José should be forced to take medical treatment, even against his will?	4.76	14.28	4.76	—	23.80	—	9.52	14.28	28.57

During the results analysis of the application of the questionnaire related to the evaluation of the medical students' answers (Table 4) on the evaluation of stigma after augmented-reality simulation, on a 1–9 scale of no/nothing and very/completely, 66.66% of the medical students marked value 9, 4.76% of the students considered 8, and 9.52% picked values 7, 6, and 5 concerning item "Would I feel sorry for José?" On a 1–9 scale of no/nothing and very/completely of item "How dangerous do you think José is?", 19.04% of the medical students considered values 8 and 7, 9.52% chose values 6, 5, and 4, 14.28% marked values 3 and 2, and 4.76% scored 1. Concerning item "How scared would you feel with José?," on a 1–9 scale of no/nothing and very/

completely, 9.52% scored 9, 5, 4, and 1, while 14.28% scored values 7 and 2; 4.76% of the medical students considered 8 and 6, and 23.80% selected value 3. On the 1–9 scale of no/nothing and very/completely of item "I think José is guilty for his present condition." 90.47% picked value 1, and 4.76% of the medical students considered values 5 and 2. In item "I think it would be better for José's community that he be admitted to a psychiatric hospital," on a 1–9 scale of no/nothing and very/completely, 19.04% of the medical students scored value 9. 9.52% chose value 6, 14.28% considered each 5 and 2, 4.76% scored 4 and 3, and 33.33% selected value 1. 4.46% of the medical students on a 1–9 scale of no/nothing and very/completely, for item "How angry would you feel about José?," chose values 4 and 2, 76.19% chose value 1, and 14.28% considered value 3. For item "How likely is it that you will help José?," on a 1–9 scale of no/nothing and very/completely, 9.52% of the medical students scored 8 and 5, 14.28% took 7 and 6, 52.38% scored value 9. 9.46% of the medical students considered, on a 1–9 scale of no/nothing and very/completely, values 8, 6, and 3, while 14.28% chose 5 and 4; 19.04% of the medical students chose 2; and 38.09% scored 1, for item "I would try to stay away from José." On a 1–9 scale of no/nothing and very/completely, 28.57% of the medical students considered value 9, 14.28% of the students chose 8 and 2, 9.52% chose 7, 23.80% scored value 5, and 4.76% chose values 3 and 1 for item "Do you think José should be forced to take medical treatment, even against his will?" Table 4 shows the analysis of the medical students' responses on the evaluation of stigma after the augmented-reality simulation.

After the simulation, as stated by the questionnaires, there was a trend to help the fictitious case patient. It is important to note that there was also an increase in the trend to hospitalize the patient and to treat him/her involuntarily.

These data indicate a change of posture after the simulation: while there was an increase in empathy, there was an apparent greater impression that the presented picture is serious. There was also an ascending trend after the simulation of considering José dangerous.

The results demonstrated an increase in the mean stigma score from 32.05 to 35.38 ($p = 0.004$), with statistical significance in pity, fear, and segregation. On the other hand, there was an increase in the average score referring to the probability of giving help, from 7.00 to 7.81 ($p= 0.034$). The tool had good acceptance, demonstrated by the average scores, for use as a teaching method (4.8), ability to increase the understanding of people with schizophrenia (4.57), realism of sound effects (4.29), realism of visual effects (3.81), and sensation of immersion in reality (3.71), on a scale from 1 (not at all) to 5 (extremely). In the analysis of the emotional impact of the tool on individuals submitted to the proposed environment, there was always some sort of symptom, and the most common one was the difficulty of maintaining focus and concentration.

Although this was an isolated intervention, there was an increase in the mean total stigma score; moreover, the simulation of psychotic symptoms through the augmented reality also resulted in increased scores of the possibility of helping a patient with psychosis. In general, the proposed system obtained a good overall evaluation. Notwithstanding these positive points, further improvements in the technique will be needed in order to decrease discomfort and improve concerns related to size and portability, so that the tool can have a large-scale usage. However, in its present form, the new tool can be used as an educational resource so that people can become more familiar with the symptoms of schizophrenia, and in doing so reducing its stigma and enhancing empathy for the patients.

The design of this study has limitations related to the long-term effect of VR in the change of attitude towards the bearer of schizophrenia. In cross-sectional analysis it is impossible to predict whether the experiment is capable of causing lasting stigma reduction.

CONCLUSION

This work presented the development of an augmented-reality environment simulating the schizophrenia psychotic symptoms as an alternative tool to help reducing the schizophrenia-related stigma so that there is no delay at the beginning of treatment. We specifically addressed the use of an augmented-reality environment through Sony HMZ-T2 glasses, which proved useful for the simulation of visual and auditory effects, managing to transmit the visual effects well with few exceptions, such as people wearing glasses, who could not see appropriately. The Panasonic RP-BTGS10 headset, which uses bone tissue to transfer sound vibrations to the nervous system, is promising, lightweight, and affordable.

According to the results, the medical students and specialist/psychiatrist included the use of the augmented-reality environment as an educational resource for health professionals as well as for family members and society in search of reducing the disease-related stigma. In the analysis of the emotional impact of the tool on individuals submitted to the proposed environment, it shall be noticed that there was always some sort of symptom, while the difficulty of maintaining focus and concentration was the most common one.

The tool developed in this work showed very promising results, and can be applied in educational environments (groups of schools, colleges, and technical training), in hospitals and clinics, and in the training and awareness-raising of groups that may come into contact with psychosis-afflicted patients, such as police officers, municipal guards, and family members, amongst many other applications. It will be necessary to further improve the technique in order to decrease discomfort and improve concerns related to size and portability, so that it can have a large-scale application. In general, the new tool can be used as an educational resource so that people become more familiar with the schizophrenia symptoms, and in so doing reducing its stigma and enhancing empathy for the patients.

Longitudinal evaluation studies with one or multiple exposures to the RV tool can demonstrate if the effects of the experiment are lasting over time, as well as determining the need to repeat the experiment to consolidate the expected effect. Future studies may also indicate whether the effect of immersion experience can be reinforced by supplementary psychoeducation measures such as short lectures on schizophrenia, for example.

AUTHORS' CONTRIBUTIONS

Rafael D. de C. Silva, Saulo G. C. Albuquerque, and Artur de V. Muniz designed the augmented-reality tool and performed the experiments, as well as investigation. Victor Hugo C. Albuquerque and Saulo G. C. Albuquerque analyzed the data. Victor Hugo C. Albuquerque, Sidarta Ribeiro, and Pedro P. Rebouças Filho are responsible for the funding acquisition and project administration. All authors contributed to and have approved the final manuscript.

ACKNOWLEDGMENTS

VHCA acknowledges the sponsorship from the Brazilian National Council for Research and Development (CNPq) via Grant no. 301928/2014-2.

REFERENCES

1. WHO, "The world health report 2001," Mental Health: New UnderstanDing, New Hope, World Health Organization, 2001, http://www.who.int/whr/2001/en/whr01_djmessage_po.pdf.
2. WHO, "Mental health," Schizophrenia, World Health Organization, 2017, http://www.who.int/mental_health/management/schizophrenia/en/.
3. C. R. Bowie and P. D. Harvey, "Cognitive deficits and functional outcome in schizophrenia," Neuropsychiatric Disease and Treatment, vol. 2, no. 4, pp. 531–536, 2006.
4. E. M. Joyce and J. P. Roiser, "Cognitive heterogeneity in schizophrenia," Current Opinion in Psychiatry, vol. 20, no. 3, pp. 268–272, 2007.
5. P. Dalgalarrondo, "Psicopatologia e semiologia dos transtornos mentais, Artmed Editora, 2009".
6. American Psychiatric Association, Diagnostic And Statistical Manual of Mental Disorders (DSM-5), American Psychiatric Pub, 4th edition, 2013.
7. N. C. Andreasen, "The diagnosis of schizophrenia," Schizophrenia Bulletin, vol. 13, no. 1, pp. 9–22, 1987.
8. D. Freeman, "Studying and treating schizophrenia using virtual reality: a new paradigm," Schizophrenia Bulletin, vol. 34, no. 4, pp. 605–610, 2008.
9. W. Veling, S. Moritz, and M. Van Der Gaag, "Brave new worlds - Review and update on virtual reality assessment and treatment in psychosis," Schizophrenia Bulletin, vol. 40, no. 6, pp. 1194–1197, 2014.
10. N. Yee and J. N. Bailenson, "Walk a mile in digital shoes: the impact of embodied perspective-taking on the reduction of negative stereotyping in immersive virtual environments," in Proceedings of Presence 2006: The 9th Annual International Workshop on Presence, Cleveland, Ohio, USA, 2006.
11. D. L. Penn, J. D. Ivory, A. Judge, and etal., "The virtual doppelganger: effects of a virtual reality simulator on perceptions of schizophrenia," The Journal of nervous and mental disease, vol. 198, no. 6, pp. 437–443, 2010.
12. M. Rus-Calafell, J. Gutiérrez-Maldonado, and J. Ribas-Sabaté, "A

virtual reality-integrated program for improving social skills in patients with schizophrenia: A pilot study," Journal of Behavior Therapy and Experimental Psychiatry, vol. 45, no. 1, pp. 81–89, 2014.

13. S.-H. Park, J. Ku, J.-J. Kim et al., "Increased personal space of patients with schizophrenia in a virtual social environment," Psychiatry Research, vol. 169, no. 3, pp. 197–202, 2009.
14. C. Hawco, L. Buchy, M. Bodnar et al., "Source retrieval is not properly differentiated from object retrieval in early schizophrenia: an fMRI study using virtual reality," NeuroImage: Clinical, vol. 7, pp. 336–346, 2015.
15. K. Han, I. Young Kim, and J.-J. Kim, "Assessment of cognitive flexibility in real life using virtual reality: a comparison of healthy individuals and schizophrenia patients," Computers in Biology and Medicine, vol. 42, no. 8, pp. 841–847, 2012.
16. S. Moritz, M. Voigt, U. Köther et al., "Can virtual reality reduce reality distortion? Impact of performance feedback on symptom change in schizophrenia patients," Journal of Behavior Therapy and Experimental Psychiatry, vol. 45, no. 2, pp. 267–271, 2014.
17. R. M. E. M. Costa and L. A. V. De Carvalho, "The acceptance of virtual reality devices for cognitive rehabilitation: a report of positive results with schizophrenia," Computer Methods and Programs in Biomedicine, vol. 73, no. 3, pp. 173–182, 2004.
18. M. Fornells-Ambrojo, C. Barker, D. Swapp, M. Slater, A. Antley, and D. Freeman, "Virtual reality and persecutory delusions: safety and feasibility," Schizophrenia Research, vol. 104, no. 1-3, pp. 228–236, 2008.
19. J. Counotte, R. Pot-Kolder, A. M. Van Roon, O. Hoskam, M. Van der Gaag, and W. Veling, "High psychosis liability is associated with altered autonomic balance during exposure to Virtual Reality social stressors," Schizophrenia Research, vol. 184, pp. 14–20, 2016, http://www.sciencedirect.com/science/article/pii/S0920996416305187.
20. P. Salgado-Pineda, R. Landin-Romero, F. Portillo et al., "Examining hippocampal function in schizophrenia using a virtual reality spatial navigation task," Schizophrenia Research, vol. 172, no. 1-3, pp. 86–93, 2016, http://www.sciencedirect.com/science/article/pii/S0920996416300895.
21. M. J. Smith, M. F. Fleming, M. A. Wright et al., "Virtual reality job

interview training and 6-month employment outcomes for individuals with schizophrenia seeking employment," Schizophrenia Research, vol. 166, no. 1-3, pp. 86–91, 2015, http://www.sciencedirect.com/science/article/pii/S0920996415002790.

22. M. J. Smith, E. Ginger, M. Wright, K. Wright, M. Bell, and M. Fleming, "Poster #S266 virtual reality job interview training," Schizophrenia Research, vol. 153, 1, p. S186, 2014, http://www.sciencedirect.com/science/article/pii/S0920996414705456.
23. W. Veling, R. Pot-Kolder, J. Counotte, and M. van der Gaag, "Psychosis liability, paranoia and distress in experimental virtual reality social environments," Schizophrenia Research, vol. 153, 1, pp. S377–S378, 2014.
24. J. Counotte, R. Pot-Kolder, A. M. Van Roon, O. Hoskam, M. Van der Gaag, and W. Veling, "High psychosis liability is associated with altered autonomic balance during exposure to virtual reality social stressors," Schizophrenia Research, vol. 184, pp. 14–20, 2017.
25. G. Thornicroft, E. Brohan, D. Rose, N. Sartorius, and M. Leese, "Global pattern of experienced and anticipated discrimination against people with schizophrenia: a cross-sectional survey," The Lancet, vol. 373, no. 9661, pp. 408–415, 2009.
26. A. H. Crisp, M. G. Gelder, S. Rix, H. I. Meltzer, and O. J. Rowlands, "Stigmatisation of people with mental illnesses," The British Journal of Psychiatry, vol. 177, no. 1, pp. 4–7, 2000.
27. D. L. Bower and W. G. Pettit, "The albuquerque policc dcpartments crisis intervention team," FBI Law Enforcement Bulletin, vol. 70, no. 2, pp. 1–6, 2001.
28. N. Rüsch, K. Heekeren, A. Theodoridou et al., "Stigma as a stressor and transition to schizophrenia after one year among young people at risk of psychosis," Schizophrenia Research, vol. 166, no. 1-3, pp. 43–48, 2015.
29. S. Sharples, S. Cobb, A. Moody, and J. R. Wilson, "Virtual reality induced symptoms and effects (VRISE): comparison of head mounted display (HMD), desktop and projection display systems," Displays, vol. 29, no. 2, pp. 58–69, 2008.
30. J. Tichon, J. Banks, and P. Yellowlees, "The development of a virtual reality environment to model the experience of schizophrenia," in Computational Science — ICCS 2003, vol. 2659 of Lecture Notes

in Computer Science, pp. 11–19, Springer, Berlin, Germany, 2003.

31. P. W. Corrigan, S. B. Morris, P. J. Michaels, J. D. Rafacz, and N. Rüsch, "Challenging the public stigma of mental illness: a meta-analysis of outcome studies," Psychiatric Services, vol. 63, no. 10, pp. 963–973, 2012.
32. F. Fernández-Aranda, S. Jiménez-Murcia, J. J. Santamaría et al., "Video games as a complementary therapy tool in mental disorders: playMancer, a European multicentre study," Journal of Mental Health, vol. 21, no. 4, pp. 364–374, 2012.
33. J. K. Luiselli and A. J. Fischer, Computer-Assisted and Web-Based Innovations in Psychology, Special Education, and Health, Academic Press, Cambridge, Mass, USA, 2016.
34. F. F. Rocha, C. M. de Lima, A. R. O. Guerra, and M. M. Marcelino, "Optimization of dense clouds to viewer softwares in virtual reality environment," in Vi National Congress of Mechanical Engineering, 2010.
35. J. Carmigniani, B. Furht, M. Anisetti, P. Ceravolo, E. Damiani, and M. Ivkovic, "Augmented reality technologies, systems and applications," Multimedia Tools and Applications, vol. 51, no. 1, pp. 341–377, 2011.

Chapter

14 Application of "Virtual Realities" in Psychotherapy: Possibilities, Limitations and Effectiveness

Dr. Christiane Eichenberg

University of Cologne (Institute of Clinical Psychology and Psychological Diagnosis) Germany

INTRODUCTION

In numerous projects, the Internet has proven to be a useful enhancement and a helpful support to psychosocial and psychotherapeutic methods. Key words such as online-therapy, e-therapy, and e-mental health are frequently used in this context (for an overview, see Bauer & Kordy, 2008; Eichenberg, 2008; Eichenberg & Ott, in press; Ott & Eichenberg, 2003; Bauer & Kordy, 2008). Another tool considered useful is mobile media, which can effectively be applied to the entire spectrum of clinical-psychological interventions

Citation: Christiane Eichenberg (January 8th 2011). Application of 'Virtual Realities' in Psychotherapy: Possibilities, Limitations and Effectiveness, Virtual Reality, Jae-Jin Kim, IntechOpen, DOI: 10.5772/12914. Available from: https://www.intechopen.com/books/virtual-reality/application-of-virtual-realities-in-psychotherapy-possibilities-limitations-and-effectiveness.

(Döring & Eichenberg, 2007). Virtual Reality (VR) technologies go one step further by enabling the creation of computer-based models of the real world that can be interacted via man-machine interfaces. VR applications can also be accessed via the Internet, but only singular and stationary programs exist so far. The observation that virtual stimuli trigger real anxiety, often accompanied by physiological symptoms (elevated blood pressure, sweating and nausea), has led to the integration of these modern applications into the spectrum of therapeutic intervention techniques.

Two conditions are necessary in order for people to experience virtual environments as "real" and thus render the environments therapeutically useful. These two conditions are referred to as "immersion" and "presence".

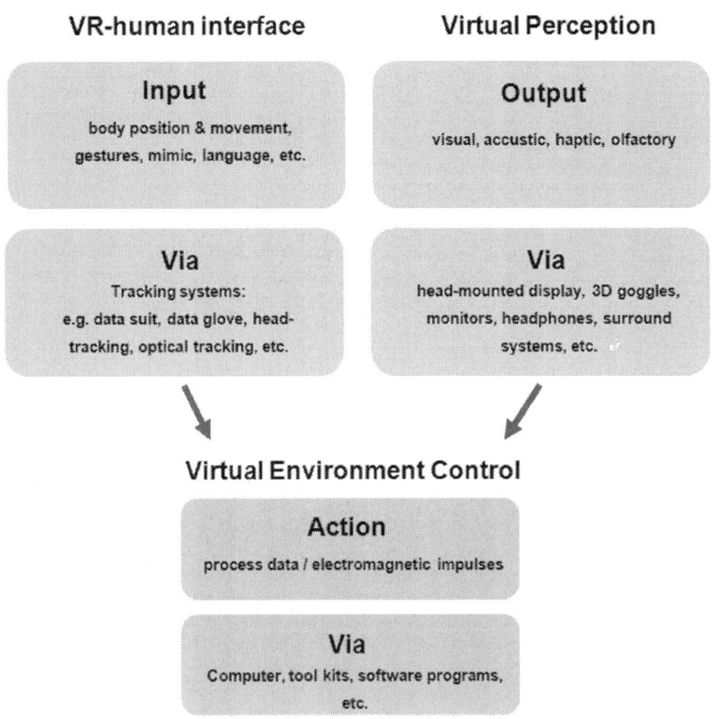

Figure 1: Technical requirements of VR applications (source: proprietary graphic).

An individual's involvement with the virtual environment due to objective, stimulating conditions is referred to as immersion. On the one hand, the virtual environment's visual, auditory, and tactile designs create the three-dimensional perception that the VR model is the real world. On the other hand, the perception of the virtual environment is facilitated by specific output devices (e.g. data-goggles, monitor) and special input devices (e.g. data gloves, voice recognition software, geolocation systems, and line-of-sight trackers). These special devices and systems enable synchronous activity and communication with the computer generated model using gestures, mimicry, language, body position, etc.

The subjective experience of physically being in a virtual environment and that this environment is real is referred to as presence. Characteristics of presence are the perception of the environment being real, blanking out real-world stimuli as well as involuntary and objectively meaningless body movements. For example, a person might crouch to feel his feet firmly planted on the real floor while crossing a virtual bridge over a virtual abyss.

USE IN PSYCHOTHERAPY

Initially, VR technologies were applied in various areas of medicine (comp. Kaltenborn, 1994). The development of a three-dimensional visualization system facilitated laparoscopic surgery. In the field of rehabilitation of physically disabled patients, carrying out everyday tasks was simplified with the aid of VR devices. Mute patients, for example, could carry on verbal conversations using a data glove that captures gestures, which are interpreted by the computer and forwarded to a language system. The language system then translates the gestures into a synthetic language.

Since 2000, VR applications have been systematically tested in the field of psychotherapy, particularly in behavior therapy and proven to be effective in the treatment of various specific phobias, as first studies show. According to the theories of behavior therapy, in order to treat phobias the anxiety provoking situation must be sought, avoidance amplifies the notion that the stimulus is dangerous and thus prevents corrective experiences. Being able to experience and tolerate anxiety is an essential part of the therapy. The aim of the treatment is to revise maladjusted concepts and to learn new behavior. There are two different forms of exposure therapy. Immediate exposure to the feared situation or object in reality is referred to as "in vivo" exposure. Exposure to the situation or object in imagination only is referred to as "imaginal" exposure. Both methods involve incremental, i.e. graduated exposure. Starting with stimuli that trigger only low levels of fear, the exposure is incrementally or massively increased. In the latter case, patients are exposed to their most extreme fear ("flooding" or, in imaginal exposure, "implosion").

EMPIRICAL EVIDENCE OF THE EFFECTIVENESS OF EXPOSURES USING VR

Most studies of the effectiveness of VR applications have examined their use in treating specific phobias such as fear of heights, fear of flying, fear of animals, and social phobias. A few studies have been made using VR to treat other disorders, though some of these applications are questionable not only ethically but also by current psychotherapeutic standards.

Firstly, two current meta analyses regarding the effectiveness of VR environments in treating anxiety disorders are summarily presented. Subsequently, exemplary studies of the treatment of anxiety disorders, including posttraumatic stress disorder, and the therapeutic VR components used in the treatments are introduced.

Meta Analyses

There are currently two meta analyses that analyze and document the present state of research on the effectiveness of VR-based exposure treatments for anxiety disorders.

N=21 evaluation studies (N=300 subjects) substantiating the effectiveness of VR-based exposure therapy were evaluated by Parsons and Rizzo (2008). All studies with pre-post measurements were included in this study; using a controlled study design was not a prerequisite for admission to the analysis. Regarding the reduction of symptoms by using VR therapies, the authors found an average effect size of d=.95 (SD=.02). Aside from fear of flying (d=1.5; SD=.05), the effect size was largest for the treatment of panic disorder with agoraphobia (d=1.79; SD=.02). The effect size was nearly identical for the treatment of social phobia (d=.96; SD=.10), acrophobia (d=.93; SD=.06) as well as arachnophobia (d=.92; SD=.12), with that of PTSD being the smallest (d=.87, SD=.01). The authors assumed a series of determining factors (e.g. degree of immersion and presence, duration of the disorder, socio-demographic aspects), but were unable to make empirically funded statements based on the data at hand, because too few studies provided information about these aspects.

Powers and Emmelkamp (2008) chose a more rigid design and used only 13 controlled studies (with N=397 subjects) as a basis. They surmised that VR treatment for anxiety disorder is highly effective (in comparison to the waiting control group: median d=1.11) and at least as effective as in-vivo therapy (median d=.34).

Overall, the findings at hand show that VR treatment for anxiety disorders is highly effective, although it seemed more effective in treating diffuse phobias (e.g. fear of flying) than more complex anxiety disorders (e.g. social phobia, PTSD). However, the weaknesses common to meta analyses (e.g. publication bias, as studies with insignificant results are less frequently published, with the consequence that effects tend to be overestimated) need to be considered. Conversely, the limitations of the studies involved need to be taken into account in particular (e.g. sample sizes that are too small, partially missing data about the time of the follow-up ratings and the conjunctive lastingness of a successful treatment). Introducing varied levels of immersion (e.g. head-mounted display or VR-cave) as independent variables and generally ensuring that no measurement instruments are used that might favor one treatment environment over the other (e.g. imaginal vs. VR) is an important consideration for future studies.

Exemplary Studies of Various Syndromes

The meta studies on hand reveal that the effectiveness of VR has been studied mainly in behavior therapy for patients with anxiety disorders. Anxiety disorders are among the most frequently diagnosed psychological disorders. In the federal health survey of 1998/99, a 12- month prevalence was established among 14.5% of the adult German population (Jacobi et al., 2004). Consequently, comprehensive research efforts to optimize existing treatment methods come as no surprise. Anxiety disorders lie within the traditional treatment range of behavioral procedures and lend themselves well to the VR setting due to their concept of exposure (as opposed to psychodynamic therapy procedures, which center on the relationship aspect). Thus, anxiety disorders present the first syndrome category for which the use of modern media such as the Internet or VR technology as a setting for interventions was scientifically evaluated (Eichenberg & Portz, 2005).

The two major diagnostic classification systems differ in their definition of anxiety disorders. While the DSM-IV (the American Psychiatric Association's Diagnostic and Statistical Manual of Mental Disorders; Saß et al., 1998) contains an individual chapter named „Anxiety Disorders", they are included in the chapter „Neurotic, Stress and Somatoform Disorders" in the ICD-10 (the World Health Organizations' International Classification of Diseases, 1991). The ICD-10 distinguishes between the subgroups of phobic disorders (agoraphobia, social anxiety disorder, as well as specific phobias) and other anxiety disorders (panic disorder, generalized anxiety disorders).

Posttraumatic stress disorder is consequently dealt with in the same chapter as anxiety disorders.

Fear of heights

The fear of situations involving heights (acrophobia) is frequently reported among the public. In a survey of over 8000 adults, 20% admitted to having experienced an exaggerated fear of heights at least once in their lifetime, but not to the extent that would meet the clinical criteria of acrophobia (Curtis et al., 1998). In the cited study, acrophobia ranks immediately behind the fear of animals, which was reported most often (22%). 5.3% of those surveyed met the criteria for diagnosis of acrophobia. Contrary to the common observation that women develop a specific phobia more frequently than men, this is not distinctively the case with acrophobia. While 55-70% of acrophobia sufferers are female, 75-90% of adults suffering from fear of animals are women (comp. DSM-IV, Saß et al., 1998).

Empirical research of VR-based exposure therapy began with individual case studies of patients suffering from acrophobia. Rothbaum et al. (1995) described an acrophobic student who had five therapy sessions after being shown anxiety reducing relaxation techniques. During these sessions, he was exposed to several virtual environments within which he could gradually move up to increasingly higher planes. On each plane, the student used relaxation techniques to habituate himself to the height. Standardized instruments (e.g. Avoidance Scale, Attitude Towards Heights) measured an improvement of his symptoms in a pre-post comparison. Even if these first studies show methodical deficits (effects of relaxation techniques were not distinguished from effects of exposure techniques), they do illustrate the fundamental advantages of imaginal confrontation. On the one hand, actual locations, in this case high bridges, can often only be reached with great effort and pedestrians can disturb the intervention. On the other hand, the stimulus can be applied in measured doses and the anxiety-provoking situation can be accessed in a safe and individually remodelable environment.

The therapeutic potential of VR exposure as part of behavior therapy to treat acrophobic patients was confirmed in a study series by Emmelkamp et al. (2001). In the first study, a within-subjects design was used. Ten acrophobic patients were gradually exposed to heights in VR during sessions and then went in-vivo to heights in the company of the therapist. The extent of their acrophobia was measured before treatment, after VR exposure, and after invivo exposure. Various scales indicated significant improvement after

VR exposure, while only one variable (Fear of Heights, Cohen) registered additional improvement after in-vivo exposure. The authors assumed that a blanket effect had happened in the sense that VR treatment was so effective that no further significant improvement could be achieved after repeated in-vivo exposures. In a second study (Emmelkamp et al., 2002), VR and in-vivo exposure were compared in a between-subject design. N=33 acrophobic patients with an average age of 44 (SD=9.3) and having suffered from the disorder for an average of 31.5 years (SD=11.3) were randomly exposed to both VR and real settings. Each exposure was graduated over the course of three sessions.

Figure 2: VR-environment used to treat fear of flying (source: A. Mühlberger).

In order to increase the comparability of the two scenarios, the real environment used for in-vivo exposures was replicated in the virtual environment. Thus, three environments – virtual or real – had to be visited: A shopping mall in Amsterdam with four floors, escalators, and bridge railings, a 50 meter high fire escape, and the roof garden on a university's grounds (65 feet high). The patients rated their anxiety levels on the SUDS-scale (Subjective Units of Disturbance) at specified points in time. Each time patients had habituated themselves to a particular situation, they were encouraged to switch to a more challenging exercise. The evaluation results demonstrated that both forms of treatment were equally effective. VR as well as the in-vivo variant lead to equally significant improvements that continued to last after six months. Krijn et al. (2004) found no differences in effectiveness regarding the dependence upon different levels of presence, i.e. operationalized with VR via Cave (high degree of presence) or head-mounted-display (low degree of presence).

Fear of flying

According to references, phobic fear of flying affects approximately 10% of the population (e.g. Nordlund, 1983). Another 20% fly with considerable unease (Institute of Demoscopy Allensbach, 2003). There is a frequent comorbidity with other disorders: According to Kinnunen (1996), 43% of those suffering from fear of flying also suffer from claustrophobia, while another 53% suffer from acrophobia. The situations that trigger fear in individuals suffering from fear of flying differ greatly. In a study with 144 subjects suffering from fear of flying (Mühlberger & Hermann, 1997), 5% of subjects reported fear of an accident happening, 29% fear of heights, 26% fear of enclosed rooms, 25% fear of an anxiety attack, 14% fear they might not receive medical attention, 12% fear of being subjected to fear itself, and just as many were afraid of their fear being noticed by others.

Schubert and Regenbrecht (2002) refer to some of these anxiety-specific characteristics that, on a conceptual basis alone, support using VR in regard to treating fear of flying. In particular, they highlight the logistical and financial expenditure that is far lower in comparison to in-vivo exposure. They also emphasize the privacy and familiarity of the treatment setting compared to the public exposure during a regular commercial flight. Mühlberger et al. (2008) add the ease of repeating VR exposure. Rothbaum et al. (2000) introduced a controlled study comparing VR supported therapy to in-vivo exposure. Fortyfive subjects with fear of flying were randomly assigned to either VR or in-vivo therapy. Both treatment environments resembled each other in the first four sessions (cognitive intervention, breathing exercises, and thought stopping training). In the next four sessions of VR treatment, patients were seated in a virtual airplane that they visualized using data goggles. The visualization was supplemented with realistic airplane ambiance noises or the simulation of turbulent weather. The patients were gradually exposed to increasingly anxiety-provoking situations (from simply sitting in a parked airplane to turbulence during takeoff, to actual flying or landing). In the in-vivo environment the subjects spent two double sessions at an airport. First they took part in flight preparation training, then they entered parked airplanes and visualized takeoff, flight and landing of the plane (combination of in-vivo and imaginal treatment). A pre-post comparison using several standardized measuring instruments showed significant improvement of symptoms in both treatment groups. No significant differences were apparent between the two treatment groups, even after the follow up rating after six months, and the improvements remained consistent. The subjects in the waiting condition showed no reduction in symptoms; however, it should be critically mentioned that the stimuli were not identical in the two treatment environments, because an actual flight was not part of the therapy.

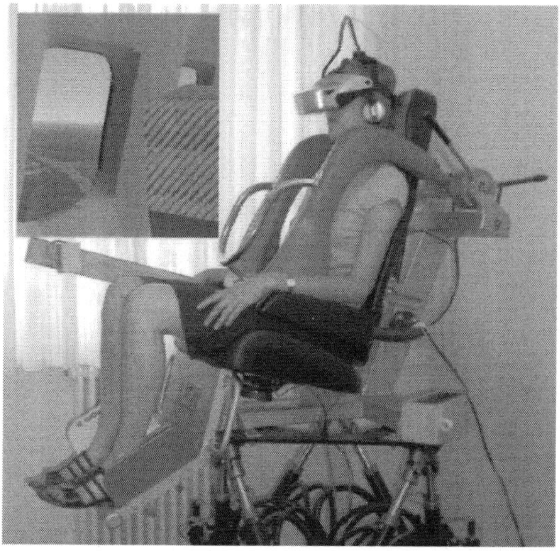

Figure 3: Fear of flying: simulator (source: A. Mühlberger).

A further study conducted by Wiederhold et al. (2003) revealed that graduated VR treatment combined with the feedback of physiological parameters (breathing, heart frequency, skin resistance) was most effective in comparison to pure VR therapy and imaginal exposure using the same graduated exposure to fear. In a randomized study, the authors found that 20% of the patients in the imaginal environment, 80% of the patients in the VR treatment and 100% of the patients who received VR exposure with additional feedback of biological parameters were able to fly again after eight weeks of therapy. Study series by German scientists from the University of Würzburg also substantiated the effectiveness of VR: Even short-term VR exposure therapy in only one session is useful for treating fear of flying in the long run. The authors demonstrated the participation in a completion flight is important for long-term therapy success, while the attendance of a therapist during this flight has little influence (Mühlberger et al., 2006). The following pictures show the simulator as well as a section of the VR (inside of the airplane) the way they were used in the Würzburg studies.

Fear of spiders

In the ICD-10, fear of spiders (arachnophobia) is assigned to the category of zoophobias, subgroup of specific phobias. Zoophobias are the most common specific phobias, the exaggerated fear of small, crawling, scuttling animals like spiders, snakes and rats being predominant. According to references, the prevalence of arachnophobia is 3.5-6.1% of the population, a large percentile of them women (Schmitt et al., 2009). A person suffering from arachnophobia will experience intense fear paired with physical reactions as well as avoidance and flight behavior when exposed to a spider. This can impede a person's daily life, such as being limited when choosing an apartment or needing help when confronted with a spider (comp. casuistic). Since spontaneous recovery is rare, behavior therapy is the preferred method in treating this disorder.

Single case studies (Carlin et al., 1997) as well as controlled studies have documented successful treatments of arachnophobia with VR.

Figure 4: VR-environment used for exposure treatment of arachnophobia (source: www.hitl.washington.edu).

Case example (from Carlin et al., 1997)

Mrs. M. (37 years old) had suffered from arachnophobia that severely affected her daily life for 20 years. Before she drove to work in the mornings, she would search her car for spiders, spray pesticide, and leave a burning cigarette in the ashtray with the car windows closed, because she had heard that spiders do not like smoke. She routinely sealed the bedroom windows with tape and the door with towels before she went to bed to make sure no spiders could enter the room. After washing her clothes, she would put each piece of clothing into an individual plastic bags, sealing the bags to make sure the clothing stayed free of spiders.

Mrs. M. took part in 12 VR sessions of 60 minutes each over the course of three months. Before the first session, she was exposed to photos and later to plastic models of spiders over the course of several hours. Despite these preparative exposures, she remained extremely phobic. The therapist saw the advantage of using VR exposure because it enabled him to control the anxiety-provoking stimulus. Virtual spiders obey commands and can be touched without risk and brought to a desired position.

During the first VR sessions, Mrs. M. was exposed to two virtual spiders in a simulated kitchen – one large brown spider and one smaller black one. One month later (5th session), the visual simulation of one of the spiders was interfaced with a furry toy spider. This spider carried a sensor so that movement of the toy resulted in the movement of the virtual spider ("tactile augmentation"). The addition of a tactile stimulus was supposed to add to a maximum degree of presence and maximum transfer to the "real world".

The combination of tactile and visual stimuli triggered intense fear responses in Mrs. M. She experienced physical symptoms such as dry mouth, uncontrollable shaking of her hands and legs, and profuse sweating.

After completion of therapy, however, she showed a visible reduction in fear towards spiders.

While her self-rating of experienced fear during the visual-tactile exposure was 7.9 on a scale of 1-10, she rated her fear at a level of 3 by the end of therapy and showed no more physical symptoms. Off the 280 students who, like Mrs. M., completed a self-rating scale of arachnophobia, 29% were just as afraid or even more afraid of spiders than Mrs. M.

Mrs. M.'s improvement is so profound that she is now able to go camping.

The success of the treatment described above was also confirmed in follow-up studies (comp. Garcia-Palacios et al., 2002). At the same time, these studies revealed that VR treatments that combine the use of tactile and visual elements are more effective than purely visual VR exposures (Hoffmann et al., 2003).

Social Phobia

The fear of being critically observed by others, leading to avoidance of social situations, is referred to as social phobia. More extensive social phobias usually occur in combination with low self-esteem and fear of criticism. Social phobias symptomatically escalate in form of blushing, shortness of breath, cramping, speech impediment and frequent slips of the tongue, shaky hands, nausea, the urge to urinate, and even panic attacks. Typically, those affected fear that their nervousness or fear could be noticed, which only increases their anxiety. In an attempt to avoid all of this from happening, individuals with social phobias often avoid situations that could expose them to being observed by others to begin with. This can have a negative impact on a person's private and career life and lead to social isolation. About 11% of the male and 15% of female population suffer from social phobia at least once in their lifetime (Maggee et al., 1996).

Studies using clinical random samples also exist for the treatment of social phobia using VR settings. In a randomized design, Klinger et al. (2005) studied the effectiveness of VR supported therapy in comparison to cognitive behavior therapy with 36 patients who had, on average, been suffering from social phobia for 15 years. Various rating scales as well as therapist ratings were used to measure the effectiveness of the treatment after 12 sessions. Both VR and cognitive behavior therapies were found to be highly effective treatment forms for this specific phobia as well, successfully reducing fear and avoidance. Distinctions between the two forms of treatment were insignificant (comp. also Roy et al. 2003). Specific VR environments have also been developed to treat public speaking fear, a potential characteristic of social phobia (e.g. Anderson et al., 2003; Herbelin et al., 2002; Pertaub et al., 2001).

The use of VR in therapy to treat further anxiety disorders (e.g. claustrophobia: see single case study by Botella, 1998) and other psychological disorders (eating disorders: see Riva et al., 2001, alcoholism: see Lee et al., 2007) was examined as well. Studies on the effectiveness of VR in treating posttraumatic stress disorder are also available.

Posttraumatic stress disorder

Approximately 30% of individuals who experience a traumatic event suffer from a psychological disorder as a result. One of these disorders is the posttraumatic stress disorder (PTSD), which has been recognized as a formal diagnosis since 1980. According to the ICD10, PTSD comprises the following symptoms: Those affected were exposed to a short or long-lasting event or situation of an exceptionally threatening or catastrophic nature, which is likely to cause pervasive distress in almost anyone. This leads to symptoms such as intrusions (flashbacks, repeating dreams), avoidance of activities and situations reminiscent of the trauma, the partial or complete inability to recall some important aspects of the event or situation, or symptoms of hyperarousal (e.g. increased startle reaction, sleeping disorders). Potentially traumatic events can be divided into two groups: manmade disasters (war, torture, and exile; sexual abuse, violent crimes, bullying) and natural disasters (e.g. earthquakes, accidents, life-threatening diseases) (Fischer, Weber & Eichenberg, in print). There are a handful of studies that examine the utilization and effectiveness of VR in treating PTSD, in particular PTSD as a result of terrorist attacks and wartime experiences.

Difede and Hoffmann (2002) developed a VR environment for patients suffering from PTSD as reaction to the events of September 11, 2001 in New York. In their initial case study, the authors describe the treatment of a 26-year-old woman whose 9/11-related posttraumatic stress disorder had not responded to traditional imaginal exposure therapy. Having witnessed the attacks from across the street, she had survived without serious physical injury, but developed severe PTSD symptoms. She suffered from flashbacks, avoidance, hypervigilance, and difficulty falling and staying asleep.

The patient was treated with six VR sessions of 45-60 minutes. She was exposed to the following virtual scenarios:

1. A jet flies over the WTC towers, but doesn't crash, normal New York city street sounds.
2. Then a jet flies over, hits building, but no explosion
3. Then a jet flies over, crashes with explosion, but no sound effects
4. Then a jet flies over, crashes with explosion and explosion sound effects
5. Burning and smoking building (with hole where jet crashed), no screaming
6. Burning and smoking building (with hole where jet crashed) and screaming
7. Burning and smoking building (with hole where jet crashed), screaming, and people jumping
8. Second jet crashes into second tower with explosion and sound effects
9. Second tower collapses with dust cloud

10. First tower collapses with dust cloud
11. The full sequence

According to standardized clinical and self-report measures, the patient's symptoms were reduced immediately following the VR exposure treatments. This result was validated in a controlled study using a small random sample (Difede et al., 2006).

In Israel, Josman et al. (2008) developed the VR environment "BusWorld" with the aim of using VR therapy to help individuals who had experienced terrorist bombings. To test the functionality of the system, they ran a pilot test with 30 healthy subjects and gradually exposed them to four levels containing a re-enacted attack. The psychotherapeutic treatment comprised of ten VR sessions of 90-120 minutes each.

There are several studies about using VR to treat patients suffering from PTSD as a result of wartime experiences. Rothbaum et al. (2001) examined the effectiveness of VR in a controlled study with 10 Vietnam veterans. The veterans were exposed to authentically recreated war scenes (e.g. flight over Vietnam accompanied by auditory and visual effects of rockets and explosions) in eight VR sessions. While they experienced a reduction in PTSD symptoms after the sessions, the intrusion-score increased after the 6-month catamnesis.

Gerardi et al. (2008) tested the environment "Virtual Iraq" in a single case study of a 29-yearold soldier who had spent a year-long tour in Iraq. He was exposed to "Virtual Iraq" in four sessions of 90 minutes each; the exposure included olfactory elements (e.g. the smell of burnt rubber).

Figure 5: "BusWorld" (source: research.haifa.ac.il).

Overall these study designs give rise to ethical concerns. Exposing Vietnam veterans suffering from severe PTSD symptoms to authentically recreated war scenarios or exposing witnesses of the 9/11 attacks to the same, dramatic virtual situation is a form of exposure that is contra-indicated as far as current research on trauma therapy is concerned. Several phases (i.a. stabilization, developing a therapeutic relationship, resolution of the traumatic memory, where the course of the traumatic situation is outlined and thus encapsulated) must precede re-experiencing and processing the traumatic experience (comp. Fischer, 2000; 2007). None of these phases were considered in the studies referred to here. Therefore, the risk of re-traumatization in VR exposure therapy is higher than the likelihood of successful processing of the traumatic experience. (For more critical issues, e.g. risk of renewed traumatization because the presented stimuli do not exactly depict the traumatic situation that the patient experienced, see Wagner & Maercker, 2009). At the same time, VR can be used to educate health professionals about recognizing symptoms by practicing adequate negotiation using a simulated case (see Kenny et al., 2008).

CONCLUSION

First studies show that virtual realities are an effective instrument within behavior therapy treatment of anxiety disorders. There are no indications that VR treatment of fear of heights and fear of flying, for example, are less effective than traditional in-vivo exposure therapy. Meanwhile several aspects that are immanent to a VR setting seem to accommodate some patients, for example in their willingness to be exposed to anxiety-provoking stimuli in the first place. There are also advantages to therapists that are summarized in Table 1.

At the same time, however, VR applications hold a number of restrictions and disadvantages for patients because of the risk of new or re-traumatization and ethical considerations and to therapists because VR technology requires technical equipment and the familiarization with this equipment.

Table 1: Advantages and disadvantages of using VR in psychotherapy

Possibilities	Limitations / Risks
For the patient • Increased willingness to be confronted with the anxiety-provoking stimuli (increased subjective perception of safety and control over the presented stimuli) in the first place • A more private atmosphere, lower logistic and financial expenditure (fear of flying) • For patients with limited ability to visualize: VR aids the imagination of the anxiety-provoking situation	**For / To the patient** • „Simulator sickness" • Risk of new traumatization if the specific VR does not reflect the patient's traumatic situation accurately • Risk of re-traumatization if certain phases (i.a. stabilization) do not precede re-experiencing and processing the traumatic experience • Habituation to war and violence: Ethics?!
For the therapist • Exposure is possible in the practice • Possibility of subtler graduation in progression and intensity • In training: learning by simulated cases	**For / To the therapist** • Technology-based treatment: interference-prone • Acquisition is expensive • Training is necessary

Overall, the results at hand are definitely in need of additional data if they are to be considered validated and differential evidence of the effectiveness of VR. The number of studies and random samples is too small to make general statements; moreover, they have pilot study character. In addition, long-term catamneses are missing. Examining personality variables (e.g. attitude towards technology, comprehension of reality and identity, ability to visualize) as possible moderators in order to develop criteria for the intra- and interindividual integration of VR in psychotherapy is advised. With the integration of any kind of media application in therapy, the effects on therapist and patient variables as well as the effects on the therapeutic relationship should be examined.

VR exposure should be seen as a media reception, where the individual experiencing it plays an active and constructive role. The presented stimuli are processed on a cognitive level and assembled to a mental model that is linked to memories and conceptions. Hence, the research results of perception and media psychology are important fundaments in the further development of VR therapy settings. One prerequisite for the effectiveness of VR treatments is that the virtual world has to reflect the real world in a way that enables coherent cognitive and emotional processing. This means that the presentations of VR worlds are enhanced to provide ideal visual, auditory, and tactile stimuli. The VR applications so far have been prototypes. They have not been widespread enough, nor has the technical equipment involved been affordable enough so that VR could be used by behavioral therapists in regular practices to benefit their patients.

Although VR exposure therapy is the traditional domain of behavior therapy, psychodynamic therapy has been expanded with the conceptual integration of media-based interventions and training techniques. For an in depth report, refer to Eichenberg (2007). This reference states that media can also be integrated in psychodynamic therapies as long as the primacy "establishment of a relationship comes before technology" is ensured. (For an example see the integration of the self-help book "New ways out of trauma" [Fischer, 2005] in psychodynamic trauma therapies (refer to Angenendt, 2003).

REFERENCES

1. Anderson P, Rothbaum BO, Hodges LF (2003) Virtual reality exposure in the treatment of social anxiety. Cognitive and Behavioral Practice 10: 240-247
2. Angenendt G (2003) Entwicklung eines Beratungs- und Therapiemanuals zur Begleitung der Selbsthilfebroschüre "Neue Wege aus dem Trauma". Dissertation an der Philosophischen Fakultät der Universität zu Köln
3. Bauer S, Kordy, H. (Hrsg.) (2008) E-Mental-Health. Neue Medien in der psychosozialen Versorgung. Springer, Berlin
4. Bering R (2005) Verlauf der Posttraumatischen Belastungsstörung. Grundlagenforschung, Prävention, Behandlung. Shaker, Aachen
5. Botella C, Banos RM, Perpina C, Villa H, Alcaniz M, Rey, A (1998) Virtual reality treatment of Claustrophobia: a case repot. Behaviour Research and Therapie 36: 239-246
6. Botella C, Quero S, Baños RM, Perpiña C, Garcia-Palacios A, Riva G (2004) Virtual Reality and Psychotherapy. In: Riva G, Botella C, Légeron P, Optale G (Hrsg) Cybertherapy, Internet and Virtual Reality as Assessment and Rehabilitation Tools for Clinical Psycology and Neuroscience. IOS Press, Amsterdam
7. Carlin AS, Hoffmann HG, Weghorst S (1997) Virtual reality and tactile augmentation in the treatment of spider phobia: a case study. Behaviour Research and Therapie 35: 153-158
8. Curtis, GC, Magee, WJ, Eaton, WW, Wittchen, H-U & Kessler, RC (1998) Specific fears and phobias. Epidemiology and classification. The British Journal of Psychiatry 173: 212-217
9. Difede, J., Cukor, J., Patt, I, Giosan, C. & Hoffman, H. (2006) The Application of Virtual Reality to the Treatment of PTSD Following the WTC Attack. Ann. N.Y. Acad. Sci. 1071: 500-501
10. Difede, J & Hoffman, HG (2002). Virtual Reality Exposure Therapy for World Trade Center Post-traumatic Stress Disorder: A Case Report. CyberPsychology & Behavior 5(6): 529- 535
11. Döring N, Eichenberg C (2007) Klinisch-psychologische Interventionen mit Mobilmedien: Ein neues Praxis- und Forschungsfeld. Psychotherapeut 2: 127-135
12. Eichenberg C (2008) Bedeutung der Medien für klinisch-psychologische Interventionen. In B. Batinic, & M. Appel (Hrsg.), Medienpsychologie

(S. 503-530). Springer, Berlin

13. Eichenberg, C (2007). Der Einsatz von „Virtuelle Realitäten" in der Psychotherapie: Ein Überblick zum Stand der Forschung. Psychotherapeut 5: 362-367
14. Eichenberg, C & Ott R (in press) Klinisch-psychologische Intervention im Internet: Ein Review zu empirischen Befunden störungsspezifischer Angebote. Psychotherapeut
15. Eichenberg C, Portz K (2005) Angststörungen: Information und Intervention online. Psychotherapie im Dialog 4: 452-458
16. Emmelkamp P, Bruynzel M, Drost L, van der Mast C (2001) Virtual realitiy treatment in acrophobia: a comparison with exposure in vivo. Cyberpsychologie and Behavior 3: 335-341
17. Emmelkamp P, Krijn M, Hulsbosch L, de Vries S, Schuemie MJ, van der Mast C (2002) Virtual reality treatment versus exposure in vivo: a comparative evaluation in acrophobia. Behavior Research and Therapie: 509-516
18. Fischer G (2000) Mehrdimensionale Psychodynamische Traumatherapie MPTT. Manual zur Behandlung psychotraumatischer Störungen.Asanger, Heidelberg
19. Fischer, G (2005) Neue Wege nach dem Trauma - Erste Hilfe bei schweren seelischen Belastungen. Düsseldorf: Patmos.
20. Fischer G (2006) Kausale Psychotherapie. Ätiologieorientierte Behandlung psychotraumatischer und neurotischer Störungen Manual zur Behandlung psychotraumatischer Störungen. Asanger, Heidelberg
21. Fischer, G, Weber, T & Eichenberg, C (in press) Posttraumatische Belastungsstörung. In S. Letzel & D. Nowak (Hrsg.), Handbuch Arbeitsmedizin. Landsberg: ecomed MEDIZIN.
22. Garcia-Palacios A, Hoffman H, Carlin A, Furness TA III, Botella C (2002) Virtual reality in the treatment of spider phobia: A controlled study. Behaviour Research and Therapy 40: 983-993
23. Gerardi, M, Rothbaum, BO, Ressler, K & Heekin, M (2008) Virtual Reality Exposure Therapy Using a Virtual Iraq: Case Report. Journal of Traumatic Stress 21(2): 209-213
24. Herbelin B, Riquier F, Vexo F, Thalmann D (2002) Virtual Reality in Cognitive Behavioral Therapy : a preliminary study on Social Anxiety Disorder, 8th International Conference on Virtual Systems and Multimedia, VSMM2002. [Online Available]. http://vrlab.epfl.ch/

Publications/pdf/Herbelin_and_al_VSMM_02.pdf

25. Hoffman HG, Garcia-Palacios A, Carlin C, Furness TA III, Botella-Arbona C (2003) Interfaces that heal: Coupling real and virtual objects to cure spider phobia. International Journal of Human-Computer Interaction 16: 283-300
26. Institut für Demoskopie Allensbach (2003) Allensbacher Berichte Nr. 16: Wieder mehr Flugreisen. Institut für Demoskopie Allensbach.
27. Jacobi F, Klose M, Wittchen H–U (2004) Psychische Störungen in der deutschen Allgemeinbevölkerung: Inanspruchnahme von Gesundheitsleistungen und Ausfalltage. Bundesgesundheitsblatt -Gesundheitsforschung Gesundheitsschutz 8: 736- 744
28. Josman, N, Reisberg, A, Weiss, PL, Garcia-Palacios, A & Hoffman, HG (2008) BusWorld: an analog pilot test of a virtual environment designed to treat posttraumatic stress disorder originating from a terrorist suicide bomb attack. Cyberpsychol Behav. 11(6): 775-777
29. Kaltenborn K-F (1994) Virtuelle Realität – Anwendungen, Möglichkeiten und Grenzen einer neuen Computertechnologie. Biomedical Journal 39: 4-14
30. Kenny, P, Parsons, TD, Pataki, C, Pato, M, St-George, C, Sugar, J & Rizzo, A (2008) Virtual Justina: A PTSD Virtual Patient for Clinical Classroom Training. Annual Review of CyberTherapy and Telemedicine 6(1): 113-118
31. Klinger, E, Bouchard S, Légeron P, Roy S, Lauer F, Chemin I & Nugues P (2005) Virtual Reality Therapy Versus Cognitive Behavior Therapy for Social Phobia: A Preliminary Controlled Study. Cyberpsychology and Behavior 1: 76-88
32. Kinnunen, P (1996) Flugangst bewältigen. Weinheim: Psychologie Verlags-Union. Krijn, M, Emmelkamp, PM, Biemond, R, de Wilde de Ligny, C, Schuemie, MJ & van der Mast, CA (2004). Treatment of acrophobia in virtual reality: the role of immersion and presence. Behav Res Ther. 42 (2) 229-39
33. Lee, J-H, Kwon, H, Choi, J & Yang, B-H (2007) Cue-exposure therapy to decrease alcohol craving in virtual environment. CyberPsychology & Behavior 10 (5): 617-623
34. Maggee, WJ, Eaton, WW, Wittchen, H-U, McGonagle, KA & Kessler RC (1996) Agoraphobia, siple phobia and social phobia in the National Comorbidity Survey. Archives of General Psychiatry, 53 (2): 159-168

35. Mühlberger,A&Hermann,MJ(1997)AllgemeinerFlugangstfragebogen. Unpublished Manuscript, Julias-Maximilians-Universität Würzburg.
36. Mühlberger, A, Krebs, H & Pauli, P (2008) Expositionsbehandlung von Flugphobie mithilfe virtueller Realität. In Bauer, S & Kordy, H (Hrsg.), E-Mental-Health. Neue Medien in der psychosozialen Versorgung (pp. 163-173). Berlin: Springer.
37. Mühlberger, A , Weik, A., Pauli, P. & Wiedemann, G (2006) One-session virtual reality exposure treatment for fear of flying: 1-Year follow-up and graduation flight accompaniment effects. Psychotherapy Research 16(1): 26-40
38. Nordlund, CL (1983) A Questionnaire Study of Swedes´s Fear of Flying. Scandinavian Journal of Behaviour Therapy 12: 150-168
39. Ott R, Eichenberg C (2003) (Hrsg.). Klinische Psychologie und Internet. Potenziale für klinische Praxis, Intervention, Psychotherapie und Forschung. Hogrefe, Göttingen
40. Pertaub DP, Slater M, Barker C (2001) An experiment on fear of public speaking in virtual reality. Studies in Health Technology and Informatics Bd. 81: 372-378
41. Powers MB, Emmelkamp PMG (2008) Virtual reality exposure therapy for anxiety disorders: A metaanalysis. Journal of anxiety disorders 22 (3): 561-569
42. Riva G, Bacchetta M, Baruffi M, Molinari E (2001) Virtual Reality–Based Multidimensional Therapy for the Treatment of Body Image Disturbances in Obesity: A Controlled Study. Cyberpsychology & Behavior 4: 511-526
43. Rothbaum BO, Hodges LF, Kooper R, Opdyke D, Williford J, North M (1995) Virtual reality graded exposure in the treatment of acrophobie: a case report. Behavior Therapie 26: 547-554
44. Rothbaum, BO, Hodges, L, Ready, D et al. (2001) Virtual reality exposure therapy for Vietnam veterans with posttraumatic stress disorder. J Clin Psychiatry 62: 617-622
45. Roy S, Klinger E, Légeron P, Lauer F, Chemin I, Nugues P (2003) Definition of a VR-Based Protocol to Treat Social Phobia. CyberPsychology & Behavior 6: 411-420.
46. Saß, H, Wittchen, H-U & Zaudig, M (1998) Diagnostisches und Statistisches Manual Psychischer Störungen (DSM-IV). Göttingen: Hogrefe.

47. Schmitt, WJ & Müri, RM (2009) Neurobiologie der Spinnenphobie. Schweizer Archiv für Neurologie und Psychiatrie 160(8) 352–355
48. Schubert T, Regenbrecht H (2002) Wer hat Angst vor virtueller Realität? Angst, Therapie und Präsenz in virtuellen Welten. In: Bente G, Krämer N, Petersen A (Hrsg.) Virtuelle Realtitäten (S. 255-274). Hogrefe, Göttingen
49. Thönes P (2006) Der Einsatz bibliografischen Materials in der kardiologischen Rehabilitation – eine qualitative Studie. Unveröffentlichte Diplomarbeit am Institut für Klinische Psychologie und Psychotherapie der Universität zu Köln
50. Wagner, B & Maercker, A (2009) Neue Medien für die Intervention bei Traumafolgestörungen. In BU Stetina & I Kryspin-Exner (Hrsg.), Gesundheit und Neue Medien. Psychologische Aspekte der Interaktion mit Informations- und Kommunikationstechnologien (S. 135-155). Wien: Springer.
51. Weltgesundheitsorganisation (1991) Internationale Klassifikation psychischer Störungen. ICD-10 Kapitel V (F). Klinisch-diagnostische Leitlinien. Bern: Huber. 978-3456841243
52. Wiederhold BK, Gevirtz RN, Spira JL (2003) Virtual Reality Exposure Therapy vs. Imagery Desensitization Therapy in the Treatment of Flying Phobia. In Riva G, Galimberti C (Eds), Towards CyberPsychology: Mind, Cognitions and Society in the Internet Age (Kap. 14). IOS Press, Amsterdam

Chapter 15 Research in Neuroscience and Virtual Reality

Beatriz Rey and Mariano Alcañiz

Instituto Interuniversitario de Investigación en Bioingeniería y Tecnología Orientada al Ser Humano, Universidad Politécnica de Valencia Spain

INTRODUCTION

Virtual reality is one of the most challenging applications of computer graphics and is currently being used in many fields. Participants of immersive virtual environments have unique experiences which were never before possible. Although they know from a cognitive point of view that the virtual environment is not a real place, they act and think as if the virtual environment were real. Virtual environments take advantage of the imaginative ability of

Citation: Beatriz Rey and Mariano Alcañiz (January 8th 2011). Research in Neuroscience and Virtual Reality, Virtual Reality, Jae-Jin Kim, IntechOpen, DOI: 10.5772/13198. Available from: https://www.intechopen.com/books/virtual-reality/research-in-neuro-science-and-virtual-reality.

people to psychologically transport them to other places.

In this chapter, we are going to analyze the two-way relationship between virtual reality and neuroscience.

First, it will be described how virtual reality can be a useful tool in neuroscience research, as long as it can be used to create controlled environments where participants can perform tasks while their responses are monitored in order to achieve a more detailed understanding of the associated brain processes. Previous work and research in this field will be detailed and discussed.

Secondly, the applications of neuroscience in the virtual reality field will be analyzed. There are aspects of the virtual reality experience such as presence that can be an object of study for neuroscientists (Sanchez-Vives & Slater, 2005). Results from neuroscience studies can help virtual reality researchers to improve their knowledge about the processes that occur in the brain during the exposure to virtual environments and generate more compelling and effective versions of the virtual environments that they develop.

At the end of the chapter, some general conclusions and implications that the research in virtual reality and neuroscience may have for future work will be described.

The different kinds of studies that will be described in this chapter are listed in Table 1.

VIRTUAL REALITY FOR NEUROSCIENCE

Virtual reality can be a perfect tool to generate controlled environments that can be used to observe human behaviour. Different aspects can be analyzed from a neuroscience perspective, including perception, control of movement, learning, memory, and emotional aspects.

Usually, in order to analyze human responses to different kinds of events or tasks, the participant behaviour has to be monitored in a real situation or during the execution of experimental tasks designed to analyze the influence of specific variables on human behaviour.

Table 1: Classification of previous studies combining virtual reality and neuroscience

Virtual reality for neuroscience	Study of human navigation with highly immersive virtual environments	(Warren et al., 2001; Tarr & Warren, 2002; Kearns et al., 2002; Foo et al., 2004; Foo et al., 2005; Waller et al., 2007; Richardson & Waller, 2007)
	Virtual versions of classical neuroscience tests to study navigation and spatial memory	(Astur et al., 1998; Jacobs et al., 1997; Jacobs et al., 1998 ; Driscoll et al., 2003; Astur et al., 2004; Astur et al., 2005; Duncko et al., 2007; Cornwell et al., 2008)
	Animal navigation	(Astur et al., 2003; Hölscher et al., 2005; Harvey et al., 2009)
	Human social interaction	(Bailenson et al., 2001; Schilbach et al., 2006; Slater et al., 2006)
Neuroscience for virtual reality	Presence research - Electroencephalogram	(Schlögl et al., 2002; Baumgartner et al., 2006; Kober, 2010)
	Presence research - functional magnetic resonance	(Hoffman et al., 2003; Baumgartner et al., 2008; Jäncke et al., 2009)
	Presence research - Transcranial Doppler	(Alcañiz et al., 2009; Rey et al., 2010)
	Virtual representation of the body	(Slater et al., 2008)

Those previous approaches have both positive and negative points that have to be taken into account when applying them to study human behaviour.

Laboratory experimental tasks allow the controlled study of any of the variables that may be having an influence on the participant's responses. However, the situation presented to the user is not realistic, and usually the participant has to execute the task in a laboratory setting and isolated from other contextual factors that are also associated with the situations or tasks that are being analyzed.

On the other hand, the analysis of human responses in real situations is complicated because the stimuli that are intervening in the experience cannot be controlled (or, at least, not completely controlled) by the experimenter.

However, with virtual reality, it is possible to design a virtual environment and situation with key elements analogous to those of a similar situation in the real world, but, in this case, the presentation of stimuli to the participant can be controlled in a precise way. Furthermore, virtual reality can also be used to create virtual versions of classical neuroscience tests that had only been applied to animals because of their characteristics. Virtual reality allows that the virtual version of the test can be conveniently applied to human participants. In the following subsections, different kinds of studies about human behaviour that have been conducted up to now with the help of virtual reality settings will be described:

- Study of human navigation with highly immersive virtual environments. Behavioural neuroscientists have been interested in analyzing how humans learn routes to get from one place to another. Highly immersive virtual environments provide a virtual laboratory where this kind of studies can be conducted and easily controlled.
- Virtual versions of classical neuroscience tests to study navigation and spatial memory.
- Animal navigation. In these cases, neural circuits underlying navigation have been studied in animals such as mice using specifically designed virtual environments.
- Human social interaction. There are other aspects, apart from navigation and spatial memory, that have been analyzed with virtual reality settings. Studies that have analyzed the neural correlates of social interaction will be described.

Study of Human Navigation with Highly Immersive Virtual Environments

Human navigation is one of the issues that have been analyzed using virtual environments. Users can navigate in a virtual reality system with specific goals, while their behaviour is analyzed to obtain conclusions about how humans learn routes to get from one place to another.

Tarr & Warren (2002) considered that three sources of information were available for this learning process: visual information in the form of optic flow (the pattern of visual motion at the moving), visual information about objects distributed in the environment (which can be used as landmarks) and body senses including vestibular and proprioceptive information. In order to analyze the influence of each of those factors, it is necessary that the subject moves through an environment where the experimenter can manipulate aspects such as the optic flow and the objects that appear in the environment. Virtual reality can be used to generate this controlled environment where the participant can navigate freely.

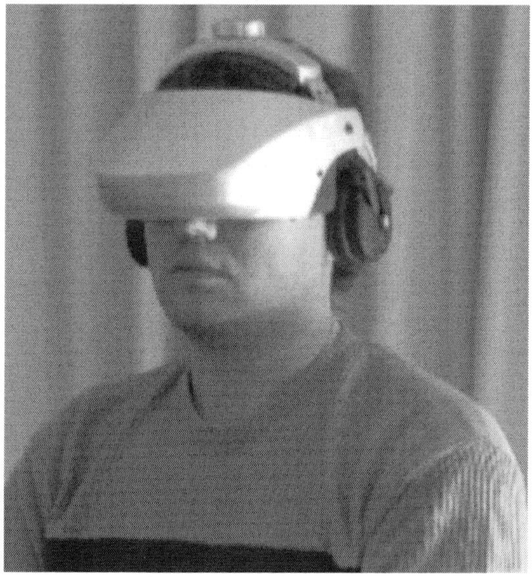

Figure 1: Subject of a virtual reality experiment wearing a head mounted display.

Tarr & Warren (2002) created a highly immersive virtual reality system, which they called VENLab, in which users visualized the environment using a stereo head mounted display. A photograph of a subject wearing a head mounted display is shown in Figure 1. Participants navigated in the VENLab using real walking (a wide-area head tracker was attached to the head tracker)

In different studies conducted with the VENLab, they analyzed the role of each of these sources of information while participants navigated in a virtual world where optic flow and landmarks could be controlled by the experimenter.

In one of the studies, Warren et al. (2001) analyzed if optic flow information is actually used when users have to walk towards a goal. Two different hypotheses had been proposed in the literature. The optic flow hypothesis indicated that the observer would walk to cancel the error between the heading perceived from optic flow and the goal navigation. On the other hand, the egocentric direction hypothesis considered that the observer just walks in the perceived visual direction of the goal with respect to the body. As the two hypotheses usually predict the same behaviour, it was fundamental the use of a virtual environment to be able to dissociate them. The virtual environment that was designed made it possible to displace the heading direction specified by the optic flow by an angle from the actual direction of walking. Different experimental conditions with growing levels of optic flow were analyzed, including an initial condition where no surrounding flow was available. It was found that subjects walked in the visual direction of a target, but increasingly relied on optic flow as it was added to the display.

In another study, Kearns et al. (2002) analyzed the role of visual information and body senses during a homing task. In this kind of tasks, the participant must be able to return to a home location after following a trajectory in the environment. Path integration is defined in this context as a navigation strategy in which information about one's velocity or acceleration is integrated on-line to estimate the distance travelled and the angles turned from an initial point (Loomis et al., 1999). Both optic flow information and body senses information (such as vestibular information and proprioception from receptors in muscles, tendons and joints) can provide information about distances and rotations. In order to analyze the role of the different variables, three experiments were proposed in the study. The task was a triangle completion task, in which participants walk two specified legs of a triangle and then they have to return to the starting position. In the first two experiments, only optic flow was analyzed, by making users navigate in a virtual environment using a joystick during the homing task. In the third experiment, the combined influence of visual and body senses was analyzed, by making the user navigate in the virtual environment with real walking. Results from the first two experiments showed that optic flow can be used for path integration in a homing task. Results from the third experiment showed a different pattern of results. Participants were more consistent, exhibited a pattern of overturning instead of underturning, and had similar responses independently of the presence of optic flow. These results seemed to indicate that, even if participants can perform path integration from optic flow if it is required, they usually rely more on body senses if this information is available.

Later, Foo et al. (2004) analyzed the influence of landmarks in navigation when compared with path integration. The task was also a triangle completion one. Four repetitions of the task with different triangles were conducted. In the first and last repetition, no landmarks were available. In the intermediate ones, a red post was placed near the starting position, but slightly displaced, with viewing angles from the final point ranging from 0 to 28 degrees. The participants did not notice the displacement, and followed the direction of the landmark. In a second experience, they were told that the landmark was unreliable, and in this case, they used path integration instead. It seems that, even if both systems provide information for homing tasks, landmarks are the factor that usually dominates navigation.

In a more recent study, Foo et al. (2005) continued the comparison of landmarks with path integration. In this case, they analyzed if the participant was able to find shortcuts in different environments during a triangle completion task. The subjects were trained on the two legs of the triangle and the angle between them in the context of a specific environment. After training, they had to find a shortcut between the endpoints of the two legs of a triangle. The first virtual environment that was used was a virtual desert world, which contained minimal optical aids. Optic flow and body senses information provided information for path integration, but no other sources of information were present. It was compared with a forest environment that contained multicoloured posts, to provide the user with a landmark strategy that could be used for navigation. Participants could not find successful shortcuts in the desert environment, but they could find them in the forest with multicoloured posts. These results seem to support that subjects rely on the potential landmarks when they are available and use them as a reference to guide navigation.

Apart from the VENLab, other special virtual reality systems have been developed to study spatial cognition. One of them is the HIVE - Huge Immersive Virtual Environment (Waller et al., 2007). This system consists of a large tracking area that lets users move through virtual worlds as they would in the real world, thus allowing the analysis of mental processes that require extensive movements through an environment. The system makes it possible to include in the experiments body-based sources of sensory information (such as vestibular and proprioceptive data), as happened also with the VENLab. Technically, the HIVE is based on an eight-camera optical tracking system that monitors user's position data, which are sent wirelessly to a rendering computer worn by the user. The environment is shown to the participant using a head-mounted display. The system is completed with an orientation tracking device. The HIVE has been used, for example, to analyze the influence of a user's physical environment on distance underestimation in immersive virtual environments. Previous research has found that egocentric distances are underestimated in immersive virtual environments (i.e., Lampton et al., 1995; Witmer & Kline, 1998). Using systems like the HIVE, it is possible to analyze if this underestimation occurs also when navigation is controlled by real physical walking. Richardson & Waller (2007) conducted an experiment which showed that the execution of an interaction task in the immersive virtual environment significantly corrected the underestimation that has been observed in previous studies.

All the studies described in this section have in common two main factors:

- The user can navigate using real walking in a wide area. Tracking systems designed to monitor the user position in large areas are used.
- The appearance and responses (such as optical flow) of the virtual environment can be controlled and changed between the different experimental conditions.

These are issues that should be taken into account when designing a virtual environment for the study of human navigation.

Virtual Versions of Classical Neuroscience Tests to Study Navigation and Spatial Memory

Virtual reality has also been used by other researchers to create virtual versions of classical neuroscience tests to study navigation.

In previous non-human research, the gold standard for analyzing place learning ability in rodents is the Morris water task (Morris, 1981). In this task, the rat has to swim to a fixed hidden platform (that cannot be seen, heard or smelt) in a circular pool, making use of distal spatial cues outside the pool. The apparatus used when this task was first applied was a circular pool with dimensions of 1.30 m diameter by 0.60 m high (Morris, 1981). The platform used in the experiment was put at a specific location in the pool, either visible or invisible (under water). Research has found that the ability to learn to navigate in this task is highly influenced by the integrity and plasticity in the hippocampus (Sutherland et al., 1982).

In order to apply the Morris water task in human research about navigation and spatial learning, practical difficulties appear. One requisite would be that humans and non-human animals should be tested in comparable spatial domains. A big pool would be required, and the manipulation of the platforms and monitoring of the experiment in this real pool would be more difficult than in the small circular container used in the experiments with rats. Furthermore, participants would probably find the task uncomfortable.

However, with virtual reality, virtual versions of the Morris water task can be prepared and applied in experiments about the analysis of place learning and spatial memory in humans. The advantages that virtual reality can provide are the following:

- A virtual pool environment with adequate dimensions for human participants can be generated and applied in the experiments.
- Subjects can navigate using virtual reality hardware for navigation. There is no necessity to physically swim.
- As the navigation occurs in a controlled computer system, it is possible to program it to easily control experimental variables such as the initial position of the participant, the position of the platforms inside the pool and the position of any visual cues in the environment.
- Furthermore, as the instantaneous position of the subject at each moment is known by the system, it is possible to store the exact trajectories that the participant has followed until arriving to the platform, allowing posterior analyses about different aspects such as the required time to find the platform or the length of the followed trajectory.

Astur et al. (1998) developed a computerized version of the test to analyze if the observed results in experiments with rats would generalize into the human domain. In their experiment, the virtual environment consisted of a circular pool in a room where several distal cues were present. No local cues were used. Participants had to swim in the pool navigating with a joystick. They had to find a platform hidden under the surface of the water from different initial locations. The fact of starting from different locations requires that a cognitive map is formed using the distal cues on the surrounding walls. Performance can be established using objective values that can be calculated, such as the path length or the required time to reach the platform. Different studies with a virtual version of the Morris water task have been developed and have shown the feasibility of applying it in human research (Astur et al., 1998; Jacobs et al., 1997; Jacobs et al., 1998; Driscoll et al., 2003; Duncko et al., 2007). These studies have shown that it is possible to apply a computerized Morris water task in human research. Each of them has focused on a different aspect of the experience. Differences in the performance of the Morris water task have been found associated to different factors such as sex, age or stress.

Posterior studies have combined the virtual Morris water maze with a virtual analogue of another task that has been used classically to analyze spatial memory in animals: an eightarm radial maze. Radial arm mazes are composed of a central area with a number of identical arms radiating outwards (Olton & Samuelson, 1974). A schema of the eight arm radial maze has been represented in Figure 2.

In the eight-arm radial maze, four of the arms have food at the end, but the other four arms do not have anything. In the first experimental trial, the rat should be able to find the food that is placed in four of the arms. Afterwards, the animal is removed from the maze. In the following experimental trials, the location of the food is maintained. With training, the rodents learn to find the food without entering in the empty arms.

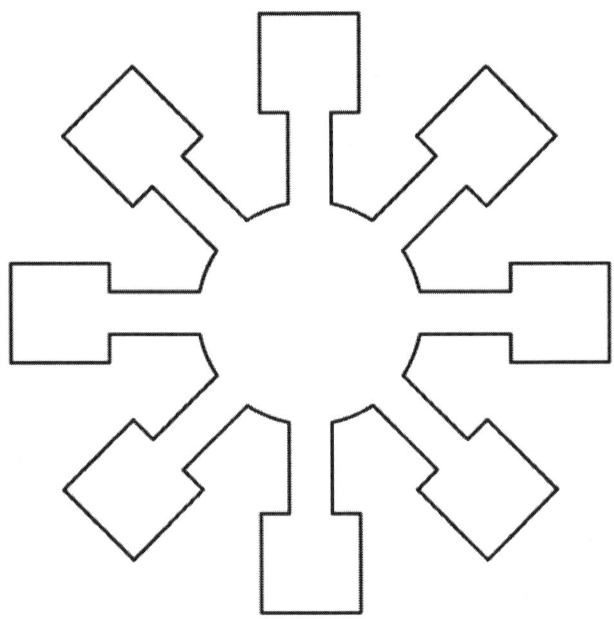

Figure 2: Distribution of the eight arm radial maze.

Astur et al. (2004) combined the virtual Morris water maze with an eight-arm radial maze. The virtual eight-arm radial maze consisted of a virtual room that had eight runways extending out of a round middle area. Participants knew that in four of the runways there was an award at the end, and that in the other four runways there was not. They had to retrieve all the awards as soon as possible. Results of the study showed that men performed significantly better than women when trying to find the hidden platform in the virtual Morris water task. However, there are no sex differences in working memory errors, reference memory errors or distance to find the rewards in the virtual radial maze. These results seemed to indicate that the virtual Morris water task and the virtual eight-arm radial maze assess spatial memory in different ways. Other studies with the virtual Morris water task and the radial mazes have monitored brain activation associated with these tests, specially analyzing the activity in the hippocampus. Cornwell et al. (2008) recorded neuromagnetic activity using magnetoencephalography (MEG), which is a technique that records magnetic fields produced by electrical activity in the brain and that can be used for mapping brain activity. Participants had to navigate to the hidden platform in a virtual Morris water task. The objective was to determine if hippocampal / parahippocampal theta activity was related to behavioural performance on the virtual Morris task. Source analysis of the MEG data captured during the study showed an increase in the power in the theta band of the spectrum (4-8 Hz) in hippocampus and parahippocampal structures during goal-directed navigation. It was also found a linear relationship between these theta responses and navigation performance on the virtual Morris task.

Astur et al. (2005) conducted an experiment with a radial arm maze to assess the function of the hippocampus and to see if the results from non-human research could be extrapolated to humans. Participants of the study had to perform a virtual radial arm task during functional magnetic resonance imaging (fMRI). An image of an fMRI machine can be visualized in Figure 3.

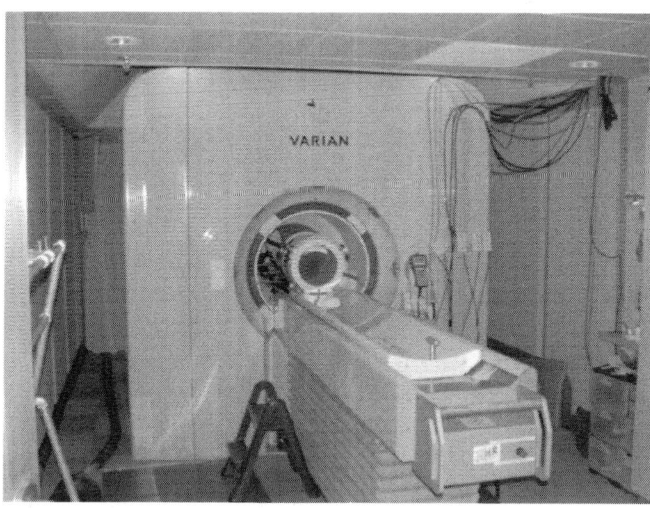

Figure 3: 4T fMRI, part of the Brain Imaging Center, in: Helen Wills Neuroscience Institute at the University of California, Berkeley.

fMRI is used for the study of metabolic and vascular changes that accompany changes in neural activity. The technique is based on the Blood

Oxygen Level Dependent method (BOLD), which measures the ratio of oxygenated to deoxygenated haemoglobin in the blood across regions of the brain. As oxygen is extracted from the blood, increases in deoxyhaemoglobin can lead to an initial decrease in BOLD signal. However, this is followed by an increase, due to overcompensation in blood flow that tips the balance towards oxygenated haemoglobin. It is this that leads to a higher BOLD signal during neural activity. fMRI is not a tool that can be easily combined with virtual reality environments. First of all, a test platform has to be developed to allow the exposition to the virtual environment while capturing the fMRI images without altering in a significant way any of both technologies. Moreover, the user has to be inside the magnetic resonance machine in supine position and with minimum head movement, and devices used to navigate and interact in the virtual environment have to work inside high magnetic fields with minimum electromagnetic interference.

Astur et al. (2005) used an fMRI-adapted joystick to allow participants to navigate in the virtual environment. As happened with other previous studies, significant changes were found in the activity of the hippocampus during the performance of the task. However, a decrease in activity occurred during the spatial memory component of the task. On the other hand, frontal cortex activity was also found, which could indicate activity associated to working memory circuits.

Animal Navigation

Virtual reality has also been used in neuroscience experiments with non-human animals. There have been some studies that have shown that primates, similarly to humans, can also interpret interactive two-dimensional projections as a virtual environment in which they can move (Leighty & Fragaszy, 2003; Nishijo et al., 2003; Towers et al., 2003). Astur et al. (2003), for example, examined if rhesus monkeys could learn to explore virtual mazes. In their experiment, four male macaques were trained to locate a target in a virtual environment. The monkeys controlled the navigation by moving a joystick. They completed successfully the task, and were able to locate the target. The search pattern that the animals followed within the maze was similar to the navigation pattern observed on more traditional twodimensional computerized mazes and was in accordance with predictions made from actual patterns in physical space.

But not only primates have been immersed in virtual reality experiences to analyze navigation patterns and spatial memory. Recently, it has been proven that rats are also able to navigate in virtual environments. Hölscher et al. (2005) built a virtual reality set-up and tested it with rats. It was shown that rodents could learn spatial tasks in this virtual reality system. One important point that had to be taken into account in the design of the virtual reality setting was to consider the wide-angle visual system of rats into account. That is why, while immersed in the virtual environment, the rat was surrounded by a toroidal screen of 140 cm diameter and 80 cm height. This screen covers a large part of the rat's visual field (360° azimuth, -20° to +60° of elevation).

Recently, Harvey et al. (2009) used this kind of virtual reality system to study the neural circuits underlying navigation in mice. The purpose was to measure the intracellular dynamics of place cells during the navigation in a virtual environment. However, intracellular recording methods require a mechanical stability which cannot be obtained when the animals can move freely in the real world. In this study, the mouse was allowed to run on top a spherical treadmill while its head was maintained stable using a head plate. Regarding the projection of the virtual environment, similarly to the previous study, the environment was projected on a toroidal screen that surrounded the rodent and that was designed to cover a wide area according to the large field of view of the animal. The movements of the mouse were measured as rotations of the spherical treadmill using an optical computer mouse. The mice were trained to run along a virtual linear track (180 cm long) with local and distal cues in the walls. Small water rewards were given to the animal when it has run between opposite ends of the track. The intracellular dynamics of hippocampal place cells were measured during the navigation with precision, because the mouse's head was stationary. The observed dynamics in the hippocampal place-cells had similar properties to those recorded in real environments.

Human Social Interaction

Virtual reality can also be a technology that can help to analyze other aspects of human behaviour. In this subsection, some studies that have been made in the social cognitive neuroscience field will be summarized.

There are several factors that contribute to make virtual reality a useful technology to address questions related to human behaviour in social situations. Participants of virtual reality experiences can feel that they are present in the virtual environment. This means that they have the sense of being in the virtual environment instead of being in their physical location, for example, the experimental room (Held & Durlach, 1992; Schumie et al., 2001). Presence is a multi-dimensional concept, and one of the dimensions that are analyzed when studying this complex experience is social presence, which occurs when part or all of a person's perception fails to accurately acknowledge the role of the technology that makes it appear that s/he is communicating with other people or entities. Virtual characters convey social information to human participants of virtual reality experiences. Furthermore, they are perceived by the participants as social agents, who exert social influence on human subjects that participate in the virtual reality experience (Bailenson et al., 2003).

Consequently, virtual reality has started to be applied in social psychological research (de Kort et al., 2003). In the following paragraphs, different studies that have analyzed several aspects of human interaction using virtual reality will be described.

Bailenson et al. (2001) analyzed the equilibrium theory specification (Argyle & Dean, 1965), which specified an inverse relationship between mutual gaze and interpersonal distance. In order to analyze this theory, participants were exposed to a virtual environment in which a male virtual character stood. The users were told to remember certain features about the agent's shirt. The participants' positions were tracked by the system, so the distance between participants and the virtual agent were continuously monitored. The results showed that the space between the participant and the virtual character was higher than the distance between the participants and objects with similar size and shape, but without human appearance. On the other hand, the interpersonal distance was higher in the case of women interacting with agents who did engage them in eye contact than with agents who did not. This effect was not observed in men. Results seem to indicate that factors such as non-verbal expressions of intimacy are in the origin of changes in the personal space.

Schilbach et al. (2006) studied the differences between being personally involved in a social interaction or being just a passive observer of a social interaction between other people, using virtual characters to generate the social situations. The virtual characters that were used in the study would gaze directly to the human observer, or look away towards a third person situated at an angle of approximately 30º (and not visible by the human participant). The virtual characters would show changing facial expressions similar to the ones that they would have in real-life social interaction situations or they would show arbitrary and socially irrelevant movements.

fMRI was used to monitor brain activity while the participants of the study observed the virtual characters. The sequences were projected onto a screen inside the fMRI scanner. After each repetition of the task, the participant had to answer two questions about how s/he has interpreted the behaviour of the virtual character. In order to allow this interaction inside an fMRI scanner, compatible keypads were used. Eye movements during conditions were also monitored using an infrared video-based eyetracking system. The results showed that higher neural activity was found in the anterior medial cortex when the virtual character was looking at the participant. Furthermore, if facial expressions were perceived as socially relevant, increased neural activity was observed in the ventral medial prefrontal cortex. Finally, the perception of arbitrary facial movements activated the middle temporal gyrus. Globally, the results showed that different regions of the medial prefrontal cortex contributed differentially to social cognition.

The interaction with a virtual character in an extreme social situation such as the conflict created within Milgram's paradigm (Milgram, 1963) has also been studied. This paradigm creates a social dilemma in which participants try to follow the experimenter's commands to administer pain to another person, but at the same time they feel that they have to avoid causing any harm to that person. This paradigm has been partially replicated within an immersive virtual environment (Slater et al., 2006). The participants of the virtual reality experience showed discomfort and increased arousal over the course of the conflict, and some of them stopped administering pain to the avatar, or expressed that they did not want to continue with the experience.

NEUROSCIENCE FOR VIRTUAL REALITY

In the previous section, a review of studies in which virtual reality has been applied as a tool for neuroscience has been presented. However, as has already been stated, neuroscience tools can also be used in virtual reality studies and can provide useful information for researchers in this field.

Some of the studies in which neuroscience has been a tool for virtual reality research are going to be described. They have been grouped in two different fields of application:

1. Presence studies. Neuroscience research can provide useful information to better understand the concept of presence in virtual environments. Different techniques and their combinations have been proposed and used to measure presence in virtual environments (Insko, 2003). These techniques have been

classified in two main groups: subjective tools and objective tools. Subjective techniques have been mainly based on the application of psychological measurement instruments like rating scales and subjective reports. On the other hand, objective techniques include behavioural measures and physiological measures. These measures are usually obtained during the virtual reality experience rather than following it, so they can be used for real-time monitoring during the exposure. However, although they are called objective, they do not generate a direct measure of presence. Instead, presence is assumed to be related in some way with the degree of change in parameters that can be obtained from physiological measures or from behavioural observation. It has been only in recent years that it has been studied applying neuroscience tools. Different neurological measures have been applied to analyze brain activity during the exposure to virtual environments in order to look for brain correlates of the presence experience. Three main neurological measures have been applied:

a. Electroencephalogram (EEG).
b. Functional magnetic resonance imaging (fMRI).
c. Transcranial Doppler (TCD).

In the following subsections, the advances in the presence research field that have been obtained in recent years using these three different techniques will be described.

2. Virtual representation of the body. Other works have applied neuroscience tools to analyze the interpretation of participants of virtual reality experiences about the virtual representation of their own body. For virtual reality researchers, it is necessary to know the interpretation that the participants of the experience attribute to the virtual representation of their bodies. The studies in this area will also be summarized in the following points.

Presence Research: Electroencephalogram

Electroencephalogram (EEG) reflects the brain's electrical activity, and in particular postsynaptic potentials in the cerebral cortex. Scalp-recorded EEG signals are thought to be generated by the addition of excitatory and inhibitory post-synaptic potentials in the cortical pyramidal neurons (Speckman et al., 1993). EEG signals always represent the potential difference between two electrodes, an active electrode and the reference electrode. This technique has a high temporal resolution, which makes it possible to analyze both fluctuations of EEG dependant of task demand, and differentiate between functional inhibitory and excitatory tasks.

EEG was proposed as a possible tool for obtaining objective indicators of presence, to detect brain states and transitions in the user, who can feel present in the virtual world and then change to feel present in the real world (Schlögl et al., 2002).

Baumgartner et al. (2006) were the first to use EEG to analyze neural correlates of spatial presence in arousing virtual environments without interaction. The virtual environment used was a virtual roller coaster scenario. Twelve children and eleven adolescents participated in the study. There was a control session, with a horizontal roundabout track, and several realistic rides (with ups, downs and loops). EEG and skin conductance were captured during the experience. It was found in both groups that spatial presence was higher in the realistic rides (when compared with the control condition). Furthermore, this was accompanied by increased electrodermal reactions and activations in parietal brain areas known to be involved in spatial navigation. Parietal processing centres in turn stimulated the insula as the core region for generating body sensations and the posterior cingulated which is strongly involved in emotion processing. On the other hand, children showed higher spatial presence, but less activity in some prefrontal areas than adolescents. These prefrontal areas are involved in the control of executive functions. The higher increase in spatial presence observed in children can have its origin on the fact that their frontal cortex function is not fully developed.

Recently, preliminary results from a study to analyze the parietal activity in interactive virtual reality were presented (Kober, 2010). The goal of the study was to analyze if the parietal activity that was found in the study from Baumgartner et al. (2006) would also appear during a free navigation in a virtual environment. The environment was a virtual maze in which the participant performed a wayfinding task while EEG activity was monitored. Results showed that parietal activation also occurred in this interactive virtual reality.

Presence Research: Functional Magnetic Resonance Imaging

In the first fMRI study related to virtual reality and presence (Hoffman et al, 2003), subjects reported experiencing an illusion of presence in virtual reality via a magnet-friendly image delivery system despite the constraint of lying down with their head immobilized in an enclosed environment. fMRI results were not reported in the study.

Recent works (Baumgartner et al., 2008; Jäncke et al., 2009) have complemented the previously described study that used the roller coaster scenario as stimulus and EEG to monitor brain activity. These recent works have analyzed fMRI data captured during the exposure to the same virtual environment. Each ride lasted 102 s in total, whereas the different phases where divided into the following time scheme: anticipation phase 30 s, dynamic phase 60 s and end phase 12 s. In total, eight different roller coaster rides were presented, four High Presence and four Low Presence roller coaster rides. Results from the fMRI analysis show that the presence experience evoked by the virtual roller coaster scenario is associated with an increase in activation in a distributed network, which comprises extrastriate areas, the dorsal visual stream, the superior parietal cortex (SPL) and inferior parietal cortex (IPL), parts of the ventral visual stream, the premotor cortex (PMC), and the brain structures located in the basal and mesiotemporal parts of the brain. The network is modulated by the dorso lateral prefrontal cortex (DLPFC). The DLPFC activation strongly correlates with the subjective presence experience (the right DLPFC controlled the sense of presence by down-regulating the activation in the egocentric dorsal visual processing stream, the left DLPFC up-regulated widespread areas of the medial prefrontal cortex known to be involved in self-reflective and stimulus-independent thoughts). In contrast, there was no evidence of these two strategies in children. This difference is most likely attributable to the prefrontal cortex that is not fully matured in children.

Presence Research: Transcranial Doppler

Transcranial Doppler monitoring (TCD) has also been applied recently to analyze cognitive states related with presence during the exposure to virtual environments in different immersion and navigation conditions. TCD is a secure and non-invasive ultrasound diagnosis technique with high temporal resolution which is used to analyze hemodynamic variations in the brain. It monitors blood flow velocity in the main vessels of the brain: the left and right Middle Cerebral Arteries (MCA-L and MCA-R), the left and right Anterior Cerebral Arteries (ACA-L and ACA-R) and the left and right Posterior Cerebral Arteries (PCA-L and PCA-R). These velocity variations constitute a reliable source of information about brain activity. When the neurovascular coupling is adequate (Iadecola, 1993), the velocity variations that are detected by TCD reflect changes in regional cerebral blood flow due to brain activation in the brain areas supplied by the monitored vessel (Daffertshofer, 2001). Consequently, the spatial resolution of the technique is delimited by the size of the cortical areas supplied by the vessels selected for a particular study. In order to apply the measurement, two probes (transducers) are required, one for each cerebral hemisphere. In functional studies, each probe is placed in its correct location by attaching it to a headpiece that the user has to wear during the whole experiment.

Alcañiz et al. (2009) used the TCD technique to compare two different navigation conditions (user-controlled vs. system-controlled navigation) potentially associated with different levels of presence in the participants of the study. The study was carried out in a CAVE-like environment with four sides (three walls and the floor), using a wireless joystick and an optical tracking system to navigate in the environment. The virtual environment that was used in the study was a maze composed of several rooms and corridors. The virtual maze was designed specifically for this task. An image of one of the rooms of the virtual environment can be visualized in Figure 4.

Results from the study showed that it was possible to use TCD to monitor brain activity during virtual reality studies. The percentage variations between mean blood flow velocity in the user-controlled navigation and its preceding baseline (repose period), and between the mean blood flow velocity in the system-controlled navigation and its preceding baseline, were positive in all the arteries under study (MCA-L, MCA-R, ACA-L and ACA-R). Significant differences between the percentage variations in the two navigation conditions were observed in the case of the left arteries: MCA-L and ACA-L. Motor tasks to control the joystick with the right hand might be the origin of the observed variations in MCA-L blood flow velocity. However, the variations in ACA-L are not directly related to this issue, and can only be explained by other factors related to the virtual reality experience, such as decision making and emotional aspects. In fact, it is expected that the user may be more emotionally involved in the free navigation condition. Furthermore, during this experimental condition, more decisions have to be made, specially associated to navigation factors. All these issues are related with the level of presence that the user is experiencing during exposure to the different navigation conditions. Presence questionnaires confirmed that the level of presence was significantly higher during the free navigation condition.

Rey et al. (2010) compared the same navigation conditions (user-controlled vs. systemcontrolled), but in two different immersion configurations (corresponding to two different virtual reality settings: the CAVE-like system and a single projection screen). In this case, only MCA-L and MCA-R were considered. The navigation factor had a significant influence on the observed blood flow velocity variations in both monitored vessels. Higher percentage variations were observed in the free navigation condition than in the automatic navigation condition.

Figure 4: Image of one of the rooms of the virtual maze that was used in the studies that analyzed presence in virtual environments using TCD

As in the previous study, the observed differences in MCA-L can have their origin in the motor tasks differences between navigation conditions. On the other hand, a possible explanation of the differences in MCA-R percentage variations between navigation conditions could be found in the higher degree of involvement of the user in the creation of a motor plan in the free navigation condition. Results from questionnaires also found higher values of presence during the free navigation condition.

Virtual Representation of the Body

Other works have applied neuroscience tools to analyze the interpretation of participants of virtual reality experiences about the virtual representation of their own body. Virtual reality can be used to replace a person's real body by a virtual representation. For example, a virtual limb can be made to feel part of the participant's body if appropriate multisensory information is provided. Slater et al. (2008) created this illusion on participants of a virtual reality experience using a tactile stimulation on a person's hidden real right hand while, simultaneously, a 3D virtual arm was projected out of their shoulder. Questionnaire responses and behavioural analyses showed that participants were experiencing the virtual arm as part of themselves. These results open up the possibility that the whole virtual body could be interpreted by participants as part of themselves in the future.

CONCLUSION

This chapter has summarized the contributions and implications that advances on the virtual reality field may have for behavioural neuroscience studies. Virtual reality can provide a virtual laboratory where experiments can be conducted in a controlled way and with the desired conditions. Applications in neuroscience studies related to spatial navigation and social interaction have been described. Based on the results of these studies, it can be foreseen that virtual reality may be the basis to develop further studies about human behaviour in the following years.

On the other hand, neuroscience tools have provided the virtual reality research field with new techniques that may contribute to the understanding of human factors and human responses during the virtual reality experience. Although neurological correlates of virtual reality experiences have still to be further analyzed, advances in this area may help virtual reality researchers to design more compelling and effective versions of the virtual environments that they develop.

The two-way cooperation between virtual reality and neuroscience can be the basis of many advances in these research areas in the following years. Both fields of research can take advantage of the results from the studies that combine the use of virtual environments with neuroscience techniques that study aspects of human behaviour inside these environments.

REFERENCES

1. Alcañiz, M.; Rey, B.; Tembl, J. & Parkhutik, V. (2009). A Neuroscience Approach to Virtual Reality Experience Using Transcranial Doppler Monitoring. Presence: Teleoperators & Virtual Environments, 18(2), 97-111.
2. Argyle, M. & Dean, J. (1965). Eye-Contact, Distance and Affiliation. Sociometry, 28:289-304.
3. Astur, R.S.; Ortiz, M.L. & Sutherland, R.J. (1998). A characterization of performance by men and women in a virtual Morris water task: A large and reliable sex difference. Behavioral Brain Research, 93, 185-190.
4. Astur, R.S.; Tropp, J; Sava, S; Constable, R.T. & Markus, E.J. (2004). Sex differences and correlations in a virtual Morris water task, a virtual radial arm maze and mental rotation. Behavioral Brain Research, 151, 103-115.
5. Astur, R.S.; St. Germain, S.A.; Baker, E.K.; Calhoun, V.; Pearlson, G.D. & Constable R.T. (2005). fMRI hippocampal activity during a virtual radial arm maze. Applied Psychophysiology and Biofeedback, 30: 307-317.
6. Bailenson, J.N.; Blascovich, J.; Beall, A.C. & Loomis, J.M. (2003). Interpersonal distance in immersive virtual environments. Personality and Social Psychology Bulletin, 29: 819- 833.
7. Baumgartner, T.; Valko, L.; Esslen, M. & Jäncke, L. (2006). Neural correlate of spatial presence in an arousing and noninteractive virtual reality: an EEG and psychophysiology study. CyberPsychology & Behavior, 9(1), 30-45.
8. Baumgartner, T.; Speck, D.; Wettstein, D.; Masnari, O.; Beeli, G. & Jäncke, L. (2008). Feeling present in arousing virtual reality worlds: prefrontal brain regions differentially orchestrate presence experience in adults and children. Frontiers in Human Neuroscience, 2: 8.
9. Cornwell, B.R.; Johson, L.L.; Holroyd, T.; Carver, F.W. & Grillon, C. (2008). Human hippocampal and parahippocampal theta during goal-directed spatial navigation predicts performance on a virtual Morris water maze. The Journal of Neuroscience, 28(23): 5983-5990.
10. Daffertshofer, M. (2001). Functional Doppler testing, In: Cerebrovascular ultrasound: Theory, practice and future development, S. Meairs & M.G. Hennerici (Eds.), 341-359, Cambridge University

Press, ISBN 0 521 63223 4, Cambridge.

11. de Kort, Y.A.W.; IJsselsteijn, W.A.; Kooijman, J. & Schuurmans, Y. (2003). Virtual laboratories: Comparability of real and virtual environments for environmental psychology. Presence: Teleoperators & Virtual Environments, 12(4): 360-373.
12. Driscoll, I.; Hamilton, D.A.; Petropoulos, H.; Yeo, R.A.; Brooks, W.M.; Baumgartner, R.N. & Sutherland, R.J. (2003). The aging hippocampus: cognitive, biochemical and structural findings. Cerebral Cortex, 13: 1344-1351.
13. Duncko, R.; Cornwell, B.; Cui, L.; Merikangas, K.R. & Grillon, C. (2007). Acute exposure to stress improves performance in trace eyeblink conditioning and spatial learning tasks in healthy men. Learning & Memory, 14: 329-335.
14. Foo, P.; Harrison, M.; Duchon, A.; Harren, W.H. & Tarr, M.J. (2004). Humans follow landmarks over path integration. Journal of Vision, 4(8), article 892.
15. Foo, P.; Harren, W.H.; Duchon, A. & Tarr, M.J. (2005). Do humans integrate routes into a cognitive map? Map- versus Landmark-based navigation of novel shortcuts. Journal of Experimental Psychology: Learning, Memory, and Cognition, 31(2), 195-215.
16. Harvey, C.D.; Collman, F.; Dombeck, D.A. & Tank, D.W. (2009). Intracellular dynamics of hippocampal place cells during virtual navigation. Nature 461, 941-949.
17. Held, R. & Durlach, N. (1992). Telepresence. Presence: Teleoperators & Virtual Environments, 1(1): 109-112.
18. Hoffman, H.G.; Richards, T.; Coda, B.; Richards, A. & Sharar, S.R. (2003). The illusion of presence in immersive virtual reality during an fMRI brain scan. CyberPsychology & Behavior, 6(2):127-131.
19. Hölscher, C.; Schnee, A.; Dahmen, H.; Setia, L. & Mallot, H.A. (2005). Rats are able to navigate in virtual environments. Journal of Experimental Biology, 208: 561-569.
20. Iadecola, C. (1993). Regulation of the cerebral microcirculation during neural activity: Is nitric oxide the missing link? Trends in neuroscience, 16(6): 206-214.
21. Insko, B.E. (2003). Measuring presence: Subjective, behavioural, and physiological methods, In: Being there: Concepts, effects and measurement of user presence in synthetic environments, G. Riva,

F. Davide & W. IJsselsteijn (Ed.), 109-120, IOS Press, ISBN 978-1586033019, Amsterdam.

22. Jacobs, W.J.; Laurance, H.E. & Thomas, K.G.F. (1997). Place learning in virtual space. I. Acquisition, overshadowing, and transfer. Learning and Motivation, 28: 521-541.
23. Jacobs, W.J.; Thomas, K.G.F.; Laurance, H.E. & Nadel, L. (1998). Place learning in virtual space. II. Topographical relations as one dimension of stimulus control. Learning and Motivation, 29:288-308.
24. Jäncke, L.; Cheetam, M. & Baumgartner, T. (2009). Virtual reality and the role of the prefrontal cortex in adults and children. Frontiers in Neuroscience 3(1): 52-59.
25. Kearns, M.J.; Warren, W.H.; Duchon, A.P. & Tarr, M.J. (2002). Path integration from optic flow and body senses in a homing task. Perception 31, 349-347.
26. Kober, S. (2010). Cortical correlate of spatial presence in 2-D and 3-D interactive virtual reality: An EEG study. Proceedings of the 3rd RAVE (Real Actions, Virtual Environments) Workshop, Barcelona, March 2010.
27. Lampton, D.R. ; McDonald, D.P.; Singer, M. & Bliss, J.P. (1996). Distance Estimation in Virtual Environments, Proceedings of the Human Factors and Ergonomics Society Annual Meeting, pp. 1268-1272(5), ISSN 1071-1813, San Diego, California, October 1995, Human Factors and Ergonomics Society, Santa Monica, CA, USA.
28. Leighty, K.A. & Fragszy, D.M. (2003). Primates in cyberspace: using interactive computer tasks to study perception and action in nonhuman animals. Animal cognition, 6: 137- 139.
29. Loomis, J.M.; Klatzky, R.L., Golledge, R.G., Cicinelli, J.G., Pellegrino, J.W., Fry, P.A. (1993). Nonvisual navigation by blind and sighted: assessment of path integration ability. Journal of Experimental Psychology: General 122: 73-91.
30. Milgram, S. (1963). Behavioral study of obedience. Journal of Abnormal Psychology 67, 371-378.
31. Morris, R.G.M. (1981). Spatial localization does not require the presence of local cues. Learning and motivation 12: 239-260.
32. Nishijo, H.; Kazui, K.; Hori, E.; Tabuchi, E.; Umeno, K.; Sasaki, K. & Ono, T. (2003). Spatial correlates of monkey hippocampal neurons during navigation in a virtual space. Society of Neuroscience Abstracts,

32: 717.14.

33. Olton, D.S. & Samuelson, R.J. (1976). Remembrance of places passed: spatial memory in rats. Journal of Experimental Psychology: Animal Behavior Processes, 2(2): 97-116.
34. Rey, B.; Alcañiz, M.; Tembl, J. & Parkhutik, V. (2010). Brain Activity and Presence: a Preliminary Study in Different Immersive Conditions Using Transcranial Doppler Monitoring. Virtual Reality 14, 55-65.
35. Richardson, A.R. & Waller, D. (2007). Interaction with an immersive virtual environment corrects users' distance estimates. Human Factors 49, 507-517.
36. Schilbach, L.; Wohlschlaeger, A.M.; Kraemer, N.C.; Newen, A.; Shah, N.J.; Fink, G.R. & Vogeley, K. (2006). Being with virtual others: Neural correlates of social interaction. Neuropsychologia 44(5): 718- 730.
37. Schuemie, M.; van der Straaten, P.; Krijn, M. & van der Mast, C. (2001). Research on presence in virtual reality: A survey. CyberPsychology & Behavior, 4(2): 183-201.
38. Slater, M.; Antlye, A.; Davison, A.; Swapp, D.; Guger, C.; Barker, C.; Pistrang, N. & SanchezVives, M.V. (2006). A virtual reprise of the Stanley Milgram obedience experiments. PLoS ONE 1, e39.
39. Slater, M.; Perez-Marcos, D.; Ehrsson, H.H. & Sanchez-Vives, M.V. (2008). Towards a digital body: the virtual arm illusion. Frontiers in Human Neuroscience, 2: 6.
40. Schlögl, A.; Slater, M. & Pfurtscheller, G. (2002). Presence research and EEG, Proceedings of Presence 2002, 5th Annual International Workshop on Presence, pp. 9-11, Porto, October 2002.
41. Speckman, E.J.; Elger, C.E. & Altrup, U. (1993). Neurophysiologic basis of the EEG, In: The treatment of epilepsy: Principles and practices, E. Wyllie (Ed.), 149-164, Lippincott Williams & Wilkins, ISBN 978-0781723749, Philadelphia.
42. Sutherland, R.J.; Kolb, B. & Whishaw, I.Q. (1982). Spatial mapping: definitive disruption by hippocampal and frontal cortex damage in the rat. Neuroscience Letters, 31: 271-276.
43. Tarr, M.J. and Warren, W.H. (2002). Virtual reality in behavioral neuroscience and beyond. Nature neuroscience 5, 1089-1092
44. Towers, D.; Ellmore, T. & McNaughton, B. (2003). Spatial navigation by Rhesus monkeys in a virtual environment by exclusively visual cues. Society of Neuroscience Abstracts, 32:518.6.

45. Warren, W.H.; Kay, B.A.; Zosh, W.D.; Duchon, A.P. & Sahuc, S. (2001). Optic flow is used to control human walking. Nature Neuroscience 4, 213-216.

46. Waller, D.; Bachman, E.; Hodgson, E. & Beall, A.C. (2007). The HIVE: A huge immersive virtual environment for research in spatial cognition. Behavior Research Methods 39(4), 835-843.

47. Witmer, B.G. & Kline, P. (1998). Judging perceived and traversed distance in virtual environments. Presence: Teleoperators & Virtual Environments 7, 144-167.

INDEX

C

D

E

F

G

U

V

W